AMERICAN GOVERNMENT, POLITICS, AND POLICY MAKING

THIRD
EDITION

AMERICAN GOVERNMENT, POLITICS, AND POLICY MAKING

David R. Berman
Arizona State University

Prentice Hall, Englewood Cliffs, New Jersey 07632

Library of Congress Cataloging-in-Publication Data

Berman, David R.
  American government, politics, and policy making.

    Bibliography: p.
    Includes indexes.
    1. United States—Politics and government—1945-
I. Title.
JK274.B52 1988   320.973   87-17500
ISBN 0-13-027434-8

Editorial/production supervision and
 interior design: Joe O'Donnell Jr.
Cover design: Lundgren Graphics, Ltd.
Manufacturing buyer: Margaret Rizzi
Photo research: Page Poore

Chapter opening photo credits: Chapter 1: Marc Anderson. Chapter 2: The New York Public Library. Chapter 3: Stan Wakefield. Chapter 4: Stan Wakefield. Chapter 5: Stan Wakefield. Chapter 6: Marc Anderson. Chapter 7: Prentice Hall. Chapter 8: Rick Bloom. Chapter 9: Reproduced from the collection of the Architect of the Capitol. Chapter 10: Stan Wakefield. Chapter 11: Anita Duncan. Chapter 12: UPI/Bettmann Newsphotos. Chapter 13: A. Devaney, Inc., New York.

 ©1988, 1983, 1979 by Prentice-Hall, Inc.
A Division of Simon & Schuster
Englewood Cliffs, New Jersey 07632

Printed in the United States of America

10 9 8 7 6 5 4 3 2

ISBN 0-13-027434-8 01

Prentice-Hall International (UK) Limited, *London*
Prentice-Hall of Australia Pty. Limited, *Sydney*
Prentice-Hall Canada Inc., *Toronto*
Prentice-Hall Hispanoamericana, S. A., *Mexico*
Prentice-Hall of India Private Limited, *New Delhi*
Prentice-Hall of Japan, Inc., *Tokyo*
Simon & Schuster Asia Pte. Ltd., *Singapore*
Editora Prentice-Hall do Brasil, Ltda., *Rio de Janeiro*

In memory of
Barney and Frances Berman

CONTENTS

PART THREE
OUTPUTS

PREFACE

This edition of *American Government, Politics, and Policy Making*, like the earlier editions, strives to cover what students need to know about the national government of the United States and to do so clearly and concisely. Among the major revisions are an expanded discussion of the policy systems model and a new chapter on citizen inputs, which covers political socialization, opinion, participation, and public control of government. To improve the flow and organization of the book, I have eliminated the chapter on global and domestic conditions found in earlier editions. Much of the material in that chapter has been shifted to other chapters, where it is more effectively used. In keeping with the model developed in Chapter 1, the text strives to examine (1) the broader environment in which national policy makers function; (2) citizen inputs and linkage mechanisms; (3) the activities of policy makers and policy-making institutions; and (4) the outputs or public policies they produce. I would like to thank the scholars who reviewed drafts of this book and the earlier editions. For this edition, those include Douglas Camp Chaffey, Christopher Rhines, Sheryl Robinson, and Roger Schaefer.

David Berman

AMERICAN GOVERNMENT, POLITICS, AND POLICY MAKING

INTRODUCTION:
THE POLICY SYSTEM

When United States Senator Russell Long was a student at Louisiana State University he reportedly asked his uncle, Governor Earl Long, for advice on an upcoming debate. "What's the topic?" his uncle asked. "Should ideals be used in politics?" his nephew replied. "Why heck yes, son," the political veteran responded. "I think you should use ideals—and anything else you can get your hands on."[1]

The notion that politics is somewhat corrupt and at best a necessary evil has a long history in the United States. Yet in reality politics is an indispensable way of achieving common goals and resolving conflicts among individuals and groups.

Textbooks that attempt to explain what happens in the political world differ greatly in their emphasis. Some authors stress the importance of constitutional principles, others are more concerned with political behavior, and still others focus on policy-making institutions, especially the presidency. Traditional texts also vary in their emphasis on how governments in the United States relate to their social and economic environments and on what the nature and effects of their public policies are.

There is, indeed, a great variety of material to cover if we are to understand government, politics, and public policy-making in the United States. One of the most useful approaches to the problem of integrating the various political activities, policy-making institutions, public policies, and social and economic environments into a coherent framework for study is systems analysis.[2] In a governmental policy-making system officials respond to various stimuli or inputs and convert these into outputs or public policies. This activity occurs within a broad environment that feeds into the system and into which the outputs are fed back. Systems theorists consider a policy output to be functional if it leads to supportive (favorable) attitudes for the political system or for those who happen to be in office, dysfunctional if it has the opposite effect. Political systems are constantly in motion as their different elements interact with the environment and each other to produce public policies. Systems analysis offers a framework for examining relationships among the various system components and for evaluating the overall function of each component.

This book examines politics and policy making at the national (often referred to as the *federal*) level of government in the United States through the use of the policy systems model shown in Figure 1–1.

The broad environment consists of global conditions (e.g., problems and developments affecting the security of the nation) and domestic economic, social, cultural, and constitutional conditions. Environmental conditions shape both the nature of the policy system and the policy demands on government officials.

[1] Quoted in Chris Kenrick, "Congress: Three Look Back," *Christian Science Monitor*, September 15, 1978, p. 2.

[2] See for example, David Easton, *The Political System* (New York: Knopf, 1972).

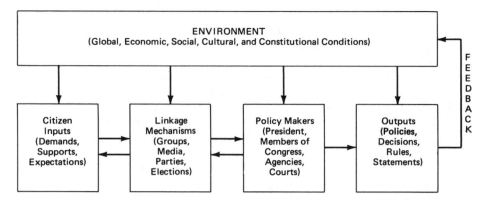

Figure 1-1. Policy System Model

Citizen inputs into the system consist of supports and expectations as well as demands for policy change. Supports consist of favorable attitudes toward the system and an acceptance of the right of those in power to make binding decisions. Supportive public attitudes are required if those in public office are to govern without resorting to force to impose these decisions. Supportive attitudes depend in part on whether government is perceived to be performing up to expectations (thus the expectations input). Governments may be in trouble if, for example, they fail to provide basic services or fail to fairly allocate the costs and benefits of public policy. Public support may also diminish when government leaders are found to be saying one thing and doing the opposite, as in the case of the sale of arms to Iran by the Reagan administration.

Citizen sentiment on policy matters—whether in regard to a relatively new problem, something government has done, or something government is considering—is communicated to public officials by a variety of linkage mechanisms. Letters, personal contact, and public opinion polls, are examples. More central linkage mechanisms include interest groups (often called *pressure groups*) the media, political parties, and elections. These institutions and organizations, do not simply enable citizens to contact officials; they also inform citizens about government activities and enable officials, most noticeably in the case of the media, to communicate their views back to the public. Given the central roles of linkage mechanisms, it comes as no surprise that questions concerning how they perform these functions—for example, whether the media are biased—are hotly debated.

The policy makers of concern in our model are presidents and their advisers, members of Congress, federal agency heads and personnel, and federal judges, particularly those in the U.S. Supreme Court. One finds each branch involved in just about every area of policy. In any given area, however, a certain branch may play a particularly prominent role. For example, the president has generally played a leading role in foreign policy, and the courts, for much of the nation's history, have been particularly significant in the area of civil liberties.

Focusing on how officials go about making policy involves, in part, tracing various processes, such as how a bill becomes a law in Congress. More basically, political scientists have been concerned with the behavior of individual policy makers. How, for example, does this behavior reflect personal characteristics such as party identification or the group atmosphere in which decisions are made?

The various national policy makers collectively produce a single output—a package of policies that is fed back into the environment. On another level, outputs are produced by the different branches or agencies of government. These policies take the form of presidential statements or directives, acts of Congress, administrative rules, and judicial decisions. Presidential statements are included in this list to indicate that a policy may be symbolic—that is, simply an expression of the government's position—as well as legally binding. Symbolic outputs may be significant, for example, in reassuring the public that government cares about a problem or is in control of a situation.

Whatever their specific form, policies are fed back into the environment, where they may have a number of effects. Ideally, they will satisfy a demand or settle a controversy. On the other hand, a disappointed group may challenge them by appealing to another policy-making body. Some policies give rise to "copycat" demands. For example, a congressional decision to regulate or deregulate a particular industry is likely to create pressure to do the same thing to another industry. Havoc may also result because of unforeseen consequences of a policy decision. During the mid 1980s, for example, a program to deinstitutionalize people with mental problems, though well intended, ultimately had the effect of putting may of those people on the streets without a home. Given the controversial nature of much of what government does and the often unintentional or unforseen effects a policy can have, one usually can expect a policy output to generate further demands. In this sense, government makes its own business.

This book is organized around the various components of the policy systems model. Part I deals with the policy-making setting. It begins with a discussion of the constitutional context of policy-making and proceeds to citizen inputs and the various linkage mechanisms. Part II examines policy makers and policy-making institutions. In Part III we turn to several areas of public policy—how the national government raises and spends money, manages the domestic economy, defends the nation, and protects our basic civil liberties.

2

CONSTITUTIONAL
CONDITIONS

The setting in which the national government functions is shaped by public institutions and by laws that confer, distribute, and limit governmental authority. The basic document on these subjects is the United States Constitution. In this chapter we first consider the development and nature of the Constitution. We then examine the basic constitutional concepts of federalism and popular control of government.

DEVELOPMENT OF THE CONSTITUTION

The United States Constitution reflects the thinking of a number of European political theorists and the influence of several historical events, including a century and a half of colonial government and the Revolutionary War. The framers of the Constitution were especially familiar with the theories of John Locke (1632–1704) and Baron de Montesquieu (1689–1755). Locke popularized the ideas that government rested upon a compact with the people and that the goal of government was to protect the natural rights of individuals to life, liberty, and property. Montesquieu's influence derived from his notions that governmental powers should be fragmented to prevent a tyrannical concentration of authority and that government should give representation to different social and economic interests.

By the time of the Constitution's framing, Americans had considerable experience with implementing these concepts. Charters and compacts, for example, had been used during colonial times to structure government and to confer and limit its authority. The use of bicameral (two-house) legislatures to furnish representation to different segments or classes of society (for example, the wealthy in one house and the not-so-wealthy in the other) and the separation of legislative and executive branches also date back to colonial times.

Many of these concepts were also evident in the state constitutions adopted shortly after the Revolutionary War. The framers of the Constitution often drew on these documents for general principles and details. Many of the framers, however, objected to the emphasis commonly found in state constitutions on legislative supremacy. Legislatures in most states were not effectively checked by either the executive or the courts. Governors were commonly restricted to one-year terms and denied the power to veto acts of legislatures. Distrust of a strong executive showed a long history of conflict between the colonists and governors appointed by English kings.

In the years immediately preceding the Constitutional Convention, the status of governors improved. This improvement came in part from reformers' efforts to curb legislatures, which to their way of thinking had produced such bad laws as the one resulting in the issuance of cheap paper money. In the late 1780s legislative activity also prompted some state courts to exercise the power of judicial review—that is, to invalidate legislation that they found to conflict with natural rights or principles in state constitutions.

The Confederation Period

The immediate problem facing the framers of the Constitution was the weakness of the national government formed in 1781 by the Articles of Confederation. The Articles were the nation's first constitution. They created what amounted to a league of state governments, each of which "retained its sovereignty, freedom and independence, and every power, jurisdiction and right which is not by this confederation expressly delegated" to the national government.

Under the Articles, full authority was vested in a single national legislative body known as Congress. Although the states sent from two to seven delegates to the Congress, each state could cast only a single vote. The one-state–one-vote rule demonstrated the principle of state equality. Important decisions—for example, those on war, finance, or treaty making, required the approval of at least nine of the thirteen states, and the consent of all the states was needed to amend the Articles. More routine matters were settled by simple majority rule of seven states. Conflict between the states occurred along a number of lines, such as north versus south, large versus small, and agricultural versus commercial. Competition and conflicting interests made it difficult for the states to agree on important matters.

The Articles did not provide for a chief executive. A member of Congress was selected to serve one year as "president" but this position amounted to little more than presiding over the assembly. The managerial functions of the national government were performed by congressional committees. Some of these, such as the Committee on Foreign Affairs and the Marine Committee, eventually developed into governmental departments headed by a secretary. In this respect the national government took on the appearance of a parliamentary or cabinet system, in which there is no separation between the legislative and executive branches. The full evolution of this system, however, was cut short by the adoption of the United States Constitution. A central problem throughout the life of the Articles was the absence of a single executive or committee to direct the various departments.

Lack of a national judiciary was another weakness of the Articles. Congress did establish temporary courts to deal with such matters as land disputes between the states. State courts, however, handled most of the litigation and, indeed, could refuse to allow the laws of Congress to apply in their states.

Among the powers expressly delegated to the Congress under the Articles were those to conduct foreign relations, enter into treaties, regulate Indian affairs, and operate a post office. These functions were undertaken without the aid or involvement of state governments. Congress could levy taxes but lacked the power to collect them. It had to rely on the willingness of the states to contribute to the national treasury, a willingness not often forthcoming. Congress also lacked the powers to regulate commerce among the states and to establish a uniform national currency. State governments, free to act as sovereign nations, coined and printed their own money and erected trade barriers to safeguard their industries from competition from other states.

In the 1780s a depression prompted a number of debtor riots and a demand for cheap paper money to pay off debts. The most important of these uprisings occurred in Massachusetts in 1786–87, when debtor farmers led by Daniel Shays (a former captain in the Revolutionary army) forcibly prevented state officials from taking their property to pay creditors. "Shays's Rebellion" frightened creditors throughout the country and spurred the move toward a central government strong enough to prevent further outbreaks and to shore up the country's currency and credit policies.

Efforts to strengthen the national government, spearheaded by reformers such as Alexander Hamilton and James Madison, led to a meeting attended by representatives of five states in Annapolis, Maryland, in 1786. This gathering was called for the stated purpose of bringing about an agreement among the states on trade and tariff matters. Hamilton and Madison, however, used the occasion to urge all the states to send delegates to a constitutional convention to revise the Articles of Confederation. The following year, fifty-five delegates from twelve states attended this convention, held in Philadelphia at the Pennsylvania State House (now called Independence Hall). Rhode Island, called by its critics "Rogue Island" because of its debtor-dominated legislature, refused to participate.

The delegates to the Constitutional Convention were a distinguished group. Indeed, as one scholar has noted, they were, "in fact or by inclination, members of the economic, social, and intellectual aristocracies of their respective states."[1] They were relatively young (average age approximately forty-two) and well educated (twenty-five had college degrees). By profession, thirty-four of the fifty-five delegates were lawyers. Most of the others were prominent businessmen engaged in banking, shipping manufacturing, and the like. The delegates, in short, did not represent a cross section of the American people. Absent were representatives of the small farmers and the artisan, who constituted the great bulk of the people, and the poor and debtors.

Nearly all the delegates had been active in state politics. Several, as state legislators, helped write the first constitutions for their states. Though eight of the delegates had signed the Declaration of Independence, many who had agreed to that document and led the Revolutionary War effort did not attend the convention. Patrick Henry, for example, declined to serve as a convention delegate, declaring that he "smelled a rat," and later he opposed ratification of the new constitution.

Certainly, the framers as a group were not revolutionaries. Many felt

[1] Merrill Jensen, *The Making of the American Constitution* (New York: D. Van Nostrand, 1964), p. 8.

that democracy meant class war, between the rich and the poor, and that the American state governments of the time had been far too democratic. To most of the delegates, a stronger national government was needed to control the "leveling spirit" that had arisen in the states since 1776 as a result of the Revolution and that, among other things, threatened the property rights of the affluent.[2]

Some historians have concluded that the framers of the Constitution sought reform as a means of protecting and promoting their own economic interests.[3] Many delegates were creditors who had much to gain by creating a strong national government that would guarantee payment of debts. And the businessmen among the delegates would benefit from improved protection of their property rights and a government that would encourage the development of a national economy. Both defenders and critics of the new constitution, however, had such interests. Other factors, such as regional divisions, also appear to have influenced the behavior of the delegates.[4]

On the whole, the framers of the Constitution distrusted the concentration of governmental authority, believed in the existence of inalienable natural rights, and felt government should be limited by higher laws of nature. Like many future Americans, the framers believed that undesirable aspects of human nature, including the desire for power, could be controlled by proper structural and organizational arrangements. In short, as James Madison argued, "in framing a government which is to be administered by men over men, the great difficulty lies in this: you must first enable the government to control the governed; and in the next place oblige it to control itself."[5]

The Constitutional Convention

The Philadelphia convention took place from May to September, 1787. Committees did much of the detail work and George Washington presided over the general meetings of the convention. Each state had a single vote on items brought before the body. One of the convention's first decisions was to bar the public and press from its meetings. Secrecy was defended on the grounds that it would promote openness in discussion and minimize external pressures. Much of what is known about the convention comes from notes taken by James Madison, which were not made public until several years later.

The official function of the convention was to revise the Articles of

[2] *Ibid.,* p. 9.

[3] A classic statement of this view was made by Charles A. Beard, *An Economic Interpretation of the Constitution* (New York: Macmillan, 1969).

[4] See, for example, Forrest McDonald, *We the People: The Economic Origins of the Constitution* (Chicago: University of Chicago Press, 1958); and Richard Hofstadter, *The American Political Tradition and the Men Who Made It* (New York: Knopf, 1973).

[5] *The Federalist,* No. 51.

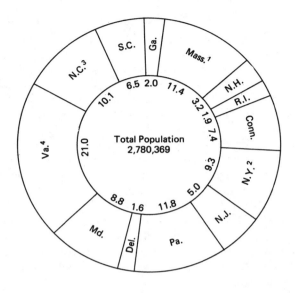

Figure 2–1   Population of the American Colonies, 1780 (Percentages)

Source: U.S. Bureau of the Census, Pocket Data Handbook, 1976 (Washington, D.C.: Government Printing Office, 1976), p. 372.

[1] Includes Maine   [2] Includes Vermont   [3] Includes Tennessee   [4] Includes Kentucky

Confederation, but the delegates soon turned to developing an entirely new constitution. They generally agreed on the need for a stronger national government, notably one that would regulate commerce among the states and promote a national economy. Within this broad consensus several areas of disagreement developed that necessitated compromise solutions. One of the most basic was the conflict between large and small states (Figure 2–1) over representation in Congress. The large states favored basing representation on the size of a state's population, a decision that would give them more representatives. The small states favored giving each state the same number of representatives, regardless of differences in population. After lengthy negotiations, the delegates reached a compromise: one chamber of Congress, the Senate, would give the states equal representation (two senators each); the other chamber, the House of Representatives, would be based on the principle of population, with each state guaranteed at least one representative. This compromise, commonly known as the Connecticut Compromise because of the role played by delegates from that state in securing agreement, was instrumental in obtaining the support of the smaller states for a stronger national government.[6]

[6] Some scholars have argued that the crucial division at the constitutional convention was not between large and small states, but between those who wanted a small republic and

The executive office was a second major area of compromise. Though some delegates wanted to vest executive duties in a body of three or more people, most favored a single chief executive or president. Most of the debate over the presidency had to do with the selection process. Some delegates proposed that Congress choose the president. Others advocated selection of the "chief magistrate" by state legislatures. Choosing the president by direct popular election was discussed but not seriously considered. As George Mason of Virginia contended, voicing the views of many delegates, "it would be unnatural to refer the choice of a proper character for Chief Magistrate to the people, as it would to refer a trial of colours to a blind man. The extent of the Country renders it impossible that the people can have the requisite capacity to judge of the respective pretensions of the candidates."[7] In addition to doubting the electorate's competence, delegates from small states feared that direct popular election would give too great an advantage to large states in national elections.

The compromise solution was the electoral college, under which state legislatures were to select electors equal in number to their representation in Congress. The electors, in turn, would vote for president and vice-president. The delegates expected that the electors would vote for many candidates and that no candidate (after George Washington) would receive a majority of the votes. If this happened, the choice would be made by the House of Representatives from among the candidates who had received the most votes.[8] In essence, the compromise called for state electors to nominate candidates for president. The House would then select the president from among the leading candidates.

Other compromises at the convention illustrate further divisions and additional time-honored methods of resolving conflicts. Some delegates, especially those from coastal areas, were concerned about losing control of the new government to the states that would be formed in the West (which was then east of the Mississippi River). Accordingly, they proposed that new states not be admitted on an equal basis with the older states in terms of representation. This motion was opposed by delegates who favored western expansion and enlargement of the Union. The compromise was a simple one: do nothing at the convention and let the new Congress decide.[9]

A number of compromises addressed the differing interests of northern

those who wanted a large one. See Martin Diamond, "What the Framers Meant by Federalism," in Robert A. Goldwin (ed.), *A Nation of States* (Chicago: Rand McNally, 1963), pp. 24–41. For a critique of this argument, see Christopher Wolfe, "On Understanding the Constitutional Convention of 1787," *Journal of Politics* 39 (February 1977): 97–118.

[7] Quoted by Max Farrand, *The Framing of the Constitution of the United States* (New Haven: Yale University Press, 1962), p. 116.

[8] Originally the House was to select a president from the five candidates receiving the most votes. The Twelfth Amendment, adopted in 1804, reduced this to the three leading vote getters.

[9] In later years Congress often imposed conditions prerequisite to statehood. Utah was admitted in 1896, for example, only after it had pledged to abolish polygamy.

and southern states. The South, which produced for export raw materials such as cotton, wanted free trade with other nations. The North desired tariffs to protect its developing industries. The framers therefore agreed to prohibit export taxes but gave Congress authority to levy tariffs. To insure that the South would have a voice in treaty making, the framers required that two–thirds of the Senate approve such agreements. On another North–South issue, the framers agreed not to ban the importation of slaves until 1808. How the slave population was to be counted in determining a state's tax levy and its representation in the House of Representatives was decided by a highly pragmatic agreement to consider each slave as three-fifths of a person for both purposes.[10]

Ratification of the Constitution

The document produced by the Constitutional Convention departed greatly from the plan of government in the Articles of Confederation. Most people had expected some relatively limited revisions of the Articles and were caught off guard because of the secrecy of the convention.

Having already exceeded their mandate, the framers went on to override provisions in the Articles that required the approval of amendments to tha document by the legislatures of all the states. Sensing the difficulty, if not the impossibility, of securing the consent of all the state legislatures, the framers provided for the Constitution to be ratified if it were approved by popularly elected conventions in nine of the thirteen states. Somewhat surprisingly, this procedure was agreed to by the Congress operating under the Articles.

Elections to state-ratifying conventions were characterized by contests between delegates who supported the new document (known as Federalists) and those who opposed it (Anti-Federalists). In the populous states of Massachusetts, New York, Pennsylvania, and Virginia the Federalists were well organized in their efforts to get delegates favorable to ratification selected. Alexander Hamilton, James Madison, and John Jay furthered the cause of ratification by writing a number of pro-Constitution essays known as *The Federalist* papers, which were published by several newspapers.

In several states the proposed constitution encountered resistance because it failed to guarantee certain freedoms found in state constitutions. The framers had felt that such declarations, or bills of rights, were neither necessary nor desirable. Hamilton argued that a bill of rights might lead Congress to assume powers it had not been given. For example, to say that Congress could not abridge the freedom of the press might be taken to mean that, short of interfering with its basic freedom, Congress could regulate the press.[11] To win

---

[10] The three-fifths provision was eliminated by the adoption of the Fourteenth Amendment in 1868.

[11] See the argument by Alexander Hamilton in *The Federalist*, No. 84.

over delegates, however, the Federalists finally committed themselves to support constitutional amendments providing for a bill of rights. The ratification struggle in the states began in the fall of 1787 and ended on June 21, 1788, when New Hampshire became the ninth state to ratify the document.

THE CONSTITUTION: STRUCTURE, POWER, AND CHANGE

The Constitution allocates authority among the branches of the national government and between the national and state governments. The document also imposes limitations on the authority of both national and state policy makers. The various local governments are regarded in the Constitution as deriving their authority from the states and thus are subject to the same limitations imposed on the exercise of state authority.

The precise nature of the allocation of governmental authority has been subject to debate. Dividing governmental powers among branches of government and between different governments was intended to avoid the concentration of authority and prevent hasty public action. Over the years, however, changes in domestic economic and social conditions and in the role of the United States in world affairs have expanded the authority of the national government and increased presidential power. Neither of these trends has resulted in complete dominance, either of the national government over the states or of the president over other branches of government. Since the 1970s, moreover, a number of efforts have been made to reverse or halt these trends. General efforts to improve the status of state and local governments in the federal system, including President Reagan's New Federalism, are discussed later in this chapter. Improvements in the position of Congress relative to the president in such matters as budgeting and war powers are discussed in later chapters.

Governmental Structure

The Constitution provided for a single chief executive chosen for a four-year term by presidential electors, a House of Representatives whose members would be elected by popular vote for two-year terms, a Senate whose members (two from each state) would be chosen for six-year terms by state legislatures, and a Supreme Court and other federal courts whose members would be nominated by the president, confirmed by the Senate, and allowed to serve for terms of "good behavior" (subject only to removal following impeachment).

The anticipated role of presidential electors was undermined in the early decades of the nineteenth century as state legislatures permitted voters to select electors pledged to particular presidential candidates. Without any change in the Constitution, the president in effect became popularly elected, though the candidate with the most popular votes does not necessarily win. A second change in the original plan was the direct election of United States senators. This modification came with the adoption of the Seventeenth Amendment in 1913.

The three branches of the national government are separated from one another in the sense that one branch either cannot at all or cannot easily remove a member of another branch from office. Congress is the only body that has such removal power. Through impeachment proceedings it may remove a president or a judge from office. The branches are also separated by the ban on members of one branch holding office in another. In these two respects, the governmental system in this nation contrasts with a cabinet or parliamentary system, such as that found in England and other modern democracies. There the chief executive (prime minister) and department heads (cabinet officials) are members of the legislature and assume their office by legislative vote.

In the United States the branches of government also have separate, though often interrelated, powers. The powers of Congress, enumerated in Article I, Section 8, of the Constitution, range from borrowing money to declaring war. Article II gives the president a general "executive power" (the existence and extent of this power have been debated), as well as more specific powers such as those to act as commander in chief of the armed forces and to make treaties. Article III simply states that "the judicial power of the United States, shall be vested in one Supreme Court, and in such inferior courts as the Congress may from time to time ordain and establish." The Constitution does not explicitly give courts the power of judicial review. This authority, however, was asserted soon after adoption of the Constitution,[12] and the practice has been accepted. Judicial review has been necessary both as a means of implementing the idea that government is limited by higher laws and in resolving conflicts between the national and state governments.

While the branches are independent, they also interact with one another. Presidents, for example, may veto acts of Congress. On the other hand, Congress may impose numerous checks on the president, such as refusing to confirm presidential nominations for office or withholding appropriations (grants of money) for programs he favors. The courts can invalidate the actions of both the president and Congress. At the same time, Congress may take away part of a court's jurisdiction or, with the concurrence of the states, reverse a court's decision by a constitutional amendment.

The national government, in essence, consists of separate institutions that share power and impose checks and balances upon one another.[13] Extra-constitutional entities such as political parties and interest groups help fill in the gaps among these institutions, especially the void between the legislature and the

---

[12] See *Marbury* v. *Madison*, 1 Cranch 137 (1803).

[13] See Richard E. Neustadt, *Presidential Power* (New York: John Wiley, 1960), p. 33.

executive. The institutions are frequently in conflict, yet the relationships have also been cooperative and agreeable.

Constitutional Powers

Generally the Supreme Court has held that the national government has inherent powers, even beyond those granted in the Constitution, in the area of foreign affairs and broad but limited powers in domestic matters. The inherent powers of the national government in external affairs are derived from the simple fact that the government represents a sovereign nation. The national government would have, for example, the inherent powers to wage war and make treaties even if these powers were not conferred by the Constitution.

Many powers of the national government are enumerated in the Constitution. Congress, for example, is expressly authorized to levy and collect taxes, borrow money, and regulate commerce among the states. Over the last several decades the Supreme Court has generally interpreted these powers liberally. In addition to its enumerated powers, Congress has implied the powers to make "all laws which shall be necessary and proper for carrying into execution" its enumerated powers. The "necessary and proper clause" in Article I, Section 8 (sometimes called the *elastic clause*) has been interpreted to give the enumerated powers an added dimension. A landmark case in this regard was *McCulloch v. Maryland* (1819), in which the United States Supreme Court under Chief Justice John Marshall, held that Congress could establish a national bank, even though the Constitution did not expressly empower it to do so.[14] The authority, Marshall concluded, was implied as being a necessary and proper way for Congress to carry out its enumerated powers, such as the powers to levy and collect taxes, borrow money, and regulate commerce among the states.

State powers are not expressly stated in the Constitution. State governments exercise all authority not exclusively delegated to the national government or denied them by the Constitution (Table 2–1). States, in other words, have residual or reserved powers. In other federal systems, such as that of Canada, the subnational governments have only specifically delegated powers while the national government exercises residual authority. The principal reserved power of the state governments in the United States is a general police power to protect the health, safety, and welfare of their citizens. Some powers, such as that to conduct foreign affairs, belong exclusively to the national government. Others, such as the ability to tax and spend money are concurrent—that is, shared by the national and state governments.

Under Article VI (known as the *supremacy clause*),

> the Constitution, and the laws of the United States which shall be made in pursuance thereof; and all treaties made, or which shall be made, under the

[14] 4 Wheaton 36 (1819).

Table 2–1 Specific Limitations on State Powers

A. *Article I, Section 10:*
  1. States cannot enter into any treaty, alliance, or confederation with a foreign government.
  2. States cannot coin money, issue paper money, or impair the obligation of contracts between individuals.
  3. A state cannot enter into agreements or compacts with another state without the consent of Congress. (In practice, consent has commonly not been required).

B. *Article IV (Interstate Relations):*
  1. Each state is required to give "full faith and credit" to "acts, records, and judicial proceedings of every other state." (For example, each state is to recognize marriages performed in other states. Under Supreme Court decisions, however, a divorce granted in one state does not have to be recognized by another state.)
  2. Citizens are not to be denied the "privileges and immunities" of citizens in other states. That is, they are not to be discriminated against simply because they are residents of other states. (The payment of out-of-state tuition is one of the several recognized exceptions to this rule.)
  3. States are required to return fugitives wanted in other states. (By judicial interpretation, this is a discretionary power of the governor in the state to which a felon has fled.)

C. *Constitutional Amendments (Civil Rights):*
  1. States are subject to the requirements of due process and equal protection (Fourteenth Amendment).
  2. States cannot deprive people of the right to vote on the basis of race (Fifteenth Amendment).
  3. States cannot deny the right to vote on account of sex (Nineteenth Amendment).
  4. States cannot impose a poll tax as a condition of voting in federal elections (Twenty-fourth Amendment).
  5. States cannot deny the vote to those eighteen years of age or older simply on the basis of age (Twenty-sixth Amendment).

---

authority of the United States, shall be the supreme law of the land; and the judges in every state shall be bound thereby, anything in the constitution or laws of any state to the contrary notwithstanding.

State constitutions, laws, and practices found by the courts to conflict with the national constitution or national laws and treaties become null and void. In view of this, the courts' broad interpretations of the powers of the national government have reduced the residual powers of the states.

The authority of both the national and state governments is subject to several limitations, the nature of which has depended on how the courts have interpreted the Constitution. Of particular importance during the last several decades have been limitations on the ability of governments of infringe upon the basic civil liberties of individuals and groups. The Bill of Rights, among other things, prohibits the national government from infringing upon the freedom of religion, speech, and assembly and extends certain basic rights to person accused of crime. Over the years the due process clause of the Fourteenth Amendment has been used by the courts to forbid the states from infringing upon most of the civil liberties guaranteed in the Bill of Rights.

Constitutional Change

The United States Constitution is a brief and flexible document generally confined to fundamentals of government. Its length, including amendments, of about 6,000 words contrasts markedly with the constitutions of most state governments, several of which have more than 100,000 words.

The Constitution is a living document that has been interpreted and reinterpreted in light of changing conditions. The most prominent role in its interpretation has been taken by the United States Supreme Court, though both the president and Congress have often acted on the basis of their interpretations of their powers.

The need to interpret the Constitution arises chiefly from the vague language contained in the document. What, for example, are the meanings of "commerce," of "necessary and proper" action, of "the general welfare," and of "due process"? In many cases, it is difficult or impossible to discover the precise intent of the framers of the Constitution. Obviously, on many questions the nation has had to decide over two centuries, such as whether to regulate commercial airlines, the framers had no opinion. The survival of the Constitution has rested largely on the framers' having made it flexible enough to serve the needs of future generations.

Besides change by interpretation, the Constitution may be altered by amendment. Under Article V of the Constitution, amendments may be proposed by a two-thirds vote in both houses of Congress or by a constitutional convention called by Congress at the request of two-thirds (thirty-four) of the state legislatures. Once an amendment has been proposed, it may be ratified by the approval of three-fourths of the state legislatures or by the consent of ratifying conventions in three-fourths (thirty-eight) of the states. Thus far, among the amendments that have become part of the Constitution, all but one (the repeal of Prohibition) have been approved by state legislatures. Congress decides the method of ratification, and in the case of Prohibition it felt that repeal would be easier to secure through conventions rather than state legislatures.

From time to time state legislatures have petitioned Congress to call a constitutional convention. On three occasions advocates of change came close to receiving the support of the required two-thirds of the state legislatures. One issue was the direct election of U.S. senators, which Congress proposed as the Seventeenth Amendment after twenty-six states requested a constitutional convention. In the 1960s a proposal for a constitutional convention to overturn the U.S. Supreme Court's decisions on legislative reapportionment fell one state short of the needed number of petitions. Since the late 1970s a number of states have petitioned Congress to call a constitutional convention that would develop an amendment requiring the national government to balance its budget. If thirty-four or more states send Congress valid petitions for a constitutional convention, members of the House and Senate would then have to determine how the delegates would be chosen, what rules would govern the operation of the convention, and whether delegates could consider amendments other than that specified in the state petitions. Some legal observers fear a runaway convention, one in which delegates would feel free to revise any aspect of the Constitution they desired. But other legal experts, including a study committee of the American Bar Association, believe that Congress has the power in calling a constitutional convention to limit the deliberations of that body to the subject designated by the legislatures.

Amending the Constitution has been a difficult process. Only twenty-six amendments have been ratified in two centuries. The first ten, the Bill of Rights, came as a package shortly after ratification of the Constitution. The 1970s and early 1980s witnessed a considerable effort to adopt an amendment providing that "equality of rights under the law shall not be denied or abridged by the United States or by any state on account of sex." This Equal Rights Amendment (ERA) was proposed by Congress in 1972. Supporters of the amendment originally had until March 22, 1979, to secure its ratification by thirty-eight states. Many states rapidly ratified the amendment. As time went on, however, the proposal became more controversial, and by March 1979 only thirty-five states had ratified. Momentum against the ERA was also evidenced in the 1970s by the decision of four state legislatures to rescind (take back) their approval of the amendment. To date, neither Congress nor the courts have ruled on the validity of the rescinding votes. Congress in 1978 voted to extended the ratification deadline to June 30, 1982, but the amendment again failed to secure ratification.

Opposition to the ERA came from fundamentalist religious bodies and conservative groups, many of which were affiliated with the national STOP ERA organization headed by Phyllis Schlafly. Opponents argued that the amendment would help destroy the family (some linked it with liberalized laws on abortion and gay rights) and deprive women of many of the benefits they now enjoy, such as draft exemption and eligibility for alimony or child support. Opponents also contended that existing laws, including many on the state level, adequately protect women against discrimination. Proponents of ERA contended that sex discrimination did exist; because current laws were full of loopholes and lacked comprehensive coverage, a general protection was needed in the U.S. Constitution. Some supporters also said that a major source of opposition to the amendment was businesspeople who feared they would have to give women equal pay for equal work, meaning more pay, if the amendment were adopted. In the early 1980s women were earning about fifty-nine cents for every dollar earned by men.

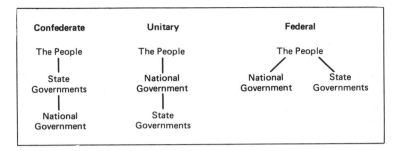

Figure 2–2   Alternative Methods of Distributing Governmental Authority in the United States.

FEDERAL-STATE RELATIONS IN THEORY AND PRACTICE

Figure 2–2 outlines three possible methods of distributing governmental authority in the United States—confederate, unitary, and federal. In a pure confederation the national government is a creation of sovereign states. The national government has only those powers given it by the states and has not direct relations with people. Under a unitary system the situation is reversed. The national government has full sovereignty, creating and delegating certain powers to states or other subnational governments. Under a federal system of government, as found in the United States, power is divided between the national and state governments. How power is divided and who should do the dividing have been subjects of dispute.

Until the Civil War intense debate rated over whether the Union created by the Constitution was a confederation or a federation. The argument that the Constitution was merely an improved version of the Articles of Confederation, a compact among sovereign states, was used by (1) the Jeffersonians to fight the programs of the Federalists; (2) several New England states to oppose the War of 1812; and (3) the southern states to oppose high tariffs and attempts to abolish slavery.

The historical and legal evidence favors those who argued against the compact or confederation theory. The Constitution states in its preamble that it derives its authority from "the people" rather than from the state governments. The Constitution was ratified by elected conventions rather than by state legislatures, and it gave the people instead of the states the right to choose the members of the House of Representatives. The Constitution also omitted the state sovereignty article found in the Articles of Confederation, placed numerous prohibitions on state activity, and made the U.S. Constitution, and national laws and treaties the supreme law of the land.

The view that the Union was a compact among the states from which they could withdraw at will was not disposed of in courtrooms, but on the battlefields of the Civil War. Following this war and until the late 1930s, the allocation of authority among the national and state governments was determined mainly by the judicial application of the doctrine of *dual federalism*. Under this doctrine each of the two types of government had a separate sphere of authority. The Supreme Court assumed much of the task of deciding which governmental function fell within the sphere of state authority and which belonged to the national government.

Under dual federalism, for example, foreign policy was regarded as the concern of the national government, while public education was to be handled by state governments or their local subdivisions. Responsibility for the regulation of business was divided, the national government regulating business activities involving more than one state (interstate commerce) and state governments controlling activities within a single state (intrastate commerce). The court frequently invalidated acts of Congress on the grounds that they fell into the states' sphere of authority. Likewise, certain state activities were declared illegal on the basis that they conflicted with the national government's authority.

The concept of dual federalism continues to play a role in legal theory and, more importantly, in how many people view national–state relations. Elements of dual federalism, moreover, appeared in the early 1980s in President Reagan's New Federalism, which calls for a transfer of several federal programs to the states. Under Reagan's proposal, the states would ultimately be able to finance these programs through tax resources given up by the national government. Initially, the New Federalism, if approved by Congress, would involve a sorting out of functions between the national and state governments—for example, national assumption of all health programs and state assumption of welfare programs.

The idea of dividing functions among levels of government conflicts with the pattern of cooperative federalism that has evolved since the 1930s. Under *cooperative federalism* the various functions of government are not divided among levels of government; instead a number of governments perform the same functions.[15] Currently all levels of government in the United States are engaged in such basic domestic programs as education, housing, law enforcement, pollution control, transportation, and welfare. In many of these areas the chief role of the national government is to help fund the state and local units. The national government also commonly sets regulations and standards of performance that the states and their subdivisions are expected to meet—for example, those established to clean up air pollution or carry out meat inspection. At times the threat of losing federal aid has been used to "encourage" states to follow certain policies. During the 1970s and most of the 1980s, for example, states that failed to enforce a 55-mile-per-hour limit ran the risk of losing federal

---

[15] For the theme that American federalism has always been a system of shared functions, see Morton Grodzins, *The American System* (Chicago: Rand McNally, 1966).

highway funds. The same inducement was used in 1985 to encourage states to raise their minimum drinking age to twenty-one.

Federal Aid Programs

The chief instrument of modern cooperative federalism has been federal aid to state and local governments. Currently this aid consists of categorical grants-in-aid and block grants. Categorical grants are given upon application by state and local officials for specific purposes, such as building a sewer system, and can be used only for those purposes. Block grants provide funds that states and localities can use as they choose for general purposes such as community development.

Because of changes in federal policy, state and local governments have generally become less dependent on federal aid since the 1970s. In 1978 federal grants constituted 27 percent of state and local expenditures; by 1985 that figure had declined to around 20 percent. Declines in federal aid, as one might expect, have not been altogether welcomed on the state and local level, especially in hard-pressed large cities. In 1986 Mayor Cisneros of San Antonio, Texas, offered an assembly of local officials this view on further proposed cuts in federal aid:

> This year all of us together face a new problem . . . . It is a disastrous dismantling of the federal-local partnership. It is a meat-axe chopping of the domestic obligations of government . . . . We must be determined to stand up for what is right in the face of what I can only call disrespect: a disrespect for our cities, disrespect for the people who govern them, and disrespect for the people who live in them.[16]

The Politics of Federalism

Conflict between national and state governments has been a continual feature of American politics. The case for vesting most responsibilities in state governments and their local subdivisions has rested in part on legal theories of federalism. But it is also based on the propositions that state and local governments should have jurisdiction over major areas of domestic policy because they are closer to the people and that governmental policies and programs should reflect the diverse needs and values of different parts of the country. Some doubt, however, has been expressed about the relative closeness of state and local governments to the people. On the whole, for example, people are likely to pay far more attention to national than state or local politics[17] and to participate more extensively in national elections than in state and local contests.

[16] Quoted in *Congressional Record*, March 25, 1986, p. E916.
[17] See M. Kent Jennings and Harmon Ziegler, "The Salience of American State Politics," *American Political Science Review* 64 (June 1970): 523–535.

Conflict over which level of government should do what has not generally emanated from disagreement over abstract principles. Often those who have championed the principle of states' rights have believed that state government is more favorably disposed to their interests. A corporation, for instance, may prefer to be regulated, if at all, at the state rather than the national level, if it perceives the states as being easier to influence and less likely to adopt effective regulations.

The choice of which government should carry out a certain function is not politically neutral. On the national level there is far more competition among business interests, more countervailing influences from organized labor and other groups, and more public attention to political matters than are found in most states and localities. Reformers have generally looked to the national government rather than the states or localities for protection of minority rights. They have also often criticized state regulation for fragmenting the treatment of national problems and for subverting public goals by vesting responsibility in nonprofessional regulators who are easily swayed by local political interests.

Determining which matters require uniform national treatment and which should be treated in light of the values and interests of particular areas of the country has been difficult. On a number of occasions the Supreme Court has ruled that basic civil liberties, such as the right to vote, must be recognized nationally. The argument has also been made that problems such as pollution control and crime spill over the boundaries of states and local governments and thus require coordinated national action. Currently at issue are these kinds of questions: Should welfare rights be one thing in New York and another in Mississippi? Should educational funding per pupil be greater in some states than others, or in some parts of a state than others?

State and local governments in this country have long been freer from interference by the national government than have subnational governments in European nations, most of which have unitary systems. State and local units have also played a major part in determining how much money is to be spent on various programs. When federal aid is counted as state and local expenditures (after all, the states and localities do make the final spending decisions), state and local governments control more than 60 percent of the funds spent on domestic programs. The largest categories of expenditures for state and local governments are education, public welfare, and highways, in that order. On the revenue side, state and local governments raise about 80 percent of the revenues they spend. The remaining 20 percent, as noted earlier, comes from federal aid. In terms of employees and payroll, state and local governments have been growing while the federal government has been relatively stagnant (see Figure 2–3).

In addition to making a number of decisions affecting domestic programs, state and local units function to limit the scope of national government activity. As one long-time participant in intergovernmental affairs has noted, there generally "must be a reasonable showing of state and local inability or

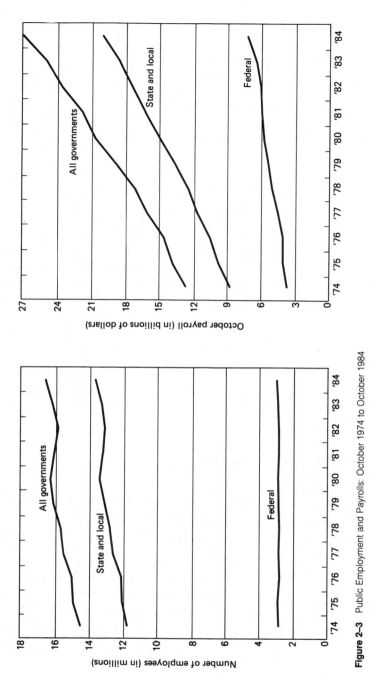

Figure 2–3 Public Employment and Payrolls: October 1974 to October 1984

Source: U.S. Bureau of the Census. Public Employment in 1094. (Washington, D.C.: Government Printing Office. 1985), p. vi.

unwillingness to act before a new federal program can be passed through the Congress."[18] Congress, which is composed of individuals who represent states and localities has also on occasion reversed U.S. Supreme Court decisions and conferred responsibilities on the states. For instance, it has allowed the states to regulate insurance companies operating in interstate commerce. More important, on policy matters ranging from school segregation to environmental protection, the national government relies on the cooperation of state and local officials in implementing policies.

Although states and localities play important roles in the governmental system, these roles are subject to change. For the most part Congress determines what role each level of government will play in the performance of domestic functions. Since the 1930s, the Supreme Court has generally refused to interfere with the sharing of governmental functions and has allowed the national government to become involved in matters once thought to be the exclusive concern of state and local governments. The Supreme Court has from time to time recognized states' rights. In the case of *National League of Cities* v. *Usery* (1976),[19] for instance, the Court invalidated legislation by Congress that would have extended federal labor regulations on hours and minimum wages to state and local employees. Its reasoning was that this legislation conflicted with the sovereign rights of the states. Nine years later, however, the Court reversed this decision and declared that the question of whether these labor standards should apply to state and local governments was to be answered by Congress rather than the courts.[20] This decision appears to have given Congress blanket authority over the states.

SUFFRAGE AND POPULAR CONTROL OF GOVERNMENT

Although the Constitution declares the source of governmental authority to be "the people," it makes scant provision for popular control of government. The framers were generally distrustful of democracy, which they associated with mob rule, and were particularly fearful that government "by the people" would lead to infringement of individual rights, especially property rights.

Originally, the only national government body to be directly elected by the voters was the House of Representatives. The Senate, to be chosen by state legislatures, was envisioned by many framers as an autocratic body that would check the excesses of the more democratic House. Additional checks on majority rule were to be provided by the president, chosen by electors, and by the appointed Supreme Court. As political scientist Robert Dahl has pointed out,

[18] William G. Coleman, "Rhetoric and Reality," *National Civic Review*, July 1970, p. 360.
[19] 426 U.S. 833 (1976).
[20] *Garcia* v. *San Antonio Metropolitan Transit District*, 105 1005 (1985).

"this country's commitment to democracy came after and not before the formation and adoption of the Constitution."[21]

Certain reforms following the election of Andrew Jackson as President in 1828, reforms that were continued by the Populist movement of the late nineteenth century and the Progressive movement of the early twentieth century, produced considerable democratization of the electoral process. This is particularly evident in the selection of the president and U.S. senators and, on the state level, the election of many officials, including judges in some states. The federal judiciary and many state courts remain appointive and thus not directly accountable to the voters. Even so, some scholars content that appointed judges actually do follow election returns in making decisions (see Chapter 9).

Along with the democratization of the election of many public officials has come an increase in the number of people who are eligible to vote. Historically, who may vote in national as well as state and local elections has been determined by state governments. As far as the framers of the Constitution were concerned, people not allowed to vote in a state election could not vote in federal elections. At the time the Constitution was adopted, the states restricted suffrage to adult white males and in some cases imposed religious and property-holding requirements. The latter two restrictions had been eliminated by the time of Andrew Jackson, except for property-holding requirements for certain elections (such as bond elections), which survived until relatively recent years.[22]

Barriers to voting have been removed chiefly by amendments to the U.S. Constitution, U.S. Supreme court decisions, and acts of Congress. The Fifteenth Amendment, adopted in 1870, banned discrimination in voting on the basis "of race, color, or previous condition of servitude." The Nineteenth Amendment (1920) extended the vote to women, and the Twenty-sixth Amendment (1971) lowered the voting age to eighteen in all elections.

The most difficult of these amendments to implement has been the Fifteenth. During the Reconstruction period after the Civil War, newly enfranchised blacks in southern states exercised their voting rights and elected twenty black members of Congress. At the end of Reconstruction, however, blacks were quickly disenfranchised through a variety of legal devices, and violence and intimidation by white-supremacy organizations were directed against those who dared attempt to vote. Some states required people whose grandfathers could not vote before the adoption of the Fifteenth Amendment (1860) to pass a literacy test in order to vote. Most blacks, of course, were required to take the literacy test and nearly all of them failed, usually because of the unfair manner in which the test was administered. The Supreme Court invalidated the use of

---

[21] Robert A. Dahl, "On Removing Certain Impediments to Democracy in the United States," *Political Science Quarterly* 92 (Spring 1977): 4.

[22] The Supreme Court invalidated the property requirement for municipal bond elections in *Phoenix* v. *Kolodoziejski*, 399 U.S. 204 (1970).

"grandfather" requirements in 1915.[23] The literacy test, however, continued to be used in a discriminatory manner for several more decades. Charles Evers, later to become the first black mayor of Fayette, Mississippi, recalled that when he first tried to register in 1946 he was told by a white registrar he could do so if he could pass a simple literacy test of one question: "How many bubbles in a bar of soap?"[24] The use of such literacy tests or those requiring blacks to give "reasonable interpretations" of state constitutions were not eliminated until the Voting Rights Acts of 1965 and 1970.

Other practices declared illegal were the white primary and the poll tax in state and local elections. Several southern states allowed the major political parties to determine who could or could not vote in primary elections. Thus, though blacks would vote in the general election, they were excluded from voting in the Democratic primary. Because candidates nominated in the Democratic primary were seldom opposed in the general election, blacks were deprived of any choice among candidates. The white primary was invalidated by the Supreme Court in 1944.[25] The poll tax, a tax on each individual who wished to vote, was used to discourage poor whites as well as poor blacks from voting. The use of poll taxes was prohibited in federal elections by the Twenty-fourth Amendment (1964) and in state and local elections by a U.S. Supreme Court decision in 1966.[26]

Through a series of civil rights laws starting in 1957, Congress also sought to protect the voting rights of blacks and other minorities. The most important legislation was the Voting Rights Act, first adopted in 1965 and since extended and amended on several occasions. The act not only prohibits the discriminatory use of literacy tests and other devices for determining voter eligibility, but provides for federal examiners to supervise the voting process when necessary and requires that ballots and voting materials be made available in languages other than English where an area is heavily populated by non-English-speaking groups. The act also requires state and local governments in areas with a history of voting discrimination to get federal permission for changes that affect voting rights, ranging from moving a polling place to altering election-districting arrangements. Since the passage of the 1965 Voting Rights Act millions of blacks have registered to vote. From 1965 to 1975 alone about 1.5 million blacks in the South were added to voter registration lists. The growth of black voting in the South has been accompanied by rising numbers of blacks seeking and winning public office.

As a result of Supreme Court decisions and acts of Congress the requirements for voting are basically the same from state to state. In order to

---

[23] *Guinn* v. *United States*, 238 U.S. 347.
[24] Quoted in *Congressional Record*, June 9, 1981, p. E284.
[25] *Smith* v. *Allwright*, 321 U.S. 649.
[26] *Harper* v. *Virginia Board of Elections*, 383 U.S. 663.

vote, one must be at least eighteen, a United States citizen, a resident of his or her state, country, or precinct for a certain period (the courts may invalidate lengthy residency requirements), and registered to vote. Regulations regarding registration vary from state to state. Some states make the process difficult—for example, by severely limiting the number of days during which people can register or the hours in which registration offices are open. Such practices can discourage people, especially the less educated and affluent, from participating.[27]

The right to vote is fundamental in a democracy. The liberalization of suffrage, however, does not guarantee that government will adhere to the principle of majority rule. As discussed in Chapter 3, it can be argued that "the people" have little influence on those who govern. There are, moreover, constitutional precepts and institutions that make it difficult to achieve a government that is responsive to the majority will. The principle of majority rule, for example, has often been frustrated by the insistence of government, particularly the Supreme Court, that certain minority and individual rights be protected. At one time the Court was particularly concerned with the protection of individual property rights. More recently it has been concerned with the rights of racial and religious minorities and individuals accused of crime. Majority rule has also been frustrated by the allocation of governmental authority among levels and branches of government. This fragmentation makes it difficult for government to respond quickly to what a majority of the people in the nation may demand.

SUMMARY

1. The immediate problem facing the framers of the Constitution was the weakness of the national government formed under the Articles of Confederation (1781–1788). The Articles emphasized state sovereignty, failed to provide for a chief executive and an effective national court system, and did not give the national government the power to tax, regulate commerce among the states, or manage the nation's currency and credit problems.

2. The framers of the Constitution came from the socio-economic elite of the population. Their views were shaped by such influences personal and regional interests, the writings of European political theorists, the colonial experience, and the performance of state governments under constitutions adopted shortly after the Revolutionary War. On the whole, the framers feared the concentration of power and favored the subordination of government to higher laws of nature.

[27] Steven J. Rosenstone and Raymond E. Wolfinger, "The Effect of Registration Laws on Voter Turnout," *American Political Science Review* 72 (1978): 22–30.

3. Framing the Constitution required a number of compromises. One of the most important was the compromise between large and small states on representation in the new Congress. Additional compromises were made on the selection of the president and between various regions of the country. A further compromise—the addition of a bill of rights—was made to secure ratification of the Constitution.

4. The United States Constitution is a relatively brief document that has been changed by interpretation and amendment to accommodate the needs of different generations. It created a set of separate national institutions that share power and impose checks and balances on one another. It also allocated authority between the national and state governments, but exactly what authority is allocated to which level has been a matter of debate. In the long run, however, governmental power has gravitated from the states to the national government and, within the national government, from Congress to the President.

5. Under the Constitution the Supreme Court has found the national government to have inherent powers in foreign policy. The Court in modern times has also broadly interpreted the enumerated powers of the national government and has added to these the concept of implied powers. State governments have residual or reserved powers. From time to time the powers of both levels of government have been limited by Supreme Court interpretations of the Constitution.

6. There are at least three different interpretations of federal–state relations: confederate, unitary, and federal systems. Over the last several decades the cooperative pattern has dominated, and the national, state, and local governments have shared responsibility for a number of functions. In recent years, however, there has been a proposal for a new sorting of functions, and under President Reagan's New Federalism state and local governments would be doing more by themselves through their own tax resources.

7. The Constitution made little provision for popular control of government. Over the years the presidency and the United States Senate have been democratized and the proportion of the population who are eligible to vote has increased. Throughout American history, majority rule has been balanced with concern for the rights of individuals and minorities.

3

CITIZEN INPUTS: OPINION, PARTICIPATION, AND CONTROL

Having examined the development and basic characteristics of our constitutional system, we can now begin to consider the political attitudes and behavior of the American people. We begin by exploring theories and findings on the development of general political orientations and by outlining the nature of public or mass opinion in this country. We then turn to political participation and questions concerning government "of the people, by the people, and for the people," to quote Abraham Lincoln's famous phrase in the Gettysburg Address.

GENERAL POLITICAL ORIENTATIONS

Political Socialization

Much of what people think about politics is acquired early in life through the process of political socialization.[1] Through this process children acquire both political knowledge (cognitive socialization) and political attachments or feelings (affective socialization). Major agents of political socialization include parents, schools, peer groups, and the mass media.

It is in the family setting that children first become socially aware of their national, community, racial, religious, ethnic, and class identities. The politically significant characteristic of political-party identification (including identification as an independent) is also commonly acquired at an early age from the family. It may be that a majority of fourth graders are committed Democrats or Republicans because of what they learn at home though they have only vague ideas about political parties or the differences between them. Young people also tend to pick up a general orientation toward political activity from their parents. Children whose parents are active in political life are also likely to become active. In families where parents ignore political life, children are unlikely to vote or engage in other forms of political activity.

Early schooling generally supplements this family influence by fostering positive feelings toward the political system. Supportive affective attitudes result from rituals such as saying the Pledge of Allegiance, singing patriotic songs, and learning about national heroes of the past. Along with learning about "our history" and "our country," children are introduced to widely shared values such as those found in the Declaration of Independence and the Constitution.

Studies suggest that "government" to young children is personified by the president of the United States, who, with exceptions such as Richard Nixon during the Watergate scandal, is viewed positively as a powerful but benevolent authority figure. Children also develop a similar awareness of officials such as police officers and mayors. This sense of trust and support tends to diminish somewhat over time. As children become older they become more knowledge-

[1] See, for example, Richard E. Dawson et al., *Political Socialization* (Boston: Little, Brown, 1977).

able about the real world and more cynical about political figures and institutions, though they remain basically supportive.

As children enter their teens, peer groups and the media assume more importance in shaping their political opinions. By this time, however, much of how they think about politics has already been set. Relationships formed with school friends are far more likely to be important in influencing social rather than political attitudes and behavior. Like their parents, they consider television a highly credible source of political information. On the other hand, teenagers spend considerably less time than their parents viewing news programs.

Political socialization or learning continues throughout life. Basic political orientations may change, for example, with changes in income, education, or peer-group affiliations. Events such as a severe economic crisis, an unpopular war, or a political scandal may also prompt changes in political viewpoints. The media, and television in particular, play a particularly important role in shaping "the picture in our heads" of what the world is like. As the following chapter indicates, however, the media's impact is less important in directly reshaping general political orientations or attitudes.

What is most remarkable about general political orientations is not that they change, but that those acquired early in life have remarkable staying power. Evidence suggests, for example, that as many as two of every three people continue to identify with the political party which they first identified as children.[2] Most people also maintain the reverence for the flag and the Constitution that they acquired in school, even though they may occasionally become highly critical of the performance of government.[3]

Political orientations persist largely for two reasons. One is the tendency of people to associate with those of similar attitudes and thus to constantly find their viewpoints reinforced by others. The other reason is people's tendency to engage in selective perception—that is, to believe information that supports their political views and to screen out information that conflicts with these views.

The socialization process helps explain both why there are differences among individuals and groups and why, at the same time, there are certain ties among them. It also helps explain how values and beliefs are handed down from one generation to another—albeit imperfectly, since social disruptions may cause a generation gap. From a systems viewpoint, early socialization is highly functional in facilitating agreement on basic values, avoiding conflict, and installing supportive attitudes toward the political system.

---

[2] See Angus Campbell, Philip E. Converse, Warren E. Miller, and Donald E. Stokes, *The American Voter* (New York: John Wiley and Sons, 1960).

[3] See Donald J. Devine, *The Political Culture of the United States* (Boston: Little, Brown, 1972).

Public Opinion

Research indicates that there is, indeed, broad agreement among Americans on what are called *core values*. And although the signals are somewhat weak and mixed, there is also evidence of support for the system. In general, however, we do not find Americans to be particularly well informed on political matters or consistent in their beliefs.

Survey data suggest that the core values that are widely shared in this country include equality, freedom, democracy, private enterprise, and individual initiative.[4] These values are far from being completely realized in American political life. The notion that people in the United States are rugged individualists, for example, has been countered by scholars who see Americans as essentially other-directed people who desire to conform and are easily swayed by others.[5] Similarly, the quest for wealth may have less to do with rugged individualism than with people's desire to "keep up with the Joneses" and to impress others with what they can afford to purchase.[6] As the chapter on government, politics, and civil rights indicates, the commitment to the value of equality has not been deep enough or broad enough to prevent discrimination against various groups, and despite a general belief in free speech, people have not been particularly tolerant of the right of those with whom they disagree to have their say.

While not perfectly implemented, core values do affect the language and style of politics and may limit the scope of governmental action. In terms of style, for example, notions of democracy and equality in American culture have encouraged politicans to at least give the impression of caring about "the common person" and have fostered officials who act like public servants in the literal sense rather than like royalty. In some cases, moreover, widely accepted values may limit alternative courses of action. A widespread belief in private enterprise (or fear of socialism), for example, will give those who see the need to nationalize industries an uphill battle.

Supports, Expectations, Information

As noted in the Introduction, supportive public attitudes are needed if those in power are to govern without having to resort to force. Political scientist V. O. Key once suggested that government must cultivate a cheerful and willing obedience among the public.[7] Many governmental officials would settle for

---

[4] Devine, op. cit.

[5] See David Riesman, *The Lonely Crowd* (New Haven: Yale University Press, 1950).

[6] See Thorstein Veblen, *The Theory of the Leisure Class* (New York: Mentor Books, 1953).

[7] V. O. Key, Jr., *Public Opinion and American Democracy* (New York: Knopf, 1961), pp. 411–431.

public apathy or indifference—anything short of hostility—as an indicator of general public support. Indeed, as we will see, apathy may be taken as an indicator of satisfaction.

Survey research indicates that feelings toward the political system and those in power vary over time. During the early 1980s the vast majority of people in this country were "very proud" to be Americans, had confidence in the future of the United States, and were satisfied with the way things were going in the nation. These feelings contrasted somewhat with the general sentiment of the 1970s.[8] Yet even when people appear satisfied with the condition of the country and their own lives, they are apt to take a dim view of the political world. Opinion polls over the past several years have frequently shown that a majority of the American people, at times a substantial majority, agree with the statements "Special interests get more from government than the people do," "People running the government don't really care what happens to you," and "Quite a few of the people running the government are a little crooked."

The public expects government officials not only to perform certain functions—for instance, to protect the nation and to provide quality education—but to act properly (be honest, hardworking, moral in their conduct), and it has often found reason to be disappointed on both of these grounds. Presidents found to be saying one thing and doing another, as Ronald Reagan did on the subject of dealing with terrorists, are likely to suffer in public opinion polls. More persistently, the American people appear to have relatively low opinions of politicians. In terms of ethical standards, members of Congress and state and local officeholders seldom receive high rankings from more than 25 percent of the public. In this regard they lag far behind a variety of people in other occupations, including the clergy, doctors, college teachers, and television reporters (see Table 3–1).

Although the American people are somewhat critical of public officials, their own interest in politics and level of information on political matters leave much to be desired. Politics simply is not all that important to many people. Less than half of all adults, for example, have taken the time to learn the name of the person who represents them in Congress. Opinions expressed on issues, as in response to a pollster's questions, may well be based on little or no familiarity with the problem. Public opinion is also likely to be inconsistent. For example, a person may be liberal on one issue and conservative on another, or a self-proclaimed conservative may consistently favor liberal programs. The more education one has, the more likely he or she is to view issues in light of a consistent set of beliefs (that is, from an ideological perspective). In general, however, people tend to look at issues one at a time.

[8] *Gallup Report*, June 1986, p. 12.

Table 3-1   Honesty and Ethical Standards (Rankings Given by Public to 25 Occupations)

	COMBINED VERY HIGH, HIGH
Clergymen	67%
Druggists, Pharmacists	65
Medical Doctors	58
Dentists	56
College Teachers	54
Engineers	53
Policemen	47
Bankers	37
TV Reporters, Commentators	33
Funeral Directors	31
Journalists	31
Newspaper Reporters	29
Lawyers	27
Business Executives	23
Senators	23
Stockbrokers	20
Building Contractors	20
Congresspersons	20
Local Political Officeholders	18
Realtors	15
State Political Officeholders	15
Labor Union Leaders	13
Advertising Practitioners	12
Insurance Salesmen	10
Car Salesmen	5

Source: Gallup Report No. 239 (August, 1985) p. 3. Reproduced with permission.

POLITICAL PARTICIPATION

Participation in politics takes a number of forms. Communication directly with public officials on policy matters, joining an association that makes demands on government, helping a political party or a candidate for office, and running and holding public office are all examples of political participation.

Given our discussion of Americans' level of interest in politics, it is no surprise that under normal conditions the number participating in politics is limited. Even in the most common form of participation—voting in presidential elections—attracts little more than half of all eligible voters. Turnout in these elections, moreover, has generally declined since 1960, when nearly 59 percent of the eligible voters turned out; less than 50 percent have participated in recent elections.

Voter turnout levels are lower in the United States than in many European nations. Americans, though, appear to be more inclined than Europeans to engage in collective political activity.[9] But the vast number of organized groups in this country are actually run by only a small fraction of their membership.[10] Only about 6 percent of the adult population in the United States contribute to political campaigns (other than through the one-dollar checkoff on U.S. income tax returns, in which over 30 million taxpayers voluntarily participate),[11] and an even smaller proportion pursue the time-consuming task of running for office.

What accounts for this lack of participation? Scholars believe nonparticipation reflects both alienation and contentment with the existing political situation. In the first case, people fail to vote or otherwise get involved in politics because they think it will be a waste of time. They have low estimations of their ability to change things. Contentment, on the other hand, has also been linked with political apathy. If people were unhappy, the theory goes, they would vote and engage in other forms of political activity. That they are apathetic therefore means that they are reasonably content with the status quo.

Who Participates?

Whether nonparticipation is due to alienation or to contentment, it is clear that some people participate more regularly than others. Research in general suggests that voter turnout is greater among whites than blacks or Hispanics and increases with age (up to sixty-five and older) and with educational attainment. At one time a higher percentage of men than women voted regularly. This difference has all but disappeared. And although unemployment may be an important political issue (see Chapter 11), the unemployed themselves are less likely than those with jobs to vote or, indeed, otherwise get involved in politics. They are typically far too occupied with holding body and soul together to engage in what appears to be a remote concern.[12]

Generally, political participation is directly related to an individual's social class as measured by wealth, education, and occupational status.[13] People from the wealthier and better-educated segments of society are more likely than others not only to vote but to make campaign contributions, join groups that

[9] See Gabriel A. Almond and Sidney Verba, *The Civic Culture* (Princeton, N.J.: Princeton University Press, 1963).

[10] David Truman, *The Governmental Process* (New York: Knopf, 1971).

[11] See David Adamany, "The Sources of Money: An Overview," *Annals* 450 (May 1976): 19–20.

[12] Steven J. Rosenstone, "Economic Adversity and Voter Turnout," *American Journal of Political Science* 26 (February 1982): 25–46.

[13] See Sidney Verba and Norman H. Nie, *Participation in America* (New York: Harper & Row, Pub., 1972).

Table 3–2   Participation in Interest Groups

	GAVE MONEY	MEMBER	EITHER/ BOTH
National	23%	13%	26%
Sex			
Men	25	15	28
Women	20	10	23
Education			
College	34	21	38
High school	21	11	24
Grade school	4	2	5
Region			
East	21	12	23
Midwest	23	12	27
South	21	2	24
West	27	l5	31
Age			
18–29 years	24	16	29
30–49 years	27	15	29
50 and older	17	8	20
Family Income			
$25,000 and over	32	22	38
$15,000–$24,999	25	12	27
Under $15,000	15	7	17
Politics			
Republican	23	13	26
Democrat	20	10	23
Independent	24	14	28

Source: *Gallup Report,* August 1981, p. 45.

pressure government (Table 3–2), and run for office. Social class, however, is not the only variable related to political activity. Group consciousness, for example, has tended to encourage blacks and other minorities to participate at a greater rate than their social status would otherwise indicate.[14]

To some extent, participation also varies by political periods. During the late 1960s and early 1970s, for example, the young and people on the ideological left were unusually active in politics.[15] Since the mid 1970s those on the ideological right have become more active. Participation by ideological groups seems to be enhanced by their perception of improved opportunities to secure the types of reforms they favor.

Participatory differences according to sex and race are most apparent when we consider who holds public office. Although a case may be made that the

[14] Ibid.

[15] Paul Allen Beck and M. Kent Jennings, "Political Periods and Political Participation," *American Political Science Review* 73 (1979): 737–750.

civil service as a whole is roughly representative of the American people, this is not true of top-level appointive positions. In these positions, women and blacks are underrepresented. That is, the proportion of these positions held by blacks and women is less than their percentage of the total population. The same two groups are also underrepresented in elective offices. Blacks, who account for about 10 percent of the population, hold less than one percent of the more than 500,000 elective positions in this country. And despite gains since the mid 1960s, women, who make up more than half of the nation's population, fill only 7 percent of all elective offices. Women who occupy elective and appointive offices are generally middle-aged with grown children. Their interest in politics is related largely to having been raised in politically active families.[16]

The significance of the unrepresentativeness of officeholders has been subject to debate. Some people have argued that women, blacks, and other underrepresented groups have special points of view on policy matters that are ignored unless their members hold office. Others counter that the underrepresented, particularly women, are far from united over policy questions and that what policy preferences they share may also be held by many people who are not members of underrepresented groups. Data suggest that an officeholder need not be black to favor programs that aid blacks or be a woman to support programs intended to benefit women. Increased representation, however, may be valuable in itself as a symbol that government does represent a cross section of the people.

THE INSIDERS

The data just presented suggest that the upper-class, middle-aged, white males have an insider's status in American politics, though their position has been increasingly challenged by women and certain racial and ethnic minorities in the last few decades. With respect to occupations, successful business people and professionals such as doctors, scientists, and lawyers have long occupied a special status in the political system. Studies on local government has generally found prominent business people to be influential in community politics.[17] On the state and national levels, the participation of individuals with business interests has been most evident in the interest groups discussed in the following chapter.

The political significance of persons with professional or technical training rests mainly on their claim to expertise in various areas of public policy. Thus, doctors employed both in and outside of government have had an impact

---

[16] For a brief report on women officeholders, see Marilyn Johnson and Kathy Stanwick, *Profile of Women Holding Office*, (New Brunswick, N.J.: Eagleton Institute of Politics, Rutgers University, 1976). For an in-depth study of women in state legislatures, see Jeane Kirkpatrick, *Political Woman* (New York: Basic Books, 1974).

[17] See, for example, Edward Banfield and James Q. Wilson, *City Politics* (New York: Random House, 1966).

(though not always a decisive one) on food, drug, and health-care policies. Similarly, scientists have been deeply engaged in policies affecting the space program and the development of weapons systems. As the tasks of government have become more complex there has been a corresponding reliance on research and development specialists, economists, and various technicians.

Lawyers deserve attention here because they have long played basic and diverse roles in politics and policy making. Many people have chosen the legal profession as the first step in pursuing their political inclinations.[18] Lawyers are the occupational source from which prosecutors, judges, and many legislators, chief executives, and administrators are drawn. Lawyers make, interpret, and enforce the laws and advise others of their legal rights and responsibilities. They are also important as individuals and groups seeking their own political ends, as advocates for those who wish to make or prevent policy changes, and as advisers to private as well as public policy makers.

A long-standing, semiserious conspiracy theory is that lawyers use government not so much to make public law as to make business for themselves. Thus, lawyers make laws that nobody can understand so that others will have to hire attorneys to defend their interests before judges who are also lawyers. Along with this theory is the belief that, at least on some issues, lawyers unite to protect their own economic interests. For example, one critic has contended that "lawyer-legislators keep an eye out for proposed bills which threaten the interest of their past, present and future clients, and vote them down.[19] Research suggests, however, that lawyer-legislators seldom vote as a bloc and that their policy preferences are on the whole, not much different from those of legislators who are not lawyers. Lawyers in office, in other words, are a diverse group who belong to different political parties and possess political philosophies ranging from the very conservative to the very liberal.

"THE PEOPLE":
A QUESTION OF INFLUENCE

Classical democratic theory assumes that the average citizen is informed about policy issues, eager to participate in political life, and, along with his or her fellow citizens, able to control those who hold political office. But as we have seen, research indicates that citizens in this country generally fall far short of these expectations. Some people are far more active and far more influential than others. Generally, high social status, wealth, and specialized knowledge give people an advantage over others in influencing public policy.

---

[18] Ibid.

[19] Melvin L. Wulf, (legal director, American Civil Liberties Union), "How Good Are Lawyers as Legislators?" *Signature*, September 1972, p. 8.

Some observers of politics in this country argue that despite these disparities, political power ultimately resides in "the people," or at least a majority of them. Although they concede that most people have little interest in or influence on most decisions made by government, those who champion this view believe that people can exert their will through elections and other forms of political participation when they feel it is necessary. Democracy, from this perspective, exists not in the number of decisions the people make but in the importance of these decisions, such as who is to hold office and major questions of policy.[20] Those who win elections acccording to this view, are given a consensus to do just about anything they want, but the people reserve the right to withdraw their support. Governmental leaders thus have considerable leeway to experiment and address complex questions, but ultimately they are accountable to the majority of citizens for what they do or fail to do.[21]

The existence of public opinion is difficult to document. Little actual force may be needed to keep leaders in line, because they share the same basic values as the general public and thus are not apt to stray far from public opinion in the first place. The possibility of a split in opinion is diminished further by the tendency, noticed in even the most repressive governments, for leaders to keep in touch with what "the people" are thinking and to make necessary adjustments.

On the other hand, it is difficult to deny that, to some extent at least, public opinion can be manipulated by verbal or other symbolic action, such as appeals to patriotism or the passage of laws that are not enforced, and by the indoctrination of people into a value and belief system supporting those in power. Perhaps the most appropriate conclusion about this problem of control is found in another quote from Lincoln: "It is true that you can fool all the people some of the time; you can even fool some of the people all the time; but you can't fool all the people all the time."

SUMMARY

1. Political socialization is the process by which people acquire political beliefs, attitudes, and opinions. Families and schools are important agents of political socialization for young people. Political attitudes formed by the early teens are difficult to change.

2. Americans agree on certain core values, such as freedom and private enterprise. Although these beliefs have not been completely realized in American political life, they influence the style and language of politics and may place certain boundaries on governmental action.

[20] See E. E. Schattschneider, *The Semi-Sovereign People* (New York: Holt, Rinehardt & Winston, 1960).
[21] Key, op. cit.

3. Americans are not particularly well informed about public affairs or consistent in their opinions on policy issues. Even though they may be satisfied with the condition of the nation and their own lives, they are apt to take a dim view of the political world and its participants.

4. Some people are more politically active than others. Generally, participation grows with increased wealth, education, and occupational status.

5. The public as a whole may be looked upon as giving governmental leaders a consensus to make decisions. This support, however, may be withdrawn.

4

GROUP POLITICS
AND THE MEDIA

Although one might argue that "the people" in some sense ultimately rule, the more ordinary course of governing involves adjusting to demands made by those relatively few people who represent organized interests. This chapter looks into the diversity of interest groups, the ways in which they attempt to influence public policy, apparent factors in their success, and the overall function of interest groups in the political system. The final section of the chapter deals with a subject of growing importance—the political functions of the mass media. More will be said about the media in the chapters covering elections, the presidency, and civil rights.

THE DIVERSITY OF INTEREST GROUPS

Benjamin Franklin wrote in the 1735 edition of his *Poor Richard's Almanack*, "God helps them that help themselves." Today, one of the most noticeable characteristics of politics in the United States is the large number of organized groups that attempt to help themselves by influencing official policy makers. There are, for example, close to 4,000 political action committees (PACs), which pour millions of dollars into political campaigns to advance the goals of corporations, labor unions, and a wide assortment of other interests (see Figure 4–1). Since the 1960s the number of organized groups has grown to the extent that just about any policy decision is bound to anger some group. Politician's lives have become even more difficult because many of the groups with which they deal are uncompromising on particular issues, such as abortion or gun control. Policy makers who fail to please the demands of such single-issue groups are apt to find themselves the targets of considerable opposition, regardless of the stands they take on other issues or the merits of their overall records.

Economic Groups

Among the most conspicuous groups engaged in politics are those that represent the views of business people, farmers, employees, (or workers) and the various professions. The term *business* applies to a number of enterprises—for example, large and small firms, manufacturers, wholesalers, and retailers. Each of the groups in the business community has its own set of problems and complaints, and within a particular industry there may be a number of forms of competition among individual firms. Business people commonly compete with each other for government favors and often disagree over specific policy matters.

Many businesses, especially the larger corporations, undertake much political activity on their own, including directly contacting policy makers or conducting public relations campaigns aimed at influencing public opinion on policy matters. Business interests are also represented by about 1,600 national

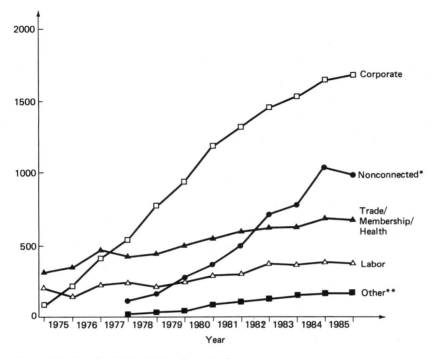

Figure 4–1 Growth of Political Action Committees

Source: Record (Federal Election Commission), March 1986, p. 4-1.

trade associations, such as the American Petroleum Institute and the National Automobile Dealers Association. Trade associations are voluntary nonprofit alliances of competitors in a single industry that often coordinate political activity and, in particular, "advance corporate interests in areas where a single company does not wish to be publicly identified."[1]

The interests of business people are further represented by organizations such as the U.S. Chamber of Commerce and the National Association of Manufacturers. The U.S. Chamber of Commerce is a national federation of 70,000 companies, 2,500 state and local chambers of commerce, and about 1,200 trade and professional associations. The National Association of Manufacturers represents the larger corporations. Since the late 1970s large corporations have also banded together to undertake lobbying activity through organizations known as the Business Council and the Business Roundtable.

[1] Larry Finkelstein, "Some Tough Question About Trade Associations," *Business and Society Review*, September 1973, p. 21. See also Edwin M. Epstein, *The Corporation in American Politics* (Englewood Cliffs, N.J.: Prentice-Hall, 1969), pp. 46–60.

The nation's farmers have trade associations that champion the distinct interests of dairy, tobacco, vegetable, cattle, wheat, and other types of farming. Larger groups have been created too. For instance, the American Farm Bureau Federation represents the more prosperous commercial farmers, and the National Farmers Union fights for the interests of small family farms. Marketing cooperatives have also been politically active in recent years. Beginning in the 1920s, cooperatives were organized with governmental encouragement as a form of collective bargaining to boost farm income. Some cooperatives are now extremely large. The three biggest dairy cooperatives, for example, produce about a quarter of the nation's milk supply. Over the years these cooperatives have contributed several million dollars in political campaigns, with a central objective of increasing milk price supports.

The major labor union in American politics is the American Federation of Labor–Congress of Industrial Organizations. The AFL–CIO has about 17 million members and conducts much of its political activity through its Committee on Political Education (COPE). Two large unions not associated with the AFL–CIO are the Teamsters, with approximately two million members, and the United Automobile Workers, with a membership of more than a million and a half. Unions historically have supported not only labor legislation such as public works expenditure to increase employment, but also measures in areas such as civil rights and consumer protection.

Among professional groups, the viewpoints and interests of lawyers are expressed by organizations such as the American Bar Association and the Trial Lawyers Association. The American Bar Assocation has taken a leading part in shaping laws (especially on crime and regulatory matters), structuring the legal system, and making recommendations for judicial positions. Although the national and state bar associations have striven for a "nonpolitical image," they have often turned to politics to protect their professional and economic interests. This effort has produced, among other things, state regulations that limit the number of lawyers and raise the income of those who do practice. Associations of trial lawyers have also sought to influence state and national legislation or regulations that they regard as affecting their economic interests. A recent example has been the opposition of trial lawyers to no-fault automobile insurance, whereby people in an automobile accident can collect from their own insurance companies without having to hire a lawyer, go to court, and establish liability.

Another professional association, the American Medical Association, to which about half of the nation's physicians belong, has regularly made known its views on federal food, drug, and health-care policies. Although the AMA has had influence, especially on the policies of the Federal Food and Drug Administration, it has lost some policy disputes. In the 1960s, for instance, it spent millions of dollars in an unsuccessful effort to prevent the adoption of the

Medicare program. The AMA has since mellowed on this issue, having seen that Medicare has contributed a great deal to the growth of the health industry.

Social Groups

In addition to these basically economically oriented organizations are voluntary citizen groups that claim to represent the interests or demands of a broad category of people. Nationality groups, such as those representing Polish-Americans, have attempted to influence United States policies regarding their ancestral homelands. Historically, religious groups have sought to influence morality issues such as those connected with liquor, gambling, and birth control.

Of particular importance in recent years has been the new Christian Right. Leaders of some evangelistic organizations have occupied the forefront of various causes, such as movements opposing the Supreme Court decisions on abortion and school prayer, and have urged their followers to support conservative candidates. According to one leader, Jerry Falwell, the movement grew

> because we touched a raw nerve in the American electorate. Pro-moral people, who felt disenfranchised, saw a rallying point, an organization that would speak to the issues they were concerned with but could never get discussed through the liberal-controlled media.[2]

Critics of the new religious right included some traditional conservatives. One of these, Barry Goldwater (R–Ariz.), announced on the floor of the Senate,

> I am frankly sick and tired of the political preachers across this country telling me as a citizen that if I want to be a moral person, I must believe in "A," "B," "C," and "D." Just who do they think they are? And from where do they presume to claim the right to dictate their moral beliefs to me?[3]

Numerous organizations with different tactics have emerged over the years to champion the causes of blacks, Hispanics, and American Indians. The black civil rights movement, for example, turned militant in the late 1960s and early 1970s as organizations such as the Student Nonviolent Coordinating Committee and the Congress of Racial Equality abandoned the goal of racial integration in favor of black nationalism. By the early 1980s, however, such activist groups had faded and the leadership of the movement was reassumed by

---

[2] Quoted in *Conservative Digest*, January 1981; Reprinted in *Congressional Record*, February 25, 1981, p. E704.

[3] Quoted in *Congressional Record*, September 15, 1981, p. S9682.

more traditional organizations such as the National Urban League and the National Association for the Advancement of Colored People (NAACP).

At various times young people, particularly college students, have formed activist organizations. Youth protest was last manifested on a large scale in the 1960s, when students from relatively affluent white middle-class families became active in the environmental protection and antiwar movements. At the other end of the age scale, membership increases since the 1960s in such groups of the American Association of Retired Persons and the National Council of Senior Citizens attest to the growing political cohesiveness of the "gray lobby."

The women's liberation movement has its roots in the feminist movement, which began in 1848 at a convention in Seneca Falls, New York. This meeting also marked the beginning of the suffragette movement, which ultimately led to the adoption of the Nineteenth Amendment to the U.S. Constitution in 1920, which gave women the right to vote. Since the 1960s the women's liberation movement, led by groups such as the National Organization for Women (NOW), have pressed for changes on issues ranging from day care to health insurance. The rise of one group tends to produce a countergroup, and, thus, one can also find a number of antifeminist organizations, such as Stop ERA.

Public Interests Groups

A public interest group has collective benefits as its chief goal. The term *collective benefits* refers to goals that directly benefit the general public, such as clean air, consumer protection, and honest government. Chief among the political reform groups in recent years has been the "citizens' lobby," Common Cause. This organization, financed by 300,000 dues-paying members, has focused on campaign finance reform, open public meetings, and related means of making government more accountable to the public. Explicit in the formation of this organization and other citizen groups has been a belief in the effectiveness of popular movements in bringing about fundamental change. John W. Gardner, founder of Common Cause, has contended, "What we are seeing is the beginning of a powerful movement to call the great institutions of our society into account."[4]

The largely middle- and upper-middle-class members of Common Cause have not only been interested in political reform, but have also lobbied in Washington, D.C., for tax changes, environmental and energy measures, and specific consumer reforms, including health insurance, new consumer-protection agencies, and no-fault insurance. The Washington, D.C., organization (Common Cause groups have been formed in several states) usually concentrates on two or three issues each year, though it supports different groups working on consumer and other public-interest causes.

[4] John W. Gardner, *In Common Cause* (New York: W. W. Norton & Co., Inc., 1972), p. 75.

Ralph Nader has been a leader of the citizen reform movement since the mid 1960s. A Harvard Law School graduate, Nader emerged as the nation's leading consumer advocate after the publication of his *Unsafe at Any Speed* in 1965. This book brought forth a series of congressional hearings into automobile safety and led to the National Traffic and Motor Vehicle Safety Act of 1966. Nader's activities also prompted an ill-conceived General Motors investigation of his personal life, which further injured the image of the corporation and resulted in a $425,000 out-of-court settlement to Nader. The settlement, Nader promptly announced, would be used partly to monitor GM's progress on safety, pollution, and consumer education. Altogether, this reformer is associated with nineteen organizations. Included are Public Citizen Litigation, concerned with court action, and Congress Watch, concerned with lobbying Capitol Hill.

Government Groups

In addition to pressure by private citizens, national public officials receive demands from officers of other governments. State and local office-holders, like private citizens, engage in organized lobbying at the national level. Local executives and legislators, in particular, have sought greater federal aid for their cities and counties. Among the groups representing states and localities are the National Governors Association, the National Association of Counties, the United States Conference of Mayors, and the National League of Cities.

Exhortations by foreign governments may come in the form of public statements or secret communiqués. Besides their formal diplomatic representatives, many foreign nations have hired Washington lobbyists (including former high-ranking federal administrators and members of Congress) to represent their interests to current members of Congress and the executive branch. Foreign countries concerned about United States defense expenditures, arms sales, foreign aid, trade, and other areas have lobbied extensively to influence U.S. policies in these areas. The scope of these efforts is suggested by the allegations made in the late 1970s that the South Korean government had engaged in illegal lobbying, including bribing members of Congress, to influence U.S. foreign policy.

GROUP TARGETS AND TECHNIQUES

Direct Contact With Public Officials

In the United States the wide dispersal of authority among various levels and branches of government gives interest groups numerous opportunities to find an official or a public body to consider their causes favorably. A group bent on policy change, for instance, might appeal to the courts if Congress is opposed to its position. Similarly, a group may take its demands to Congress after failing to receive what it wants on the state level. The scattering of power may also work to the advantage of those seeking to prevent change. For example, those who fail to prevent congressional action can appeal to the courts or try to hinder administrative agencies' efforts to implement the policy.

The nature of the interaction between interest groups and policymakers varies with the branch of government. Though judges are not immune from political pressure, they are generally not lobbied in the same ways that legislators and administrators are pressured. Reaching the courts requires that an attorney be hired, formal proceedings be followed, and grievances be expressed in appropriate terminology. Often the key to success in a court case is finding the precise words to use in an argument. For example, political scientist Lynton Caldwell has reported that in the early years of the environmental movement

> Advocates of aesthetic reform in the human environment found that abuses could often be successfully attacked upon grounds of health and safety. Courts that rejected qualitative or aesthetic grounds for public action would often sanction in the same action if the physical well-being of the people were at stake.[5]

Interactions between group representatives and public officials other than judges are more overtly political. Many interest groups maintain Washington, D.C., offices staffed with people who keep track of developments in the legislative and administrative branches and attempt to influence their activities. Some groups pay for the services of Washington-based law firms in dealing with legislators or administrators. These firms provide expertise in such policy areas as antitrust and tax regulations and use their personal contacts with important public officials on behalf of their clients. Some of the most effective contact people in Washington are former members of Congress and high-ranking public administrators. Such officials in effect cash in on their public service by selling clients their access to government. Ethical and legal problems growing out of this practice became apparent in the mid 1980s when Michael Deaver, former aid to President Reagan, was found to have commanded high fees from corporations and foreign governments eager to take advantage of his ready access to the president.[6]

Some legislative lobbying may be social, as at parties and dinners held for particular legislators. At times, favors may be won by the promise of campaign contributions, or less frequent, direct bribery. More routine tasks of the legislative lobbyist include drafting bills, finding friendly legislators to

---

[5] Lynton K. Caldwell, *Man and His Environment: Policy and Administration* (New York: Harper & Row, Pub., 1975), p. 27.

[6] Among other things, the Ethics in Government Act prohibits high-ranking officials from lobbying their former department or agency within a year of leaving office.

introduce them, testifying at legislative hearings, and using knowledge of the legislative process or close friendships to make important contacts. At the heart of lobbying is communicating information on a specific policy matter. The lobbyist first contacts those legislators likely to support his or her group's position. The strength of a group depends partly on the presence of its members in a significant number of legislative districts. Some groups, such as home builders or automobile dealers, are politically important in nearly every congressional district.

Lobbying in the executive or adminstrative branch resembles that in the legislature. In addition, interest group influence, especially that of business people, has been built into administrative decision making through interest group representatives' membership on public advisory boards or committees. As one legislator has pointed out, "Industry committees perform the dual function of stopping the government from finding out about corporations while at the same time helping corporations get inside information about what the government is doing."[7]

More broadly, many executive agencies, including the national Labor, Agriculture, and Commerce departments, have very close relationships with well-organized clientele groups such as the AFL–CIO, Farm Bureau, and U.S. Chamber of Commerce, which look upon these agencies as means of promoting their interests. Clientele groups are often consulted in the selection of key personnel for executive agencies, and in some cases members from these groups may fill some of the positions.

In recent years much effort has been directed toward strengthening the regulation of lobbying. Under current law, contained in the Federal Regulation of Lobbying Act of 1946, all persons whose main job is to influence legislation must register with the House and the Senate and file financial and other data, such as information on what types of legislation they are trying to affect. The goal of these regulations has been to subject lobbying to greater public exposure. The 1946 act, however, contains various loopholes, and attempts have been made to strengthen the registration requirement and secure greater information. Thus far, reform has been stymied by extensive lobbying, as would be expected.

Efforts to reform lobbying in the administrative process have produced a review of the advisory committee system and, probably more important, the passage of a "sunshine act" in 1976 that limits the ability of federal agencies to hold closed meetings with those whose interests are directly affected by their decisions.

[7] Quoted in Lee Metcalf, "The Vested Oracles: How Industry Regulates Government," in Charles Peters and James Fallows (eds.), *Inside the System*, 3rd ed. (New York: Praeger, 1976), p. 261.

Appeals to the Membership and the Public

Groups, particulary those experiencing difficulties in securing direct access to policy makers or getting their support, often use more indirect lobbying methods. These include appeals to their membership and the public, attempts to influence political parties and elections, and protests.

Group leaders commonly call upon the members of their organizations to contact their representatives in Congress or key policymakers they may know and present the group's position on a pressing issue. Many of the letters, phone calls, telegrams, and visits that members of Congress receive from their constituents are initiated by interest groups.

Many groups concentrate on influencing public opinion. This is a major objective of groups that use protest to bring about reform. Other groups, notably the economically oriented ones, use the media primarily for defensive purposes—that is to prevent adverse policy changes. Public relations campaigns may be directed toward cultivating favorable opinion for a group. For example, they may incorporate advertisements that show what the group is doing to benefit America or that demonstrate the group's position on a specific policy matter. Political scientist V. O. Key once suggested that business people "are soft touches for publicity men" and are frequently convinced that they can sell their positions on public policy in much the same way they can sell goods. Key concluded that public relations personnel often "succeed in separating business-men from large sums of money to propagate causes, often in a manner that sooner or later produces a boomerang effect."[8]

Attempts to Influence Political Parties and Elections

Political parties are another focus of interest groups. They attempt to influence the platforms adopted by the two principal parties and, more significantly, the choice of candidates nominated by these parties. Many of the major interest organizations have more friends and influence in one political party than in the other. For instance, the Democratic party has generally been friendlier to the goals of organized labor, and the Republican party has been more receptive to the objectives of big business.

At times interest groups have participated in the formation of third parties. In 1976, the antiabortion Right to Life organization took advantage of federal matching funds to nominate a candidate for president. Its goal, however, was not to win the presidency but to educate the public to its cause. Generally, interest groups do not nominate candidates on their own. Instead, they endeavor to secure the election of the candidates most favorable to their causes.

Campaign aid from interest groups takes the form of direct monetary payments and various "in-kind" donations, including personnel for registration

---

[8] V. O. Key, Jr., *Public Opinion and American Democracy* (New York: Knopf, 1961), p. 529.

drives or the free use of a group's postage meter. Businesses contribute far more money than any other type of group, including organized labor. On the other hand, labor furnishes substantial in-kind services. Most business aid goes to Republicans, most labor assistance to Democrats.

Rating candidates by their stands on certain issues is another electoral activity carried out by some interest groups. This may be done by surveying a candidate's opinions or by examining an incumbent's voting record. Ratings are currently made by about fifty organizations, including the liberal Americans for Democratic Action and the conservative Americans for Constitutional Action. Candidates rated high by one of these two groups are likely to be rated low by the other.

The effectiveness of ratings by interest groups is difficult to determine. A high rating on a given list might help a candidate, especially in securing the backing of the rating group, but it may also constitute a "kiss of death" for attempts to gain the support of other groups. A liberal senator from Missouri once remarked that his high standing in the ADA's ratings was "about as politically useful in Missouri as a pro-Arab position in New York."[9] Environmental groups have in recent years focused on defeating the reelection bids of a "dirty-dozen" national legislators who are perceived to be "antienvironmental." About 70 percent of these members of Congress have been defeated.[10] More recently, groups from the "Moral Majority" have sought the election of legislators who are sympathetic to their viewpoints.

Protests

Protests, which involves marches, sit-ins, strikes, and boycotts, dramatically illustrate, with the media's help, a group's problems or policy objectives. Generally protests, along with rioting, have been viewed as the tools of people who are unable or unwilling to engage in more conventional pressure techniques such as lobbying, or who regard such channels as useless. Racial minorities, poverty organizations, antiwar groups, and opponents of nuclear power have employed protest techniques in recent years. Much of this activity is designed to generate favorable media coverage and, through this, the support of organizations and persons important in the eyes of decision makers. For minority groups and the poor, effecting political change has been linked to gaining allies in America's white middle class, where power is thought to reside.

The young, the poor, and minority groups have not been the only ones to use protests such as strikes and boycotts. The strike has long been a central tactic of organized labor, including unions of public employees, in pursuing political and economic goals. In the mid 1970s doctors went on strike seeking

---

[9] Thomas Eagleton (D–Mo.), quoted by Carol S. Greenwalk, *Group Power: Lobbying and Public Policy* (New York: Praeger, 1977), p. 127.

[10] Greenwalk, op. cit., p. 127.

governmental relief from malpractice insurance costs. Boycotts have been used by consumers protesting high prices. The national meat boycott of 1973 is an important example. A Gallup Poll found that better than one of every four people surveyed had participated in the boycott, either reducing or giving up consumption of meat. This protest was very strong in large cities and in the East. The boycott brought retail slumps and layoffs in the meat industry, and it helped prompt President Nixon to place a ceiling on meat prices. The controls, however, caused a meat shortage as farmers cut back their supply.

Some research suggests that groups using disruptive methods such as protests are often successful in bringing about policy change.[11] Yet, as the example of the meat boycott suggests, governmental action may be more symbolic than real. It is also clear that disruptive activities may generate bitter conflict and invite resentment against the protesters.

Effectiveness

In general, the effectiveness of an interest group is related to such factors as its financial and informational resources, whether it is on the offense or defense, and its status in the eyes of decision makers. Financial resources determine the ability of a group to support court suits, lobbying, public relations campaigns, and election and information-gathering activities. Groups with minimal staff and access to expertise may make problems important through protests but are likely to have little impact on framing solutions to these problems. Groups on the defensive have an advantage over groups trying to bring change: whereas the latter must overcome several obstacles in the policy-making process, the former may frustrate change at any of several points in the process.

The influence of a group depends, most fundamentally, on its status in the eyes of a decision maker. A group is particularly influential where a decision maker is affiliated with the group (for example, when farm groups talk to legislators who are farmers), where the group is viewed as important to the decision maker's constituency (either the one from which he or she was elected or the one from which he or she hopes to be elected), and where the group is recognized as a legitimate and reliable source of information.

The competence of a group of influence policy is also enhanced by its ability to bring about social or economic disruptions. Threats of disaster or crisis are common techniques of agenda building (making an issue important) and influence. Threats of disorder, disruption, and violence have at times been effective weapons for relatively powerless groups. Threats of a decline in the supply of medical service, food, or energy have been used to influence governmental policy. Producers who allege a potential crisis in the supply of a product or service can usually restrict its supply to create the crisis. Whether a supply

---

[11] William Gamson, *The Strategy of Social Protest* (Homewood, Ill.: Dorsey, 1975).

crisis is natural or contrived, it is potentially beneficial to the supplier of a highly valued product or service. Energy-producing companies have often used a supply crisis to justify "raising prices, reducing quality, and securing special privileges" from government.[12] More recently, energy-supply problems have been employed to justify the removal of price controls on oil and natural gas.

The capability of a private group to create a crisis, whether a social disorder, an economic slowdown, or a shortage of a valued product or service, gives it considerable clout in the political process. Crisis avoidance is exchanged for such things as more social programs, higher wages, and increased profits.

INTEREST GROUP FUNCTIONS

Many political scientists have found interest groups valuable to individuals, policy makers, and the political system as a whole. Belonging to a group that takes an active interest in public affairs is consistent with constitutional guarantees of free speech and the petitioning of government. Joining others multiplies one's political influence and thus makes the exercise of these constitutional rights more meaningful. Interest groups are useful to policy makers as well, providing information, support, and the opportunity to consult with those whose cooperation is needed in implementing policies.

In the political system as a whole, interest groups supplement the electoral system, which represents geographical areas, with representation of other interests, such as occupations. The presence of a large number of interest groups has been considered valuable for dispersing political power and providing checks and balances on governmental authority.

On the other hand, interest groups have been subject to numerous criticisms. As mentioned, the existence of a large number of uncompromising groups greatly increases the problems of governing. Another problem is that some groups, most noticeably economic interests, have more influence than others and can control various areas of public policy. In this system of "private subgovernments" or "interest group liberalism," for example, farmers control farm policy and the petroleum industry controls governmental oil policies.

According to pluralist theory, not all groups are formally organized. Some exist only as potential groups, but should an important interest be neglected, individuals and formal organizations will emerge as its advocates. Pluralists scholars, led by political scientist Robert Dahl, have contended that the political system in this country is open enough so that all groups who demand to be heard have an opportunity at some critical stage in the policy-making process

[12] David Howard Davis, *Energy Politics* (New York: St. Martin's Press, 1974), p. 9.

to influence the policies affecting them.[13] Critics of pluralist theory, however, have pointed to the unequal distribution of political influence among groups and to the numerous difficulties of out-groups—for example, those representing poor people—in breaking into the "pressure system." That system, it would appear, has a definite bias toward the middle- and upper-income classes.

POLITICAL ROLES OF THE MASS MEDIA

Advocating Interests

The mass media (newspapers, magazines, radio and television stations) in this nation function in part as an interest group. Each of the mass media is a business and, like other businesses, has a direct interest in various areas of public policy. The media, for example, have had the general goals of securing freedom-of-information and open-meeting laws, which facilitate their access to news, and legislation or court decisions that will allow them to protect the confidentiality of news sources. Associations such as the National Association of Broadcasters are regularly concerned with activities of the Federal Communications Commission, which controls the licensing of television and radio stations.

The media, of course, also speak out on a wide range of policy matters that have no direct relation with the interests of the industry. Newspaper editorials give advice to public officials and recommend candidates for office. Television and radio stations perform similar activities but have been far more restricted by requirements that they must offer an opportunity for contrasting viewpoints to be aired on controversial issues.

Conveying Political Information

Besides being independent sources of policy views, the media function as conduits, though not altogether impartial ones, for others who would shape policy. As we have noted earlier in this chapter, groups commonly direct their efforts toward receiving favorable media coverage. Wealthier associations purchase media time or space to foster goodwill or to align public opinion behind their causes.

Government officials and candidates for elective office also attempt to use the media to secure policy support and a favorable image. Among these officials, the president has the greatest access to the media. Indeed, his unique ability to command the spotlight has, in the opinion of some analysts, given him an "electronic throne" from which he can outshine his opponents, eclipse other policy-making institutions, and define the directions of public policy.[14]

---

[13] Robert A. Dahl, *A Preface to Democratic Theory* (Chicago: University of Chicago Press, 1956).

[14] See Newton N. Minow and others, *Presidential Television* (New York: Basic Books, 1973).

The media also function as channels by which officeholders communicate with each other. As one writer has said, "a President often finds it effective to tell the press what he has decided in order to demonstrate that his mind is made up."[15] On the other hand, legislators and administrators may reach the ear of the chief executive by publicly exposing problems and policy proposals about which he might not otherwise hear, and, in some cases, about which he might not want to hear.

Checking Government

At times public officials have attempted to prevent the media from reporting stories. The Nixon administration for example, attempted unsuccessfully to prevent publication of *The Pentagon Papers* on the grounds that it contained classified information concerning the war in Vietnam. This "classified" study of Vietnam War policies had been leaked to the press by Daniel Ellsberg, who had been employed in the Pentagon. The government in this case failed to convince a majority of the Supreme Court justices that censorship was necessary in the interest of national security.[16]

In publishing *The Pentagon Papers*, newspapers were playing the sometimes controversial role of the media as a "fourth branch of government" that imposes checks and balances on the other branches. One long-standing journalistic norm is that reporters be adversaries of government. While this role is imperfectly played, journalists do commonly proceed on the assumption that public officials generally try to manage the news in their favor by claiming more credit than they deserve for good news, concealing their mistakes, and withholding damaging information from the public.

In their adversary role, reporters champion the public's "right to know" and are reluctant merely to rewrite press releases or act as cheerleaders for public officials. The adversary role requires that reporters penetrate official secrecy, uncover facts through investigative journalism, and publicize all the news whether it reflects favorably or unfavorably on public officials.

Investigative reporting has been stimulated in recent years by the example set by *Washington Post* reporters Robert Woodward and Carl Bernstein in uncovering the Watergate scandals. Much investigative reporting relies upon deliberate leaks of information by governmental insiders. Not all of this information is publicized. Reporters, for instance, may hold back information an official does not want released in order to get that officer to reveal further information. Reliance upon tips or leaks from governmental insiders (often known to the public only as "authoritative sources") raises certain problems.

---

[15] Leon V. Sigal, "Bureaucratic Objectives and Tactical Uses of the Press," *Public Administration Review* 33 (July/August 1973): 340.

[16] *New York Times Company* v. *U.S.*, 403 U.S. 713 1971.

Reporters are seldom in a position to check the accuracy of leaks, and by publicizing them they may inadvertently be helping their sources to punish political enemies.

Informing the Public

Informing the public is the broadest and most basic function of the media. Considerable controversy has developed over how well that function has been exercised and how the media affect political attitudes and behavior. One of the oldest criticisms, of television in particular, is that the media place far too much stress on entertainment and far too little emphasis on world conditions and developments. Several years ago Federal Communications Commissioner Newton Minow declared television to be a "vast wasteland" of game shows, violence, commercials, and boredom.

Television, in the opinion of some, may still not be carrying enough news. It is, however, the chief source of political information for most people. A more recent concern about television is its supposedly biased coverage. The national networks in particular have been judged by various people to stress social conflict, violence, and other unpleasant news and to be overly critical of major public and private institutions. One analyst has concluded that viewers are likely to be left with the impression that "none of our national policies work, none of our institutions respond, none of our political organizations succeed."[17]

Reporters can help determine what events should be reported and how they shoud be emphasized and interpreted. What finally gets into the news, however, is not a matter simply of the whims of reporters. News is shaped by limits on the amount of time allocated to research a story and, on television, to report a story. Budgetary constraints also limit the news-gathering effort, often forcing reporters to rely on government handouts. Reporters, moreover, may find their stories rejected or modified by news editors. The editors, in turn, are restrained by station owners, network executives, and publishers.

Television has a gigantic audience. Like other media, its influence is probably greatest where people have no intense, preexisting attitudes. To cite an extreme example, it would be difficult for the media to change the minds of those in the Right to Life movement about abortion. For many people, particularly the well educated, the influence of television is also somewhat offset by the information they receive from other sources, such as newspapers and magazines. Those on the lower end of the educational scale are less likely to seek out other information, and thus are more heavily influenced by television.

---

[17] Michael J. Robinson, "Public Affairs Television and the Growth of Political Malaise: The Case of the 'The Selling of the Pentagon,'" *American Political Science Review* 70 (1976): 429.

SUMMARY

1. Government officials are in contact with the representatives of a wide variety of interests. Many observers have said that the most influential advocates are those who represent the economic interests of business, labor, employee, and professional groups. There is, however, frequent conflict within each of these broad groups (for example, between small and large businesses) and between these groups (for instance, between business and labor). Along with pressure from economic groups, policy makers are confronted with demands from citizen groups bent on reform and from representatives of other governments, both domestic and foreign.

2. All levels and branches of government are subject to interest group pressure. Contact between interest groups and legislators or administrators is generally much less formal than the contact of such groups with the courts. Lobbyists meet legislators and administrators personally, going first to those they feel are most likely to support their group's position. The interests of many groups are built into the administrative process through advisory boards or committees and through administrators' recognition of groups as legitimate clients having the right to influence the selection of agency personnel.

3. Groups that find it difficult to secure direct access to public officials or official support for their positions use indirect methods of applying pressure, such as appealing to their members and the general public and protesting. Working within political parties and attempting to influence the election of candidates are other indirect interest group tactics.

4. Interest groups as a whole are considered valuable because they help citizens influence public policy and they provide checks and balances on governmental authority. On the other hand, they have been the subject of numerous criticisms, the most important being that powerful interests have a disproportionate share of influence on public policy. The effectiveness of individual interest groups depends on their financial and informational resources and their status in the eyes of public officials. In these respects, most economically oriented interest groups enjoy an advantage over other groups. However, protest tactics, including threats of disorder and the skillful use of the media, can give substantial influence to groups that are otherwise relatively powerless.

5. The mass media function in part as an interest group. They are also influential as an independent source of political information on matters not directly related to the interests of the media industry, as a means through which interest groups and governmental officials attempt to influence policy, and as an adversary of government. There is considerable debate over how well the media play these roles and what their overall effects on public opinion are.

5

PARTIES,
CAMPAIGNS,
AND ELECTIONS

To complete the setting in which public policy is made, we must consider the work of political parties and the frequently hectic scrambles among candidates for office. In this chapter, we examine the national party system, party organizations, and campaigns and elections for national office.

THE PARTY SYSTEM

The amount of competition among political parties is one of the most significant indicators of political life in any geographical area. The right to choose among candidates, central to democracy, is nonexistent in many nations because one party nominates all the candidates. In the United States there have been localities, even entire states, where one party has dominated elections, experiencing only token, if any, competition. Within the dominant party, however, struggles have often developed among candidates and opportunities have emerged for choice in primary elections (nominating elections in which citizens choose party candidates).

Development

The United States Constitution makes no mention of political parties. Many of the framers felt such organizations would create divisions in a developing country that required unity. Such fears were expressed by George Washington in his Farewell Address to the nation in 1797. To Washington, the division of the people into rival political parties would only serve the interests of "cunning, ambitious and unprincipled men" who would distort differences among groups and sections of the country to gain office and, in the process, destroy respect for the new government and encourage disobedience to its decisions.

Party divisions had begun to develop early in Washington's administration when Thomas Jefferson, then secretary of state, opposed policies advocated by Alexander Hamilton, the secretary of the Treasury. Hamilton became leader of the Federalist party, which championed a strong national government, concentration of authority in the president, and public policies designed to promote economic development, manufacturing, and commerce. Jefferson resigned from Washington's administration and formed what was initially known as the Anti-Federalist party. The Anti-Federalists countered the Federalists with demands for a limited national government, legislative supremacy, and policies that favored farmers, workers, and small shopkeepers.

In an effort to oust the Federalists, Jefferson and his followers began to cultivate the support of the electorate. Federalists, on the other hand, tended to avoid electioneering, considering it to be 'bad form" and a dangerous activity that would "rouse the rabble" and thus menace the stability of the nation. The

60

consequences of these divergent attitudes toward electioneering were predictable: in 1800 Jefferson and his party came to power, and the Federalist party began to fade from the political scene.

Until 1860 the party founded by Jefferson, eventually known as the Democratic party, largely dominated national (presidential and congressional) elections. From the 1820s to 1860, however, the party was sometimes successfully challenged for the presidency by the National Republican party, which evolved into the Whig party. The Whigs were a loose coalition of sectional and economic interests (for example, eastern manufacturers and bankers, southern slaveholders, and westerners who wanted the national government to finance improvements in transportation) who disapproved of policies pursued by Democratic president Andrew Jackson. The Whig party was torn apart by slavery and other issues and disappeared as the nation headed toward the Civil War.

The modern Republican party emerged in the 1850s out of spontaneous movements of middle-class people in many parts of the North. The main objective of the new party, officially founded in 1854, was to prevent the extension of slavery into the territories controlled by the United States. Many northern Whigs and northern Democrats became Republicans. Also joining the new party were many laborers, small business people, and farmers. As political scientist Clinton Rossiter observed, "whatever the Republicans were to become in later years, they were far from being a conservative, business-oriented party in infancy."[1]

Republicans captured the White House for the first time with the election of Abraham Lincoln in 1860. From the 1860s to the late 1920s the Republicans generally dominated national politics. Of the eighteen presidential elections held from 1860 through 1928, Republican candidates won fourteen times. Republicans were also generally able to control the Senate and, to a lesser extent, the House of Representatives in this period. For several decades following the Civil War, Republican candidates "waved the bloody shirt" to remind the voters that their party had led the struggle to save the nation.

Republican success rested in part on being identified with the cause of the North and in part on providing benefits to various groups. Among the latter were pensions to Union soldiers, tariff protections to manufacturers, and free land in the West to railroads and farmers. By the late nineteenth century the party had become closely allied with large manufacturing and financial interests, although the progressive or liberal faction of the party was critical of big business.

Until the great economic depression that began in 1929 and extended into the 1930s the Republican party was generally regarded as the party of

---

[1] Clinton Rossiter, *Parties and Politics in America* (Ithaca, N.Y.: Cornell University Press, 1960), p. 79.

economic prosperity. The depression brought a reversal of this view and ushered in an era of general Democratic dominance, which continues, though somewhat shakily, to this day. Since 1932 Democratic candidates have won eight of fourteen presidential elections and have lost control of both houses of Congress only twice—in the Eightieth Congress (1947–49) and the Eighty-third Congress (1953–55). Democrats have drawn their strength from the coalition of interests first put together by Franklin Roosevelt in 1932. This coalition has consisted of large numbers of white southerners, blacks, nationality groups such as the Polish and the Italians, religious minorities (Catholics and Jews), blue-collar workers, lower-income groups, and intellectuals. The ability of party leaders to rally these groups around Democratic candidates has varied from election to election.

Over the past few decades the balance between the two parties has not been shaken by any dramatic or sudden change such as the upheaval that produced the 1930s depression. There have, however, been what appear to be some relatively long-term changes in the balance.[2] One of the most noticeable long-term changes in the original New Deal coalition has been the growth of Republican strength among white southerners, many of whom opposed the commitment of the national Democratic party to the civil rights causes that took root in the late 1940s and early 1950s. To some extent, Democratic losses among whites in the South have been offset by gains in the registration of black voters.[3] A large percentage of the latter usually vote for Democratic candidates. Prior to the 1930s blacks were a stable block in the Republic party, the party of Lincoln.[4]

In the last few presidential elections, however, Republicans have also made steady gains with blue-collar workers, Catholics and fundamentalist Protestants, and young voters. In the mid 1980s the number of eligible voters who declared they were Republicans fluctuated between 32 and 35 percent and at times nearly equaled the percentage who said they were Democrats. In the 1930s there were three times as many Democrats as Republicans. As recently as 1980, surveys showed that Democrats outnumbered Republicans two to one.

At this point it is difficult to determine if the nation has been steering toward a new party alignment. To some extent the popularity of the Republican party in the mid 1980s reflected the popularity of President Reagan. Reagan's overwhelming reelection in 1984 was not, however, accompanied by a landslide for other Republican candidates, and in 1986 the GOP lost control of Congress. Republican popularity also reflected the belief that the party was once again the

---

[2] See Everett Carll Ladd, "On Mandates, Realignments, and the 1984 Presidential Election," *Political Science Quarterly* 100 (Spring 1985): 1–25.

[3] On changes in the Democratic party, see John Frederick Martin, *Civil Rights and the Crisis of Liberalism: The Democratic Party 1945–1976* (Boulder, Colo.: Westview Press, 1979); and Alexander P. Lamis, *The Two-Party South* (New York: Oxford University Press, 1984).

[4] See Nancy J. Weiss, *Farewell to the Party of Lincoln* (Princeton, N.J.: Princeton University Press, 1983).

party of prosperity. This image could change rapidly with a downturn in economic conditions.

What seems to be a more fundamental limit to large-scale party realignment is that voter ties to political parties are generally much weaker now than they have been in the past. Some 30 percent of the electorate do not affiliate with either major party. Of the 60 to 70 percent who do, many, particularly younger voters, do not appear to be strongly attached. We can therefore expect to find constant shifts in support for candidates of the major parties.

Party Identification:
Republicans, Democrats, and Independents

People "join" a political party by registering with the party of simply by considering themselves members. People who identify with a political party are likely to have done so early in life. As we saw in Chapter 3, identification as a Republican or a Democrat is something many people inherited from their parents. In general the psychological attachment to a political party may not be what it used to, but for many people party attachments are very difficult to break.[5] This does not mean, however, that even strong identifiers will always vote for the candidates on their party's ticket. In any given election a number of voters may switch to support candidates of the opposing party. Many "partisans" also engage in split-ticket voting—that is, voting for a candidate of one party for one office and a candidate of the opposite party for another office. In recent presidential elections around 60 percent of the electorate has split its vote between the two parties.

In terms of socioeconomic characteristics, those who identify with the Republican party tend to be relatively well educated wealthy professional or business people. Many people with these characteristics are also found among the Democrats. But the Democrats, as we have seen, have had a particularly strong appeal to blacks and other minorities and to those with limited incomes and education (see Table 5-1). There are liberals and conservatives in both parties, but on a national level Republicans are more conservative than Democrats on issues involving governmental social programs and regulation of business.

As noted, the decline in party identification has been particularly pronounced among younger voters. Youthfulness has been a dominant characteristic of the independent voter. Some observers have viewed this as a life-cycle phenomenon, contending that as young people grow older they will tend to

---

[5] See Angus Campbell and others, *The American Voter* (New York: John Wiley, 1960). A number of studies have suggested, however, that party identification is less stable than commonly assumed. See, for example, Kenneth J. Meier, "Party Identification and Vote Choice: The Causal Relationship," *Western Political Quarterly* 28 (September 1975): 496–505.

Table 5–1 Political Party Affiliation

Question: *In politics, as of today, do you consider yourself a Republican, a Democrat, or an Independent?*

	JANUARY-JUNE, 1986			
	REPUBLICAN	*DEMOCRAT*	*INDEPENDENT*	*NUMBER OF INTERVIEWS*
National	32%	39%	29%	5,929
Sex				
Men	33	36	31	2,980
Women	31	42	27	2,949
Age				
Total under 30	35	33	32	1,241
18-24 years	34	33	33	593
25-29 years	36	34	30	648
30-49 years	30	38	32	2,258
Total 50 and older	32	45	23	2,405
50-64 years	31	44	25	1,223
65 and older	35	45	20	1,182
Region				
East	32	39	29	1,486
Midwest	31	35	34	1,529
South	31	43	26	1,748
West	37	38	25	1,166
Race				
Whites	35	35	30	5,327
Nonwhites	12	68	20	602
Blacks	9	73	18	525
Hispanics	24	49	27	330
Education				
College graduates	39	31	30	1,223
College incomplete	40	31	29	1,449
High school graduates	30	39	31	1,975
Not high school graduates	23	53	24	1,262
Occupation of CWE				
Professional and business	39	31	30	1,745
Clerical and sales	35	36	29	407
Manual workers	27	42	31	2,160
Skilled workers	29	38	33	1,039
Unskilled workers	26	45	29	1,121
Household income				
$50,000 and over	38	32	30	635
$35,000-$49,999	39	32	29	863
$25,000-$34,999	34	35	31	1,039
$15,000-$24,999	30	40	30	1,276
$10,000-$14,999	26	47	27	847
Under $10,000	28	47	25	954
$25,000 and over	37	33	30	2,537
Under $25,000	28	44	28	3,077
Religion				
Protestants	36	38	26	3,499
Catholics	27	43	30	1,636
Labor Union				
Labor union families	26	44	30	1,150
Nonlabor-union families	34	38	28	4,779

Source: Gallup Report (July, 1986), p. 21 Reprinted with permission.

associate with a party. Other observers have argued that the failure to identify with a party represents a generational change. In their view, there is a fundamental difference of opinion on the value of existing parties between younger and older voters. According to this latter view, even as younger voters grow older they will continue to resist party identification unless one or both of the major parties become more responsive to their views.[6]

Third Parties

Although the Democratic and Republican parties have played the most prominent role in modern party politics, there have also been various minor parties, commonly called *third parties*. Some of these, such as the Communist party and the Socialist Workers party, have advocated ideologies that have not appealed to many voters. Most other third parties have confined their efforts to a single cause, such as prohibiting drinking (Prohibition party) or restricting abortions (Right to Life party), that is neglected by the major parties. Parties of the latter type are probably more accurately regarded as interest groups.

There have been many third-party candidates for the presidency. The most successful in recent years was Governor George Wallace of Alabama, the candidate of the American Independent party, who in 1968 received nearly 10 million votes (13.5 percent of the total vote) and carried five southern states with a total of forty-six electoral votes. Twelve years later John Anderson, who had been a member of the House of Representatives from Illinois, ran as an independent in the belief, supported in early polls, that many U.S. voters were unhappy with the choice between the Democrat Carter and the Republican Reagan. Anderson asked voters to "take a leave of absence" from their parties and support his candidacy. Though polls showed Anderson favored by 20 percent or more of the voters during the campaign, he received only about 7 percent of the ballots cast on election day and failed to carry a single state or obtain any electoral votes.

Third parties and their candidates have to compete with the traditional allegiances many people feel toward the two main parties. Furthermore, if their policy proposals prove attractive to many voters, the major parties may advance similar proposals and in effect absorb the third party. Election practices also impede the development of third parties. In the electoral college method of selecting the president, for example, the winner takes all; votes cast for losing candidates do not count for anything. Many voters may therefore conclude that a vote for a third party's candidates is likely to be wasted. Likewise, without a good chance of victory it is difficult for third parties to attract financial backers.

[6] See Paul R. Abramson, "Generational Change and the Decline of Party Identification in America: 1952–1974," *American Political Science Review* 70 (1976): 469–478.

Organization

Political party organizations exist on the national, state, and local levels. They are run by a small number of party workers who spend most of their energy on election activities such as recruiting candidates, raising funds, and attempting to influence voter choices. Party organizations, however, do not have a monopoly over any of these functions. Indeed, as we will see, they have become less important in these respects.

Party organizations, like many interest groups, are voluntary associations of people who have come together for political purposes. Compared with interest groups, however, they are concerned less with specific matters of public policy than with electoral victories. Compared with other associations of citizens, party organizations are also subject to considerably more governmental regulation. State laws, for instance, outline the basic structure of parties and determine such internal organizational matters as the method of selecting party officials.

The base of the political party structure consists of precinct committee members. Usually elected by party members, they spend the bulk of their time on election duties–for example, getting out the party vote on election day. A precinct is the smallest voting district in an election area (for example, a city). Above the precinct level one may find party organizations at the ward (from which city council members are elected in some cities), city, county, congressional district, and state levels.

State party organizations are weak coalitions of independent county organizations that participate in fund raising and statewide campaigns. State organizations still use state party conventions to write party platforms and, in some states, to make nominations for public office, choose who will represent the state party on the national party committee, and select delegates to national party conventions. In most states and counties, however, nominations for office are made through direct public primary elections. Similarly, delegates to national conventions have increasingly been selected in presidential primaries and open caucuses rather than by state party conventions.

In presidential election years delegates from every state (chosen by convention caucus or primary) assemble in a national convention of their party. Besides nominating the party's presidential and vice-presidential candidates and performing other election-year functions, the delegates formally select a national committee and someone to chair it. In practice, these conventions merely ratify their state party's choice of national committee members and approve whomever their party's presidential nominee chooses for national chair.

The national committees meet only two or three times a year. The committee chairs, however, devote full time to their jobs and are aided by permanent Washington staffs. In presidential election years the national chair and Washington staff work full time to get their party's nominee elected.

What the national chair and the staff do between elections depends largely on which party has won the White House. When the president is of their party, the chair and staff build party and general public support for the president and further his campaign for reelection. When the party is out of power, the national chair becomes a broker among the various factions in the party, building party unity, strengthening party organization, and raising funds for the next election.[7]

People who are active in political party organizations have traditionally been viewed as political hacks who are interested primarily in securing material benefits, such as a public job, for their efforts. Indeed, at one time a major reward for party activity was a governmental position in the event the party's candidates won. For much of the nation's history public positions were filled on the principle "to the victor belongs the spoils." Late in the nineteenth century, however, this spoils system was finally replaced with a merit system of governmental employment; at present the supply of patronage or spoils appointments is much smaller.

Contemporary party activists are generally well-educated, successful people with a relatively high socioeconomic status. Most, therefore, do not have to rely upon political activity to make a living. Party activists today seem more concerned with issues and broad matters of public policy than activists in the past.[8] The chief exceptions are party workers (especially at the precinct levels) in some large cities where patronage still provides an incentive.[9]

The years have witnessed a decline in the role of party organizations in the political system. The classic urban political machines that once dominated nominations for local, state, and congressional offices have largely disappeared. Two factors in this decrease have been a reduction in patronage, upon which many local organizations were built, and the advent of primaries, which limit the party organization's control over nominations. Another historical role of urban political parties, that of providing for the poor and newcomers to the city, has been undercut by the growth in governmental welfare programs.

Party organizations continue to exercise important functions in the election system. For instance, they recruit candidates, raise funds, and inform and activate voters. A number of other institutions, however, also perform these functions. Many candidates are recruited by interest groups or are self-recruited. Rather than attempting to secure the support of party leaders, these candidates may run against the party bosses in primary elections.

Candidates who acquire a party nomination place little value on the

[7] See Frank J. Sorauf, *Party Politics in America*, 3rd ed. (Boston: Little, Brown, 1976), p. 119.
[8] See James Q. Wilson, *Political Organizations* (New York: Basic Books, 1973).
[9] See Sorauf, op. cit., p. 99. See also Charles W. Wiggins and William L. Turk, "State Party Chairmen: A Profile," *Western Political Quarterly* 23 (June 1970): 321–332.

assistance offered by party organizations.[10] Most candidates build their own campaign organizations. Those who can afford the cost purchase the talents of public-relations firms, campaign specialists, and pollsters. The candidate-oriented committees may obtain some aid from the party organizations, but they depend largely on their own efforts.

Finally, the mass media have become far more important than party organizations in the election process. This has been especially evident in presidential nominations and elections. As one analyst has concluded, "the standing of candidates is now certified not by state party leaders but by small groups of reporters and commentators."[11]

PRESIDENTIAL CAMPAIGNS AND ELECTIONS

The Constitution requires of a presidential candidate only that he or she be a natural-born citizen (not a naturalized citizen), at least thirty-five years old, and a resident of the United States for fourteen years (though not fourteen consecutive years) before the election. In the real world, of course, the road to the White House is filled with numerous obstacles that can be overcome only with considerable skill, hard campaigning, and good fortune.

The Electoral College

Technically, American voters cast their ballots not for presidential candidates but for *electors*, who in turn vote for president and vice-president. Under Article II, Section 1, of the Constitution, each state legislature is required to select, in any manner it desires, a number of electors equal to its representation in Congress. Thus, a state with two senators and four Congress members would have six electors, each of whom casts one electoral vote. Under the Twenty-third Amendment, the District of Columbia is given three electoral votes. The total number of electors (known as the electoral college) and electoral votes is 538. A presidential candidate must receive not less than 270 electoral votes to win.

Electors (whose names may be on the ballot) are generally party regulars who are chosen by state party officials or through party primaries. Each party selects a complete slate of electors, and voters choose between the slates (though they may consider themselves to be choosing between presidential candidates). Electors on the slate that receives the most votes are the ones who cast the official

---

[10] See, for example, Jeff Fishel, *Party and Opposition: Congressional Challengers in American Parties* (New York: D. McKay, 1973), pp. 99ff.

[11] Gerald M. Pomper, "The Nominating Contests and Conventions," in Gerald M. Pomper (ed.), *The Election of 1976* (New York: D. McKay, 1977), p. 33.

ballots for president and vice-president. The only exception to this process is in Maine, where each congressional district awards one electoral vote to the winner of that district; two additional electoral votes are awarded to the statewide winner.

If no presidential candidate receives a majority of the electoral votes, the election becomes the responsibility of the newly elected House of Representatives. The House chooses the winner from among the three candidates who have received the most electoral votes. In electing the president, each state delegation in the House has a single vote. A state loses its vote if its delegation is equally divided on the candidates. Because voting is done by states, it is possible for twenty-six states with less than 20 percent of the nation's population to determine the winner.

If no candidate for the vice-presidency has a majority of the electoral votes, the decision is made by majority vote in the Senate. Each senator votes as an individual for one of the two leading contenders. If the House is unable to decide on a president by the day of the presidential inauguration, the vice-president chosen by the Senate becomes acting president until the House decides. Should the Senate fail to select a vice-president by inauguration day, the Speaker of the House of Representatives becomes acting president.

As noted in Chapter 2, this complex system of electing a president emerged as a compromise among the framers of the Constitution. The system has proved less than perfect. For one thing, only a few states legally require electors to cast their ballots in accordance with the vote of their state. It has happened, though very rarely, that an elector has cast his or her vote for someone other than the candidate preferred by a majority of the state's voters. A simple remedy to this problem would be to abolish the position of elector and require the electoral votes of a state to be automatically cast for the candidate who obtains the most votes in the state.

A more important indictment of the electoral college system is that it is undemocratic. In three elections (those of 1824, 1876, and 1888) a candidate was elected president who had fewer popular votes than one of his opponents. The only sure way to avoid this situation is to abolish the system and give the election to the candidate who receives the most popular votes.[12]

Efforts to secure a constitutional amendment for direct popular election of the president have encountered strong resistance. Some people have argued that the Electoral College, like Congress, demonstrates the principle of federalism by recognizing the equality of the states. Abolishing the electoral college, it is feared, would reduce the impact of smaller states in presidential elections.

---

[12] Other proposals made over the years have been to split up the electoral vote by (1) having two electors chosen by the statewide vote and the remainder by the vote in each congressional district (as in Maine) and (2) making the electoral vote proportional—that is, if two candidates receive approximately the same number of votes in a state with twelve electoral votes, each candidate would receive six votes.

From another point of view, some liberals have feared that abolishing the Electoral College system would make presidential candidates less sensitive to the problems of people in large metropolitan areas. The system has encouraged presidential campaigning in these areas because they are less likely than smaller locales to be committed in advance to the candidates of one party.

Primaries and Conventions

The initial task of a would-be president is to win the support of a majority of the delegates at the national party convention. Each state sends a number of delegates to the Democratic and Republican conventions. The number is roughly proportional to a state's electoral vote. Both parties, though, give additional delegates to states that have demonstrated their party loyalty— for example, by voting Democratic or Republican in recent presidential elections and by electing Democratic or Republican governors or members of Congress. Democrats have adopted rules insuring that prominent party leaders and party members holding important elective offices be seated as delegates. The national Democratic party also requires that the states divide their delegations equally between men and women. Republicans do not have rules affecting the seating of prominent party members or women.

In the majority of the states, convention delegates are chosen in presidential primaries. In most states primaries are *closed*: only registered Republicans can vote in Republican primaries, only registered Democrats in Democratic primaries. A few states have *open* presidential primaries, in such states people can participate in the primary of their choice regardless of their party affiliation. In states without presidential primaries, local caucuses of party activists usually select delegates to district and state conventions. Delegates to the national convention are chosen at the state convention.

From time to time reformers have contended that the present primary system should be scrapped in favor of a national presidential primary where, on the same day, voters in every state would vote for their choice for the presidential nominee of their party. Supporters of this reform argue that it is fairer in that everyone, not simply people in particular states, would be allowed to vote. A presidential primary is also thought to be an improvement in that voters could choose among all the candidates for nomination. Under the present arrangement the identity and number of candidates in a primary vary from state to state. A national vote on all the candidates, it is contended, is a better test of who is likely to be the strongest contender in the national election. Another alleged benefit of this reform would be a national campaign that is shorter, less expensive, and less demanding on the candidates (not to mention the public).

Critics of the national primary respond that it would tend to favor candidates who are well known and have ample financial and organizational resources. Excluded from meaningful participation would be dark-horse candidates, who under the present system can take their case to the public state by state in a quest for national viability and support.

The use of presidential primaries, whether state-by-state, regional, or national, has had several repercussions. In the first place, primaries have in theory made the nomination system more democratic in that more people can participate. Yet in practice only a small percentage of the eligible voters turn out for these elections. It may thus be an unrepresentative, highly motivated, ideological minority that chooses the party's standard bearer. Party officials have also had to worry about *raiding*, whereby people who belong to one political party vote in the primary of the opposite party. Even in closed-primary states it is not difficult to qualify as a voter in the opposition party's primary. As a result of this flexibility, candidates who face an uphill struggle in their own party may get a substantial boost from voters from the other party. In 1976 and 1980, for instance, Ronald Reagan's candidacy for the Republican presidential nomination benefited from the votes of conservative Democrats in Republican primaries. Presidential primaries may also lead to party divisiveness, as they did in the contest between Jimmy Carter and Ted Kennedy for the Democratic nomination in 1980. This tough primary battle made it difficult for supporters of the defeated candidate to rally around the primary winner.

Another effect of the presidential primaries has been to decrease the control of state and local party leaders over the choice of national convention delegates. At times party leaders have attempted to gain a measure of control by placing a slate of unpledged delegates or a slate of delegates pledged to a "favorite son" (often the state's governor) on the primary ballot. These techniques give state and local party leaders a bloc of votes they can use for bargaining purposes at the convention—votes they can throw to a candidate in exchange for the promise of the vice-presidency or a position in the presidential administration if the candidate is successful. Voters, however, do not appear to be attracted to unpledged delegations. The favorite-son device is typically unattractive unless that person is perceived as a serious national candidate.

Presidential primaries have also made it easier for candidates representing an ideological wing of the party and even well-organized unknowns adept at attracting media coverage to secure the nomination. The success of several presidential campaigns—notably those of Goldwater for the Republican nomination in 1964, McGovern for the Democratic nomination in 1972, and Carter for the 1976 Democratic nomination—had much less to do with the support of party officials than with timely primary victories. Yet, should an individual become president by this route, the absence of a strong partisan constituency in Congress and on the state and local levels may make it very difficult for the "outsider" to govern. Several observers, for example, have attributed many of President Carter's problems to the lack of a firm base of support among leading members of his own party.

Finally, presidential primaries have severely reduced the importance of the national convention in the nominating process. In the past, conventions were controlled largely by party members who held public office or led party organizations. Nominees for president were selected in "smoke-filled rooms," out of public view, as a result of bargaining among party leaders. Often it took multiple ballots on the convention floor to secure a nomination. The growth in the number of primaries has meant that the winners of the nomination are now likely to be known before the national conventions. The last convention in which more than one ballot was necessary was held in 1952. Only when candidates have closely split the primary vote, as did Gerald Ford and Ronald Reagan in 1976, does a convention have a meaningful role in the nomination process.

Many issues concerning the role of conventions in the nomination process were aired at the 1980 Democratic National Convention during the debate over whether to reject a rule that required delegates to vote on the first ballot for the presidential candidate to whom they were pledged in their primaries or caucuses. Rejection of the rule would have allowed delegates to vote for whom they wanted on the first ballot. Freeing the delegates would have raised the possibility of Jimmy Carter being denied the nomination he apparently had wrapped up by his success in the primaries and caucuses. Carter's supporters contended that lifting the rule would cheat millions of voters who had supported Carter in the primaries. Backers of the rule change (which included Senator Edward Kennedy, Carter's principal rival in the primaries) argued that the convention should be an "open one" in which delegates were free to debate and vote their consciences rather than a meeting place where "programmed robots" automatically cast their ballots. Moreover, supporters of the open convention argued that the delegates should be free to change their minds as political circumstances changed rather than being bound by primary decisions made as long as six months earlier. Open-convention advocates reminded the delegates that Carter had slipped badly in public opinion polls since his early primary victories and that because of this they should reconsider their support for him. The debate ended when the convention, dominated by delegates loyal to Carter, rejected the motion to change the binding rule.

Conventions may be split fairly evenly between rival factions (such as liberals and conservatives) or candidates. At such times, conflicts may develop over the legitimacy of various delegations and the content of the party platform (a statement of the party's principles and stands on various issues) formally adopted by the convention. Platforms have commonly been viewed by political commentators and citizens as sets of meaningless generalities and promises. Researchers, however, have found that platforms commonly contain specific pledges of governmental action that are important to various groups and thus help enlist group support for parties and their candidates. Moreover, many specific promises made in party platforms eventually become public policy because successful candidates are likely to try to honor these commitments.

One of the most important functions of the convention is to choose the vice-presidential nominee. This choice is important in large part because the vice-president can move up to the presidency. The odds are about two to one that a vice-president will eventually become president by filling a vacancy or being elected to the office. In practice, delegates to the national convention simply approve the presidential nominee's choice of a running mate. Most presidential nominees have declared that a chief criterion in their selection is the candidate's ability to serve as president. Equally important, if not more so, is the desire of the presidential nominee to balance the ticket. For example, if the presidential nominee is from the South, a vice-presidential nominee from the North may help balance the ticket. In 1984 the Democrats made history by balancing the ticket with a woman, Geraldine Ferraro, as vice-presidential nominee. Although this move was an advance for women's rights, it appears to have had little effect on the 1984 presidential vote.[13]

Campaigns

One of the chief factors in campaigning for the presidency is whether an incumbent president is seeking his party's nomination. Incumbent presidents seeking reelection normally have little reason to worry about securing the nomination of their party. There are exceptions, however, such as the strong challenge, made by Ronald Reagan to Gerald Ford in the 1976 Republican state primaries and national convention and to Jimmy Carter by Ted Kennedy in 1980. Most presidents spend a great deal of time and effort in their first term attempting to insure their renomination and reelection.

At any given time there are a number of would-be presidential candidates. Some politicians have made the presidency a lifelong ambition. Candidates may begin to develop plans for winning the presidency and to build a campaign organization immediately after the defeat of the party in a presidential election or even during the second term of a president who belongs to their party. An early start was particularly important in the success of George McGovern and Jimmy Carter in gaining their party's nomination.

Where an incumbent is not a candidate, there is likely to be much competition for the nomination. Some candidates may test the political winds for party, interest-group, and financial support and decide that the effort is not worth making. Such was the case with Senator Walter Mondale in 1975. Mondale was subsequently placed on the Carter ticket and elected vice-president.

Other candidates drop from the race in the first few months of the delegate-selection process. The first presidential primaries, caucuses, and state party conventions at which delegates are chosen are especially important because

---

[13] Ladd, op. cit., p. 16.

they give the winners further visibility and help generate momentum or possibly build a bandwagon effect (the desire to join a likely winner) for their campaigns.

Having secured the nominations, the rival candidates build up the organizations that helped give them the nomination and attempt to enlist the campaign aid of the political party and other organizations. In the general-election campaign the winner-take-all effect of the electoral college system encourages candidates to ignore states where they seem sure to win or lose and concentrate their efforts on large, populous states where the race appears close.

Nationally televised presidential debates highlighted the presidential campaigns of 1960, 1976, 1980, and 1984. Most presidential candidates with an edge in the polls have been unwilling to debate their principal opponent in the belief that this could jeopardize their leading position. Although the evidence is not conclusive, it is commonly believed that the televised debates in 1960 between John Kennedy and Richard Nixon helped Kennedy win the election. Over 80 percent of the voters watched at least one of the three Ford–Carter debates in 1976. Viewer surveys showed Ford to be the winner in the first debate and the loser in the second and third. More systematic research suggests that most viewers who favored one of these two candidates before the first debate did not change their minds thereafter. Generally, Republicans tended to see Ford coming out ahead in the debates while Democrats felt Carter did better. Most affected by the debates were political independents (those not committed to a candidate or party); among this group, Carter made the most substantial gains.[14] Surveys suggest that Ronald Reagan, the "great communicator," was considered by a majority of viewers to be a clear winner over Jimmy Carter in 1980 and a closer victor over Walter Mondale in 1984.

CONGRESSIONAL CAMPAIGNS AND ELECTIONS

In every even-numbered year, all 435 House seats and one third of those in the Senate are scheduled for election. When a House seat is vacated, because of the death or resignation of the incumbent, the governor of the state represented may call a special election in an odd-numbered year. Vacancies in the Senate are filled by gubernatorial appointment (appointment by the governor), and the appointee serves out the predecessor's term.

The Election Setting

Senators are chosen in statewide elections. Though House members could be selected the same way, they are usually elected from districts within

[14] Donald T. Cundy and John J. Havick, "Impact of the 1976 Presidential Debates: A Preliminary Analysis" (paper prepared for the annual meeting of the Western Political Science Association, Los Angeles, 1978). See also Robert E. Gilbert, *Television and Presidential Politics* (North Quincy, Mass.: Christopher Publishing House, 1972).

their states. The exceptions have been in states with only one representative. State legislatures are responsible for determining the boundaries of congressional districts. The Supreme Court ruled in 1964, however, that these districts must be as nearly equal in population as is practical.[15] The Court's decision signaled the end of the common practice of giving rural areas far greater representation in Congress than was warranted by their populations. Before this judicial decision a House member from an urban area commonly represented two or three times the number of people represented by a House member from a rural area. The effects of the Court's decision were to increase substantially the number of House members elected from urban areas, especially from suburbs near large cities, and to reduce the number from rural sections.

Gerrymandering is a districting problem the courts have thus far failed to address effectively. The term refers to the drawing of district lines in a manner that discriminates against a group of people or a political party. Though districts may be relatively equal in population, they can be designed so as to disperse the black vote or the Democratic vote, for example, into a number of districts, thereby preventing these people from constituting a majority in any one district.

Every other congressional election coincides with a presidential election. Those held in the second year of a presidential term, such as 1978 or 1982, are known as *midterm* or *off-year* elections. Scholars have long been interested in how presidential and congressional elections influence each other. Some studies suggest that a presidential candidate who wins by a large margin is able to carry a number of his party's candidates for Congress into office. This coattail effect has appeared in some elections. At times a reverse effect has developed: congressional candidates have run ahead of a presidential candidate and added to his vote totals. As we will see, however, the influence of one election upon the other may be diminishing. Presidential and congressional candidates have been developing independent electoral coalitions, and many incumbent members of Congress have been able to hold their jobs regardless of what happens to the national ticket.

Midterm elections have had two characteristics. First, voter turnout is lower at midterm than in presidential-election years. Presidential contests bring out a number of people who would not otherwise vote in congressional contests. Second, the president's party usually loses congressional seats in midterm elections. To some extent the midterm election functions as a national referendum on how the president has performed, particularly in managing the economy, in his first two years.[16]

---

[15] *Wesberry* v. *Sanders*, 376 U.S. 1.

[16] See William J. Keefe and Morris S. Ogul, *The American Legislative Process*, 3rd ed. (Englewood Cliffs, N.J.: Prentice-Hall, 1973), pp. 105–107; and Edward R. Tufte, "Determinants of the Outcomes of Midterm Congressional Elections," *American Political Science Review* 69 (September 1975): 812–826.

The Candidates

The formal eligibility requirements for election to Congress are few. Under the Constitution, a senator must be at least thirty years old, a U.S. citizen for nine years, and a resident of the state from which he or she is elected. To qualify for the House of Representatives an individual must be twenty-five or older, a citizen of this nation for at least seven years, and a resident of the state from which he or she is elected. The Constitution does not stipulate that representatives must live in the districts from which they are elected, but custom and the poor possibility of victory by a nonresident in effect make district residency a requirement.

Candidates for congressional office must, of course, meet more demanding informal qualifications if they are to have a chance of success. Among such requirements are deep roots and relatively high socioeconomic status in their community and ample time and money for their campaign.

As indicated in our discussion of party organization, candidates for Congress are recruited in several ways. Some recruit themselves by circulating petitions to get their names on the ballot and seeking out organizational and public support. Other candidates are recruited by party officials, party leaders in government, and interest groups. In the last-named case, a successful candidate in effect becomes an elected lobbyist.

The Primaries

The primary system used for congressional nominations (and nominations for state and local offices) varies among the states. The majority of states have closed primaries. As we have seen, voters in such states can cast ballots only in the primary of the party to which they belong. Voters may declare their party affiliation when they register or, in a few states, when they appear at the polling place. In open-primary states, voters do not have to proclaim their affiliations and can choose among either (but not both) of the party tickets. Some states have a *blanket primary*, in which voters can choose candidates of different parties—for example, a Republican candidate for Congress and a Democratic candidate for governor.

Congressional primaries have encountered the same problems that we noted in presidential primaries. Congressional primaries have been characterized by only minimal turnout and—though this has been difficult to document—the raiding of one party's primary by voters of another party. The limited public visibility of primaries and the limited citizen involvement in them may play into the hands of an intense minority. During the 1986 elections, for example, supporters of extremist Lyndon LaRouche placed several nominees for Congress and other positions on Democratic primary ballots. Raiding, of course, is easier in open-primary states, but not impossible in states that, in theory at least, are closed. The motivations behind raiding are difficult to determine. One theory is that raiding is undertaken to secure the nomination of a candidate who can be easily defeated in the general election. Another theory is that people enter the opposition's primary simply to vote for a candidate they would like to see elected.

Another problem with primaries is that they may lead to intraparty conflicts that hinder party unity in the general election. Party leaders may attempt to avoid primaries in which bitter competition is likely, by discouraging a candidate from running. They may do this by refusing to circulate his or her nominating petitions or by pledging to support the candidate for another office.

A divisive primary does not guarantee defeat in the general election. It is, however, apt to leave wounds that are difficult to heal, particularly among those who actively worked on behalf of defeated primary candidates. One study found that about one of every five activists who worked for a defeated candidate may help the other party's candidate in the general election. More commonly, these activists may vote for the victorious candidate in the general election but refuse to assist him or her in that contest.[17]

Competition for Seats

The number of candidates in any given congressional primary depends mainly on whether an incumbent is running for reelection and on the party's electoral strength in the district. Incumbents who wish renomination are often unopposed in the primaries. When an incumbent is not running for reelection, the primary of a party with considerable popular support in the district or the state is likely to have two or more candidates for the nomination. Where a party has little hope of winning the general election, party leaders may encounter difficulty in coming up with a candidate. Under such circumstances, the candidate is likely to be a party loyalist willing to run in the hope that doing so will eventually help build the party's strength.

Competition among candidates in general elections is similarly affected by incumbency and party strength. In about 10 percent of all elections for seats in the House of Representatives in recent years, candidates have run unopposed. Moreover, congressional elections in which the victorious candidate receives less than 55 percent of the vote are infrequent. Accordingly, only about one of every four House seats can be said to have been competitive.[18] Since the mid 1950s incumbent members of Congress in both parties have generally been difficult to defeat. Incumbents have had an advantage over challengers in staff, access to campaign finances, and public visibility. Even more significantly, they have built a coalition of support among members of the dominant political party in their district, and this support safeguards their seat.

[17] Donald Bruce Johnson and James R. Gibson, "The Divisive Primary Revisited: Party Activists in Iowa," *American Political Science Review* 68 (1974): 67–77.
[18] See Keefe and Ogul, op. cit., pp. 100–102.

CAMPAIGNS AND ELECTIONS:
CONCLUDING OBSERVATIONS

Campaigning for the Voters

Over the years campaigns for the presidency, and to a lesser extent other offices, have become more professional. Yet most campaigns have less organization and planning than meets the eye. As political scientist Frank Sorauf has noted,

> the conventional wisdom seems to suggest . . . that most political campaigns are run on a master battle plan adhered to with almost military discipline and precision. In reality most American political campaigns lurch along from one improvisation to another, from one immediate crisis to another. They are frequently underorganized, underplanned, and understaffed—and consequently, often played by ear on a surprising lack of information.[19]

During campaigns, candidates strive to cultivate a favorable public image, to discredit their opponents, or both. They "point with pride" at their own records and proposals and "view with alarm" those of rivals. "Dirty tricks" are sometimes employed, such as the infiltration of an opponent's campaign organization to secure confidential information and the hiring of hecklers to disrupt a rival's rallies. Mudslinging (personal attacks) are sometimes made (but seldom at the presidential level): opponents are said to have lied about their educational and occupational achievements, to be "secret drunks," or to be tied to political radicals or organized crime. Many campaign activities are designed to demonstrate a candidate's affinity with various areas or various segments of the population. Candidates may be found waiting outside factory gates to shake hands with workers, milking a cow in Wisconsin, and parading on a horse in Texas.

One of the most prominent characteristics of modern political campaigns has been the use of the media to communicate with voters. Many campaigns are managed by technicians skilled in marketing candidates through the media in much the same way toothpaste and other products are sold.[20] Such advertising has only a minimal effect on the many voters who are predisposed to vote a certain way and who thus will believe only political information that supports their predispositions. On the other hand, political advertising may have a great influence on those with only a minimal interest in politics.[21] The less

---

[19] Sorauf, op. cit., p. 249.

[20] See, for example, Dan Nimmo, *The Political Persuaders: The Techniques of Modern Election Campaigns* (Englewood Cliffs, N.J.: Prentice-Hall, 1970); and David Lee Rosenbloom, *The Election Men: Professional Campaign Managers and American Democracy* (New York: Quadrangle, 1972).

[21] See Nimmo, op. cit.

interested voter appears to be particularly influenced by short "paid political announcements" that are repeated a number of times.[22]

More broadly, political campaigns as a whole generally do not function as much to convert voters as to stimulate those predisposed toward a candidate to show up at the polls. Many voters apparently make up their minds quickly once they know the identity of the candidates. Others are predisposed to vote a certain way because of their party affiliation or membership in a particular social group or class. In a particular election, however, the number of voters who are converted can make the difference between winning and losing.

Voter Behavior

The importance of determinants of voting behavior such as the candidates' characteristics, party affiliation, and the policy issues in the campaign is difficult to pinpoint. All may be involved in the decisions of individual voters. The importance of each factor can be expected to vary from voter to voter and from campaign to campaign. Party affiliation, for example, was not very significant in the 1972 presidential election, where 40 percent of those who identified themselves as Democrats voted for Republican Richard Nixon, and in 1980 and 1984, where there was a large Democratic vote for Reagan. It was important, however, in the 1976 presidential election, where party identifiers tended to support the candidate of their party. Likewise, the characteristics of the candidates, such as their religion, experience, and personality, may be more important to some voters and in some elections.

Often voting is based on a negative evaluation of a candidate: voters in effect vote *against* someone rather than *for* someone else. Thus, it might be said that the more voters saw of Carter, the better Reagan looked. One factor that seems highly important in the voter's decision, particularly in congressional elections, is whether a candidate is an incumbent. As suggested previously, incumbents normally have an advantage.

It seems safe to say that a certain number of people will vote for a Democratic candidate or a Republican candidate simply because he or she belongs to their party. Such partisan voting is more likely in races for the House than in races for the Senate or the presidency because candidates for the House receive far less publicity and there are fewer specific issues to which voters can relate. Party affiliation is also likely to affect voter decisions when other factors, such as the candidates' personalities and the campaign issues, do not lead the voter to a conclusion. Thus the act of voting may be looked upon as follows:

> The voter canvasses his likes and dislikes of the leading candidates and major parties involved in an election. Weighing each like and dislike equally, he votes for the candidate toward whom he has the greatest net number of favorable

---

[22] Thomas E. Patterson and Robert D. McClure, "Television and the Less-Interested Voter," *Annals* 425 (May 1976): 88–97.

attitudes, if there is such a candidate. If no candidate has such an advantage, the voter votes consistently with his party affiliation, if he has one.[23]

The ability of voters to evaluate candidates on the basis of their stands on issues requires the taking of such stands. But presidential candidates commonly blur their stands on issues, because they seek the support of various sectional, economic, ethnic, and other interests which may be conflicting with one another over basic issues. Major candidates for president often sound much alike on major issues because they attempt to please the same groups and tap the same broad spectrum of opinion. Candidates who have been more issue-oriented or ideologic, such as George McGovern and Barry Goldwater, have suffered by being identified as extremists. Thus a candidate may be criticized for avoiding issues or for taking both sides on a policy matter, but he or she is likely to suffer even more by taking firm stands on controversial subjects. Although voters appeared to be concerned about some of candidate Ronald Reagan's statements, he was able to avoid being labeled an extremist.

Campaign Finance

Since the late 1960s campaign finance has been a favored target of political reform groups. Their major fear has been that those who contribute large amounts of money to a campaign will have undue influence over public policy. As one analyst has wisely observed, "almost as important as the fact of excessive financial influence over the political process is the appearance of such influence, since it erodes public confidence in the integrity of the electoral system and in the legitimacy of the officials selected under this system.[24]

As mentioned in Chapter 4, candidates and campaign organizations have traditionally depended on the financial support of a few "fat cat" contributors, such as wealthy business people and labor unions. The unions pioneered the practice of organizational contributions, collecting funds from their members and channeling it through political action committees (PACs) to favored candidates. Organizational contributions are now made by nearly every conceivable group. In the mid 1980s there were more than 4,000 PACs, among which businesses had become more prevalent than unions. PAC spending in federal elections increased from $12.5 million in 1974 to over $100 million in 1984. In the latter year, about 26 percent of all funds spent in congressional races came from PAC contributors and about one third of those running for Congress received half of their contributions from this source.[25]

---

[23] Stanley Kelly, Jr., and Thad W. Mirer, "The Simple Act of Voting," *American Political Science Review* 67 (June 1974): 574.

[24] Edwin M. Epstein, "Corporations and Labor Unions in Electoral Politics," *Annals* 425 (May 1976): 36.

[25] *Congressional Record*, December 3, 1985, pp. S16678ff.

Candidates for national office who are unknown may have to rely heavily upon large contributors for the start-up funds they need to gain visibility. Small as well as large contributions are likely to be easier to obtain for candidates who do well in a primary or, in the case of presidential contenders, in several primaries. Some candidates are sufficiently wealthy to avoid, or at least minimize, dependence upon contributions. In recent years, it has been common to find twenty or more millionaires in the U.S. Senate.

Candidates of the two major parties generally have different bases of financial support. For example, people in the higher income brackets are more likely to give to Republican candidates than to Democratic contenders. Because of this, Republicans generally are in a better position than Democrats to raise campaign funds.

A number of contributors, however, may give to the candidates of one party in a certain year and to the candidates of the other party in the next. Contributors in any particular year may also give to candidates running against each other for the same office. Apparently the most flexible of all contributors are business and other groups that rely on public spending programs or whose welfare is affected by governmental regulations. Taking no chances, they may contribute to anyone who is not an implacable enemy.

On the whole, more money is contributed to candidates in contests whose outcome is uncertain. Incumbents tend to receive more money than nonincumbents, and among incumbents in Congress those who hold key committee positions are more likely than others to receive the financial backing of interest groups.

People, groups, and institutions contribute to political campaigns for a number of reasons. Some contributors, most notably those who make small contributions, may act out of party loyalty, friendship for the candidate, or agreement with the candidate's policy views. Those who give large amounts may expect specific favors in return—for example, the candidate's support for a particular piece of legislation if he or she is elected. Some large contributors may expect a job, such as an ambassadorship, from a president they have supported. Probably more realistically, large contributors expect no more than that an officeholder they supported will think kindly of them and be willing to listen to their demands.

The presidential election of 1972 witnessed a number of well-publicized scandals concerning campaign finance. Many of them involved the fund-raising activities of the Committee to Re-elect the President (CREEP), formed on behalf of Richard Nixon. Fund raisers for Nixon were eventually accused of accepting millions of dollars from dairy cooperatives in exchange for the administration's help in such matters as increasing milk price supports; dropping an antitrust suit against the giant International Telephone and Telegraph Corporation; and in effect extorting millions of dollars from corporations that do business with the national government or are subject to its regulations.

These and related abuses of campaign financing led to the far-reaching and complex Federal Election Campaign Act of 1974. This law (1) limited the amount of money that can be contributed by individuals or organizations to each candidate for federal office, (2) required candidates to make reports (open to public inspection) disclosing the identity of those who contributed $100 or more to their campaigns and revealing the nature of all expenditures over $100, and (3) created the Federal Election Commission to implement campaign-finance laws.

The 1974 law also provided federal grants for the primary and general-election campaigns of presidential candidates. The money comes from a presidential campaign fund established in 1971 that is built on a voluntary federal income tax checkoff. Although candidates do not have to accept the grants, those who do are limited in the amount they can spend.

Since 1974 the financing of presidential campaigns has consisted largely of taxpayer contributions. Similar legislation has been introduced for congressional campaigns. Without such financing, candidates for Congress will continue to be dependent on a few large contributors and on political action committees for funds.

SUMMARY

1. Political parties are not mentioned in the Constitution, many of whose framers feared that the rise of parties would cause disruption and disrespect for the new government and its laws. Nevertheless, from the earliest days of George Washington's administration to the present national politics has been characterized by struggles for power between political parties. The party founded by Jefferson, which has come to be known as the Democratic party, has contended with the Federalist and Whig parties and, since the 1850s, with the Republican party. The Republican party was the dominant force in national politics from the 1860s to the late 1920s. Since the 1930s the Democratic party has dominated elections for national office.

2. The United States has a national two-party system in which both parties try to build winning coalitions of diverse social, economic, and regional interests. Third or minor parties in this country have at times articulated issues neglected by the major parties. Third parties, however, have faced a number of difficulties (such as those imposed by the election system) in attracting voters. The major parties in this country are highly fragmented. Being a member carries no obligations, not even that of voting for the party's candidates for office. Relations among party workers, candidates for office, and public officeholders are not necessarily close or harmonious.

3. Liberals and conservatives are found in both parties. Studies suggest, however, that Democrats and Republicans tend to differ on some policy matters, with

Democrats leaning to the more liberal side and Republicans tending to be more conservative.

4. Political party organizations perform a variety of important functions in the political system, such as recruiting candidates, raising campaign funds, activating voters, and attempting to influence voter choices. People who are active in contemporary party organizations are far more concerned with public policy matters than their predecessors were. Party organizations as a whole, however, have lost much of their control over the recruitment and nomination of candidates and the conduct of campaigns. Many candidates for office are self-recruited and rely on their own campaign staffs or on hired professionals to win primary and general elections.

5. Central among the institutions that condition presidential campaigns and elections is the electoral college. The major criticism of the electoral college has been that it allows the possibility of electing a president who has fewer popular votes than an opponent. The institution has been defended on the grounds that it reflects the federal principle by recognizing the equality of the states.

6. Presidential primaries in various states have become the principal means through which presidential candidates win delegates to their party conventions. The growing use of primaries has reduced the importance of national conventions in the nominating process. A convention, however, may be the scene of much conflict and bargaining if the delegates are closely divided among the candidates.

7. Incumbent presidents normally have little difficulty in getting their party's nomination for reelection. In recent years candidates making their first bid for the presidency have often begun campaign preparations several months before the first presidential primary. Many candidates drop out of the race in the first few months of the campaign for delegates. Early primary victories are important in generating publicity, building momentum, and creating a bandwagon effect. The candidates who secure the nomination pay particular attention to large states where it appears the vote will be close.

8. Congressional elections are held every two years. Campaigns for House seats are usually waged within districts designed by state legislatures. District lines may be gerrymandered to give an advantage to the candidates of one party over those of another. Every other congressional election coincides with a presidential election, and the two elections may influence each other. A popular presidential candidate, for instance, may help some of his party's candidates for Congress get elected. On the other hand, presidential and congressional candidates have in recent years been developing independent electoral bases, which have minimized the effect of one type of election on the other. Congressional elections held independently of presidential elections attract fewer voters than those held

in conjunction with presidential elections, and they usually result in the president's party losing seats in Congress. Many voters in these midterm elections apparently base their votes on how well the president has performed.

9. Candidates for Congress usually have to meet informal requirements, such as the time and funds necessary to wage a campaign, as well as satisfy the formal requirements set in the Constitution. Candidates seek the nomination of a political party by entering primary elections, which in most states are closed—that is, confined to voters who have registered with a particular party. Primaries have been criticized because they usually attract only a limited number of voters and often lead to conflict within the party among rival candidates. One of the most striking recent characteristics of congressional elections is that most incumbents who seek reelection are victorious.

10. Modern political campaigns have become more professional, although they may seem to be more organized and planned than is actually the case. In many elections, especially for the presidency, media specialists are employed to "sell" candidates much like they would sell a commercial product. Television political spots may be a very effective way to reach voters who have only a minimal interest in politics. However, campaigns generally do not change many minds. Instead they tend to stimulate those individuals predisposed for or against a candidate to come to the polls. The characteristics of the candidates, party affiliation, and policy issues all influence voter behavior, the first two being generally more important than the last.

11. One of the most difficult problems of political campaigns has been their financing. Although contributors have a number of reasons for giving money to candidates, there has been a long-standing fear that large contributors in effect purchase favors from victorious candidates whom they support. Responding to this problem, Congress placed regulations on campaign financing. Since 1976 financing of congressional elections has been proposed but not adopted.

PRESIDENTIAL
POLITICS
AND POLICY MAKING

Thus far we have been concerned with the general character of American politics and the setting in which public policy is made. In chapters 6–9 we focus on official policy makers and policy-making institutions. We begin in this chapter with the presidency, which, though provided for after Congress in the U.S. Constitution, has emerged as the focal point of the national government. We first examine the various provisions of the Constitution and acts of Congress that pertain to the presidency. We then turn to the occupants of the office and the presidential establishment, discuss presidential influence, and offer some concluding observations on the presidency.

NATURE OF THE OFFICE

The American presidency has been shaped in part by numerous provisions in the U.S. Constitution and acts of Congress relating to qualifications, terms, succession, disability, and removal. Law and tradition also have created certain roles or responsibilities for presidents.

Legal Conditions

Presidents are elected to four-year terms. Although it might be argued that a president should serve as many terms as the voters desire, the Twenty-second Amendment, adopted in 1951, stipulates that no person can be elected to the office more than twice. The amendment imposes special restrictions on those who become president by filling a vacancy in the office. If they serve more than two years in completing someone else's term, they are eligible for only one elected term. If they serve two years or less, they are eligible for two elected terms. Thus, a person can serve ten years as president. A number of students of the presidency, including four former presidents (Johnson, Nixon, Ford, and Carter), have suggested a single six-year term for the office. They argue that six-year presidents freed from reelection concerns would have a better chance of completing the goals of their administration. On the other hand, as political scientist Thomas Cronin has argued, "with a six-year term we'd get two extra years of the weak presidents and two years less of those who were very competent and able and had the quality to provide leadership for the nation."[1]

Under the Constitution the vice-president serves as president if the incumbent dies, resigns, or becomes unable to carry out the duties of the office. By act of Congress the line of succession after the vice-president is the Speaker of the House, the president pro tempore of the Senate, and the heads of the executive departments, beginning with the oldest department (State) and proceeding to the newest (Education).

[1] Quoted in *Common Cause*, October 1980, p. 23.

The possibility of a vacancy in the vice-presidency has been substantially reduced by the Twenty-fifth Amendment (1967). It requires the president to fill the vacancy by nominating an individual for the position. The president's nominee takes office after being confirmed by a majority vote of both houses of Congress. The law was first applied in 1973 when Vice-President Spiro Agnew resigned and was replaced by Gerald Ford. After Richard Nixon's resignation Ford became president, and the system was used once again in the selection of Nelson Rockefeller as vice-president.

Another section of the twenty-fifth Amendment deals with the problem of presidential disability. If a president feels unable to perform his duties, he is to so inform the president pro tempore of the Senate and the Speaker of the House in writing. The vice-president becomes acting president until such time as the president informs the leaders of the two houses that he is able to resume his duties. President Reagan followed the procedure just described in making a temporary transfer of power to Vice-President George Bush in 1985, though he did not formally invoke the Twenty-fifth Amendment.

The Twenty-fifth Amendment also provides if a president cannot inform Congress of his disability the vice-president and a majority of the members of the Cabinet may submit a written declaration to Congress that the president is unable to serve. The president may resume his duties by submitting a message that he is capable of serving. Such a message, however, may be challenged by the vice-president and a majority of the Cabinet. In this case the conflict is settled by a vote in both houses of Congress; a two-thirds vote is required in each house to sustain the position of the vice-president and Cabinet majority. Thus far, occasion for the use of this provision has not arisen.

The ultimate check upon the president (and other administrative officials as well as judges) is provided for in Article II, Section 4, of the Constitution: removal from office "on impeachment for, and conviction of, treason, bribery, or other high crimes and misdemeanors." Impeachment is the bringing of charges against an official. This responsibility is vested by the Constitution in the House of Representatives. If the House votes to impeach a president, the charges are tried in the Senate, which for this purpose is presided over by the Chief Justice of the United States (who is also the presiding officer of the U.S. Supreme Court). Conviction requires a two-thirds vote of the senators present and results in removal. After removal a president may be tried in the regular courts on criminal charges.

Thus far only one president has been impeached—Andrew Johnson in 1868. Johnson escaped conviction in the Senate by a single vote. In 1974, the House Committee on the Judiciary concluded nearly six months of investigation by voting in nationally televised hearings that Richard Nixon be impeached by the full House for (1) obstructing justice in an attempt to cover up an unlawful entry into the Watergate headquarters of the Democratic National Committee; (2) abusing his power by, among other things, using confidential information contained in income tax returns for political purposes; and (3) acting in contempt of Congress by refusing to comply with its subpoenas. Nixon resigned before the articles of impeachment could be voted upon by the House.

Presidential Roles

Presidents have commonly been viewed as performing a variety of leadership roles, among them chief legislator, chief administrator, chief diplomat, commander in chief, chief of party, chief magistrate, and chief of state. The designation of the president as chief legislator reflects the fact that since the administration of Woodrow Wilson (1913–21) many of the most important bills introduced in Congress have been formulated by the president or elsewhere in the executive branch. In addition, presidents can help determine the fate of legislation initiated by others. For example, they can help line up congressional votes for a measure, give its proponents access to the technical resources of the bureaucracy, and publicize the proposal. Presidential resources can also be used to block or blunt the development of new policies.

Presidential involvement in the legislative process stems partly from other roles of the chief executive, such as national leader, chief administrator, and party chief. The Constitution and various acts of Congress also involve the president in legislation by authorizing or requiring him to send various messages to Congress (such as State of the Union, budget, and economic messages), call special sessions of Congress, and veto legislation.

The veto power is a particularly valuable tool. It enables presidents both to prevent unwanted policies from becoming law and, through the threat of a veto, to deter Congress from even considering certain proposals (see Chapter 7). One power the president does not have is the line-item veto. This power, possessed by several state governors, would enable the president to veto appropriations for specific programs. President Reagan in 1986 proposed that presidents be given this power so that they can cut unnecessary or wasteful programs and reduce the national debt. Speaking to Congress in his state of the union message of that year, he declared, "Give me the authority to veto waste, and I'll take the responsibility, I'll make the cuts, I'll take the heat."[2] Opponents of the line-item veto contend that the chief executive already has ample power over spending (this power will be discussed shortly). More important, they argue, the line-item veto would concentrate too much power in the president and radically diminish the role of Congress in the budgetary process.

In addition to working through Congress, presidents can in effect legislate on their own by issuing executive orders. These are rules or regulations made by presidents to implement acts of Congress and treaties and to fulfill their various constitutional responsibilities. Many executive orders have been directed

---

[2] Quoted in *Congressional Record,* February 5, 1986, p. S1050.

at changing the organization or procedures of administrative agencies. Such orders may pave the way for broader policy changes. The civil rights movement, for example, received a boost from an executive order by Harry Truman that ended segregation in the armed forces. Similarly, "equal opportunity" legislation can be traced in part to an executive order issued by John Kennedy in 1961 that created the Equal Employment Commission to protect individuals against discriminatory practices in the federal civil service.

In theory the president sits at the head of a vast federal bureaucracy of close to 3 million civilian employees and oversees the expenditure of $900 billion annually. As one observer has concluded, "being President of the United States is the single largest management job in the world."[3] The most basic responsibility of the president as head of the administrative branch, according to Article II, Section 3, of the Constitution, is to "take care that the laws be faithfully executed." Yet it is clear that presidents may be less than enthusiastic about implementing laws or programs with which they disagree. Several presidents have shown their disagreement with congressional policy by impounding (refusing to spend) funds appropriated by Congress for various programs. President Kennedy, for example, once refused to spend funds earmarked for racially segregated hospitals and other facilities. Several years later President Nixon impounded much of the money Congress had appropriated for social and environmental programs, on the grounds that they contributed to inflation. In reaction to the latter experience Congress placed limits on the ability of chief executives to control spending. Under a 1974 law, a presidential decision to defer spending can be rejected by either house of Congress and the decision of a president to cut off funds for a program must be approved by both houses. These controls, however, do not appear to have greatly hindered presidents bent on reducing expenditures. During Ronald Reagan's first two years in office, for example, Congress agreed to better than 75 percent of White House requests for recissions in spending. From this some $20 billion dollars were saved.[4]

Recent Supreme Court rulings appear to give the president a limited right under the doctrine of executive privilege to withhold information from Congress, especially information on sensitive national security issues.[5] The Supreme Court has also recognized that presidents are immune from private lawsuits. In a five-to-four decision in 1982 the Court reasoned that because of the singular importance of the office of president, diversion of the president's energy by private lawsuits would endanger the effective functioning of govern-

---

[3] Donald Haider, "Management and the Presidency: From Preparation to Performance," *Presidential Studies Quarterly*, 6 (Winter and Spring 1976): 5.

[4] *Common Cause*, July/August 1985, p. 45.

[5] For example, *United States* v. *Nixon*, 418 U.S. 683 (1974). Some authorities, it should be noted, have argued that "executive privilege" is a myth. See Raoul Berger, *Executive Privilege* (Cambridge, Mass.: Harvard University Press, 1974).

ment. The proper remedy for presidential misconduct, the Court concluded, was impeachment rather than payment of damages. Presidential appointees, though, have only "qualified protection" against private suits: they can be sued if their conduct violates well-established rights.[6]

Several provisions of the Constitution and the realities of modern global politics have given presidents a leadership role in foreign policy. Under the Constitution the president is chief diplomat with the duties, among others, of making treaties (subject to approval by the Senate) and receiving foreign ambassadors and thereby recognizing foreign governments. The President also acts as commander in chief of the U.S. armed services. This military power, however, is shared with Congress, and the specific allocation of responsibilities has been a matter of dispute (see Chapter 12).

At a less lofty level is the presidential role of political party leader. Although partisanship is not in keeping with the idealized role of national leadership, it is difficult for a president to forget that he is a Republican or a Democrat. Party workers expect their "man in the White House" to look after the welfare of the party. Regular party members whose support is needed for presidential nominations or renominations may also insist that a president perform as a true conservative or liberal. These expectations may have a substantial effect on policy. During the months leading up to the 1976 Republican presidential nominating convention, for example, many conservative policy positions taken by President Ford were apparently directed toward wooing Republican workers and potential convention delegates away from Ronald Reagan.

The status of the president as party chief is limited by the decentralized nature of political parties. Presidents are seldom able to control their party's nominations of candidates for Congress and other offices, and quite frequently they find that legislators with the same party affiliation oppose their policies.

The principal powers of the president as chief magistrate are granting reprieves, pardons, and amnesties or crimes committed against the United States. A reprieve is a postponement of punishment when, for example, new evidence is found in a case. An absolute pardon restores an individual's full rights and civil liberties; a conditional pardon carries certain restrictions. A pardon may be given prior to a trial, during a trial, or after a person has been convicted. President Ford's 1974 pardon of former president Nixon for any crime he might have committed under federal law, though highly unpopular, was nevertheless legal. Amnesty is in effect a blanket pardon of a group of people, such as draft resisters.

Whereas the role of chief magistrate calls for difficult decisions, the role of chief of state is a considerable drain on the time and energy of presidents. As chief of state the president is the symbolic head of government, responsible for

---

[6] *Fitzgerald* v. *Nixon*, 457 U.S. 731 (1982).

the ceremonial duties—hosting foreign dignitaries is an illustration—performed by a king or queen in such countries as England. In many nations the symbolic role is carried out by an official called a president while a prime minister or a premier actually heads the government. In the United States the president plays both roles.

What presidents do with their time is shaped by their attitudes and inclinations, the demands made upon them, their legal responsibilites, and the formal and informal roles they are called upon to assume. Many matters with which presidents concern themselves are not of earthshaking importance. President Franklin Roosevelt, for instance, took a direct interest in postage-stamp designs (this stemmed from his hobby of stamp collecting). Specific demands and issues of concern to presidents vary over time. Since the 1930s, presidents have tended to give priority to foreign policy and broad national economic problems such as inflation and unemployment. In fulfilling his legal obligations the president and his staff must spend much time on such chores as searching for personnel to fill various offices and determining which legislation should be vetoed and which signed into law. Further time is consumed in preparing a legislative program, the executive budget, and various messages to Congress. Ceremonial and public-relations activities also use up many presidential hours. Finally, presidents frequently attempt to resolve conflicts among their staff advisers or executive departments. As a sign on Harry Truman's desk stated, "The Buck Stops Here."

PRESIDENTIAL STYLES, ADVISERS, AND DECISIONS

The Presidents

What types of people have been elected president? Thus far all presidents have been white and male; most have been lawyers; veterans of military service; English, Scottish, or Irish by ancestry; and members of a Protestant denomination. The only Catholic to be elected president was John F. Kennedy in 1960.

In terms of style, some presidents, such as Jimmy Carter, seem to involve themselves personally in the details of public policy and thus may be criticized for failing to see the "big picture." On the other end of the involvement scale, some presidents—an example is Ronald Reagan—appear to be concerned only with general policy directions and, having delegated much authority to others, often seem uninformed about specific developments within their own administrations.

Presidents have also varied in their powers and responsibilities. Weak or passive presidents subscribe to President Taft's view that they can exercise only those powers specifically granted or reasonably implied in the Constitution or an act of Congress.

Strong or active presidents have generally followed Andrew Jackson's lead in declaring themselves to be the tribunes of the people. This special relationship with the people is based on the fact that the president is the only major official in the country who has a national constituency. Under the stewardship theory, as articulated by Theodore Roosevelt, the president is a steward of the people and has an obligation to do all he can for them. Toward this end, Roosevelt asserted, the president may take any action not forbidden by the Constitution or the laws.

Going considerably further in terms of power is the executive prerogative theory. Basically, this is the belief that in emergencies the president may act beyond his authority and, indeed, in violation of the law. Presidents sometimes apply the prerogative theory in wartime.

In recent years increasing attention has been given to the psychological makeup of presidents. Personality studies of presidents have added further insights into the character of the men who have held that office. Woodrow Wilson, for example, appears to have gone through a regular sequence of stages following his assumption of major executive roles as university president, governor, and president of the United States. In each case there was a period of dramatic accomplishment followed by controversy and ultimately failure, largely of his own making, especially the inability to make minor concessions. Wilson has been appraised as flexible and pragmatic in seeking power, but far more rigid and dogmatic in exercising it. Some of his causes, such as the League of Nations, were perceived by Wilson to be "holy," nonnegotiable objectives. Those who opposed these causes were to be overwhelmed and routed.[7]

Political scientist James David Barber's studies of presidential character have resulted in a fourfold classification of presidential styles.[8]

1. Active-positive presidents (such as Franklin Roosevelt, Harry S. Truman, and John Kennedy) work very hard, are flexible, and enjoy their activities. They savor the politics of persuasion and bargaining, and they compromise to get results.

2. Active-negative presidents (such as Woodrow Wilson, Herbert Hoover, Lyndon Johnson, and Richard Nixon) are highly industrious but tend to be aggressive against what they see to be a hostile environment and frequently find the work irritating and punishing. Active-negatives are not apt to be good

[7] Alexander L. George and Juliette L. George, *Woodrow Wilson and Colonel House: A Personality Study* (New York: Dover, 1964). This and related studies are discussed by Fred I. Greenstein, *Personality and Politics* (Chicago: Markham, 1969), pp. 73–93.

[8] James David Barber, *The Presidential Character: Predicting Performance in the White House*, 3rd ed. (Englewood Cliffs, N.J.: Prentice-Hall, 1985).

listeners, or to appreciate those who ask the "wrong" questions or give answers that conflict with the president's position or predispositions.

3. Passive-positive presidents (such as William Howard Taft and Warren G. Harding) are relatively slow-moving, agreeable, and anxious for approval.

4. Passive-negative presidents (such as Dwight D. Eisenhower and Calvin Coolidge) are inactive, are anxious to avoid controversy or hard decisions, and dislike being bothered about political matters. Said Calvin Coolidge, "One of the most important accomplishments of my administration has been minding my own business."

It should be noted that the assignment of presidents to particular classifications is a difficult task and is likely to provoke disagreement. Some scholars, for example, have looked upon Ronald Reagan as being rigidly attached to conservative values and the goal of implementing these values. This orientation makes him an active-negative type.[9] A more recent image of Reagan, inspired in part by the Iran-Contra controversy, suggests a passive, uninformed, and uninvolved president who nevertheless enjoys the job, especially making public appearances. From this perspective, he is a passive-positive type.

Barber has argued that it is important to look into the backgrounds of those who seek the presidency in an effort to predict their behavior under given circumstances. To Barber, the active-positive type is clearly preferable to the others in terms of being able to accomplish objectives and to endure the strain of office.

The Presidential Establishment

Surrounding the modern president are a vast number of advisers and assistants who form the presidential establishment and compete for access to the chief executive. The relationship between the president and one of these individuals, the vice-president, has varied greatly from administration to administration. Traditionally, vice-presidents have gained their positions only because they balanced the party's ticket, and once in office they have been virtually ignored by their presidents. Thomas Marshall, vice-president under Woodrow Wilson, told the following story; which reflects the views of a number of others who have held the office: "There were once two brothers. One ran away to sea. The other was elected Vice President and neither was heard of again."[10] Humorist Finley Peter Dunne, writing as Mr. Dooley, observed, "Th' prisidincy is th' highest office th' gift iv th' people. Th' vice-prisidincy is th' next highest an' th' lowest. It isn't a crime exactly. Ye can't be sint to jail f'r it, but it's a kind iv a

---

[9] See, for example, Robert Dallek, *Ronald Reagan: The Politics of Symbolism* (Cambridge, Mass.: Harvard University Press, 1984).

[10] Quoted by Alvin Shuster, "The Vice President," *Election Handbook* (New York: New American Library, 1968), p. 89.

disgrace. It's like writin' anonymous letters."[11] Though still the object of jokes, modern vice-presidents such as Walter Mondale and George Bush have been personally close to their presidents and thus have been given important assignments, the right to sit in on important meetings, and the opportunity to give advice on major decisions.[12]

Other presidential assistants include Cabinet officers and a large number of people working in the Executive Office of the President. The Cabinet consists of the heads of the thirteen executive departments, who are appointed by the president with the consent of the Senate. No specific provision for a cabinet is made in the Constitution, but since George Washington presidents have consulted with their department heads individually and collectively in Cabinet meetings. Eisenhower used his Cabinet more than all other presidents since World War II. The Eisenhower Cabinet met regularly to discuss important issues, and often during the sessions each member asked for advice on a wide range of matters other than those of concern to his or her department. Since Eisenhower, Cabinet meetings have been relatively infrequent, though somewhat revived under Carter and Reagan. Kennedy regarded collective meetings of department heads as an anachronism and felt that the nature of a problem, not mere Cabinet status, should determine who was to be brought into a discussion.

Loyalty to the president, managerial ability, political philosophy, and acceptability to party, congressional, and interest-group leaders appear to be among the most important criteria in the selection of Cabinet members. Newly elected presidents often ignore federal administrators as potential Cabinet members and choose people from business, state and local governments, or universities. Going to the outside gives a president a chance to reward those who aided his or her election, institutionalize the policy thrust of the administration, bring new ideas as well as new faces into government, and, by selecting prominent people, give more credibility to the administration. During an administration several Cabinet positions are likely to become vacant for one reason or another. In contrast with the initial appointees, replacement Cabinet members have frequently been federal officials who were promoted from within the department they were selected to head or from a position such as undersecretary in another department. This pattern of replacing "outsiders" with "insiders," which has been evident in several recent administrations, enables presidents to secure greater managerial expertise and Washington experience.

The ability to manage Cabinet-level bureaucracies appears to be a rare quality, and those with this talent may be shifted from department to department to solve management problems. An example of this type of administrator is Elliot Richardson, who moved from undersecretary of state to secretary of

---

[11] John Bartlett, ed., *Familiar Quotations* (Boston: Little, Brown, 1968), p. 892.

[12] Paul C. Light, *Vice-Presidential Power: Advice and Influence in the White House* (Baltimore: Johns Hopkins, 1984).

health, education and welfare (now two separate departments) to secretary of defense and finally to attorney general in the Nixon administration. Richardson resigned as attorney general rather than obey Nixon's order to fire Archibald Cox (who was investigating the Watergate scandal) but returned as secretary of commerce under President Ford.[13]

Political scientist Thomas Cronin distinguishes between inner and outer Cabinet positions.[14] The *inner Cabinet* has included the heads of the State, Defense, Treasury, and Justice departments. These heads have generally been selected on the basis of their personal loyalty to the president and have worked closely with him and his top staff. The attorney general performs numerous duties of interest to presidents; the others are knowledgeable in the basic areas of national defense and general economic policy. Even the secretary of state, however, may be eclipsed by presidential advisers. Such was the fate of Secretary of State William Rogers when Henry Kissinger was Nixon's presidential adviser on national security.

The remaining department heads have usually been in the *outer Cabinet*. Their departments (Agriculture, Interior, Transportation, Health and Human Services, Education, Housing and Urban Development, Labor, Commerce) deal mostly with domestic programs, which have been of less concern to recent presidents than foreign and broad economic problems. The selection of the department heads in the outer cabinet has often reflected an effort to satisfy groups who are served by their departments. Although competence has not been ignored, the appointment of these heads has also been influenced by the desire to give a balanced appearance to the administration—for example, to represent various parts of the country, women, and racial and ethnic minorities. Department heads in the outer Cabinet are not likely to be close to the president. They are more apt to function as advocates for the needs of their departments than as employees of the president who execute his orders.

The Executive Office of the President was created by an executive order of President Franklin Roosevelt in 1939 as a staff arm of the presidency. The number of people in the Executive Office has ranged from 1,175 members in 1954[15] to approximately 5,000 to 6,000 since the 1970s. The growth has occurred mainly through the increased role of the president in foreign and domestic affairs. Expansion has also been related to the reluctance of presidents to rely on the permanent federal bureaucracy for policy advice and implementation and to their desire to keep highly sensitive matters secret.[16]

Within the Executive Office are the president's immediate assistants and

[13] See James J. Best, "Presidential Cabinet Appointments: 1953–1976," *Presidential Studies Quarterly* (Winter 1981): 62–66.

[14] Thomas E. Cronin, *The State of the Presidency* (Boston: Little, Brown, 1975), pp. 177–210.

[15] Thomas E. Cronin, "The Swelling of the Presidency," *Saturday Review,* February 1973, pp. 30–36.

[16] Ibid.

advisers, known as the White House Office, and a number of more specialized agencies, such as the Office of Management and Budget (formerly the Bureau of the Budget), the Council and Economic Advisers, and the National Security Council.

The Office of Management and Budget undertakes a vital role in coordinating the spending and legislative proposals of agencies within the executive branch. Much of this is done in the course of developing the budget recommendations the president submits to Congress each year. The Council of Economic Advisers is headed by three economists appointed by the president with the consent of the Senate. These economists and their staff help prepare the president's annual economic report to Congress and regularly advise the president on economic affairs.

The National Security Council (NSC) is composed of the secretaries of state and defense, the vice president, the president's national security adviser, and others who meet with the president and advise him on foreign and military policy. The National Security Council is intended to be an advisory group that assists in developing broad policy goals. At times, however, the staff employed by the NSC have become directly involved in implementing programs. During the Reagan administration, for example, a number of staffers associated with Lt. Col. Oliver North became deeply enmeshed in a number of secret operations, among which were the highly controversial selling of arms to Iran and the diversion of profits from that sale to rebels in Nicaragua (see Chapter 12).

Of the approximately 500 people on the White House staff, many perform relatively routine clerical duties or chores such as answering the mail. Others are speech writers, press secretaries, and legal counsels. Still others are lobbyists who work with legislators, private groups, or both.

Some presidents have preferred a large specialized, hierarchical staff headed by a chief of staff. This was especially true of Eisenhower—no doubt because of his military background—and of Nixon. The Nixon White House staff, headed by H. R. "Bob" Haldeman, raised stout barriers to those, including legislative leaders and department heads, who wished contact with the president. Similar problems occured in the Reagan years when chief of staff Donald T. Regan, who was known as the "Prime Minister," was able to control access to the president and, to a considerable extent, how much the president knew about developments within his own administration. The result of the "palace guard" mentality, particularly evident in the Nixon and Reagan administrations, is to isolate the president and to cut him off from advice and information he might not like but should hear.

Presidential Decision Making

The characteristics, values, and beliefs of a president are important factors in presidential decision making. Presidents, like other policy makers, have private as well as public goals. Thus while they may be genuinely concerned with issues of public policy and committed to specific causes, they are also concerned with their own career and prestige. During his first term much of what a president does reflects his desire for reelection. In his second term a president may worry less about his constituents and more about his place in history. Presidential decision making is also affected directly and indirectly by the citizenry, the media, Congress, the federal bureaucracy, major interest groups, officials from other nations, and, possibly most important, the inner circle of advisers who help the president deal with these various constituencies.

Although some presidents have been far more accessible than others, all have allowed only a relatively few individuals into their inner circle of advisers. Some people qualify as presidential advisers because they are viewed by the president as highly knowledgeable in a particualr subject. Others are likely to be people he has known for a long time and with whom he feels comfortable. Many advisers and assistants have worked in the president's campaign and have proved their loyalty to him, as, for example, President Carter's staff from Georgia and President Reagan's advisers from California.

Presidential advisers may provide the chief executive with honest and blunt advice. On the other hand, they may tell the president only what he wants to hear because of their reverence for him or because they must retain his favor to keep their positions.

The chief executive and his advisers may sometimes engage in what Irving Janis has termed *groupthink*.[17] In a groupthink situation group loyalty and team play are emphasized and each participant attempts to maintain the approval of the others, especially the leader. Group members are thereby constrained from being critical or expressing their doubts about the wisdom or consequences of a proposed course of action. Janis developed the groupthink concept to help explain gross miscalculations by groups of policy-makers, such as the ill-fated Bay of Pigs invasion, the failure to be prepared for Pearl Harbor, the invasion of North Korea, and the escalation of the Vietnam War. Janis found the same type of detrimental group process to be at work in each of these decisions.

PRESIDENTIAL INFLUENCE

Influencing the Public

Presidents devote much time tending to their popular image, often with the aid of media and public relations specialists. Like most people, they want to be loved and appreciated. Popularity is also sought to enhance reelection

[17] See Irving L. Janis, "Groupthink and Group Dynamics: A Social Psychological Analysis of Defective Policy Decision," *Policy Studies Journal II* (Autumn 1973): 19–25; and Irving L. Janis, *Victims of Groupthink* (Boston: Houghton Mifflin, 1972).

opportunities and to give presidents an advantage in dealing with Congress and other officials such as those in foreign countries.

American presidents commonly attempt to depict themselves as hard-working, knowledgeable, decisive executives who are in control even though everyone else may be confused. Presidents often also cultivate the image of a person who has the "common touch," who is concerned about the problems of the average American and interested in what he or she has to say.

Prominent among the presidents who have attempted to project the latter image was Jimmy Carter, who committed himself in his presidential campaign to a "direct, intimate relationship" with the American public. After his election Carter took a crowd-pleasing impromptu walk down the inaugural-parade route. Once in office he reinstituted Franklin Roosevelt's fireside chats with the public; conducted the first presidential radio talk show, in which he answered questions from people across the nation; presided over a mock New England town meeting; stayed overnight with an "average" American family; and began to cut down on the number of limousines and other symbols of the imperial presidency. Carter undertook this campaign in part to build up greater public support than had been apparent in his narrow victory over Gerald Ford in 1976. By the end of his first three months in office Carter had secured a 75 percent approval rating from the public—though this rating might have climbed even without his attempts at image building. By the end of Carter's first two years in office his popularity had declined to under 50 percent. Some commentators attributed the drop to an excess of symbolism: the president seemed to be all style and no substance. Others contended that the American people actually preferred the imperial style. Acting on that assumption, President Reagan restored much of the pomp and ceremony of the presidency—for example, trumpets heralding his appearance, white-tie dinners, and a marine guard in uniform at the entrance to the White House.

Efforts to build support with the public have often brought presidents and their assistants into conflict with the press. Not surprisingly, presidents have attempted to exaggerate their accomplishments and minimize or conceal their mistakes or failures. White House reporters, whether from large daily papers, the wire services, newsmagazines, or the television networks, rightly suspect that there is often more to the news than what is contained in administration press releases. Reporters who wish to be something other than presidential cheerleaders engage in investigative journalism—for example, by getting tips from high administration sources.[18]

Interactions between reporters and the president take place on a fairly routine basis in presidential news conferences. Presidents have control over the number, time, location, and format of news conferences. Before the advent of television, news conferences were often informal and the president's remarks

---

[18] George E. Reedy, "The President and the Press," *Annals* 427 (September 1976); 67.

could be kept "off the record," or out of print. Televising news conferences has made them far more formal and staged. Frequently, presidents attempt to get specific messages across to the viewing audience by making opening statements and by planting questions with cooperative reporters. Some presidents, such as Eisenhower, disliked press conferences and limited their number. Presidents may avoid having their views filtered through the White House press corps by going directly to the public through radio or television. Presidents such as Richard Nixon who have attempted to circumvent reporters in this manner have been irritated by "instant analysis" of their presentations by media commentators.

Some presidents, such as Franklin Roosevelt and John Kennedy, enjoyed good relations with the press. Others had more difficulty. Lyndon Johnson, according to his press secretary, George E. Reedy, regarded journalists

> as people who had to be bamboozled, bullied, cajoled, or bribed with entertainment . . . He regarded newspapers and newscasts as partisan arenas in which contending politicans struggled for an advantage. . . . As a result, every newspaper reference to him was examined painstakingly to determine whether it was favorable or unfavorable. Unfortunately, his concept of favorable was a story carrying flattering adjectives topped by a picture in which his hair was neatly combed, his suit was freshly pressed, and his left profile was prominent. Anything that fell short of this ideal was "unfavorable" and the writer marked down as an enemy. . . .[19]

Whatever the effect of specific efforts to gain public approval popular support for presidents tends to follow a consistent pattern. In their first few months in office presidents generally stand high in public opinion polls as the American people rally behind the new chief executive. A new president is likely to find that the percentage of the public that approves of how he is handling his job is far higher than the proportion of the electorate that voted for him. The first few months are characterized not only by public support but also by "honeymoon" relations between the president and the press and Congress. Presidents who come to office by accident—that is, who move up from the vice-presidency because of a vacancy in the presidency—find the same supportive environment at first.

After this early stage presidential popularity fluctuates but generally follows a downward trend. Popularity increases if the president is reelected but then declines again.

Fluctuations in presidential popularity are related principally to major events. Presidential involvement in a dramatic international crisis generally increases popular support, even if, as after the Bay of Pigs invasion, the president was perceived by many people as having blundered. General economic

[19] Ibid., p. 66.

problems such as inflation or unemployment, on the other hand, customarily reduce presidential popularity.

Long-term declines in presidential popularity may be due mainly to the alienation of specific groups over a period of years to the point where a sizable coalition of interests has developed against the president. Apparently, the more a president attempts to do, the more likely he is to alienate a succession of groups.[20]

Influencing Congress

Presidential recommendations regarding new legislation, the funding of existing programs, treaties, and appointments to top-level positions must all be approved by Congress. In addition to attempting to get Congress to do certain things, presidents also have frequently been anxious to prevent Congress from acting on a specific program or spending what the president considers to be an excessive amount of money.

Much of the work of "selling" the president's position in Congress is assumed by White House lobbyists or department personnel. In working for the approval of his programs the president may personally contact individual legislators. Congressional leaders may be invited to breakfast with the president or to attend informal dinners at the White House. On major issues special strategy sessions are held with legislative leaders. Occasionally the president phones individual legislators whom he feels may be persuaded to tip the balance on a close vote in the president's favor. Presidents may also seek the aid of important groups, businesses, or newspapers in a legislator's constituency in securing his or her support.

Presidential dealings with Congress may be characterized by threats of a veto or promises of increased rewards. Those who aid the president, for example, may be given a voice in determining who should fill particular positions in the national government. Support may also be followed by presidential assistance in a legislator's campaign, the granting of a public contract to a business in a particular congressional area, or a presidential pledge to support a particular bill in Congress.

Presidents can also influence congressional votes through appointments. As chief administrator the president makes about 3,000 appointments to federal office. In addition, presidents make appointments to federal judicial positions. Judicial appointments and many top-level administrative appointments require the approval of the Senate. Traditionally, appointments have been used as rewards for those who helped the president get elected and as means by which

---

[20] See John E. Mueller, "Presidential Popularity From Truman to Johnson," *American Political Science Review* 64 (March 1970): 18–24; John E. Mueller, *War, Presidents and Public Opinion* (New York: John Wiley, 1973); and Samuel Kernell, "Explaining Presidential Popularity," *American Political Science Review* 72 (June 1978): 506–522.

the president can bargain with members of Congress—for instance, by offering a position to a person sponsored by a senator in exchange for the senator's vote in favor of a presidential policy.

The ability of presidents to influence Congress either positively or negatively depends on a number of factors. Some of these are situational. Presidents, for example, may take advantage of the temporary support given them in their "honeymoon" period or in an emergency to push through legislation. A presidential declaration of an energy crisis or any other crisis does not necessarily mean, however, that the public or Congress will concur with this view and support government action. Under unfavorable conditions presidents may wisely choose to make only a relatively few demands on Congress. This selective strategy minimizes the possibility of embarrassing defeats and allows the president to conserve his limited resources (such as patronage favors and goodwill) for use on the most important issues. Making a limited number of demands on Congress, moreover, minimizes the possibility of a backlash from legislators anxious to demonstrate that the legislative body is not merely a rubber stamp for the president.

Two other variables that may condition the president's success with Congress are his popularity with the people and the partisan composition of the legislative body. Legislators are reluctant to publicly oppose a president who is popular with the public or, more particularly, with the legislator's constituents.[21] A highly favorable ranking in public opinion polls, however, is only a potential means of influence. Some popular presidents, such as Eisenhower, did not take advantage of their popularity in providing policy leadership. Others, such as Kennedy and Carter, found that a high ranking in public opinion polls was not enough to allow them to have their way in Congress.

All other things being equal (which they seldom are), a president is better off in working with Congress if his party has a majority in both houses. Even this situation, however, does not guarantee smooth sailing. Legislators are subject to different pressures—for example, those of a constituent nature. Many have electoral bases independent from that of the president and thus do not see their political futures tied to his. At the same time, there is such a thing as party loyalty—that is, a desire to see the "party" do well in the eyes of the public. Likewise there is a spirit of party opposition. A congressional-liaison man for President Carter once charged, for example, that Republican members of Congress were voting "against their own interests just for the sake of making the President look bad."[22] A president confronted with two houses controlled by the other party can expect difficulty simply on the basis of partisanship.

---

[21] See George C. Edwards III, "Presidential Influence in the House: Presidential Prestige as a Source of Presidential Power," *American Political Science Review* 70 (March 1976): 101–113.

[22] Quoted in "The Hard View From the Hill," *Newsweek*, October 10, 1977, p. 30.

Along with the general political climate, the status of the president in public opinion polls, and partisan considerations, the influence of the chief executive may vary with policy issues. For most of the period since the Second World War, presidential influence in Congress has been greater in foreign policy than in domestic policy. Presidential influence in the foreign area has been based chiefly on control of the information the president receives from the State and Defense departments and from intelligence agencies. Many legislators have not only been willing to defer to the judgment of presidents on foreign policy but also, as in the activities have often preferred not to know what is happening. Since the Vietnam War, the easing of tensions with the Soviet Union and the People's Republic of China, and the Watergate revelations, Congress has been more critical of presidential foreign policy proposals.

Finally, presidential success in Congress has varied to some extent with the personal styles and skills of the chief executive. Lyndon Johnson is generally regarded as an outstanding example of a president who knew how to deal with Congress. Johnson was a veteran of Congress, where he served for several years as Senate majority leader. As president he used his personal contacts with legislators and his intimate knowledge of the ways of Congress to achieve his objectives. President Carter, on the other hand, came to Washington as a political outsider and had several problems with Congress during much of his administration. Congressional leaders commonly complained that Carter did not consult enough with Congress before submitting his proposals, tried to force through too much legislation at once, wasted his efforts and bargaining powers on lost causes, and did not "stroke" legislators enough (that is, try to build close personal relationships with them or do favors for them in return for votes).

Among the factors that condition a president's success in Congress, the most important appear to be his ability to master the support of influential people or groups in a legislator's constituency and to either help or hurt a legislator's standing with the people he or she depends upon for electoral support. On that basis, some scholars have concluded that the president can influence congressional decisions only on a limited number of legislative matters and that most members of Congress tend to vote the same way no matter who is president or which party the president belongs to.[23]

Influencing Administrators and Judges

Career administrators and judges are, as later chapters indicate, by no means easy to push around. At the same time, they are not entirely immune from the pressure for reform that can be generated by a popular and skillful president. More directly, presidential influence within the administrative and

---

[23] See, for example, Aage Clauson, *How Congressmen Decide: A Policy Focus* (New York: St. Martin's Press, 1973).

judicial systems derives from the chief executive's ability to make appointments. Since the Kennedy years of the early 1960s, White House staff, rather than national party leaders, have taken responsibility for recruiting candidates for major positions. White House staffers have been more concerned with making appointments that will help the incumbent president gain control over the large and unwieldy bureaucracy.[24] More traditional uses of patronage—strengthening the party organization by making appointments recommended by party leaders or rewarding people who have helped in the president's campaign—have not been ignored, but the most important objective has been finding people who can be trusted to implement the president's program.

Among recent administrations, White House assistants to Ronald Reagan were particularly concerned with screening top-level appointees to make sure of their ideological compatibility with the president. In several cases, this meant that people who had a record of opposing the policies of particular agencies were appointed to important positions within those agencies. To a considerable extent, the real "Reagan Revolution" was manifested not so much in abolishing agencies but in reducing their budgets and appointing people to administrative positions, as in the Environmental Protection Agency, who either relaxed or failed to implement the laws. Reagan's use of the appointment power also gave him, as it did earlier presidents, the opportunity to reshape the federal judiciary along lines more to his liking (see Chapter 9).

CONCLUDING OBSERVATIONS

The American presidency has been looked upon both as a relatively weak institution and as a source of great power. The weaknesses of the office are seen in the frequent inability of presidents to rally the people around a given goal, such as energy conservation, or to get their own legislative programs through Congress. There may well be a considerable gap between what most of the public feel presidents can do and what they are actually able to do on matters of public policy. As Lincoln pointed out in 1864; "I claim not to have controlled events, but confess plainly that events have controlled me." Many decades later Harry Truman added, "Being a President is like riding a tiger. A man has to keep on riding or be swallowed."

Over the years, historians and political scientists have made a number of rankings of how presidents have performed.[25] A composite ranking of the greatest presidents has Lincoln first followed by Washington, Franklin Roosevelt, Jefferson, Wilson, Theodore Roosevelt, and Jackson in that order. On the

[24] See, for example, Roger G. Brown, "Party and Bureaucracy: From Kennedy to Reagan," *Political Science Quarterly* 97 (Summer 1982): 279–294.

[25] See the review by Elmer Plischke, "Rating Presidents and Diplomats in Chief," *Presidential Studies Quarterly* 15 (Fall 1985): 725–742.

negative side, Harding leads the list, followed by Grant, Pierce, and Buchanan. Recent presidents—Johnson, Nixon, Ford, Carter, and Reagan—have not been included in enough evaluations to be ranked with their predecessers. Presidents who emerged as leaders in times of great stress have generally been evaluated positively. Those, such as Nixon, whose adminstrations were tarred by major scandals have been negatively evaluated. Scholars have also tended to give higher rankings to active presidents who followed the Theodore Roosevelt model than to passive ones who followed the Taft model.

Presidential reputations among scholars, it should be noted, may vary over time. President Eisenhower, for example, though immensely popular with the public while in office, was regarded by earlier historians and political scientists as an ineffectual, passive figurehead who failed to address major problems such as poverty and racial discrimination. But after the turmoil of the 1960s and early 1970s under "imperial" presidents, many scholars looked back with fondness at the relatively tranquil 1950s and the laid-back presidency of Eisenhower. More recently, Eisenhower has also been regarded by some scholars as a skillful politician who worked behind the scenes to bring about policy changes. Changing concepts of the presidency and of Eisenhower's involvement in the office have combined to improve his ranking among scholars.

A very sensible approach to ranking presidents is to consider them in the context of the period in which they served. According to one study, for example, some presidents served at a time that called for laying the groundwork for change, whereas others were called upon to actually make changes and still others to consolidate and refine changes already made. Presidents who served during these three stages of politics and policy—the preparation, achievement, and consolidation phases—are to be judged by different standards. Thus one can regard John Kennedy as a highly successful president because he performed well in a preparation phase by being innovative and laying the groundwork for reform; Franklin Roosevelt was likewise highly successful because of the abilities he demonstrated in an achievement phase; and Dwight Eisenhower was successful because he performed well in guiding the country through a consolidation phase.[26]

Over the long run, the office of president has increased in importance, albeit unevenly, as strong presidents have sometimes been followed by weak or nonassertive ones. Likewise, throughout American history the holders of the office have been called upon to assume an increasing amount of responsibility. One reason for this has been that the president is the only important public official elected nationwide. The relationship between the president and the electorate gives the nations's chief executive the image of a "tribune" or

[26] Erwin C. Hargrove and Michael Nelson, *Presidents, Politics, and Policy* (Baltimore: Johns Hopkins, 1984).

spokesperson for all the people rather than, as in Congress, a geographically restricted number of people.

On a broader level, presidential power has expanded as the result of changes in domestic economic and social conditions and in the role of the United States in world affairs. Faced with increasingly complex domestic and international problems, both Congress and the public have turned to the president for leadership on major policy questions. Presidential leadership may be particularly related to a widely shared view that the world is in a constant state of anarchy and is filled with menace. Consequently, a leader is needed who will plan, look after things, and take swift and decisive action when necessary. Other widely shared views supporting presidential leadership have been that the president must help initiate major policy changes and that the president is the only one who can "put it all together" by giving direction to both Congress and the massive federal bureaucracy.

Presidents who have chosen to exert leadership or who have been compelled to do so by emergencies such as wars or economic crises have generally found ample authority for their actions. While the framers of the Constitution were fearful of executive power, they also recognized the need for "energy, dispatch and responsibility" in a single chief executive and designed the Constitution accordingly. The assumption that the highly respected George Washington would be the first president undoubtedly made it easier for many framers to leave room for the exercise of presidential leadership. Presidents have commonly acted on the premise that they have an inherent power to take whatever action is necessary in the interest of national security or in response to emergencies. In many instances Congress has delegated powers to the president and to administrative agencies under his official direction.

Though Vietnam, Watergate, the Iran-Contra affair, and other policy failures may have considerably damaged the prestige of the presidency, it may be said that

> the office has a kind of prestige that it did not know under Washington and lacked as late as the turn of the twentieth century. Washington, after all, lent his prestige to the presidency, but today quite the reverse process takes place when a man becomes President. He becomes the great figure in our system because the office is the great institution.[27]

There is little doubt that the president is in a position to do more than any other individual public official in the nation. The legal status, prestige, informational resources, and high visibility of the presidency give whoever occupies the office an extraordinary opportunity to determine what problems will receive public and governmental attention and what will be done about

[27] Clinton Rossiter, *The American Presidency*, 2nd ed. (New York: Harcourt, Brace & World, 1960), p. 83.

them. Moreover, as former White House adviser Theodore Sorenson has remarked, the president's

> decisions do not merely differ in degree from the decisions of others. No one else faces so many complex issues where the solutions are so remote, so dependent on the undependable, and so tinged with potential disaster.[28]

SUMMARY

1. The Constitution and laws of Congress (1) set various qualifications for the presidency, (2) limit to ten the number of years a president can serve, (3) outline procedures to be followed in case a president should die, resign, or become disabled, in case a vacancy occurs in the vice-presidency, and in case an attempt is made to remove a president from office.

2. One of the most important roles played by presidents, is that of chief legislator. Though not always dominant in the legislative process, the president can also do some legislating on his own through executive orders. The formal status of the president as chief administrator does not give him as much control over the bureaucracy as one might expect, but he can use his administrative powers to frustrate the implementation of congressional policy. Other roles played by the president are chief diplomat, commander in chief, chief of party, chief magistrate, and chief of state.

3. Four types of presidential styles have been proposed: active-positive (hard-working, enjoying the job), active-negative (hardworking, not enjoying the job), passive-positive (relatively inactive, enjoying the job), and passive-negative (relatively inactive, not happy in the job). Presidents have also differed in their powers and responsibilities, some feeling limited to specific authorizations of power, others believing they could do what is not forbidden by the law, and still others feeling they may do what is necessary even if it should violate the law. Among the general factors affecting presidential decision making are the president's values, beliefs, and private goals, various constituents, and presidential advisers. In any given situation, however, it is extremely difficult to pinpoint which factors influence a presidential decision.

4. Among the advisers and assistants to the president are the vice-president, Cabinet members, and a large number of people working in the Executive Office of the President. Within this "presidential establishment" the inner cabinet and the White House staff are particularly close to the president. The president and his inner circle of advisers may engage in groupthink, a principal

---

[28] Theodore C. Sorenson, *Decision-Making in the White House* (New York: Columbia University Press, 1963), p. 12.

effect of which is to overlook possible adverse effects of a proposed course of action.

5. Attempting to secure popular support for the president and his programs and attempting to influence Congress are two of the most time-consuming and important presidential activities. Generally, popular support for presidents declines from a high level of initial approval as presidents alienate one group after another. Success with Congress is influenced by a great many factors—for example, the general political climate, the president's popularity, the partisan composition of Congress, specific issues, and the personal style and skills of the chief executive. A president's chief resources may be his popularity in a legislator's constituency and his ability to either help or harm a legislator's standing with his or her constituents.

6. The office of president has grown in importance because of the image of the president as a spokesperson for all the people and because of changing economic, social, and world conditions that have created a greater need for leadership.

7

CONGRESSIONAL
POLITICS
AND POLICY MAKING

Article I, Section 1, of the U.S. Constitution provides that "all legislative powers herein granted shall be vested in a Congress of the United States, which shall consist of a Senate and House of Representatives." The powers of Congress, often listed in vague terms in the remainder of Article I, have made it one of the foremost legislatures in the world. Within this country, however, Congress has often found itself battling with the president for the final say on matters of public policy. This chapter considers the structure and organization of Congress, the environment in which it functions, and the policy-making activities and roles of that body.

THE STRUCTURE AND ORGANIZATION OF CONGRESS

Congress consists of two separate bodies, the Senate and the House of Representatives. They differ in several respects and are eager to protect their privileges and powers from each other.

All members of the House serve two-year terms and stand for election at the same time. The shortness of this term has been objected to, especially by House members themselves, because reelection campaigning distracts them from their legislative duties. However, representatives generally have far safer seats than senators, and many find reelection to be nearly automatic.[1]

The House members are apportioned among the states on the basis of population, though each state is guaranteed at least one representative.[2] The number is fixed by act of Congress at 435. After each decennial census, the apportionment of representatives among the states normally changes: the states with the fastest-growing populations gain representation, and those with little or no population growth or with declining populations lose representation. As pointed out in Chapter 5, members of the lower house are normally elected from districts within the states; the making of such districts by state legislatures may give rise to cries of discrimination.

U.S. senators are not bothered by apportionment or districting. Each state is entitled to only two senators and these offices are filled by statewide elections. Senate terms are six years. Unlike House terms, Senate terms are staggered so that only one-third of the Senate seats are up for election every two years.

As noted in Chapter 2, the creation of two houses was looked upon by the framers of the Constitution as an element of a system of checks and balances. The framers generally felt that the Senate, originally selected by state legisla-

[1] See Albert D. Cover and David R. Mayhew, "Congressional Dynamics and the Decline of Competitive Congressional Elections," in Lawrence C. Dodd and Bruce L. Oppenheimer (eds.), *Congress Reconsidered* (New York: Praeger, 1977), pp. 54–72.

[2] The House also includes nonvoting delegates from the District of Columbia, Guam, the Virgin Islands, and Puerto Rico.

tures, would check the passions or liberal excesses of the lower house, which was the only national institution elected directly by the voters. At times, however, the Senate has clearly been the more liberal body. During the 1960s and 1970s, for example, the Senate was far more likely than the House to tax and spend for domestic social programs and to impose regulations on businesses in the interest of the environment and the consumer. Differences between the two houses in constituencies, elections, and terms may help explain why, all other things being equal, the Senate might be more liberal on policy matters.[3] Senators generally have larger and more urban constituencies than House members and usually have far more competition for their seats. Senate candidates are thus more likely to have liberal constituents and to have to outpromise competitors to get their votes. The longer senatorial terms is also thought to give senators a greater opportunity to propose and support liberal programs.

Other distinctions between the Senate and the House exist in organization, procedure, and regular activities of members. The House is more tightly organized and operates under more rigid rules. Debate is strictly limited in the House but virtually unlimited in the Senate. The greater importance of hierarchy and formal rules in the House has resulted largely from the greater size of that body—435 members compared with 100 in the Senate. The latter body has frequently been compared to a "club" that conducts its activities informally. The less personal and better-organized House ordinarily performs its legislative functions in less time than does the Senate.

Congress begins its annual session in January. Congress may also be called into special session by the president, although this has rarely been done. Recent sessions of Congress have lasted ten to eleven months. Chief among the organizational elements of Congress are its presiding officers, party representation, various groupings (such as along regional lines), staffs, and committees.

Presiding Officers

The presiding officer in the House of Representatives is the Speaker of the House, who is chosen by the political party that has a majority of the members in this body. The Speaker recognizes who can speak on the floor of the House, interprets House rules, refers bills to standing committee, and appoints House members to select and conference committees (these various committees are discussed below). Historically, the Speaker has been a powerful figure in the House. In the early 1900s, for example, the rules of the House permitted the Speaker arbitrary power in recognizing those who could speak and in making appointments to standing (permanent) committees that considered legislation. The Speaker also chaired the Rules Committee (discussed below) and thus was in a potent position to control the flow of legislation in the House.

[3] See Sam Kernell, "Is the Senate More Liberal Than the House?" *Journal of Politics* 35 (May 1973): 332–363.

Constant abuse of the Speaker's powers finally led Congress in 1910 to strip the office of Speaker of much of its formal authority. The Speaker henceforth was required to recognize the right of those who wished to speak on the floor, lost control over appointments to standing committees, and was taken off the Rules Committee. Since that time the influence of the Speaker has rested less on the formal powers of the office than on the occupant's personal prestige and status as the leader of the majority party.

The Consitution designates the vice-president of the United States as presiding officer of the Senate. Few vice-presidents have devoted much time or energy to the job. The vice-president is not a member of the Senate, cannot enter Senate debate, and can vote only in the event of a tie. As presiding officer the vice-president has such duties as ruling on points of procedure, recognizing speakers, and referring bills to committees. In the absence of the vice-president these duties are ordinarily assumed by the president pro tempore of the Senate, who is elected from this body by the majority party. The president pro tempore is usually the senior senator in the majority party. First-term senators may also be asked to preside as part of their "learning experience." The presiding officer in the Senate, whoever he or she may be, is much less powerful than the Speaker of the House. Much of the leadership of the Senate is in fact exercised by those who hold party offices such as majority leader in this legislative body and who chair important committees.

Party and Other Groupings

Political parties have long played a key role in organizing the House and Senate. Members of the majority party in the two bodies meet separately in caucus (a party conference) to elect the Speaker of the House, the president pro tempore of the Senate, and the majority leaders. The House majority leader is less important than the Speaker as a party spokesperson and strategist in steering legislation. The Senate majority leader exercises a dominant role in these activities. In each body there is a majority whip and several assistant whips who work closely with the majority leader (or the Speaker) by taking vote counts on pending measures and attempting to round up party members for important votes. Majority whips are appointed by the Speaker in the House and are elected by party members in the Senate. Each whip names his or her assistants. The minority party in each house also meets in caucus and elects a minority leader and a whip. Customarily the leaders of the majority and minority parties work closely in scheduling the work of the Senate and the House. Party leaders may also work closely with the president and his advisers, especially if they are all from the same political party.

Other party organizations in Congress include committees that (1) determine who is to serve on or chair the various legislative committees; (2) help leaders develop party stands on issues and floor strategy; and (3) raise and distribute funds to help elect or reelect party members to the House or Senate.

In addition to these party groups Congress currently contains some two dozen caucuses or committees formed along regional, ethnic, ideological, and other lines. This list includes the New England Congressional Caucus (interested in problems of particular concern to this region, such as energy), the Congressional Black Caucus, the Congressional Hispanic Caucus, the Woman's Caucus, and the Ecology Caucus.

The Democratic party membership in the House includes faction called the Democratic Study Group. This organization was created in 1959 by liberal Democrats frustrated over the apparent inability of the House to pass reforms. The group has long promoted domestic causes such as national health care and civil-rights legislation. It also took a leading part in the antiwar movement in the late 1960s and in the ongoing congressional reform movement. It has fluctuated between 100 and 200 members, with a research staff that provides members with reports on pending bills. It has also had its own whip system to line up supporters for important votes.

Staffs

Congressional staffs are increasingly important in Congress. They have been valued for helping legislators to manage their work loads and make more informed decisions and for reducing legislative dependence upon the executive branch and interest groups for information.

Personal, committee, and specialized staff agencies are the three sources of staff assistance. The personal staff of a legislator generally includes an administrative assistant (AA) and one or more legislative assistant (LAs). Some offices, such as those of senators from the most populous states, include individuals who specialize in handling constituent problems, legislative research, and press relations, respectively. Committee staffs generally confine their work to policy matters. More will be said about the roles of these two types of staffs in the following section.

Chief among the specialized staff agenices are the Congressional Research Service, the General Accounting Office, and the Congressional Budget Office. The Congressional Research Service has a variety of specialists who provide research and other kinds of assistance to individual legislators and congressional committees. The General Accounting Office has become more important to Congress in recent years by providing analyses of executive-branch expenditures and program implementation. The Congressional Budget Office provides members of Congress with the financial and program data they need to prepare the annual budget.

Table 7–1 Standing Committees of the Congress

HOUSE COMMITTEES	SENATE COMMITTEES
Agriculture	Agriculture, Nutrition, and Forestry
Appropriations	Appropriations
Armed Services	Armed Services
Banking, Finance and Urban Affairs	Banking, Housing, and Urban Affairs
Budget	Budget
District of Columbia	Commerce, Science, and Transportation
Education and Labor	Energy and Natural Resources
Energy and Commerce	Environment and Public Works
Foreign Affairs	Finance
Government Operations	Foreign Relations
House Administration	Governmental Affairs
Interior and Insular Affairs	Judiciary
Judiciary	Labor and Human Resources
Merchant Marine and Fisheries	Rules and Administration
Post Office and Civil Service	Small Business
Public Works and Transportation	Veterans' Affairs
Rules	
Science and Technology	
Small Business	
Standards of Official Conduct	
Veterans' Affairs	
Ways and Means	

Source: *United States Government Manual 1985-1986* (Washington, D.C.: Government Printing Office, 1985), p. 25.

Committees

In 1885 Woodrow Wilson wrote in his classic study *Congressional Government,* "It is not far from the truth to say that Congress in session is Congress on public exhibition, whilst Congress in its committee-rooms, is Congress at work." Within Congress, Wilson concluded, the most powerful people were those who headed important committees. Indeed, Wilson felt that "a government by chairmen of the Standing Committee of Congress" was the best description of our form of government. Although congressional committees may be less significant today than they were in Wilson's time, they continue to be a vital element of Congress. Standing committees (see Table 7–1)—organized around such areas as foreign affairs, education, and agriculture—are the bodies in which the bulk of the legislative work is done.[4]

[4] In addition to standing committees, there are conference committees (discussed in the section on the lawmaking process), joint committees, and special investigative committees. Members of these committees are appointed by the presiding officers in each house. Joint committees comprise members of both houses. Some, such as the Joint Committee on

Standing committees evolved as a means by which legislators could divide their labor to cope with an increasing work load and to specialize in dealing with complex problems. In practice, the committes have been relatively autonomous power centers. The development of the committee system has given rise to fears that Congress is overspecialized, overcompartmentalized, and unable to integrate policy in a comprehensive fashion. The growth of subcommittees has furthered this fragmentation and has also tended to reduce the control possessed by committee chairpersons.

The distribution of standing committee positions among Democrats and Republicans is roughly proportionate to the parties' strength in the House and the Senate. Thus, if the Senate contains twice as many Democrats as Republicans, its committees will have approximately twice as many Democrats as Republicans. Committee chairpersons are always members of the party that has a majority in the house. In each house a group of party leaders (who constitute either a steering committee or a committee on committees) determines which Republicans and Democrats will sit on which committees.

Committee assignments are important to members of Congress because they affect their ability to take care of constituent interests, establish their role in shaping policy, and affect their status and influence in the legislative body as well as their public visibility. To a large extent committee assignments reflect a process of natural selection. It has not been uncommon, for example, to find legislators who are bankers sitting on banking committees, or those who are farmers being on agriculture committees. Although such legislators conceivably have expertise in the matters before their committees, they may also have a conflict of interest (that is, they may be in a position to adopt legislation that serves their own interests). The selection system may be based more directly on constituent interests. For example, members of the interior committees usually come from the West and those on foreign-commerce committees usually represent coastal states. The committees may also reflect distinct ideological biases. The House Armed Service Committee, for instance, has attracted a large number of representatives who are political conservatives while the House Education and Labor Committee has attracted an unusually large number of liberals.[5]

The chair of an important standing committee has long been one of the

Printing, are concerned with housekeeping functions rather than public policy. The last joint committee with authority to write legislation, the Joint Committee on Atomic Energy, was abolished in 1977. Joint committees have been given only limited opportunity to consider policy matters because neither house has been willing to share its powers. Special investigative committees—such as the Senate Select Committee on Presidential Campaign Activities headed by Senator Sam Ervin, which exposed the Watergate scandals—have played an important role in American politics. Much of the investigative function in recent years, however, has been assumed by standing committees.

[5] See Robert H. Davidson, "Representation and Congressional Committees," *Annals of the American Academy of Political and Social Sciences* 418 (January 1974): 48–62.

most highly prized positions in Congress. Though chairpersons are not free to be as autocratic as they once were, what a committee does still depends principally on what its chair wants or allows it to do.

Traditionally, chairs have been awarded by the rule of seniority, whereby the member of the majority party who has the longest continuous service on a committee becomes its chair. The seniority rule has been defended on the grounds that it avoids a mad scramble for chairs and that is ensures the granting of such posts to the most experienced members of the committee. At the same time, application of the rule has favored legislators from noncompetitive districts (for example, Democratic strongholds in the South) who tend to be conservative and, at times at least, at odds with the policy views of the majority of their fellow party members, especially in the case of Democrats, in the Senate or the House. The rule of seniority, moreover, directly rewards years of service rather than competence and, because the position is secure, has invited arbitrary behavior. Largely for these reasons the seniority rule has been partially modified in recent years and some long-time chairpersons have lost their positions. While seniority is still very important it has become clear that chairpeople must perform to the satisfaction of the majority caucus.

THE LEGISLATORS: INTERACTION AND INFLUENCE

Conduct

Mark Twain once quipped, "It could probably be shown by facts and figures that there is no distinctly native American criminal class except Congress."[6] Public opinion polls since the early 1970s indicate that many Americans consider Congress to have more than its share of people who are guilty of unethical conduct, if not illegal activities. To some extent Congress has suffered from a general decline of faith in politicians—a product of the Watergate scandals. Nixon's resignation as president on August 9, 1974, was followed by a series of other Washington scandals, many of them directly involving Congress. In the late 1970s, for example, the integrity of more than 100 members of Congress was questioned in an investigation of Korean influence buying. As the nation entered the 1980s several members of Congress were indicted as a result of the Federal Bureau of Investigation's Operation Abscam (Arab Scam). In this operation bribes for various favors were offered members of Congress by FBI agents masquerading as wealthy Arabs or their representatives. Videotapes were made of some of the members taking bribes.

Under the Constitution each house judges the conduct of its members. Historically, however, members of both houses have been reluctant to publicly

---

[6] *Pudd'nhead Wilson* (1894).

criticize or to punish a colleague. On some occasions, however, outrageous behavior or the disclosure of a scandal has prompted punitive action. In 1954 the Senate censured (publicly condemned) Senator Joseph McCarthy, who had made reckless accusations concerning communist influence in government. In 1967 Senator Thomas Dodd was censured for diverting campaign funds for his own use. The same year, charges concerning the misuse of public funds prompted the House to rule that Adam Clayton Powell was unqualified to serve in Congress. The U.S. Supreme Court, however, ruled that Powell had been duly elected by the voters in his district and could not be barred from membership because of alleged misconduct in an earlier term of office.[7] Both houses of Congress have had codes of ethics for their members. Among other things, these codes, considerably strengthened in 1977, require annual reports on the income of each legislator and limit outside income from speaking engagements, published articles, and other sources. Violation of the codes may bring censure or expulsion.

Standards of conduct in Congress, while a continuing problem, are probably no lower than standards among the public at large. By a number of other measurements, however, Congress is not a cross section of American society. Information gathered on who has served in Congress in recent years suggests that the "average" member of Congress is white, male, Protestant, approximately fifty years old, and a lawyer. The precise significance of age, racial, religious, and occupational characteristics in relation to a legislator's voting behavior is difficult to determine. Some of these factors may generally be of little importance. As noted in Chapter 3, for example, the voting behavior of lawyer-legislators is probably no different from that of nonlawyers. Even a high degree of cohesion, as among black legislators on some issues, may be related more to factors such as constituency, party identification, or political philosophy.

The number of factors that might be said to influence the behavior of congressmen and women are limitless. Some analysts have attributed a great deal of what legislators do, such as trying to get committee assignments that will make them highly visible to their constituents or trying to get their names attached to highly popular legislative proposals, as exhibiting a desire for reelection. Others have pointed out that most members of Congress have not had to worry about reelection and have been motivated more by a desire to achieve power and personal status in Congress.

Relations With Constituents

Whatever their ultimate motivation, most members of Congress and their staffs spend considerable time providing services to their constituents. Such services, or *casework*, commonly include answering requests for information

---

[7] *Powell* v. *McCormack,* 395 U.S. 486 (1969).

about governmental programs. In some cases a legislator may help someone back home apply for a government benefit or secure better service from a governmental agency with which he or she is trying to deal. Members of Congress commonly seek casework problems in the hope that solving them will result in electoral support. They may also introduce private bills to avoid an unjust application of a law to an individual. For example, a representative or a senator may sponsor a private bill to prevent an illegal alien living in his or her district or state from being deported. Only one in five of all private bills, however, becomes law.

Many communications received by legislators from their constituents involve requests for special assistance. Other communications express the views of constituents on matters of public policy—for example, instructions on how a legislator should vote on an upcoming issue or expressions of support or disapproval on a stand the legislator has already taken. The effects of this type of communication differ among legislators. Some apparently are influenced by large volumes of mail while others are impatient with those who criticize their voting decisions or urge a policy position. One of the most notable U.S. senators in the latter respect was Stephen M. Young, who responded to critical letters with replies such as the following: "I am sending you a letter received this morning, evidently from some crackpot who used your name."[8]

Members of Congress spend considerable time in their states or districts. They return home on weekends (business in Congress is usually scheduled from Tuesday to Thursday to allow long weekends) and during recess. The average member of Congress makes thirty to forty trips home a year (the frequency of trips varies with how close the district is to the capital) and spends from 130 to 140 days in his or her district. Back home, members of Congress report on important policy developments, explain their voting records, and frequently give rather well rehearsed "A Day in the Life of a Congressman or Congresswoman" speeches to any group requesting one. Many members of Congress assume that although certain policy issues are important to their constituents, the chief factors in securing political support are being trusted and liked as individuals. Accordingly they develop a home style that they hope is pleasing to their constituents. Though styles vary, a characteristic that appears to be widely shared in recent years is the attempt to enhance one's standing at the expense of other members of Congress and of the institution itself. Constituents are told, for example, that their representative was one of a few, if not the only one, to oppose the aims of big business, irresponsible liberals, or other powerful evildoers found in abundance in Congress. As a student of Congress has stated, "members of Congress run for Congress by running against Congress."[9] This

---

[8] Stephen M. Young, *Tales Out of Congress* (Philadelphia: Lippincott, 1964), p. 90.

[9] Richard F. Fenno, Jr., *Home Style: House Members in Their Districts* (Boston: Little, Brown, 1978), p. 168.

may be pleasing to constituents, but it does little for the long-term prestige of Congress.

In theory, legislators are often looked upon as caught between two conflicting roles: (1) delegates of their constituents who do what a majority of those back home desire on policy matters, and (2) trustees for their constituents who exercise their own judgment on issues that come before the legislature. In fact the delegate role can be played only imperfectly because on many issues legislators hear nothing from their constituents. When constituent opinion is expressed, moreover, it may be vague, unrepresentative of the views of the people in the district or state, or badly divided over an issue. In these situations instructions are unclear and legislators are forced to rely on their own judgement or the advice of others.

Generally, the constituency of greatest importance to a legistor is the coalition of people that put him or her into office or that is deemed necessary for reelection. Some constituents are more important than others. Legislators are likely to act in accordance with the views of that part of their constituency that can endanger their reelection. This is not to suggest that legislators are necessarily pressured into stands by certain constituents. Rather, they are likely to share the same values and policy sentiments.

Relations With Colleagues and Staff

Interaction among legislators is commonly built upon shared characteristics, such as party, region, state, ideology, and having come into the legislative body at the same time (that is, belonging to the same "freshman class"). Members of Congress commonly depend on one another for "cues" or advice on how to vote on a specific policy matter. Legislators are faced with a large volume of decisions, some of which involve highly complex matters. Reliance upon colleagues who have similar political philosophies or who are considered to have expert knowledge on a particular subject enables a legislator to cope with his or her policy-making tasks.

Frequently interaction among members of Congress takes the form of bargaining and compromising on policy matters. Those who seek the adoption of a bill set out to make the adjustments and trades that are necessary to build a coalition large enough to secure its passage. *Logrolling*—the exchange of favors— has also been a time-honored practice in legislative bodies. The most prominent example of this on the national level has been *pork-barrel* legislation, in which members of Congress exchange support for public-works programs (such as dams) in various parts of the nation. The absence of conflict, of course, depends upon whether resources are perceived as sufficiently ample for everyone having a claim to them.

Congressional aides and committee staff members play crucial roles in linking legislators to other officials and to persons outside government and in influencing the development of policy. This linkage function, while usually well performed, has presented lobbyists and others the problem of penetrating the loyal guard around a legislator. As a congressman told a group of city officials,

> You know what happens to your letters and telegrams that you send to congressmen? The staff swallows them up—they eat 'em. . . .
> Congressional staffs are sometimes too dominant; you have to get to the senator or representative directly. . . . I wish more of you would buttonhole your senators and congressmen when they're home, away from the protective cocoon of their staffs.[10]

Legislators rely upon staff members for a variety of policy-related activities. These include gathering information, originating and drafting legislation, and suggesting maneuvers on how to get the legislation adopted. This does not mean that staffers feel free to compete with legislators for the limelight. On the contrary, they strive for low visibility in their policy-making activities. The following observation by a committee staff member in Congress appears to be widely shared:

> The occupational danger of a staffer on [Capitol] Hill or elsewhere is that you often come to think that you are the Senator, or the President, and that your boss is a mere figurehead who ratifies what you do. . . . In a sense you do have that power, but the boss put you there and you remain there because you give him ideas that are in tune with his. You make the recommendation that he would make anyhow if he had the time to do it.[11]

Relations With Lobbyists

As indicated in Chapter 4, legislators meet with lobbyists who represent private groups, executive agencies, state and local governments, and foreign governments. Legislators need little or no prompting to protect certain causes, especially when economic interests important in their constituency are involved. Senator Russell Long of Louisiana once remarked, "If I didn't represent the oil and gas industry, I wouldn't represent the state of Louisiana."[12] On many issues legislators attempt to enlist the support of private groups whose cooperation is needed in securing the passage of a bill or in implementing a program. Lobbying in Congress, in short, is multi-sided: outside groups attempt to influence legislators, legislators try to influence groups, and legislators seek to influence each other.

By and large the lobbying job of the representative of a particular outside group is a matter of contacting legislators who are natural allies—that is,

---

[10] Quoted in "Senator Garn Offers Lobbying Tips," *Nation's Cities,* April 1975, p. 12.

[11] Jeremy Main, "A Backstage Activist on Capitol Hill," *Money,* February 1975, p. 36.

[12] Quoted in "Question of Ethics," *Newsweek,* July 14, 1976, p. 25.

who are likely to agree with the organization's position because they share the same interests or because the group is important in their district or state. Perhaps the most significant political resource of lobbyists is providing information a legislator might not otherwise obtain.

The most valuable service rendered by a lobbyist for his or her clients is access to legislators. A lobbyist with several business clients put it thus:

> I can't march into a Senator's office and tell him how to vote. Oh, you hear about creeps in this town bragging that they have this Senator or that commissioner in their hip pocket. Baloney. I provide my clients access, not influence. I put them in touch with someone who I know will work with them and try to come to an amicable and reasonable agreement if possible.[13]

Much of the influence of a group or its lobbyist with a legislator may come indirectly through the latter's staff. On relatively noncontroversial, routine bills, lobbyists are often content to contact committee staff members whose recommendations may carry considerable weight with the committee. On more controversial issues, most notably those that have captured public attention, the lobbyist's ability to influence either staff or legislators is considerably reduced.[14]

THE LAWMAKING PROCESS

Origin and Introduction of Bills

The function of developing legislation is shared by members of Congress with the executive branch and a wide assortment of interest groups. For several decades the executive branch has been the source of much of the most important legislation considered by Congress. To a large extent the legislative agenda is set by the president's State of the Union message. In this speech, delivered before Congress at the beginning of each congressional session, the president outlines the major actions he would like Congress to take. The message is followed by the submission of more detailed proposals from the White House to Congress.

No matter how a bill originates, it can be introduced in the House or Senate only by members of these bodies. An administration (presidential) proposal is usually presented by the chairpersons of the committees having jurisdiction over the subject involved. A bill may have several cosponsors (no more than twenty-five in the House), whose names are listed on the bill. On

[13] Quoted by David Sheridan, "The Lobbyist: Out of the Shadows," *Saturday Review,* April 8, 1972, p. 49.

[14] See Lester Milbrath, *The Washington Lobbyists* (Chicago: Rand McNally, 1963); and John M. Bacheller, "Lobbyists and the Legislative Process: The Impact of Environmental Constraints," *American Political Science Review* 71 (March 1977): 252–263.

important issues several different bills may be introduced in each chamber. Both houses may consider a bill or a series of bills at the same time, or one chamber may wait until the other has acted before considering a measure.

Committee Action

Bills are given to presiding officers or their assistants in each house and are referred by them to an appropriate standing committee. Committees have life-and-death control over legislation referred to them. When the presiding officer in the House or the Senate has a choice of committees to which a particular bill may be referred, his or her decision can determine the bill's fate.

Nine of every ten bills introduced in Congress die in committee. Committees often pigeonhole (fail to take any action on) proposed legislation. Legislators who have presented bills, especially private ones, may be willing to allow them to die in committee. Indeed, they may even informally request a chairperson to do this. This situation sometimes develops when, because of constituent pressure, members of Congress feels it is prudent to introduce legislation that they personnally consider unwise or unsound.

On other occasions the supporters of a bill may be anxious for committee action. If a committee refuses to act, there is little the bill's supporters can do. Measures can be withdrawn from committees and brought directly to the floor (that is, before the entire House or Senate) only if a majority of House members sign a discharge petition or a majority of Senate members pass a special resolution that this be done. Securing such a petition or resolution is generally difficult.

Committees often refer bills to subcommittees. A subcommittee may meet to hear testimony by members of the executive branch, legislative sponsors, private groups, and others with an interest in a proposal. This hearing is followed by a *mark-up* (drafting) session, in which bills of serious concern to the subcommittee are revised. The subcommittee then reports back to the full committee, which may hold further hearings and mark-up sessions. Under current rules of the House and Senate, most subcommittee and committee hearings and meetings are open to the public.[15]

When a committee has completed its deliberations, the bills it favors, which by now may have been considerably revised, are reported to the full House or Senate with a recommendation for its adoption. Bills not favored by a majority of a committee are usually not reported. Committee chairpersons generally strive to shape legislation that is unanimously supported in the committee. Occasionally, however, a committee report is accompanied by a minority report in which dissenters state their objections to the legislation.

---

[15] Sessions are open unless a majority of the committee, in a roll call vote, decides to close them to nonmembers. The open rule does not apply to matters involving national security or committee operations such as personnel decisions.

Committee recommendations on bills are usually adopted by the Senate and the House. If a routine bill receives favorable treatment in the committee, lobbyists who support the measure are not likely to bother contacting members of the House and Senate before the final vote.

Floor Action

In the House, bills reported by committees are placed on calendars that outline the order in which they are to be considered. When and how important measures are to be debated depends, however, on the House Rules Committee. This committee, often called the "traffic cop" of the House, has authority to set the date for the consideration of a bill and to impose limits on the nature of the debate. If may hold additional hearings on the bill, and it may decide not to set any date for debate on the floor.[16] The committee may issue an open rule, which allows unlimited amendments to a bill, or a closed or *gag* rule, which prohibits or limits amendments.

House debate on major issues is usually conducted in the Committee of the Whole, which is the full House meeting as a committee. This meeting requires the presence of only a hundred House members for a quorum (rather than the majority required for formal action) and allows debate to be informal. Until the 1970s it also offered the advantage that no roll-call votes were taken. After the Committee of the Whole makes it recommendations, the House takes final, formal action.

In the Senate there is nothing comparable to the House Rules Committee. The leaders of the majority party, who may consult with the leaders of the minority party, generally determine the Senate's agenda. Any senator, however, may request consideration of a bill.

On most issues debate in the Senate is ended by a consent agreement. If merely one senator wishes to continue the debate, a consent agreement cannot be reached. Over the years the Senate has become notorious for *filibusters*. A filibuster takes place when a senator, or more commonly a group of senators, engages in long speeches on the floor in an effort to prevent a vote on a bill. Under current Senate rules a filibuster can be ended by a vote of three-fifths of the Senate—in other words, at least sixty senators. Ending debate in this manner is known as invoking *cloture*.

A unique filibuster took place in 1977 after a cloture vote had stopped debate on legislation to eliminate federal controls on the price of natural gas. Liberal Democrats conducted a eight-day "filibuster-by-amendment," introducing more than 500 amendments to the pending legislation, each requiring time-consuming speeches and roll-call votes. The goal was to delay the vote on

---

[16] If the Rules Committee does not act on a bill within twenty-one days, the chairperson of the committee that considered the bill can bring it to the floor. A discharge petition may also bring a measure to the floor.

the deregulation measure until President Carter could muster enough votes to pass his own plan, which would have continued regulation. An agreement between Carter and the majority leader, however, forced an end to the filibuster, and the original deregulation measure passed the Senate.

As this discussion suggests, amendments to bills are often made from the floor in both the House and the Senate. Amendments may broaden a bill or offer enough concessions that a sufficiently large coalition of legislators can be built to secure passage. Amendments also may be offered by opponents of a bill who wish to prevent such a coalition from forming. Legislators who do not wish to vote directly against a bill may support efforts to recommit it (that is, to send it back for further study) to the committee that reported it. Recommital effectively kills a bill. Although technically a violation of House and Senate rules, riders may be attached to legislation. Riders concern policy matters bearing little or no relation to the subject of a bill, but they become law if the bill to which they are attached is enacted.

Conference Committees

Differences between the two houses occur on about one of every ten pieces of legislation. In such cases the presiding officers in each house establish conference committees to resolve the disagreement. Usually senior members of the committees that first considered the legislation are appointed to the conference committees.

What goes on in conference committees is shrouded in secrecy because their meetings are closed to outsiders and no record of the proceedings is kept. While each member is expected to defend the position of his or her house (as shown in the vote on the bill), the sessions frequently seem to be free of conflict. Committee members may in fact be more favorably disposed toward the version of the bill passed in the other house than the version in their own.[17] Conference committee meetings, on the other hand, can result in a stalemate, and as a consequence a bill can die in conference. If a compromise is agreed upon, it must be adopted in both houses before becoming law.

Presidential Action

After a bill is approved by both houses, it is sent to the White House. The president may sign it or allow it to become law without his signature by not acting on it within ten congressional working days. If Congress adjourns before the ten-day limit expires, however, the president's refusal to sign a bill results in

[17] See Walter J. Oleszek, "House–Senate Relationships: Comity and Conflict," *Annals of the American Academy of Political and Social Science* 418 (January 1974): 75–86. See also David Volger, *The Third House: Conference Committees in the United States* (Evanston, Ill.: Northwestern University Press, 1971).

pocket veto. This rule was adopted to prevent Congress from passing a number of last-minute measures and then immediately adjourning so that the president is unable to deliver a formal veto. Generally when a president vetoes a bill he sends it back to Congress with a statement outlining his reasons. Congress can make changes and repass the legislation, or it can attempt to override the veto. A veto override requires a two-thirds vote in each house. This requirement is heavily weighted in the president's favor because he needs the support of only one-third of each house, plus one additional member's vote, to sustain his position. The result is that few vetoes are overridden.

Legislative Voting

During the lawmaking process legislators may make a series of formal votes. Some of these are made in committee. Others occur on the floor and concern amendments, recommital motions, veto overrides, and of course the passage of legislation.[18]

In studying the voting behavior of legislators, scholars have generally focused upon their personal characteristics (for example, party affiliation, political attitudes); external pressures (from constituents, colleagues, interest groups, and so on); and situational factors (such as the nature of the decision to be made and the amount of time and information available to the legislator in making the decision). How all these factors interact at any specific time is not precisely known. For a variety of reasons a legislator may not vote for a bill he would like adopted. Conversely, a legislator may not like a bill but may feel compelled to vote for it. Former U.S. senator George Aiken confessed,

> During the 34 years of my tenure as U.S. Senator, I have committed many sins. I have voted for measures which I felt were wrong, comforting myself with the excuse that the House of Representatives, the conference committee or, if necessary, the chief occupant of the White House would make the proper corrections.
> At other times, I have voted for measures with which I did not agree for the purpose of preventing the approval of other measures which I felt would be worse.[19]

A study based on a survey of House members suggests that the most important influence on legislators' votes on a wide range of issues is the opinion of their colleagues.[20] Cue taking from colleagues may be due largely to the heavy

---

[18] Voting in Congress may take place by voice, standing, filing passed tellers, or roll call. In the House many votes are now electronically recorded. Teller votes are recorded in the House (even when it meets as a committee of the whole) if one-fifth of a quorum requests that this be done.

[19] "A Confession by a Valedictorian," *Congressional Record*, December 11, 1974, p. S21025.

[20] John W. Kingdon, *Congressional Voting Decisions* (New York: Harper & Row, Pub., 1973).

work load of Congress and to the impossibility of every legislator knowing the contacts of every bill on which he or she must vote. Legislators thus turn for advice to other legislators, though this reference group varies from issue to issue.[21]

In many cases, little if any controversy arises over a bill and serious divisions do not emerge. When there *is* conflict over legislation, it is frequently between Democrats and Republicans. The parties, however, do not hold together on all issues. Party leaders frequently find it difficult to unite their party members behind a bill. Leaders may find, for instance, that a legislator cannot support the party's stand on a bill because the measure is opposed by important interests in the member's constituency.

On many major issues since the end of the Second World War Congress has been divided into three political groups: northern Democrats, southern Democrats, and Republicans. Southern Democrats have often differed with northern Democrats on issues of foreign policy and domestic social programs and have joined the Republicans to form a conservative coalition on these matters. This coalition was evident in the first term of Richard Nixon (1968–72), helping the president on such matters as dismantling the Johnson administration's War on Poverty programs and pushing the military effort in Vietnam.[22] It reemerged when Democrat "boll weevils" joined Republicans in the early 1980s in supporting President Reagan's budget cuts in social programs and his tax reduction program.

Divisions in Congress also may reveal attachments to opposing interest groups (such as probusiness versus prolabor groups) and regional conflicts (for example, over energy policies and the distribution of federal spending and aid programs).

Politics can also bring together diverse groups behind a piece of legislation. In the adoption of a revenue-sharing bill in 1972, for example, liberals supported reform because they felt cities would get more money; conservatives backed it because they believed it would reduce the influence of the national government on states and localities. Legislators frequently agree on the desirability of a bill without agreeing on why it is desirable.[23] For those who build winning coalitions, it is how people vote, not why they vote, that is important. The result of coalition building, however, may be legislation whose utlimate aims are somewhat vague or are incompatible with one another.

---

[21] Aage Clausen, *How Congressmen Decide: A Policy Focus* (New York: St. Martin's Press, 1973).

[22] See John F. Manley, "The Conservative Coalition in Congress," in Dodd and Oppenheimer, op. cit., pp. 75–95.

[23] See Charles E. Lindbloom, "The Science of Muddling Through," *Public Administration Review* 19 (Spring 1959): 79–88.

CONGRESS AND THE COURSE
OF PUBLIC POLICY

Members of Congress perform three basic roles in the policy process. They develop policy proposals, pass upon them, and oversee the administration as laws. Senators and representatives have often been looked upon as playing a minor role in the development of policy proposals, especially in comparison with the president and the executive branch. On many major domestic issues, however, leadership has been exerted not by presidents but by certain members of Congress supported by various groups. In recent years, for example, legislators have initiated and generated support for domestic reform legislation in the areas of environmental and consumer protection and health, education, and welfare.[24]

As the preceding section suggests, there are numerous points in the process of making a bill into a law at which legislation can be lost. Those opposing charge thus have a considerable advantage over those trying to bring it about.

Policy making in Congress has usually been characterized by bargaining, compromise, and negotiation. Congress has generally responded to situations or demands with what most people would consider small, incremental changes. Rather than "great leaps forward," there has been a continuous piecemeal modification of previous policies. Congress has found it difficult to take dramatic steps into new areas. It is not likely to undertake major reform unless there is a crisis or public pressures are intense. Economic downturns, wars, intense protest movements, or electoral landslides that usher in a new group of lawmakers are examples of what is needed to spur an otherwise sluggish and fragmented institution into action.[25] Once Congress has entered a new policy area, however, demand is for further action (often to correct deficiencies in the initial legislation), and the pace of reform legislation may accelerate. This pattern has occurred, for instance, in the areas of environmental and consumer protection.[26]

Congressional policies are often adopted without regard to how they relate to previous policies. This approach leads to conflicts and confusion in overall governmental policy. Thus, in the Department of Agriculture one set of official attempts to discover means of increasing agricultural production while another group seeks to find means of limiting production. In response to the controversy over cigarettes and health the national government has spent millions of dollars to encourage people to stop smoking and several million

[24] See, for example, Gary Orfield, *Congressional Power: Congress and Social Change* (New York: Harcourt Brace Jovanovich, 1975).

[25] Barbara Sinclair, *Congressional Realignment,* 1925–1978 (Austin: University of Texas Press, 1982).

[26] See J. Clarence Davis III, *The Politics of Pollution,* 2d ed. (New York: Pegasus Press, 1975); and Mark V. Nadel, *The Politics of Consumer Protection* (Indianapolis: Bobbs-Merrill, 1971).

dollars more to support tobacco growers. Coordinated action in programs such as antitrust enforcement and transportation has often been frustrated because different agencies over the years have been given overlapping responsibilities in these areas.

The mere adoption of a law does not necessarily mean that much will be accomplished. Some laws may be only symbolic gestures, not intended to be enforced. Others are token efforts, designed to give the impression that much is being done about a problem; in this way more comprehensive legislation may be avoided. The best laws may lie dormant because the legislature refuses to give an administrative body the funds, staff, or legal authority necessary for implementation. Many laws, intentionally or unintentionally, are poorly drafted; they contain contradictions or loopholes that allow those adversely affected to circumvent compliance or to adopt strategies that nullify the expected benefits of the legislation. Laws that are vague or contradictory or that represent a radical legal departure from the past may be tied up by court challenges for years.

Policies may also falter because those entrusted with their implementation may be in no mood—for personal, ideological, or political reasons—to do so. The problem of implementation is especially difficult when the president or an administrator is called upon to execute a policy he has opposed. Congresswoman Leonore K. Sullivan explains:

> Once we enact a program—any program—particularly one pushed through over the President's objections, or veto—we are still dependent upon the President and his appointees for administration of that program. If he wants to prove our policy is wrong, he can readily find many subtle ways to make it fail.[27]

One of the most important and least well performed functions of Congress is overseeing the administration of laws. Congress has several means of performing this task. Oversight, for example, may be undertaken during annual budgetary hearings. Congress may also conduct detailed investigations into an administrative agency or into an ongoing program of concern to several agencies. Finally, Congress may check administrative decisions by subjecting them to various reviews (see chapter 8), although this is questionable on legal grounds.

In general, members of Congress have been unenthusiastic about exercising the oversight function. The failure of legislators to follow up on the implementation of laws may rest mainly on the feeling that, in the absence of a well-publicized scandal or crisis, little political mileage is to be found in oversight activity. Responsibility for much of the routine oversight effort that *is* undertaken is assumed by congressional staff aides and agencies such as the General Accounting Office.

---

[27] Leonore K. Sullivan, "Consumer Issues in the Middle-Income Housing Field," speech reprinted in *Congressional Record,* February 20, 1975, p. E625.

SUMMARY

1. Congress comprises two separate bodies, the House and the Senate. Contrary to the expectations of the framers of the U.S. Constitution, the House has not turned out to be more liberal than the Senate. The House operates under more formal rules than the Senate and has much less of a "club" atmosphere. It also generally accomplishes its business in less time than the Senate.

2. The central elements in the organization of Congress are the presiding officers, political parties, various caucuses, staffs, and committees. The presiding officer in the House is the Speaker. This person's influence rests less on the formal powers of the office than on personal prestige and status as leader of the party that has the most seats in the House. The presiding officer in the Senate (the vice-president of the United States or the president pro tempore) is much less powerful than the Speaker of the House. Central party roles are played by the majority and minority leaders in each house, who have assistants called whips. In addition to party caucuses, members of Congress are divided into regional, ethnic, ideological, and other groups. Staffers have come to play an increasingly important role in Congress, helping legislators manage their work loads and make more informed decisions and reducing congressional dependence on the executive branch and interest groups for information.

3. Much of the most important work of Congress is done by standing committees and subcommittees, whose growth has tended to fragment Congress into autonomous power centers. Committee assignments are important to individual members of Congress because they affect their policy-making role, status in the legislature, ability to serve constituents, and future political careers. Legislators gravitate toward committees in which they have a philosophical, constituent, or personal interest. Committee chairs are usually selected on the basis of seniority, a rule that directly rewards years of service rather than competence. To a considerable extent what a committee does depends upon what its chairperson wants it to do. Chairpersons, however, may be unseated by a vote of the majority caucus and have lost a measure of control through the growth of semiindependent subcommittees.

4. Members of Congress, like other politicians, have been commonly suspected of unethical if not illegal activites. Though scandals in the 1970s and 1980s have helped to reinforce this viewpoint, standards of conduct in Congress are probably no lower than standard's among the public at large. In terms of age, race, sex, and occupation, however, Congress is not a cross section of the American people.

5. Members of Congress interact with their constituents, their colleagues and staffs, and lobbyists. Much of the contact with constituents involves casework— answering requests for special assistance. On policy matters legislators have a

number of difficulties in playing the role of delegate—assuming they wish to do so. The "constituency" legislators are more apt to try to please those who put them into office or those whose support is considered necessary for reelection. Colleagues and staffers often are important to individual legislators as sources of information on policy questions. Information is also the chief resource of lobbyists for private groups.

6. Legislative proposals in Congress may be initiated by individual legislators, congressional committees, interest groups, or people in the executive branch. Ninety percent of the bills introduced die in standing committees. In the House, the fate of most bills also depends on the decisions of the House Rules Committee. In the Senate debate may take the form of a filibuster, which can be ended only by a cloture vote. Differences between the House and Senate on a particular piece of legislation are resolved (if at all) in conference committees. After a measure is approved by both houses it is sent to the president for his approval or disapproval.

7. Legislative voting reflects a number of factors, such as the personal characteristics of legislators, pressures on them from others, the amount of time and information available for decision making, and the nature of the legislation. Cue taking from colleagues appears to be a particularly important influence on how individual legislators vote. Conflict over policy issues may occur along many lines—for example, between political parties, liberals and conservatives, supporters of different interest groups, and representatives from different regions. Legislators or groups of legislators may have different and even conflicting reasons for voting for a particular piece of legislation.

8. Members of Congress have played important roles in initiating domestic policy proposals. Congress as a whole, however, has not been known to act quickly on controversial matters of public policy. It is unlikely to undertake major reforms, moreover, unless stimulated by a crisis or intense public pressure. Over the long run, congressional policies, such as those on tobacco, may conflict with each other. Many acts of Congress, finally, may never be implemented by presidents or administrators, at least in the manner in which they were intended.

8

BUREAUCRATIC
POLITICS
AND POLICY MAKING

Article II, Section 3, of the Constitution instructs the president to "take care that the laws be faithfully executed." Theoretically, this puts the president in charge of the administrative branch. Yet, most presidents since Franklin Roosevelt (1933–45) have at some time expressed frustration in trying to control the bureaucracy. Where does the bureacracy fit in the policy-making process? This chapter first looks at some viewpoints on the roles of bureaucrats over time. We then turn to the bureaucrats themselves—their personal characteristics, the conditions of their employment, and their behavioral patterns. The last sections focus on the relations between administrative agencies and those outside the bureaucracy and on agency performance in the broader political system.

THE ROLE OF THE BUREAUCRACY

Over the years the bureaucracy has been looked upon from a variety of perspectives. One of the earliest views was that administrative positions were important means of building support for a political party. Later came the notion that administrators should be independent from "politics" and well qualified to perform specific functions in implementing the law. A more contemporary viewpoint is that administrators are deeply involved in politics and policy making.

The Spoils Perspective

Until the late nineteenth century federal positions were filled predominantly on the basis of political patronage. When a political party gained control of the White House, it would fill national offices with party workers or party supporters. This practice was valued in large part because it served party goals. The prospect of receiving a job provided an incentive to participate in party politics. Once a party won office, "contributions" from those who received appointments were used to help finance campaigns and build party organizations.

From a management perspective, spoils or patronage was defended on the grounds that it helped insure that people in public positions would be loyal to the president. The spoils system was further defended on the grounds that it avoided a permanent bureaucracy—that is, a group of individuals who made a career out of public employment. President Andrew Jackson, among others, contended that people who stayed in office for a great length of time were likely to "acquire a habit of looking with indifference upon the public interests" and to make government "an engine for the support of the few at the expense of the many."[1] A permanent bureaucracy was not only undesirable but unnecessary, Jackson argued, because the work of government was simple enough for most people to handle. Because of this, one could have massive changes in the personnel of government without risking a decline in the quality of service.

Neutral Competence

The increasingly intense attacks on the spoils system during the last decades of the nineteenth century stemmed primarily from a broader campaign to reform political parties. However, the spoils system was threatened by the need for skilled personnel to cope with the increasingly complex policy problems government was called upon to resolve. The objective of getting better personnel or, to phrase it negatively, "kicking the rascals out" of the bureaucracy, gained momentum after President James Garfield was assassinated by a disgruntled office seeker in 1881. Two years later Congress passed the Pendleton Act, which created the U.S. Civil Service Commission and charged it with implementing a merit system for recruitment and advancement. Along with the merit system came restrictions on the power of presidents to dismiss employees covered by civil service, and rules and regulations that forbade covered employees from engaging in political activities. In effect, there were steps toward a large permanent bureaucracy below the level of major managerial positions, which were still subject to political appointment.

These changes in the personnel system reflected a belief, widely held by governmental reformers in the early twentieth century, that policy making and administration were separate spheres of government activity. Policy making, it was argued, ended when the legislature made laws. Bureaucrats were expected to be politically neutral but expert and efficient in their role of implementing this policy.

A Contemporary Viewpoint

Neutral competence continues to be a central theme in public employment, being manifest in the conditions under which many administrators work and in the recruitment process. One consequence of this emphasis has been the growth of a bureaucracy that is not only permanent but increasingly professional. Professionalism developed as more and more positions were filled by individuals possessing formal training and specialized knowledge in law, science, medicine, engineering, and other areas. With professionalism, the role of the administrator has in a sense become not only less political but almost antipolitical. As Frederick Mosher has noted,

[1] Quoted in V. O. Key, Jr., *Politics, Parties, and Pressure Groups*, 5th ed. (New York: Thomas Y. Crowell, 1964), pp. 348–349.

professionalism rests upon specialized knowledge, science, and rationality. There are *correct* ways of solving problems and doing things. Politics is seen as being engaged in the fuzzy areas of negotiation, elections, votes, compromises— all carried on by subject-matter amateurs. Politics is to the professions as ambiguity to truth, expediency to rightness, heresy to true belief.[2]

As the following chapter indicates, there is a similar tendency, though for different reasons, for judges to have a rather low opinion of "politics." Yet, neither administrators nor judges are in any real sense nonpolitical in what they do.

Most contemporary observers agree that no absolute lines can be drawn between politics or policy making and administration. Administrators are involved in policy formulation, interpreting vague legislative statutes, applying them to specific situations, and recommending reforms or changes in them. These individuals are part of the highly politically charged policy system, and any action they take or fail to take cannot help but affect the rights, obligations, and interests of an individual or group. Administrative agencies also "play politics" in attempting to build executive, legislative, interest-group, and public support for their operations and programs.

Overall, administrators can be viewed as functioning at various levels of politics and policy making. At the micro level, administrators within a given agency are concerned with applying the law in specific situations, be it arresting narcotics dealers, determining who gets a television station, or passing upon the request of a city government for aid to build an airport. At the subsystem level, administrators concern themselves with routine questions concerning basic programs—such as how much money should be put into what types of activities and what general rules should be imposed on how the money is used—and interact with those in Congress or various private groups who have a continuing interest in the same programs. At the macro level, administrators, particularly agency heads, are caught up in macropolitics: they attempt to promote their interests—for example, securing a bigger appropriation or preventing another agency from stepping on their turf—or defend themselves from charges of misconduct. Here the general public, Congress as a whole, and the president become involved in the agency's political life.[3]

BUREAUCRATS: THE HUMAN ELEMENT

Who are the bureaucrats? How are they selected? What generalizations can be made about bureaucratic behavior and politics within agencies?

[2] Frederick C. Mosher, *Democracy and the Public Service*, 2nd ed. (New York: Oxford University Press, 1982), pp. 118–119.

[3] For further discussion of different levels of politics, see Emmette S. Redford, *Democracy in the Administrative State* (New York: Oxford University Press, 1969), pp. 83–131.

Personal Characteristics

Approximately 3 million persons are employed by the national government. Of this total, about 36 percent serve in the Department of Defense and 25 percent in the Postal Service. More than 90 percent of all federal employees are located outside the Washington, D.C., metropolitan area. About 30 percent of federal employees are women and 20 percent are members of minority groups. Women and minorities are less well represented in the supergrades (top management positions). The people in these offices are generally white, male, well-educated professionals who come from upper-middle-class urban families.

In terms of occupational background, the federal service has a great many professionals, such as engineers, scientists, and lawyers. Indeed, many administrative agencies are dominated by professionals. Examples are the Army Corps of Engineers (civil engineers), the Department of Education (educators), the Public Health Service (doctors), and the Bureau of Labor Statistics (economists).

Conditions of Employment

Most federal employees are selected through a merit system whereby job applicants and current employees seeking advancement must meet various standards of competence. Positions are classified at different General Service (GS) grades that vary in terms of qualifications, salary, and responsibilities. The supergrades are GS 16 through 18. Exempted from merit requirements are department heads and several high-ranking positions below the department-head level. These exempt posts are filled by presidential appointment, although in practice presidents have often allowed department heads to fill the exempt positions in their departments.

Before 1979 major personnel functions concerning GS-classified employees were vested in the U.S. Civil Service Commission. This agency, headed by three commissioners appointed by the president, developed general personnel policies, recruited and examined candidates for federal positions, and heard employee grievances. The Civil Service Reform Act of 1978, signed into law by President Carter, abolished the Civil Service Commission and divided its functions between two new agencies. One of these, the Office of Personnel Management (OPM), is headed by a director appointed by the president and confirmed by the Senate and is vested with general personnel matters such as recruiting, examining, and employee training. The second agency, the Merit System Protection Board, is an independent agency headed by three members appointed on a bipartisan basis by the president and confirmed by the Senate; its principal function is to hear employee grievances. This essentially judicial function was expected to be improved by being isolated from the more managerial personnel functions.

The Civil Service Reform Act of 1978 also made it easier to fire or demote poorly performing career employees. Under the previous system, managers were reportedly reluctant to fire poor employees because of the red tape involved and because it could take two years or more before such employees exhausted their right to appeal. The new act reduced the number of appeals from three to one. On the positive side, the act created an elite corps of top managers, the Senior Executive Service, who can easily be shifted from department to department as needed, to improve the performance of career servants. Those in the Senior Executive Service and in middle-level positions, moreover, were to be rewarded for their competence by bonuses. Unfortunately for those in the Senior Service, Congress in the early 1980s cut back on the bonuses. Because of this and a general pay cap (maximum), many top managers, scientists, and engineers left the federal service for higher-paying jobs in the private sector.

About 60 percent of the federal work force is represented by unions. While the law recognizes the right of federal employees' unions to work for better conditions and to represent workers in disputes with management, it does prohibit strikes, work slowdowns, and picketing that interfere with government operations. Unions found guilty of participating in illegal strikes may be decertified or stripped of their bargaining rights. Such was the fate of the Professional Air-Traffic Controllers Organization (PATCO), which initiated a two-and-a-half month strike in 1981. These restrictions on strikes distinguish federal employment from employment in the private sector.

Federal and private employment also differ in regard to political activity. The drive for neutral competence discussed earlier has been embodied in a number of restrictions on political involvement by federal employees. Under the Hatch Act, for example, classified federal employees cannot engage in campaigns on behalf of partisan candidates for office. The act's intent is to protect federal employees from political pressure rather than to punish them. At the same time, however, restrictions on political activity have been seen by many to violate the employees' constitutional rights.

Bureaucratic Behavior

It is difficult to generalize about the behavior of the millions of people employed by federal agencies. There are, however, some findings and theories on this subject that deserve consideration. One prime objective of many career administrators is job promotion. This may produce displays of activity that give the impression that an official is very much occupied with important work. The desire for a promotion may also make administrators reluctant to give policy advice that conflicts with the stand of their superiors.[4] But not all officials are timid in dealing with those above them in their organization. Administrators in professions such as science and medicine, for example, are apt to demand a degree of autonomy from their more politically minded bosses and may insist upon the superiority of their technical findings over the political considerations of others.

Another common characteristic of bureaucratic behavior is adherence to well-developed routines and operating procedures that take politics out of decision making and depersonalize dealings with the public. The effect may be that administrators are isolated from elected officials and the public. Routines and procedures may also become ends in themselves and even more important to administrators than the goals of their agency's programs. This phenomenon is known as *goal displacement.*

These characteristics of career bureaucratic behavior may apply to those in the private sector as well. Yet, while public and private bureaucrats have much in common, the differences between their respective sectors may affect their behavior. One difference is that persons in the public service are subject to more public exposure than those in private organizations. Public expectations and numerous legal restrictions impose a more stringent code of conduct on public administrators. Federal career executives also have a particular sense of "serving a cause."[5] Compared with individuals who pursue private careers, those who take on public service careers are more attracted by the prospect of involvement in important public affairs and less attracted by material incentives such as pay and retirement programs (though the latter are also important to public administrators).[6]

Internal Politics

Politics within an agency is usually characterized by the phenomena identified in our discussion of the presidential establishment (Chapter 6), such as conflict between individuals over who is to get into the boss's inner circle of advisers. In theory, authority within an organization is derived from an individual's place on the organization chart. Authority in administrative agencies is hierarchical: the entire structure of a large organization is linked by a chain of command in which people on one level are told what to do by the person immediately above them. The devising of hierarchy, a clear definition of duties,

[4] See Morton H. Halperin, *Bureaucratic Politics and Foreign Policy* (Washington, D.C.: Brookings Institution, 1974), pp. 85–89.

[5] See W. L. Warner and others, *The American Federal Executive* (New Haven: Yale University Press, 1963).

[6] See Edward Lawler, *Pay and Organizational Effectiveness: A Psychological View* (New York: McGraw-Hill, 1971).

and adherence to certain principles of administration[7] are believed to establish the necessary controls over subordinates and to channel their energies toward coordinated and common ends.

In practice, a manager such as a bureau chief may have only limited control over his or her subordinates. The manager may have reached his or her position through the operation of the Peter Principle.[8] This means that the individual performed so well in a previous position that he or she was eventually promoted beyond his or her level of competence. Effective leadership may then be assumed by someone who is officially a subordinate. The authority of the manager is limited by civil service and the professional expertise of those supervised. The manager, therefore, is more likely to be a negotiator, communicator, or manipulator than an authority figure who shouts orders from a lofty position.

Conflict within administrative agencies may occur along several lines. Divisions may be found between political appointees tied to the current administration and career civil servants who identify with the agency's past programs. Differences may also be found between those engaged in subject-matter functions—that is, implementing the agency's programs—and those involved in staff functions such as budgeting and purchasing. Those who are determined to get the tasks of the agency accomplished may resent the emphasis on efficiency and red tape demanded by others. Another type of conflict is that between generalists and specialists. Generalists have a broad view of the agency's programs and are sensitive to external political conditions. Specialists, such as individuals in engineering or medicine, tend to have a narrower focus and may have stronger ties to their profession or peer group than to their organization.

Specialists may resist controls or limitations they see as primarily political. In 1970, for example, the chief pathologist in the Food and Drug Administration's Bureau of Science charged that middle-level bureaucrats with limited scientific training had expunged conclusions based on laboratory research from reports because these findings had cast doubt on FDA policies on food additives and pesticide safety. Similarly, in 1974 a group of FDA doctors and scientists told a Senate investigating committee that they were frequently harassed and disciplined by superiors for reporting negatively on new drugs.

---

[7] One of the commonly advanced principles of administration is the necessity for *unity of command,* which in essence means that no person should be responsible to more than one superior. For this reason, commissions and boards have been frowned upon as means of program management. Collegial bodies are best reserved for quasi-judicial regulatory functions and advisory functions. Another principle is that no one person should supervise more than a given number of people; otherwise the subordinates escape the supervisor's span of attention and control. Actually, the proper span of control can be expected to vary with the type of work being done. Structuring organizations around a limited span of control, moreover, requires multiple levels of organization, which in turn create further problems in the upward and downward flow of communications within an organization.

[8] See Laurence J. Peter and Raymond Hull, *The Peter Principle* (New York): Morrow, 1968).

Some testified that they had been pressured by FDA officials to change or modify their recommendations against the marketing of a drug.

As these examples illustrate, subordinates sometimes go over the heads of superiors. Most commonly, however, this is done through a type of guerrilla warfare in which doubts concerning the wisdom of policies are secretly transmitted to friendly legislators, reporters, or interest groups—a process known as bootlegging.[9] Some whistle blowers simply vent grudges against their superiors and suffer no retaliation. Others, however, invite punishment for "committing truth." The major dangers are detection and retaliatory action. Sanctions against dissenters may include harassment, demotions, pay cuts, firing, and even criminal and civil penalties.[10] Professionals, fearing a loss of employment, especially when the job market is tight, and eagerly wishing to protect their status, income, and retirement benefits, may be very reluctant to speak out against their employer.

AGENCY POLITICS: EXTERNAL INFLUENCES

What an agency does is affected not only by internal politics but by elements of the broader political system. In this section we are first of all concerned with matters of organization and reorganization. Theoretically, at least, an agency's performance is affected by its place on the organization chart. We then examine agency relationships with the president and his aides, Congress, and interest groups.

Organization and Reorganization

The federal bureaucracy has four main components. The largest is the executive departments. These are headed by secretaries, except for the Department of Justice, which is directed by the attorney general. The heads of the executive departments constitute the president's Cabinet and report directly to him. Each department contains numerous bureaus, divisions, and sections.

---

[9] See Francis E. Rourke, *Bureaucracy, Politics and Public Policy,* 2nd ed. (Boston: Little Brown, 1976), pp. 110–115.

[10] Under the Civil Service Reform Act of 1978, the Merit Systems Protection Board is to protect whistle blowers from reprisal by their agencies. Whistle blowers are considered by the law to be "those employees who expose practices which they reasonably believe to be a violation of law, rule, or regulation, or which they believe constitute mismanagement, gross waste of funds, abuse of authority, or a danger to public health or safety." Yet, these protections have been deemed inadequate. Representative Patricia Schroeder (D–Colo.) has noted, "We speak to the glory of the whistleblowers, we hail them as the salvation of our budget traumas, and we promise them their place in Heaven. But in fact, we have let them be eaten alive." *Congressional Record,* January 22, 1986, p. H49.

The second component of the federal bureaucracy is the independent agencies, which are located outside the executive departments. The heads of these agencies also report directly to the president. In contrast with departments, independent agencies are concerned with more specialized functions, such as veterans' affairs and environmental protection.

The third component of the bureaucracy is government corporations such as the Tennessee Valley Authority, which produces and sells electric power, and the U.S. Postal Service. These administrative units provide services that could be (and often are) supplied by private enterprise. Government corporations are usually organized much like private corporations and are headed by boards chosen by the president with the consent of the Senate.

Bureaucracy's fourth element is the independent regulatory commissions, such as the Interstate Commerce, Federal Communications, Federal Trade, and Securities and Exchange commissions. These agencies are headed by boards or commissions consisting of five to eleven members. These commissioners are nominated by the president and confirmed by the Senate. Presidential control over appointments is restricted by laws that make commissioner terms longer than that of the president (from five to fourteen years), stagger the terms commissioners serve so that all do not leave office at the same time, and limit the number of commissioners from any one political party. Once in office, commissioners do not report to the president and can be removed by him only under conditions stipulated by Congress.

Collective decision making and the semiindependence of the commissioners from presidential control have been thought necessary for the impartial performance of judicial functions by the commissions. To allow the president to intervene in decisions such as who is to be allowed to operate in the trucking or broadcasting business has been considered by Congress and others as vesting too much authority in one person and inviting political abuse.

On a broader and more positive level, independent commissions have been seen by Congress as a means of accomplishing necessary regulatory functions without increasing the president's authority. The independent commission, as former regulator James Landis wrote in 1938, "is, in essence, our generation's answer to the inadequacy of the judicial and legislative process. It represents our effort to find an answer to those inadequacies by some other method than merely increasing executive power."[11]

The U.S. Constitution contains little direction as to how the work of the national government is to be divided among various departments and agencies. These decisions have been made largely through acts of Congress. Over the last half century, however, presidents have taken a leading role in proposing new agencies and reorganizing older ones. Presidential plans to reorganize the

---

[11] James M. Landis, *The Administrative Process* (New Haven: Yale University Press, 1938), p. 75.

federal bureaucracy have commonly called for the consolidation of agencies with overlapping functions in an effort to improve administrative efficiency or save money (though reorganizations seldom achieve either of these goals).[12] New agencies formed from parts of old agencies have also been proposed as a way to coordinate efforts to solve problems that have suddenly become important, such as environmental protection and energy shortages.

Under present law major reorganization plans proposed by the president go into effect within sixty days unless they are rejected by a majority vote in either the House or the Senate. Since the 1930s, Congress has rejected about three of every ten reorganizations suggested by the president. Reorganization proposals that clear Congress often do so in highly modified form. Members of Congress are on guard particularly against proposals that would strengthen presidential control over administrative agencies at the expense of congressional influence. Another obstacle to gaining congressional support for reorganization is that the consolidation or reshuffling of agencies disrupts the jurisdiction of congressional committees. Ranking committee members are likely to resist proposed changes that would diminish their committee's authority.

Interest groups doing well under the status quo, moreover, fear organizational changes that would sever their contacts in the bureaucracy and in congressional committees. In 1966, such fears prompted legislators and interest groups representing the shipping industry to engage in an intensive and ultimately successful lobbying effort to keep the Maritime Administration in the Department of Commerce (President Johnson had proposed shifting it to the Department of Transportation).

Presidential Influence

In addition to their power to make reorganization proposals, presidents have a measure of control over the federal bureaucracy through the Office of Management and Budget, which reviews the spending and legislative proposals of the various federal departments, agencies, and commissions and conducts studies that can affect the future functioning of these units. The power of the president to appoint the heads of various administrative organizations also gives the chief executive at least a minimal opportunity to establish the general direction of agency policy.

Presidential control over the bureaucracy, however, is limited by the existence of a permanent bureaucracy protected by civil service and by the support an agency may have in clientele groups (those served by the agency), Congress, or public opinion. A more practical limitation is that no president can keep abreast of the vast amount of administrative activity. The extent to which

---

[12] See Harvey C. Mansfield, "Federal Executive Reorganization: Thirty Years of Experience," *Public Administration Review* 27 (July/August 1969): 332–345.

a president attempts to influence the functioning of an administrative agency depends mainly upon the president's own inclinations and the importance of agency actions at any given time. The absence of a scandal or a crisis an agency may be regarded by the president as not worthy of his attention.

Presidential appointees who head administrative organizations such as Cabinet-level departments face the same control problems. Generally, appointees take office with only minimal familiarity with their departments' programs and operations. This lack of expertise, along with limitations on the time available to department heads, means that a great deal of authority is delegated to subordinates. More broadly, a department head is likely to discover that each administrative unit in his or her organization has a separate statutory base, which defines its mission, a specific set of committees to deal with in Congress, its own set of friends and enemies, and its own professional standards and organizational lore. As a consequence of strong external support in Congress, organizations such as the Federal Bureau of Investigation in the Department of Justice and the Army Corps of Engineers in the Department of Defense have largely been free of effective departmental supervision.

The relationship between the chief executive and the permanent bureaucracy has varied from president to president. Most chief executives, however, have expressed frustration with the bureaucracy, finding it hostile to their policy objectives or unable to pursue efficiently any program objectives at all. Assistants and advisors in the presidential establishment concerned with policy (for example, defense or welfare) have tended to look upon the permanent bureaucrats as adversaries who must be coerced to act in accordance with presidential policies.[13]

Over the years various presidents have voiced concern over their limited ability to influence career administrators, many of whom have watched presidents and their political appointees come and go. Harry Truman once complained,

> The difficulty with many career officials in the government is that they regard themselves as the men who really make policy and run the government. They look upon the elected officials as just temporary occupants. Every President in our history has been faced with this problem: how to prevent career men from circumventing presidential policy. Too often, career men seek to impose their own views instead of carrying out the established policy of the administration. . . .[14]

Presidential efforts to further their control over the bureaucracy have taken several forms. President Eisenhower was able to reclassify a number of

[13] Thomas E. Cronin, *The State of the Presidency* (Boston: Little, Brown, 1975), p. 126.

[14] Harry S. Truman, *Memoirs*, Vol. 2, *Years of Trial and Hope* (Garden City, N.Y.: Doubleday, 1956), p. 165.

administrative positions from civil service status to Schedule C status, which made the positions appointive by the president. President Nixon and some other presidents sought greater control through reorganization plans and the placement of persons loyal to the chief executive in various administrative units with the mission of examining agency decisions in light of the president's policies. The Nixon years also illustrated that the president and members of his staff may attempt to directly influence independent agencies such as the Securities and Exchange Commission to support a campaign contributor or the Federal Communications Commission to impede the license applications of television stations owned by groups thought to be unfriendly to the administration.

Conflict between the president and the career bureaucracy may, as in the Nixon and Reagan years, reflect philosophical and partisan differences. Nixon's attempts to implement his conservative views on social programs were strongly resisted by administrators involved in this policy area who favored a more liberal approach. Nixon, a Republican, was also faced with the fact that only about 17 percent of the career administrators during his term identified themselves as Republicans; 36 percent were independents and 47 percent were Democrats. Presidential conflict with the segment of the bureaucracy that operates domestic social programs may be expected to be particularly severe when the White House is occupied by a conservative Republican.[15]

Congressional Influence

In many respects Congress is the most important institution in the political environment of federal administrative agencies. Congress makes major decisions on agency authority, appropriations, staff, organization, procedures, and location within the governmental structure. Congress may also conduct detailed investigations into an agency's operations or into a program of ongoing concern to several agencies. Another function frequently performed by Congress is to consider appeals by groups of agency decisions, such as an order by the Food and Drug Administration to take a particular product off the market. Often these appeals are successful. In 1969, for example, Congress responded to complaints from the tobacco industry about the Federal Trade Commission's attempt to put health warnings on cigarette packs by prohibiting the agency from making any decision on the matter for two years.

The goal of securing congressional support for an agency's position requires lobbying. This means the appearance of agency heads at formal meetings, such as congressional hearings. Most large agencies also have several people on their staffs who keep up with political developments and stay in touch with legislators, presidential assistants, and interest groups on a more informal

---

[15] Joel D. Aberbach and Bert A. Rockman, "Clashing Beliefs Within the Executive Branch," *American Political Science Review* 70 (June 1976): 456–468.

basis. To further cultivate legislative support an agency may adopt a policy of consulting with legislators before making staff appointments, funneling important news about agency affairs through legislators whose districts are affected, and working diligently to honor a legislator's request for information and other assistance.

Cabinet officials and the heads of various independent departments and agencies have been especially anxious to stay on good terms with congressional committees that pass upon their units' programs or appropriations. As indicated in Chapter 7 these committees usually make the final decisions on agency matters. Getting along with congressional committees may involve grueling public hearings. As one observer has noted, Interstate Commerce commissioners, for example, tend to take congressional hearings philosophically:

> The better questions by the Chairman [of the committee] are greeted by long silences or nervous glances from the Commissioners. But the Commission still views these occasions as rather unpleasant periods it must endure and then ignore. It understands that the Senator must appear antagonistic so that the folks back home will know he is doing the job. Hostile questions are accepted as part of the game.[16]

During the 1970s and early 1980s Congress tried to gain greater control over administrative rules and regulations through the use of legislative vetoes. Under this procedure Congress could prevent a rule or regulation from going into effect by rejecting it in one or both houses or by refusing to approve the administrative decision. Such vetoes were not subject to review and possible veto by the president. Critics of the legislative veto contended that the process violated the Constitution by sidestepping the president's veto power and interfering with his responsibility to execute the laws. In 1983 the U.S. Supreme Court agreed with this position in a decision that was expected to lead to the demise of more than 200 laws in which the veto device had been used.[17] Thus far, however, Congress has been able to circumvent the decision. Through a number of methods, informal as well as formal, it has kept the legislative veto alive and well.[18]

People who favor the legislative veto contend that it is needed to keep the bureaucracy responsive to Congress, which, in theory at least, is entrusted by the voters with lawmaking responsibilities. Critics of the legislative veto argue that it not only violates the Constitution but has a "chilling effect" on adminis-

---

[16] Robert C. Fellmeth, *The Interstate Commerce Commission* (New York: Grossman, 1970), p. 24. See also David Burnham's report on a study done by the Senate Government Operations Committee, "Congress Called Lax on Review of U.S. Agencies," *New York Times,* February 10, 1977, pp. 1, 15.

[17] *INS* v. *Chadha,* 462 U.S. 919 (1983).

[18] See Louis Fisher, "Judicial Misjudgements About the Lawmaking Process: The Legislative Veto Case," *Public Administration Review* 36 (November 1985): 705–711.

trators—that is, it makes regulators, for example, more cautious in regulating powerful business groups. But those who favor the veto commonly see this chilling effect to be a good thing, and have offered the veto as a cure for a runaway bureaucracy that has regulated too much.

As noted in Chapter 7, Congress has not generally been given high marks for its performance in overseeing administrative activities. Its concern over how the laws have been administered has been largely reactive—that is, in response to complaints voiced by the media, constitutents, interest groups, or disgruntled agency employees. Rather than taking a broad view of an agency's programs, many legislators are more concerned with contacting agencies on behalf of constituents, friends, or campaign contributors for information on pending applications or suits and subtly influencing agencies to act favorably. Some legislators shun detailed investigations into how the laws are being administered because they fear such probes may bring reprisals from powerful interest groups. Others are not overly zealous in their oversight activity because they have values and interests similar to those who head the agency they are charged with overseeing. For most members of Congress, the failure to implement laws may rest in the belief that this is tedious and time-consuming work that, in the absence of a well-publicized scandal or crisis, offers few political rewards. Thus, congressional staff offices and aides have assumed responsibility for much of the broader and more routine oversight activity. Especially important in recent years in this regard has been the General Accounting Office (GAO).

Interest Group Influence

Administrative agencies, like political parties, Congress, and the presidency, serve as means by which various groups in society seek to protect and promote their particular interests. Some groups, especially those representing important economic interests, have been commonly viewed as highly successful in this regard. As one reformer, John Gardner of Common Cause, has put it,

> in fact, a large part of what is called the Federal Government is not a coherent entity at all, but a collection of fragments under the virtual control of highly organized special interests in the private sector. In the Special Interest State that we have forged, every well-organized interest "owns a piece of the rock."[19]

Groups attempt to influence the selection of administrators of programs affecting their interests, lobby administrators, and often participate directly in agency activities as members of advisory boards or committees. Lobbying takes place at formal and informal meetings, where administrators may be asked to

---

[19] John Gardner, "How a President Can Beat the Special Interests," *In Common,* Fall 1976. p. 3.

speak in return for favors such as travel expenses and honoraria. Journalist Louis Kohlmeier has found this type of activity understandable in the regulatory area:

> A regulated company can hardly be blamed for using every opportunity to influence a regulator. It legitimately fears that if it doesn't a competitor will. Indeed, considering what's at stake a company would be remiss in its duty to its stockholders if it didn't try to exert influence.[20]

From the agencies' point of view, interest groups are valuable as sources of information and as contacts with those whose assistance the agencies need in order to implement administrative rules, regulations, or programs. For many agencies the support of the groups they serve is their most important resource in dealing with Congress and the White House. The American Farm Bureau, for instance, may lobby on behalf of or in conjunction with Department of Agriculture officials to get legislation through Congress. Some regulatory agencies at times have a similar relationship with business groups or industries subject to their regulation. While a regulated group may promote or defend its regulators, however, it is not likely to do so publicly. As a Federal Trade commissioner observed, "it is simply not in the pattern" for the regulated industries "to announce publicly their approval of any actions taken by their regulators. It is almost as if this might establish a precedent which could weaken their protest when the agency action was one of which they disapproved."[21]

Other scholars have concluded that regulatory agencies tend, some more than others, to go through a "life cycle" or a "rhythm of regulation" between action and inaction.[22] According to a long-standing theory, regulatory agencies emerge with great energy from the crisis that led to their creation and, finding much support from other public officials and the public, proceed to take their mission seriously. Within a matter of years, however, the glamour subsides and the agency tires of fighting and settles down to routine and peaceful relations with those subject to regulation. Eventually an agency enters into old age, and it becomes difficult to distinguish the objectives of those regulated and those who are supposed to regulate. Agencies may be rejuvenated, at least temporarily, by external pressure such as that exerted by Congress.

A number of groups, such as Common Cause and those led by Ralph Nader, regularly monitor governmental agencies, intervene in agency proceedings, and gather information that gives various agencies unfavorable publicity. Activities of these groups have led to reforms such as the Sunshine Act, which requires many federal agencies to hold their meetings in public.

---

[20] Louis M. Kohlmeier, Jr., *The Regulators* (New York: Harper & Row, Pub., 1969), p. 71.

[21] Mary Gardiner Jones, "The Role of Administrative Agencies as Instruments of Social Reform," *Administrative Law Review* 19 (May 1967): 288.

[22] See Marver H. Bernstein, *Regulating Business by Independent Commission* (Princeton, N.J.: Princeton University Press, 1955).

In an effort to strengthen and institutionalize these watchdog activities, several reform groups have sought since the 1970s to create an independent agency for consumer advocacy that could intervene in agency proceedings on behalf of consumers and challenge agency decisions in court. Their proposal would replace the several consumer offices now scattered throughout many departments with a single consumer agency unattached to any existing department or agency. Existing consumer offices have been unable to carry out an aggressive consumer role because of constraints against rocking the boat imposed upon them by the agencies in which they are located. Reformers have contended that an independent consumer agency is particularly needed to intervene in the proceedings of regulatory agencies which, because of the lack of consumer representation, normally hear only one side of a case—that of the business or corporation.

Thus far, opponents of a new consumer agency, led by business groups such as the U.S. Chamber of Commerce, have been able to prevent its passage in Congress. They have argued tht a new agency is unnecessary because consumers are adequately protected by existing agencies and laws and that the proposed agency would be another costly bureaucratic monstrosity that would institutionalize "Naderism" and thus unjustly harass business and disrupt governmental operations.

AGENCY PERFORMANCE AND SURVIVAL

Policy Functions

The policy-making functions of administrative agencies involve both the development and implementation of public policy. One example of the former is the role several agencies played in the federal government's antismoking campaign. This effort began in 1963 when President Kennedy directed Surgeon General Dr. Luther L. Terry to set up an advisory committee on smoking and health that would review relevant studies and report on the matter. This committee, comprising medical experts with prestigious credentials, reported on January 11, 1964, that "cigarette smoking is a health hazard of sufficient importance in the United States to warrant remedial action."

The committee's recommendation was supported by a number of health groups, such as the American Cancer Society and the American Heart Association. Also contributing to the growing antismoking campaign was the Federal Trade Commission, which in the mid 1960s proposed bands on the advertising of tobacco products. During this period the Federal Communications Commission facilitated the cause by requiring television and radio stations to give "significant time" to antismoking messages (one for every three cigarette commercials). The antismoking commercials prepared by public health groups proved effective in bringing a short-term decline in smoking and increasing public awareness of the problem. The result of all this activity was the passage of legislation in 1970 that banned cigarette advertising on television and radio and shortly thereafter the adoption by the Federal Trade Commission of regulations that required health warnings on cigarette packages and in printed advertisements for the product.[23]

Many policy proposals that eventually find their way to the president or Congress come in whole or in part from administrative agencies. These ideas may be rejected by one president only to be accepted by another. Planners employed by the Central Intelligence Agency, for example, were unable to secure Eisenhower's support for the Bay of Pigs invasion of Cuba but succeeded with Kennedy. Generally, however, the bureaucracy has not been looked upon by either presidents or scholars as an important source of new ideas. Indeed, agencies are most often viewed as hostile to both procedural and policy changes that would affect them. As Harold Seidman, a former budget official, has said,

> because people believe what they are doing is important and the way they have been taught to do it is right, they are slow to accept change. Institutional responses are highly predictable, particularly to new ideas which conflict with institutional values and pose a potential threat to organizational power and survival. Knowledgeable Budget Bureau officals once estimated that agency positions on any major policy issue can be forecast with nearly 100 per cent accuracy, regardless of the administration in power.[24]

In implementing policy, agencies may be controlled by zealots who take their mission (for example, fighting communism, helping the poor, or bringing electric power to farmers) seriously and take a broad view of their powers and responsibilities. New regulatory agencies tend to behave in this manner, but eventually their fervor declines. In the absence of external support or pressure many agencies are apt to be timid and to take a restricted view of their authority.[25]

As we noted at the start of this chapter, administrators have traditionally been looked upon as politically neutral agents through which elected policy makers implement their objectives. Yet it is clear that administrators may refuse to implement a clearly stated policy directive of Congress, the president, or even their own agency superiors. A number of factors are involved in this type of

---

[23] See Lee Fritschler, *Smoking and Politics: Policy-Making and the Federal Bureaucracy.* (New York: Appleton-Century-Crofts, 1975).

[24] Harold Seidman, *Politics, Position, and Power,* 2nd. ed. (New York: Oxford University Press, 1975), pp. 18–19.

[25] As one observer has noted, "the assumption of responsibility by an agency is always a gamble that may well make more enemies than friends. The easiest course is frequently that of inaction. A legalistic approach that reads a governing statute with the hope of finding limitations upon authority rather than grants of power with which to act decisively is thus common. . . ." Landis, op cit., p. 46.

behavior. One study, for example, found that government inspectors frequently disobeyed an agency rule that offers of bribes from a firm subject to regulation be reported to superiors for possible prosecution. The reason was that they feared being seen by their colleagues as "squealers" or "informers" who were simply trying to gain the favor of higher-ups.[26] Refusals to report were also apparently linked to a feeling that a bribe offer was natural and understandable, though it was wrong to accept the offer.

Refusals to obey a policy directive may reflect a disagreement with the goals of the directive, a feeling that the policy is impossible to implement, or both. They may also be based on a belief that an order is likely to be reversed. Political appointees as well as career administrators, for example, frequently delay implementation of a presidential directive, expecting that the president will change his mind. The president is often regarded by administrators as having fallen under some evil influence from which he might recover if given enough time. The result may be a situation such as this: in the 1971 war between India and Pakistan the State Department backed India while the White House supported Pakistan.[27]

From the administrators' point of view a more common problem is that congressional and presidential directives are often unclear. As one administrator has asked,

> exactly what are the "unemployability," "alienation," "dependency," and "community tensions" some programs desire to reduce? How would one know when a program crossed the line, successfully converting "poor quality of life" into "adequate quality of life"? Would anyone recognize "improved mental health," "improved local capability," or "revitalized institutions"?[28]

In the absence of clearly stated policy goals or measurements the principal means of evaluating policy is simply to test its political acceptance. Policy is deemed successful if it does not generate discontent or, more positively, if the attentive part of the public regards it as satisfactory. In some cases, as in the regulatory field, a lack of complaints may merely mean that the law is not being enforced. Those who may benefit from enforcement—the general public—may be unaware that the law is not being enforced, and those whose behavior is to be regulated by law are of course not likely to complain about lack of enforcement.

Agency Survival

Agency survival in the broader political system depends principally on one of two factors: (1) possession of information and skills needed to formulate

[26] See Peter M. Blau, *The Dynamics of Bureaucracy* (Chicago: University of Chicago Press, 1955), pp. 148–55.

[27] See Halperin, op. cit., pp. 235–260.

[28] Pamela Horst and others, "Program Management and the Federal Evaluator," *Public Administration Review* 34 (July/August 1974): 303.

an execute policy and (2) support from an external source, such as Congress, the president, interest groups, or the public.[29] An agency head may be expected to provide favors for and support policies acceptable to individuals, groups, or institutions deemed vital to the agency's survival and prosperity. Agency personnel soon develop a sense of who is important in this respect. In regard to inquiries to an executive agency, for example, "responses to the White House are typically made within 24 hours, to Congress in 3 working days and to the public 'as soon as possible.'"[30]

Like other participants in the political process, administrators anticipate the political consequences of taking a particular course of action. If they anticipate that the president, Congress, or an important group will not approve of a particular agency policy, they may abandon it. To some extent, courts, the media, and the public impose a similar restraint on administrative policy making.

External forces not only constrain administrative agencies but may prompt them to take policy actions that they otherwise might not have taken. In the late 1960s, for example, the Federal Trade Commission became subject to numerous criticisms. Two major reports, one by a Nader organization and the other by the American Bar Association, both concluded that the agency was unwilling or unable to aid consumers in any meaningful way.[31] The commission was judged to be guilty of ineffectiveness and myopia and of not even caring enough to ask Congress for more authority to make its work effective. The American Bar Association committee, established at the request of President Nixon, further suggested that the FTC either be reorganized from the top down or be abolished altogether. The president then named Miles Kirkpatrick, the author of the ABA's indictment of the FTC, the commission's new chair. Faced with the reformers' scorn and with the threat of being abolished or seeing its major functions given over to a new agency, the FTC began functioning much like it had in its earlier, aggressive days. This renewed vigor, however, aroused intense political opposition within the business community, which during the early 1980s helped prompt the agency to back off from enforcing certain policies.

The desire to survive and prosper in the larger political system undoubtedly has a large impact on how agencies perform their functions of policy development and implementation. There are other elements in administrative policy making, however, that should be pointed out. Administrators, for example, have their own goals (such as status and income), values, and political

---

[29] See Rourke, op. cit.

[30] Victor G. Rosenblum, "Handling Citizen Initiated Complaints," *Administrative Law Review* 26 (Winter 1974): 11.

[31] See American Bar Association, *Report of the ABA Commission to Study the Federal Trade Commission* (Chicago, 1969); and Edward F. Cox and others, *The Nader Report on the Federal Trade Commission* (New York: Baron Publishing, 1969).

predispositions, which may underlie their behavior. In any given organization, moreover, substantial influence may be exerted by professionals in such fields as medicine, science, engineering, law, and economics. While agency policy making is never fully divorced from politics, the expertise and factors provided by technicians and professionals may at least limit the possible courses of action.

SUMMARY

1. Career administrators have been expected to be politically neutral and competent in implementing the laws. But while they have enjoyed a measure of independence and are increasingly professional, they are in fact deeply involved in politics and doing much more than simply implementing the laws.

2. More than 60 percent of the people who work for the national government are employed by the Department of Defense and the Post Office. Most federal employees work outside the Washington, D.C., metropolitan area. Those holding the top career positions protected by civil service are generally well-educated white males. A number of professionals, such as engineers, scientists, and lawyers, are also found in the federal service.

3. Most positions in the federal service are filled in accordance with a merit system that requires various standards of competency. The Civil Service Reform Act of 1978 created two new agencies to perform personnel functions. It also made it easier to fire or demote poorly performing career employees and to reward those who are performing well.

4. Bureaucratic behavior in private as well as public organizations is shaped by a desire to please superiors and to adhere to well-developed routines and operating procedures. Compared with administrators in the private sector, those in the public sector are subject to more public exposure and more regulations on their conduct and have a greater sense of serving a cause.

5. A manager such as a bureau chief is less likely to be an authority figure who rules by command than a subtle manipulator of his or her subordinates and a person who must umpire various conflicts within the organization. Subordinates sometimes blow the whistle on their superiors, though at the risk of various forms of punishment.

6. The organization of the federal bureaucracy has been shaped by acts of Congress and reorganization plans submitted by presidents to Congress. The bureaucracy has four major components: executive departments, independent agencies, government corporations, and independent regulatory commissions.

7. Presidential control over the bureaucracy is limited by the existence of a permanent bureaucracy protected by civil service; the support various agencies

have in Congress, interest groups, or public opinion; and limits on expertise and time the president can devote to administrative matters. Presidential appointees to administrative agencies face the same limitations. Presidents and their assistants have often been in conflict with the career bureaucracy.

8. Congress sets the framework in which agencies function (for example, their organizational location, finances, and power) and may reverse agency decisions. Agency heads are particularly concerned about their relations with appropriate congressional committees. Agencies may lobby Congress and do favors for important members in order to gain their support.

9. Interest groups influence administrative agencies by the manner in which agency personnel is selected, by serving on advisory committees, and through lobbying. Administrators find interest groups a valuable source of information and support in dealing with other participants in the political process, such as Congress and the president. Attempts have been made to balance the influence of special interests or clientele groups in the administrative system with groups or institutions representing a broader public interest.

10. Administrative agencies both develop and implement public policy. Agencies, especially older ones, have been considered less responsive to new ideas and may take a limited view of their powers and responsibilities unless pressured into activity. Administrators may refuse to implement a policy. At times, agencies may have little guidance as to what they are supposed to do and whether what they do is successful.

JUDICIAL
POLITICS
AND POLICY MAKING

"The judicial power of the United States," according to Article III of the Constitution, "shall be vested in one supreme court, and in such inferior courts as the Congress may from time to time ordain and establish." This brief provision has led to the creation of a system of federal courts that coexists with court systems in each of the states and to the birth of perhaps the most powerful court in the world, the United States Supreme Court. This chapter begins with an overview of court systems in the United States and the functions of courts in the political system. The rest of the chapter is concerned with the specific role and performance of the Supreme Court.

COURTS AND JUDGES

The Courts

There are fifty-one court systems in the United States—one of federal (or national) courts and one in each of the fifty states. The bulk of the work-load in both state and federal courts consists of civil and criminal cases. Civil cases usually concern conflicts between private parties, such as litigation resulting from an automobile accident. In some civil cases the government itself may be a party to the suit. In criminal cases the government prosecutes someone who is charged with committing a misdemeanor or a felony, the latter being a more serious offense.

The structure of state and federal courts follows a common pattern. In most states there are (1) trial courts (commonly called *district courts*), where most civil and criminal cases are originally heard, often before a jury; (2) intermediate courts of appeals, which primarily review cases decided at the trial court level; and (3) a court of last resort (commonly called a *state supreme court*) whose prime responsibility is reviewing cases decided by the lower appeals courts. The basic structure of the federal court system follows the same format: there are federal district or trial courts, federal courts of appeals, and the United States Supreme Court.[1]

Federal and state court systems are largely separate from each other. Most of the nation's legal business is settled in state courts under state laws. However, state court decisions that involve a *federal question* (a question involving the Constitution or laws and treaties of the United States) may be appealed to the

---

[1] These three types of courts are known as *constitutional courts*, having been created under the judiciary article, Article III, of the Constitution. In addition there are a number of legislative courts created under the legislative article, Article I. Legislative courts generally perform more specialized functions than constitutional courts. Examples of legislative courts are the United States Court of Military Appeals, the United States Claims Court, and the United States Tax Court. The decisions of legislative courts are subject to reversal by the United States Supreme Court.

U.S. Supreme Court.[2] Such review means that the high court is in a position to make sure that the Constitution and national law have the same meaning in all of the states.

The ninety-seven federal district courts carry most of the work load of the federal courts. At least one court of this type exists in every state. A single judge usually presides. Juries are used in about half of the approximately 300,000 cases decided each year by these courts. Three-judge district courts (of which one judge is a member of a federal court of appeals) decide cases of particular importance, such as those involving the constitutionality of federal and state laws.

The several U.S. courts of appeals are immediately above the district courts in the hierarchy of the federal judiciary. The nation is divided into twelve geographically defined jurisdictions, called *circuits*. A court of appeals, which normally sits as a panel of three judges, is found in each circuit. The chief function of these intermediate courts is to review decisions by the district courts within their jurisdictions (although some district-court decisions, such as those made by three-judge district courts, may be appealed directly to the U.S. Supreme Court). The courts of appeals also are empowered to review the decisions of federal regulatory agencies, such as the Federal Trade Commission.

The United States Supreme Court, at the top of the federal court system, comprises nine members—a chief justice and eight associate justices. The Court has original jurisdiction over some types of cases and controversies—for example, those involving two or more states. The bulk of its work load, however, consists of cases coming from state courts of last resort (usually state supreme courts) and from lower federal courts. The Supreme Court has discretion in determining what cases it will review. It may, for example, refuse to hear a case from a state court on the grounds that it does not raise a substantial federal question. For a case to be reviewed by the Court, at least four of the nine justices

---

[2] The Constitution and acts of Congress establish the jurisdiction of federal courts. In some cases these courts have exclusive jurisdiction; that is, cases can be heard only in such a court. Other types of cases are shared with the states. Generally, the jurisdiction of the federal courts depends upon what and who are involved in the dispute. Concerning the former, the federal courts have jurisdiction in cases involving admiralty and maritime laws as well as in those involving federal questions.

As the parties to the dispute, the federal courts have jurisdiction (generally exclusive) in cases involving (1) foreign ambassadors or ministers; (2) the U.S. government and its agencies and officials; (3) suits brought by state governments against other states, citizens and other states, foreign governments, or citizens of other nations; and (4) suits brought by citizens of one state against citizens of another state. In the last category, Congress has provided by statute that the federal coursts may assume jurisdiction only if the case involves a claim totalling $10,000 or more. Otherwise a court of the state in which the defendant resides decides the case. For purposes of determining jurisdiction, a corporation is considered to be a citizen of the state in which it has incorporated.

must vote to do so. If a case is not reviewed by the Court, the decision of the state or lower federal court goes into effect.[3]

Judicial Selection

Whereas state and local judges are chosen by a variety of methods, all federal court judges are nominated by the president and confirmed by a majority vote in the Senate.[4] The judges in effect hold office for life, subject only to removal by impeachment and conviction. Since the beginning of the federal court system, impeachment proceedings have been initiated against only ten federal judges and only four have been removed from office.

The president commonly delegates the task of recruiting court nominees to the attorney general, who in turn usually vests the responsibility in the deputy attorney general. Also involved in the recruitment process are important politicians, especially U.S. senators, and the American Bar Association's Committee on the Federal Judiciary. The president may also consult with incumbent or sitting judges, and especially with the chief justice of the Supreme Court, in making appointments.

The influence of individual senators has been greatest in the recruitment of federal district court judges. By tradition, the president is expected to clear his nominees at the district level with senators who belong to the president's party and who represent the state where the judge is to sit. If the president fails to honor this practice of *senatorial courtesy,* the offended senator may declare the nominee to be "personally obnoxious" and call upon his colleagues to reject the nomination. Other senators, having a potential interest in seeing that the practice of senatorial courtesy is honored, can be expected to agree to this request.

The American Bar Association's Committee on the Federal Judiciary is effective in the early stages of the recruitment process, particularly for appointments to the district and appellate courts. The committee is dominated by older, more conservative, and highly successful lawyers. It investigates and rates

---

[3] Cases originally heard by state or lower federal courts get to the Supreme Court primarily by two routes: direct appeal (a statutorily granted right) and a petition for a writ of certiorari. The latter, constituting an order to a lower court to send up a record of a case for review and possible reversal, is issued when at least four of the nine justices vote to do so. Most petitions for a writ of certiorari are rejected. To some authorities the principal difference between a denial of an appeal and a denial of certiorari is in terms of precedent. When a court refuses to hear a case brought to it on appeal, it in effect sets a precedent by affirming the lower-court decision. Judges have not been of one mind on the meaning of a denial of certiorari, but it appears that such a decision generally does not constitute approval of the lower court decision and thus cannot be used as a precedent.

[4] See Henry J. Abraham, *The Judicial Process,* 3rd ed. (New York: Oxford University Press, 1975), Chapter 2. See also Abraham's *Justices and Presidents: A Political History of Appointments to the United States Supreme Court* (New York: Oxford University Press, 1974); and Harold W. Chase, *Federal Judges: The Appointing Process* (Minneapolis: University of Minnesota Press, 1972).

prospective judicial nominees and gives its findings to the Department of Justice. Its recommendations may prompt that department to either eliminate a number of candidates or to seriously consider them.

Over the years various administrations have sought the appointment of lower court judges who are ideologically compatible and can be expected to make the "right" decisions on important litigations. Because of factors such as senatorial courtesy and the influence of the American Bar Association, presidential assistants in charge of judicial appointments do not always get to pick the judges of their choice. There is no guarantee, of course, that judges hand-picked by the administration will live up to its expectations. Research does suggest, however, that very often these expectations are realized. For example, in fulfilling a pledge to appoint to the federal bench those "whose judicial philosophy is characterized by the highest regard for protecting the rights of law-abiding citizens," President Reagan filled the lower federal courts with judges who, in contrast with President Carter's appointees, were reluctant to side with defendants in criminal cases.[5]

The appointment of a justice to the Supreme Court gives a president an opportunity to make a more general impact on judicial policy. The president's choice may also be influenced by the American Bar Association and party leaders. On these nominations, however, the president plays a more decisive part than in nominations for lower federal court positions. Since the establishment of the Supreme Court, the Senate has rejected about one of every five presidential nominees for positions on that court. Since 1900, however, the Senate has refused to confirm only four of fifty such nominees. Thus, the odds are high that whomever a president nominates for the Court will take office.

Of the factors in a president's choice of a Supreme Court nominee, the most important is his desire for someone who shares his political philosophy and will, accordingly, vote as he would on issues coming before the Court. The performance of Supreme Court justices, however, is difficult to predict. Indeed, one-fourth of the justices have behaved contrary to the apparent expectations of the presidents who appointed them.[6]

In choosing a nominee for the Supreme Court, presidents usually select members of their own party and, on occasion, friends. To some extent presidents have also attempted to balance Court representation geographically (though this was done more extensively in the nineteenth century than it has in the present one). Most recent presidents appear to have reserved seats for Catholics and Jews, but no Jew has served on the Court since 1969. The

---

[5] C. K. Rowland, Robert A. Corp, and Ronald A. Stidham, "Judges' Policy Choices and the Value Basis of Judicial Appointments," *Journal of Politics* 46 (1984): 885–902. More generally, see Robert A. Corp and C. K. Rowland, *Policymaking and Politics in the Federal Courts* (Knoxville: University of Tennessee Press, 1983).

[6] See Robert Scigliano, *The Supreme Court and the Presidency* (New York: Free Press, 1971), p. 146.

appointment of Thurgood Marshall in 1967 may have established a tradition that there is to be at least one black member of the Court. No persons of Hispanic, Asian, or Indian extraction have yet been appointed. In 1981 Sandra Day O'Connor, a Reagan nominee, became the first woman on the Supreme Court. This appointment, while highly popular, was criticized by some conservatives on the grounds that O'Connor was weak on issues such as the Equal Rights Amendment and abortion because of positions she had taken while serving in the Arizona state legislature.

The Constitution contains no qualifications for the holding of a federal judicial office, even with respect to legal education, experience, and age. Supreme Court appointees, however, have shared certain features. The "average" justice has been male, white, Protestant, of Anglo-Saxon stock, from fifty to fifty-five years of age at the time of appointment, and a lawyer by training. Many justices have held elective office. Relatively few, on the other hand, have had extensive judicial experience before their appointments. More than 40 percent of those who have served on the Supreme Court, including six of the fifteen chief justices, had no judicial experience. Of those who previously served in state and lower federal courts, only about one of five held those positions for ten or more years.[7]

Courts in the Political System

As noted earlier in this chapter, the most common function of courts in the United States is to decide civil or criminal cases. But courts are also policymakers and critical institutions in the political process. Both federal and state courts have the power to review and reverse the decisions or actions taken by legislative bodies or administrators. The courts can also make an issue, whether school desegregation or abortion, important to other public bodies (sometimes requiring them to take action) and the public at large. Lower courts regularly pass judgement on the efforts of government agencies to enforce laws, ruling, for example, in antitrust suits against businesses accused of price fixing and in suits by private parties challenging the decisions of administrative agencies or their failure to implement a law, such as to register a pesticide.

As participants in the political process, judicial bodies are of concern to interest groups. The latter attempt to influence judicial policy by participating in the selection of judges initiating litigation, and entering suits as *amicis curiae* ("friends of the court").[8] Some groups have turned to the courts for policy

[7] See Abraham, *The Judicial Process*, p. 50.

[8] As Amicus Curiae, a group or individual not involved directly in a suit is brought in to advise the court on the broader implications of the controversy. Often, the views of the executive branch on matters of federal policy are represented in this manner through the Solicitor General, an official in the Justice Department.

reforms they could not secure in the legislative arenas. One group that has successfully followed this route is the National Association for the Advancement of Colored People (NAACP), which, operating through its fund for legal defense and education has won numerous Supreme Court cases on the rights of blacks in such areas as education and voting. Other groups have found the courts of value in nullifying certain legislation, such as that regulating their activities.

Courts have traditionally been called upon by various groups to provide a last-resort remedy to their problems. Since the 1960s, however, litigation has been viewed by several organizations, particularly public interest groups concerned with matters such as consumer and environmental protection, as the first step in bringing about policy change. Reform groups have frequently bypassed legislatures and executives and gone directly to court. Bringing suit has been regarded as less expensive than undertaking an intensive legislative lobbying campaign. Moreover, the chances of securing a favorable decision have been perceived to be greater in the courts because judges are more likely than members of Congress to "listen to reason" and less likely to be influenced by popular sentiment or pressures exerted by powerful interests.[9]

Laws and court rulings in the 1960s (now somewhat modified) considerably aided various people and groups in achieving *standing* (the legal right to bring a suit) in federal courts. Historically, standing has required that those who bring a case have an immediate interest in the outcome of the decision rather than simply a grievance against an existing governmental policy. In recent years, however, the Supreme Court has in some cases allowed people to sue simply on the grounds that they are taxpayers, and groups representing general public interests, such as those of consumers, have been permitted to bring suit. The Court has not yet gone to the lengths once advocated by former justice William O. Douglas—giving standing to those who represent the interests of inanimate objects, such as trees, that are threatened by environmental deterioration.

The result of these increased demands on the court system has been that the courts, especially at the national level, have become involved in decisions that were once made by other branches of government. Federal judges during the 1970s not only attempted to prod executives and legislators into action but also established guidelines for the management of schools, state prisons, and mental hospitals and decided whether nuclear power plants should be built. Some critics, such as former governor George Wallace of Alabama, declared, "Thugs and Federal Judges have just about taken charge of this country."[10] Others,

---

[9] See, for example, Roger C. Cramton, "Judicial Law Making and Administration," *Public Administration Review* 36 (September/October 1976): 551–555; Donald L. Horowitz, "The Courts as Guardians of the Public Interest," *Public Administration Review* 37 (March/April 1977): 148–154; and Donald L. Horowitz, *The Courts and Social Policy* (Washington, D.C.: Brookings Institution, 1977).

[10] Quoted in "Too Much Law?" *Newsweek*, January 10, 1977, p. 40.

while not opposed to the objectives of judicial involvement (for example, cleaner air and more humane prisons), have been concerned about the capacity of the courts to deal with such problems and, more broadly, about the appropriate role of judges in a representative democracy.

DECISION MAKING IN THE SUPREME COURT

The Setting

Much of the concern over the role of courts in the political process has focused on the Supreme Court. This august body has been surrounded by mythology to the point that many Americans appear to question whether its nine members are really human. Some books, such as *The Brethren* by investigative reporters Woodward and Armstrong, however, suggest that the justices are only too human, capable of nursing enmities, intriguing against each other, and wheeling and dealing to secure desired results.[11] On a broader level the Court is inherently involved in politics in the sense that any decision it makes, and even its refusal to make one, affects some group's rights, interests, or obligations. This court like Congress, has considerable discretion to choose the issues of public policy it will consider. Unlike Congress, however, it cannot select whichever controversy appears appropriate. Its policy-making function is exercised only after problems are brought to it in the form of litigation. The Court, moreover, by the wording of the Constitution, is to confine itself to "cases or controversies" in which there is actual conflict among opposing litigants. Unlike some state courts, the Supreme Court will not give advisory opinions.

The U.S. Supreme Court is in session for thirty-six weeks each year, from mid October through June. In emergencies it may extend its sessions or meet in special session. Justices spend several days each session reading briefs (written legal arguments) and listening to oral arguments on cases the Court has agreed to hear. About half the cases the Court handles involve the executive branch of the national government. The solicitor general or his or her staff normally argues the executive branch's position. The solicitor general is third from the top in the Department of Justice, ranking immediately behind the attorney general and the deputy attorney general. The solicitor general and various private groups may also submit briefs and participate in the oral argument, even if they are not directly involved in the litigation, by acting as an amicus curiae. The right to intervene in this manner depends on the consent of both parties to the dispute or, failing this, the approval of the Court.

When the Supreme Court justices are not hearing oral arguments they spend much of their time either working in their own offices (with the assistance

---

[11] Bob Woodward and Scott Armstrong, *The Brethren: Inside the Supreme Court* (New York: Avon Books, 1981).

of three of four law clerks) or engaging in formal and informal meetings with each other. Three Fridays a month the justices meet in conference to decide tentatively the cases they have heard argued and to determine the cases they wish to review. The chief justice presides over the conference, which is closed to all others. The Chief Justice begins by summarizing each case and stating his views as to its disposition. Other views then are given by the associate justices in order of their seniority in the Court. When a vote is taken, the junior member of the Court votes first and the chief justice last. As pointed out in the beginning of this chapter, it takes four affirmative votes to bring before the Court a case from the state or lower federal courts. Cases considered by the Court are decided by majority vote, five votes constituting a majority for cases in which all nine vote.

Congress has set rules disqualifying justices from considering cases when there is a reasonable doubt about their impartiality. An example would be a case concerning a company in which a justice holds stock. In practice, however, each justice decides whether to disqualify himself or herself from a case. When a justice refuses to participate or is physically unable to do so there may be a four–four vote in a case. In this situation the decision the Court is reviewing is affirmed.

Often the justices will issue a short, unsigned *per curiam opinion*, which simply states the Court's decision in a case without offering reasons. Other cases are assigned to an individual justice, who writes a detailed opinion giving the reasons a majority of the Court members decided the way they did. The chief justice, if he agrees with the majority on a case, may decide to write the Court's formal opinion, or he may assign this task to another justice. If the Chief Justice is in the minority, the senior justice among the majority decides who will write the opinion. The Court has written an average of about 130 full opinions each session in the past few years.

After an opinion is written and agreed upon by at least a simple majority of the justices, it is announced in open court on opinion day, which is scheduled on three Mondays a month. The majority opinion in a given case may be accompanied by concurring and dissenting opinions. Justices who write concurring opinions agree with the conclusion reached in the majority opinion but not with the reasoning that led to it. Justices who write dissenting opinions state why they disagree with the conclusion reached in the majority opinion.

In recent years two of every three cases decided with written opinions have been accompanied by at least one dissenting opinion.[12] Some dissents have eventually become majority opinions. Dissents, in the words of former chief justice Charles Evans Hughes (1930–41) are appeals "to the brooding spirit of the law, to the intelligence of a future day." Several justices and scholars,

[12] Stephen C. Halpern and Kenneth N. Vines, "Institutional Disunity," *Western Political Quarterly* 30 (December 1977): 471.

however, have not been enthusiastic about dissents, claiming that they frequently lead to confusion because they exaggerate or distort the meaning of the majority opinion. More broadly, unity has been seen as necessary to maintain the power and legitimacy of the Court and to secure compliance with its decisions. For these reasons, majority opinions are frequently rewritten, not simply to get a majority of the justices to support a decision but to get a unanimous decision. The norm of unity or minimal disagreement also apparently applies to judicial behavior in the courtroom. A strong vocal dissent may draw a reprimand from the chief justice. An example of this occurred in the Warren court when the chief justice reacted to a harangue by Justice Felix Frankfurter by remarking,

> That was not the dissenting opinion you filed. That was a lecture—a closing argument by a prosecutor to a jury. It might properly have been made in the conference room but not in this courtroom. As I understand it, the purpose of reporting an opinion here is to inform the public and not for the purpose of grading this Court.[13]

Outside the courtroom justices seldom publicly discuss the Court's deliberations on a previous case. Inside the court the justices consider cases in closed conference, as noted before, to promote a free exchange of ideas and to minimize the possibility of a premature disclosure of the Court's decision. To further protect against leaks, all opinions (draft as well as final) are printed in a shop located in the basement of the Supreme Court building. The Supreme Court is one of the most leakproof institutions of government. Yet at times, advance information about its deliberations and decisions have reached the media. For example, newspapers and newsmagazines reported the Court's 1973 abortion decision before it was publicly announced in court.

Influences on Decision Making

One of the oldest explanations of Supreme Court decision making is known as *mechanical jurisprudence*. This theory assumes that justices do not make law but find it embedded in the Constitution or a statute and apply it to a particular case. All a justice has to do, according to this theory, is lay a challenged statute alongside the Constitution to see if a conflict is present. If a conflict is found the statute is void.

Few modern legal scholars subscribe to the mechanical jurisprudence theory of decision making. Justices have much discretion in interpreting the specific meaning of legal terms such as *due process* or *equal protection* and in finding whether a particular action conflicts with the Constitution. Congressional statutes the Court is called upon to interpret are also frequently vague in their

---

[13] Quoted in Fred Rodell, "It is the Earl Warren Court," *New York Times Magazine*, March 13, 1966, p. 96.

intent, and the Court must determine their meaning. As former justice William O. Douglas observed,

> the battle that raged before the legislature is now transferred to the court. The passage of the legislation quieted the conflict only temporarily. It breaks out anew in the process of interpretation in the courts. A storm hits the court room, and the advocates take up the fight where the legislature left off. The same cleavage that appeared in legislative halls now shows up among the judges. . . .[14]

A dominant characteristic of judicial policy making is the use of the rule of *stare decisis*, or case precedent. Under this rule current cases are to be decided in the same manner as similar ones decided previously. Justices, however, may differ over which past decisions apply to a current case. Individual justices, and the Court as a whole, moreover, may choose to ignore or to reverse precedents established in earlier decisions and set out in new policy directions. In the 1954 case of *Brown v. Board of Education*,[15] for instance the Court under Chief Justice Earl Warren reversed a decision that had prevailed since 1896 defending "equal but separate" public facilities for whites and blacks. The Warren Court, in general, was less concerned with legal and historical data than with the actual effects of existing practices, such as the effect of school segregation on black children, and with fundamental problems of fairness.

As this discussion suggests, there is considerably more involved in judicial decision making than the legal criteria found in the Constitution, statutes, and previous Court decisions. Scholars have used a variety of approaches to uncover the nonlegal factors that affect judicial decision making. It is clear that Supreme Court justices, like other public officials, have political predispositions and attitudes that are reflected in their voting behavior.

Justices also may act upon well-developed perceptions of their roles as members of the Court. Holders of any office, of course, may perceive their basic roles differently. Supreme Court justices have differed over whether the Court should strive toward restraint or activism. Those disposed toward restraint attempt to restrict the range of issues the Court will consider and to avoid questioning the wisdom of the actions taken by other public officials or bodies. The need for restraint has been defended on two grounds: (1) the Court, being an appointed body, is unqualified to question the wisdom of policies made by officials who are more directly accountable to the public, and (2) problems exist that the Court can do nothing to remedy even if it is willing to try. Justices disposed toward activism have contended that the court should not stay aloof from the political system and that it has a unique role to play in protecting values and rights that might otherwise be neglected by other political institutions.

---

[14] William O. Douglas, "In Defense of Dissent," speech reprinted in Alan F. Westin (ed.), *The Supreme Court: Views From Inside* (New York: W. W. Norton & Co., Inc., 1961), p. 53.
[15] 347 U.S. 483.

Political scientist Henry Schmandt has suggested that the views of individual justices on this issue "run a continuum from insistence on virtual withdrawal of the judiciary from the policy making arena to espousal of almost total involvement in the political struggle."[16]

Judicial decision making does not occur in a political vacuum. As shown in the following section, there is evidence that many Supreme Court justices have attempted to stay in line with dominant political opinion or the mood of the country. Studies of the Court, based largely on the papers and biographies of former justices and the comments of former law clerks, suggest that there is also considerable interaction among justices that influences their decision making.[17] The Supreme Court is a small group in which decision making is affected by friendship and characterized by bargaining among justices and by efforts to persuade colleagues toward a particular policy view.

Such interaction occurs in the Friday conferences in which the Court makes a tentative decision on cases and throughout the opinion-drafting process. During the latter, copies of majority, concurring, and dissenting opinions are circulated among the justices, who are in constant communication through memoranda, the telephone, or informal meetings. As a result of this interchange, justices who were in a minority in the conference session may be able to form a majority on a case. The problem of holding a conference majority together is further complicated by the difficulty of getting five or more justices to agree on the reasons for a decision. Justices, like members of Congress, are better able to agree that something should be done than on why it should be done. As one justice has said,

> you work your brains out and you finally circulate something. Then one guy sends you a note saying, "I'd be happy to join with you in Smith v. Jones if you'll take out that paragraph on the top of page five."
> And then another guy has a whole new concept he wants in, and if you've only got a five-man majority, you have to listen to all suggestions very seriously or you might lose the whole thing.[18]

A Supreme Court opinion ultimately emerges as a group effort and is commonly the product of several draftings. Consequently, the Court's opinions, like legislation, may contain vague or even contradictory statements.

Throughout the deliberations on a case the chief justice is in a particularly advantageous position to influence the outcome. In conference, for

[16] Henry J. Schmandt, *Courts in the American Political System* (Belmont, Calif.: Dickenson, 1968), p. 44.

[17] See Walter F. Murphy, *Elements of Judicial Strategy* (Chicago: University of Chicago Press, 1964).

[18] Unidentified justice quoted by Nina Totenberg, "Conflict at the Court," *Washington Magazine*, (February 1974), reprinted in Celeste Tomiero (ed.), *Readings in American Government* (Guilford, Conn.: Dushkin Publishing Group, 1977), p. 34.

example, the chief justice expresses his views first and thus can attempt to define the issues. He is generally better informed than the other justices about applications before the Court and about what his colleagues think about a case. He receives more communications from the justices than any other justice. In addition to these institutional factors, the leadership and influence of the chief justice depend upon his ability to gain the respect of his associates. This quality played a large part in the effectiveness of chief justices such as Charles Even Hughes (1930–41) and Earl Warren (1953–69).

Certain issues can divide the justices. An examination of civil liberties cases in the 1958 court term, for example, found a recurring division between a conservative group led by Justice Frankfurter and a liberal group headed by Justice Brennan.[19] Research on voting patterns in the Court of the 1970s also found Brennan to be the leader of a pro–civil liberties bloc, which was frequently in conflict with a group headed by William Rehnquist.[20] It is not completely clear how these blocs are formed or why two or more justices vote the same way on particular issues; ideology, party identification, and personality are probably involved.

THE PERFORMANCE OF THE COURT

Judicial Review

The most basic power of the Supreme Court is to interpret the Constitution and declare legislative, executive, and administrative acts unconstitutional. The Constitution does not specifically grant this power of *judicial review* to the Court. There is evidence, however, that the framers of the Constitution expected the Court to exercise this power.[21]

The Court first asserted its right to declare acts of Congress unconstitutional in the case of *Marbury v. Madison* in 1803.[22] The case emanated from the efforts of President John Adams, who was defeated in the election of 1800 by Thomas Jefferson, to appoint as many members of his political party (the Federalist) as possible to federal court positions before he left office. Many, but not all, of these appointments were officially made before Jefferson assumed the presidency. When Jefferson became president he ordered his secretary of state, James Madison, not to deliver the remaining commissions. William Marbury, who had been promised a relatively minor position as justice of the peace in

---

[19] S. Sidney Ulmer, "The Analysis of Behavior Patterns," in Glendon Shubert, *Quantitative Analysis of Judicial Behavior* (Glencoe, IL: The Free Press, 1959), Chapter 3.

[20] C. Jeddy Levar, "The Nixon Court: A Study of Leadership," *Western Political Quarterly* (December, 1977): 484–92.

[21] See, for example, the argument by Abraham, op. cit., pp. 304–308.

[22] 1 Cranch 137.

Washington, D.C., was one of those who did not receive his commission. Marbury, drawing upon a section of a 1789 act of Congress, asked the Court to issue a writ of mandamus compelling Madison to deliver the commission.[23] In the Court's formal opinion, Chief Justice Marshall, a Federalist, scolded Madison for not delivering the commission but declared that the Court could not issue a writ of mandamus. The section of the act of Congress that gave the Court this authority was invalid because it sought to enlarge the original jurisdiction of the Court and thus violated the Constitution. Marshall argued that the Court had the authority to invalidate acts of Congress because the Constitution was the supreme law of the land and the Court, as guardian of the Constitution, could not honor any law that conflicted with the Constitution.

Since *Marbury v. Madison*, most of the important exercises of judicial review have involved the invalidation of state and local laws. Justice Oliver Wendell Holmes (on the Court from 1902 to 1932) once remarked, "I do not think the United States would come to an end if we lost our power to declare an act of Congress void. I do think the Union would be imperiled if we could not make that declaration as to the laws of the several states."[24]

The Court has been less strict in checking the actions of Congress, the president, and federal administrators than it has been in reviewing how state and local officials have exerted their powers. The Court has invalidated the provisions of only slightly more than 100 of approximately 75,000 laws passed by Congress since 1789.[25]

Similarly, the Court has done very little to limit the expansion of presidential powers. Indeed, it has often defended or rationalized the enlargement of these powers to meet emergencies. There have been exceptions, however. In 1952, for instance, the Court denied President Harry Truman the right to seize steel mills.[26] The president ordered the mills taken to avoid a strike that would supposedly have disrupted the production of weapons needed for the war in Korea. The Court was closely divided in this case. The majority decision rested largely on the fact that Congress had considered giving the president such authority but had chosen not to do so. And in *United States v. Nixon* (1974)[27] the Court denied that the president had an inherent power under the doctrine of executive privilege to withhold evidence needed for criminal proceedings. As a result of this ruling President Nixon was forced to provide special prosecutor Leon Jaworski with tape recordings of his conversations with

[23] A writ of mandamus compels a public official to perform his or her official nondiscretionary duties.

[24] *Law and the Court* (1913).

[25] Abraham, op. cit. p. 280.

[26] *Youngstown Sheet and Tube Co.* v. *Sawyer*, 343 U.S. 579.

[27] 418 U.S. 683.

aides who had been charged with attempting to cover up crimes involved in the Watergate break-in.

The Supreme Court and lower federal courts regularly review cases involving administrative agencies. The courts, however, have generally given great weight to the agencies' judgments and have reversed them only under unusual circumstances (though, as noted earlier, courts have been more active in reversing agency decisions in recent years). The Supreme Court has supported some agencies more than others. For example, it has upheld the decisions of the Federal Trade Commission more than 90 percent of the time in recent years but the decisions of the Interstate Commerce Commission only slightly more than 60 percent of the time. The major variable involved in the Court's willingness to support an agency is whether the justices agree with the policies being implement by the agency.[28]

The Court and Public Policy

The impact of the Supreme Court has been far more pronounced in domestic policy than in foreign policy. The Court has been reluctant to challenge how national officials handle foreign affairs, on the grounds that doing so would involve "decisions of a kind for which the judiciary has neither aptitude, facilities, nor responsibilities."[29] It has been highly unusual for the Court to make a decision interfering with a war effort. The power of the national government in times of war has been seen by the Court to be broad enough to enable it to do what is necessary to achieve victory. In the words of former chief justice Charles Evans Hughes, "the power to wage war is the power to wage war successfully."

The broad expansion of governmental power during wartime may even lead to actions that would clearly violate civil liberties in time of peace. One of the clearest illustrations of this occurred during the Second World War when the Supreme Court upheld the right of President Franklin Roosevelt to order 120,000 Japanese Americans on the West Coast to be taken from their homes and placed in internment camps. This action was held by the Supreme Court to be justified as a military necessity.[30]

A principal domestic concern of the court until the late 1930s was the protection of private property rights and economic enterprises from governmental regulation. The depression of the 1930s and popular support for Franklin Roosevelt's New Deal recovery program eventually pressured the Court into a position of supporting governmental programs regulating the economy. Since the late 1930s the Court has been more concerned with basic

[28] Bradley C. Cannon and Michael Giles, "Recurring Litigants: Federal Agencies Before the Supreme Court," *Western Political Quarterly* 25 (June 1972): 183–191.

[29] *Chicago and Southern Air Lines* v. *Waterman*, 315 U.S. 103 (1948), p. 110.

[30] *Korematsu* v. *United States*, 323 U.S. 214 (1944).

civil rights and liberties such as free speech, due process protections to those accused of crime, and freedom from racial discrimination. Concern with these subjects reached a high point in the court headed by Earl Warren from 1953 to 1969. Warren, a former public prosecuter and governor of California, was appointed to the Supreme Court bench by Eisenhower, who later called this appointment "the biggest damn fool mistake I ever made in my life."[31] Others, however, applauded the decisions made in this era, which among other things officially ended separate schools for blacks and whites, extended protections to criminal defendants (for example, by limiting searches and seizures), and democratized representation in state legislatures.

After Warren the Court was headed by Nixon appointee Warren Burger. The appointment of Burger, a conservative judge on the court of appeals for the District of Columbia circuit, was expected to eventually bring about a reversal of many of the Warren Court decisions. The Court under Burger, which included several appointees of Nixon and Reagan, was less inclined than the Warren Court toward judicial activism and in some areas, such as criminal law, was more conservative. Yet under Burger, the criminal law reforms of the Warren era were left mostly intact and expected rollbacks in such areas as school desegregation, school prayer, and affirmative action did not materialize. The Burger Court also entered new areas of reform, as when it liberalized abortion laws. In sum, the Court under Burger did not follow a consistent pattern of constitutional interpretation.

In 1986 Burger resigned and President Reagan appointed Justice William Rehnquist to replace him. Rehnquist, an intellectual leader among the Court's conservatives, was expected to lead the Court in a more consistently conservative direction.

The Power of the Court

The Supreme Court is probably "the most extraordinarily powerful court of law the world has ever known."[32] Its power has been derived from the deep respect generally felt for it as an institution and the underlying belief that the Court is not a political institution but a legal one. This distinction between law and politics is commonly seen as follows: "Law is stable, politics is ephemeral. Law is evenhanded, politics is biased. Law is legitimate, politics is questionable. Law is conservative, politics is often radical."[33]

The Court since John Marshall has found it desirable to perpetuate the myth of its nonpolitical character. However, it has not always been able to count

---

[31] Quoted in Alpheus Thomas Mason, "The Burger Court in Historical Perspective," *Political Science Quarterly* 89 (March 1974): 28.

[32] Alexander M. Bickel, *The Least Dangerous Branch: The Supreme Court at the Bar of Politics* (Indianapolis: Bobbs-Merrill, 1962), p. 1.

[33] Herbert Jacob, *Law, Politics, and the Federal Courts* (Boston: Little, Brown, 1967), p. ix.

on habitual obedience to its decisions. When the court faces determined defiance, the fate of its orders depends on the support of the other branches of government. The Court, as Alexander Hamilton noted, does not possess either the "sword or the purse" to enforce its policies. When physical force or sanctions such as the denial of federal aid are required to compel compliance with a Court order, they must be supplied by the executive and legislative branches. Resistance encountered in school desegregation cases, for example, led to the presidential commitment of federal troops in the 1950s and 1960s. Similarly, the 1964 Civil Rights Act authorizes all federal agencies administering grant programs to withhold federal money from state and local activities where racial segregation is practiced.

Supreme Court policy making is subject to numerous checks by other courts, Congress, and the presidency. Supreme Court decisions may be modified or in effect negated by state and lower federal courts charged with their implementation. Given the vagueness of many Court opinions, the meaning of the law depends not only on what the Court says but also on state and lower federal court interpretations of what the Court says. At other times, as in segregation cases, lower courts have refused to implement Court rulings.

Congress and the president have come to the aid of the Supreme Court by securing compliance with a strongly resisted decision, as they did in the segregation cases, but they are under no compulsion to do so. In addition, Congress may (1) change the Court's appellate jurisdiction so that it cannot hear certain types of cases, (2) increase or decrease the number of justices who sit on the Court, and (3) reverse a Supreme Court decision by legislation or through a constitutional amendment. Over the years both liberals and conservatives have threatened to impose such controls because of disagreement with Court policies. Although controls have seldom been imposed, they appear to have constrained judicial policy making.

The last time Congress actually restricted the Supreme Court's appellate jurisdiction was in 1866, when it prohibited the Court from considering cases involving Reconstruction (post–Civil War) policies. The threat of such action has been common, however, and in the early 1980s numerous proposals were made in Congress to prevent federal courts from considering cases involving school prayer, abortion, and busing for the purposes of school integration. Critics of this approach have responded that conservative groups unhappy with federal court rulings in these areas, especially those of the Supreme Court, should attempt to reverse them by constitutional amendment instead.

Efforts to enlarge the Court and to fill the new positions with justices who will vote the way the president wishes have occasionally been made. Franklin Roosevelt launched the last major attempt. His 1937 "Court-packing" proposal was defeated in Congress because many people sought to retain the independence of the Court. The battle, however, prompted a switch in the court's voting, which became more favorable to Roosevelt's policies. This adjustment by the Court is commonly known as "the switch in time that saved nine" as the number of Court members.

Reversal of Court decisions by legislation has occurred. For example, the Court ruled that interstate insurance companies could not be regulated by the states, but Congress decided otherwise. The Eleventh, Fourteenth, and Sixteenth amendments to the Constitution also reversed Supreme Court decisions.

Given the inherent political limitations on the Supreme Court's power, we may conclude that it is unable to counter the wishes of the "lawmaking majority" or the "dominant political coalition" for a substantial length of time. Viewed in this perspective, the Court's policy-making capability may be attributed to its choice of the right conditions and policies. As one authority has pointed out,

> judicial self-restraint and judicial power seem to be the opposite sides of the same coin: it has been by judicious application of the former that the latter has been maintained. A tradition beginning with Marshall's coup in Marbury v. Madison . . . suggests that the Court's power has been maintained by a wise refusal to employ it in unequal combat.[34]

The ability of the Supreme Court to make policy can appropriately be looked upon as a consequence of the fragmentation of political power in the American political system. In view of this fragmentation, a decision is unlikely to be resisted by a cohesive majority and is bound to have much support. When cohesive majorities exist or appear to exist, as in the area of national defense, the Court is likely to be cautious and self-restraining. On a much broader level, an important function of the courts, especially the Supreme Court, is to add to the legitimacy of the political system by appearing as detached, principled guardians of fundamental freedoms.[35]

SUMMARY

1. There are fifty-one court systems in the United States, one of federal courts and one in each of the states. The United States Supreme Court reviews those cases arising from state courts and lower federal courts that at least four of the nine justices feel raise a "substantial federal question."

2. Federal judges are nominated by the president and confirmed by a majority vote in the Senate. They are subject to removal only by conviction on impeachment charges. Individual senators and the American Bar Association have played influential roles in the selection of lower federal court judges. Presidents play a

---

[34] John P. Roche, "Judicial Self-Restraint," *American Political Science Review* 49 (September 1955): 772.

[35] Ibid.

more decisive part in the selection of Supreme Court justices; they usually look for candidates who share their political philosophy. Generally, securing appointment to the Supreme Court has been a matter not of working one's way up in the judicial system but of finding political favor with the president.

3. Courts in this nation, especially the Supreme Court, can make an issue important to other public bodies and the general public. They also serve as means by which groups can secure policy objectives they either have not been able to secure from other branches of government or cannot secure from those branches as easily as they can from the courts. Growing reliance on the courts for policy reform, however, has raised several questions concerning the role of the courts in relation to the more representative branches of government and the capacity of the courts to perform the tasks demanded of them.

4. The Supreme Court cannot make policy decisions directly but must wait for cases to come before it. Decisions about which cases will be heard and about the merits of cases are made in conferences closed to everyone but the justices. Justices frequently dissent from a majority opinion. This practice has been criticized on the grounds that it threatens the legitimacy of the Court, adds confusion to the meaning of its decisions, and makes it more difficult to secure compliance with a decision.

5. Supreme Court justices have much discretion in interpreting the meaning of the Constitution, statutes, and their own previous decisions. Nonlegal factors that affect judicial decisions are the justices' values, ideology, partisan identification, perceptions of their roles as judges, and interactions with one another. Many decisions result from bargaining and compromise among the justices.

6. The Supreme Court has been a far more important check on the powers of state and local governments than on the power of the national government. Its impact on policy has been far greater in domestic than in foreign affairs. Historically, the court has protected economic rights and, particularly since the late 1930s, basic civil rights and liberties. The Court's power is subject to numerous limitations. Generally, the Court may be unable to resist dominant political sentiments for a substantial length of time.

10

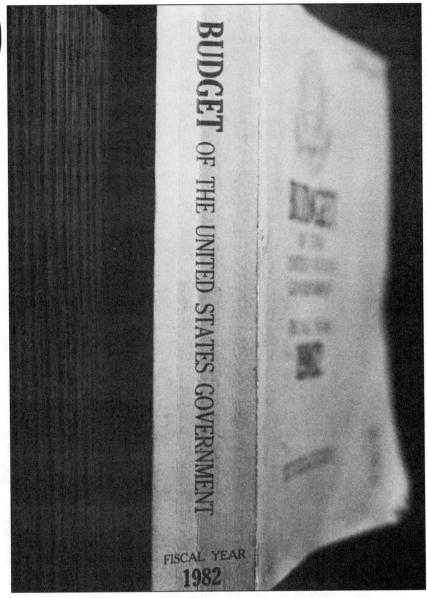

BUDGET OF THE UNITED STATES GOVERNMENT

FISCAL YEAR
1982

GOVERNMENT, POLITICS, SPENDING, AND TAXING

Table 10–1 Government Expenditures

CALENDAR YEAR	TOTAL PUBLIC SECTOR[a]	AS PERCENTAGE OF GNP	PER CAPITA IN CONSTANT (1972) DOLLARS	FEDERAL GOVERNMENT PERCENTAGE OF TOTAL[b]
1929	$ 10.3	9.9	$ 258	24.4
1939	17.6	19.3	472	45.2
1949	59.3	23.0	757	66.0
1959	131.0	26.9	1,090	64.2
1969	286.8	30.4	1,630	58.6
1974	460.0	32.1	1,872	55.5
1976	574.9	33.5	1,996	56.3
1978	681.1	31.5	2,034	56.3
1980	869.0	33.0	2,139	59.1
1981	983.6	33.3	2,186	61.1
1982	1,090.1	35.5	2,263	62.5
1983	1,167.5	35.3	2,312	62.8
1984	1,258.0	34.3	2,379	62.6
1985 (est.)	1,375.9	35.4	2,491	62.7

[a] In billions of current dollars.

[b] Federal aid programs are considered to be state-local expenditures.

Adapted from Advisory Commission on Intergovernmental Relations, *Significant Features of Fiscal Federalism 1985* (Washington, D.C.: Government Printing Office, 1985), pp. 6–9.

We have concentrated to this point on the constitutional environment of policy making, citizen inputs, linkage mechanisms, policy makers, and policymaking institutions. The last four chapters in this book analyze what the national government has done or has failed to do in various areas of public policy. In this chapter we first take a broad look at government financial trends. We then analyze the process by which the federal budget is adopted, the strategies and conflicts this involves, and general patterns in expenditures and revenues.

GOVERNMENT FINANCES

Public Sector Spending

That government in the United States (state and local as well as federal) has become more expensive over the last fifty years hardly qualifies as news. How much government spending has grown depends on the measures employed. Those fearful of big government are most alarmed by total spending. This amounted to nearly $1,376 billion in 1985 (see Table 10–1). By comparison, total spending was $869 billion in 1980 and "only" $460 billion in 1974. The figures are far less alarming when public sector expenditures are considered as a percentage of the gross national product (the total value of the goods and services produced in the nation, including both the private and public sectors) in a given year. Government expenditures as a percentage of gross national product (GNP) increased dramatically during the depression years of the 1930s, enjoyed less spectacular but steady growth through the mid 1970s, and have been relatively stable since, slightly increasing or decreasing from year to year. By another measurement, when one controls for population growth and inflation, government expenditures appear to have increased more consistently. Changes in government expenditures per capita, up to an estimated $2,491 in 1985, however, appear to have been relatively slight in recent years. As Table 10–1 suggests, all levels of government have increased their expenditures, but the biggest spender in recent decades has been the national government. Currently it accounts for around 63 percent of the money spent in the public sector.

Statistics, of course, can be used to buttress any number of arguments. Economic conservatives who contend that decisions concerning the allocation of resources should rest in private hands are apt to be quite unhappy, to say the least, that governments account for 35 percent of the goods and services produced each year. Liberals, on the other hand, have traditionally been unhappy with what they see as an overemphasis on private goods and an underemphasis on public goods. *Private goods* are those items people purchase for their own consumption. *Public goods* are those things, such as roads, law enforcement, and pollution control, that government provides to the public. Writing in the late 1950s, economist John Galbraith noted the disparity in the provision of these two types of goods:

> The family which takes its . . . air-conditioned, power-steered, and power-braked automobile out for a tour passes through cities that are badly paved, made hideous by litter, blighted buildings, billboards, and posts for wires that should long since have been put underground. They pass on into a countryside that has been rendered largely invisible by commercial areas. (The goods which the latter advertise have an absolute priority in our value system. Such aesthetic considerations as a view of the countryside accordingly come second. On such matters we are consistent.) They picnic on exquisitely packaged food from a portable icebox by a polluted stream and go on to spend the night at a park which is a menace to public health and morals. Just before dozing off on an air mattress, beneath a nylon tent, amid the stench of decaying refuse, they may reflect vaguely on the curious unevenness of their blessings. Is this, indeed the American genius?[1]

Contemporary observers likewise have seen the need for a massive infusion of public funds for cleaning up our air and water, protecting ourselves against hazardous wastes, and rebuilding much or our nation's infrastructure—its roads,

---

[1] John Kenneth Galbraith, *The Affluent Society* (New York: Houghton Mifflin, 1958), p. 253.

bridges, and various other public facilities—which are in bad repair because of underinvestment and years of neglect.[2]

In addition to conflict over how the nation's wealth should be distributed between the public and private sectors, there have been unending disputes over the allocation of funds among various public sector activities and over the financial responsibilities of the various levels of government. One classic dilemma of policy makers has been choosing between "guns and butter"—that is, defense versus domestic needs. As indicated in Chapter 2, modern-day advocates of dual federalism would shift the bulk of the responsibility for financing domestic programs to state and local governments while the national government focuses almost exclusively on foreign policy and defense. Opponents of this approach contend that hard-pressed states and localities are in no position to assume these responsibilities.

Pressure for Spending

Generally, one can trace demands for increased spending to the perception of the nation's problems both at home and abroad. Heightened concern over national security, for example, translates into pressure for a larger defense budget. Over the last several decades the defense budget has principally reflected the perceived need to confront or contain communism in various parts of the world and to engage in a seemingly unending arms race with the Soviet Union.[3] As for domestic problems, population growth by itself means additional pressure for governmental services and public facilities. The types of services that become important depend in part not only on total population growth but on how that growth takes place. Growth because of increases in life expectancy are likely to create concern over such matters as social security and health care. Increases in birth rates generate pressure for more educational expenditures. Declining birth rates can be expected, all other things being equal, to have the opposite effect.

To some extent, pressure for spending also results from public expectations that government will live up to commitments made in previous eras. Since the 1930s the national government has assumed a general responsibility for the well-being of the American people. To be sure, the strength and depth of this commitment have been questioned, but even the most conservative administration since the 1920s, that of Ronald Reagan, appears committed to maintaining the integrity of the social security system (public support for the program virtually dictates this position) and to keeping a "safety net" of federal programs for those in need.

[2] See, for example, Pat Choate and Susan Walter, *America in Ruins* (Washington, D.C.: Council of State Planning Agencies, 1981).

[3] See Charles W. Ostrom, Jr., and Robin F. Marra, "U.S. Defense Spending and the Soviet Estimate," *American Political Science Review* 80 (September, 1986): 819–842.

While people may see a number of good reasons for governmental spending, governments must live within constraints, largely political, on how much they can tax. Anxious to keep taxes at a level that prevents a full-scale taxpayers' rebellion, national policy makers have felt compelled to go into debt to meet certain pressing demands and to ignore other demands altogether. These are the kinds of decisions that have to be made in the budgeting process.

MAKING THE BUDGET

The Process

Each year the government of the United States prepares a budget estimating anticipated revenues and expenditures and allocating funds among governmental agencies and programs. This document shows the federal government's spending and income plans for each fiscal year. Under changes made in 1974, the fiscal year begins October 1 and ends the following September 30. The fiscal year is identified by the calendar year in which it ends. Thus, fiscal year 1984 is the year terminating on September 30, 1984.

Before 1921 the president had little control over the spending requests of federal agencies. The secretary of the Treasury prepared the federal budget proposal by simply transmitting the spending requests of federal agencies to Congress. No attempt was made to coordinate agency proposals to eliminate overlapping and duplicated programs or to curb extravagant agency requests. Since the Budget and Accounting Act of 1921, however, the president and his staff have reviewed and judged agency spending proposals and assimilated them into a single overall budget, which the president submits to Congress as his recommendations.

The budgeting process begins each spring when the president and his staff, particularly personnel in the Office of Management and Budget (OMB), evaluate governmental programs, establish priorities, and make revenue projections. In the fall all federal agencies and departments are required to formulate their proposed budgets for the next fiscal year in accordance with general guidelines set down by the OMB. This office then reviews agency proposals and makes recommendations to the president, who submits a budget proposal to Congress in January. Later in the year, the president may submit supplemental budget requests to cover needs not foreseen when the original budget was submitted.

A long-noted weakness of Congress in relation to the presidency has been its relative lack of control over the national budget. Although Congress controls the purse strings, it has relied mostly upon information supplied by the executive branch in making its spending decisions. It has made little effort to review the president's budget comprehensively.

In the Congressional Budgeting Act of 1974, Congress attempted to overcome these and related problems. This law created budget committees in both the House and Senate, established the Congressional Budget Office, and set up a series of procedures by which Congress is to consider the federal budget. The Congressional Budget Office provides staff assistance to the budget committees, though other members of Congress can also take advantage of its services. In many respects, the office does for Congress what the OMB does for the president in providing basic budgetary data and an analysis of alternative courses of action on budgetary matters.

The most important aspect of the post-1974 congressional budgetary procedures is the requirement that Congress set targets or ceilings for overall expenditures, levels of revenue, and public debt. Specific targets are proposed by the budget committees and are voted on by Congress. The budget committees and the budget office monitor decisions on appropriations, the authorization of new programs, and revenue bills to determine how well Congress is staying with its fiscal targets.

Appropriations committees in the House and the Senate directly consider the president's budgetary proposals. These committees do most of their work through permanent subcommittees that have authority over the budgets of particular administrative agencies. The subcommittees hold hearings in which administrative officials testify on their spending needs. Subcommittee decisions on these needs are usually accepted by the full committee, whose recommendations are in turn usually approved by the entire House and Senate.

When the October 1 deadline for congressional adoption of a new budget is missed (this happens most often because the White House and a majority of Congress cannot agree on spending priorities), Congress may adopt a continuing resolution that allows agencies to keep operating, usually at their existing levels of expenditure, until a new budget can be adopted. After the House and the Senate have agreed on the budget an appropriations bill is sent to the president. The chief executive can veto the bill, but unlike many state governors, as mentioned earlier, he does not have the power to veto specific items in appropriation bills. As noted in Chapter 6, the president does have a limited power to *impound* (refuse to spend) funds that Congress has appropriated. Massive impoundments by President Nixon, however, prompted Congress to pass a law that requires impoundments to be subject to congressional approval.

Strategies and Conflict

Budgeting is a highly political process in which strategies are mapped out and conflicts and disputes over public policy take place. Some of this activity occurs within an agency or department. The spending requests of the various divisions of an agency can generally be depended upon to add up to an amount exceeding what the OMB considers reasonable. Budgeting officials within the agency, attempting to avoid exceeding the limits set by the OMB, become involved in struggles between division heads, each wanting to have the necessary cutbacks taken from some other division's budget. Division heads may take their case to the agency head and enlist the support of outsiders such as members of Congress and interest groups.[4]

Similar activity characterizes the dealings between administrative agencies and the OMB. Agencies will almost always ask for more money than they spent the previous year.[5] Increases may result from forces beyond an agency's control. To keep a program operating at the same level, for instance, more revenue is needed inflation-produced increases in the cost of goods and services the agency must purchase. Other uncontrollable increases are necessitated by pay raises passed by Congress and expenditures produced by legislative statutes. As a matter of strategy an agency may request more than it actually needs or expects to get, anticipating cuts somewhere down the line. Such padding allows the OMB and Congress to play their watchdog roles of cutting expenses while not endangering the basic programs of each agency. The OMB staff also attempts to anticipate what Congress will do to its budget recommendations. This may lead to further padding of at least some proposed expenditures.

When the budget finally reaches Congress, each member must make his or her own calculations. Budgeting, as a member of the senate once declared, "requires each Senator to examine not only the needs of this Nation, from defense to domestic spending, but requires formulating a position on fiscal policy: the desired levels of spending and taxation. Finally, each Senator must consider carefully and represent thoroughly his or her State's varied needs."[6]

More directly, research suggests that appropriation decisions of both House and Senate members are influenced by electoral considerations and general economic conditions.[7] As election time nears, members of Congress generally attempt to improve their records by securing as many benefits as possible for their constituents. As a consequence, appropriations tend to be much higher during election years than during nonelection years. Appropriations increases are also especially likely during periods of high levels of unemployment. At these times, members of Congress tend to favor spending for various types of construction activities, such as new roads or buildings. Though such appropriations may be viewed as "budget busters" by presidents, they are

---

[4] See Peter B. Natchez and Irvin C. Bupp, "Policy and Priorities in the Budgetary Process," *American Political Science Reveiew* 67 (September, 1973): 951–963.

[5] See Aaron Wildavsky, *The Politics of the Budgetary Process*, 4th ed. (Boston: Little, Brown, 1983); and Ira Sharkansky, *The Politics of Taxing and Spending* (Indianapolis: Bobbs-Merrill, 1969).

[6] Slade Gorton (R–WASH.), quoted in *Congressional Record*, May 1, 1986, p. S5195.

[7] See Roderick Kiewiet and Mathew D. McCubbins, "Congressional Appropriations and the Electoral Connection," *Journal of Politics* 47 (1985): 59–82.

likely to be viewed by Congresspersons as providing needed employment in their districts and as improving their chances for reelection. As one congressman— who saw a $15 million bridge for his district eliminated by a presidential veto— put it: "You can bet your spring petunias that this congressman will vote to override. President Reagan, he ain't gonna be running in '88, but I am."[8]

Historically, presidents, members of Congress, and others involved in the budgetary process have simplified their work by looking at only a limited number of spending issues. Primary attention has been given to spending proposals for new programs or agencies and expenditures that represent a radical departure from the past. Generally, little attention has been given to ongoing programs, which have been allowed to grow by a certain across-the-board percentage.

The Carter administration, in attempting to cut expenses, took a different approach—zero-based budgeting. This approach requires agencies to evaluate the costs and benefits of all their programs, new or old. Zero-based budgeting was difficult to implement in the executive branch (it required a great deal more work than conventional procedures) and was resisted in Congress because it threatened established programs. It was finally abandoned in August, 1981, in the first year of the Reagan administration.

President Reagan's call for far more drastic budgetary changes, however, created a whirlwind of debate in the 1980s. Reagan's first budget, for fiscal 1982, was about $725 billion. This was not an absolute cut in spending (expenditures were only $660 billion in fiscal 1981), but it represented a cut in the rate at which the budget had grown in previous years. On the expenditure side, Reagan secured cutbacks in several social programs and large increases in the defense budget. In regard to taxation, the administration got Congress to agree to a very large 25 percent cut in income taxes over a thirty-three-month period.

Critics of Reagan's program contended that far too much was spent, and actually wasted, on national defense. Reagan, it was argued, never met a weapon system he didn't like. Another general complaint was that the budget benefited the rich at the expense of the middle class and the poor. Though Reagan argued that he had retained a "safety net" of programs for the "truly needy," most of the budget cuts did come from programs benefiting low-income people. Critics of cuts in education, job training, day care and other social-service programs argued that these cuts brought about only false economies and reflected the failure of the president to see the importance of investing in the human capital necessary for the future of the nation.

On the taxation side, it is clear that those in the highest income brackets benefited the most from the income tax reforms made early in the Reagan administration. This advantage was defended on the grounds that the wealthy

---

[8] "Overheard," *Newsweek* (April 13, 1987): 19.

would be more likely than others to invest their tax savings in projects that would improve the nation's general economic productivity. This notion, central to Reagan's "supply-side" economics, was considered by critics inside and outside of government to be nothing more than a new version of "trickle-down" economics. The notion that tax benefits to the rich would ultimately trickle down to the more needy was to critics such as Congressman Benjamin Rosenthal of New York "a little like saying, if there's more cake for the few, there'll be more crumbs for the many."[9]

A more widely shared criticism of Reagan's economic program was that large budget deficits resulted from his deep cuts in taxes and large increases in military spending (deficits and the national debt are discussed at the end of the chapter). For some time the administration argued that the debt problem would disappear with increased economic prosperity. But the national debt continued to increase, despite general prosperity, pressure to require the national government to balance its budget also continued. This led to the adoption in 1985 of the Balanced Budget and Emergency Deficit Control Act. Commonly known as the Gramm-Rudman act, the measure aimed for a balanced budget by 1991 through certain annual reductions in the deficit. The act empowered the General Accounting Office to order across-the-board reductions if the debt-cutting targets for any given year could not be achieved through the normal budgeting process. Shifting the work of budget cuts to a relatively obscure administrative agency would have helped the legislators normally responsible for that task to avoid criticism for unpopular decisions. The Supreme Court, however, has determined that Congress cannot delegate such power to the GAO. In effect, this means that all spending cuts have to be voted upon by Congress and approved by the president. Without the automatic across-the-board feature, Gramm-Rudman has been largely only symbolic in nature.

Tax Reform

Over the years, Congress, often responding to presidential initiatives, has experimented with various types of tax reform. Sometimes, emphasis has been on increasing revenue. At other times, concern has been with making adjustments that would stimulate economic activity or make the tax system fairer or less complicated. Members of Congress have been pressured from individual constitutents and local business interests who want particular exemptions or are fearful of losing existing advantages. Tax policy, as it has been hammered out, has generally been a matter of adjustment, bargaining, compromise, and shifting political objectives rather than consistently applied economic theory.[10]

---

[9] Quoted in *Congressional Record*, May 13, 1981, p. E2331.

[10] See John F. Witte, *The Politics and Development of the Federal Income Tax* (Madison: University of Wisconsin Press, 1985).

In the early 1980s, the Reagan administration and several members of Congress expressed an interest in tax reform designed, in large part, to make the system simpler and fairer. By the 1980s, it was quite apparent that a number of loopholes and special exemptions had made the individual income tax far less progressive than appeared to be the case. There was also considerable discontent with a corporate income law that had permitted so many deductions that many of the most prosperous corporations paid no taxes at all. As a broad reform, several members of Congress advanced the notion of a general or flat or proportional tax that would tax everyone at the same percentage and the elimination of virtually all special deductions.

The upshot of all this activity was the Tax Reform Act of 1986. This legislation, which took two years to get through Congress, generally lowered rates, eliminated many loopholes, and shifted more of the taxation burden from individuals to businesses. The bill was viewed by its sponsors as "revenue neutral" in that it would not bring in more revenue but simply shift the burden. As might be expected, particular reforms had their critics. Some felt, for example, that elimination of various tax shelters for businesses would discourage investment and trigger an economic slowdown.

WHO BENEFITS? WHO PAYS?

In recent years, payments to individuals have constituted the largest category of national expenditures (see Table 10–2).[11] This category includes social security, medicare (a health insurance program for the elderly), unemployment compensation, public assistance, and other social programs. Payments to individuals accounted for about 45 percent of the federal budget in 1986. Social security, the major component of this category, accounted for 20 percent of total spending. In comparison, national defense made up 28 percent, interest on the national debt, 14 percent, and grants to state and local governments, about 6 percent. A major trend during the 1980s, reflecting the priorities of the Reagan administration, has been an increase in the percentage devoted to national defense and decreases in various programs in the payments-to-individuals category (other than social security) and grant programs to state and local governments. Increasing in rather dramatic fashion has been interest payments on debt (from 8 to 14 percent of total spending 1978).

Looking at expenditures on a department-by-department basis for 1986 (Table 10–3), we find Health and Human Services, which administers social

---

[11] Expenditure categories found in official budget documents are commonly controversial. For example, considerable debate has taken place over which expenditures should be included under headings such as national defense and welfare. See James L. Clayton, "The Fiscal Limits of the Warfare-Welfare State: Defense and Welfare Spending in the United States Since 1900," *Western Political Quarterly* 29 (September 1976): 364–383.

Table 10–2 Expenditures of the National Government (Percentages of Total Expenditures)

	PAYMENTS FOR INDIVIDUALS	NATIONAL DEFENSE	GRANTS TO STATES AND LOCALITIES*	NET INTEREST
1978	46	23	12	8
1979	46	23	11	8
1980	47	23	9	9
1981	48	23	9	10
1982	48	25	7	11
1983	49	26	6	11
1984	47	27	6	13
1985	45	27	6	14
1986	45	28	6	14

* Excluding grants for payments to individuals.

Data source: Executive Office of the President, Office of Management and Budget, *The United States Budget in Brief, Fiscal Year, 1988*. (Washington, D.C.: Government Printing Office, 1987), pp. 98–101.

security programs, heading the list. It is followed by the Defense Department and the Treasury Department (the latter has charge of paying interest on the debt). While one might conclude from this that the United States government has been generous in regard to social welfare, it should be noted that by comparison with most countries in western Europe, governments in the United States (including state and local units) spend relatively little on programs of this

Table 10–3 Employment and Expenditures of Departments and Major Agencies, 1986

	EMPLOYMENT	EXPENDITURES*
Agriculture	102,997	58.7
Commerce	32,321	2.1
Defense	1,069,863	285.9
Education	4,526	17.7
Energy	16,193	11.0
Health and Human Services	128,105	334.0
Housing and Urban Development	11,720	14.1
Interior	70,657	4.8
Justice	63,307	3.8
Labor	17,931	24.1
State	25,261	2.9
Transportation	60,375	27.4
Treasury	130,845	179.2
Environmental Protection Agency	12,931	4.9
National Aeronautics and Space Administration	21,660	7.4
Veterans Administration	220,642	26.5

* In billions of dollars.

Data source: Executive Office of the President, Office of Management and Budget, *The United States Budget in Brief, Fiscal Year 1988* (Washington, D.C., Government Printing Office, 1987), pp. 109, 113.

Table 10–4 Revenue Sources of the National Government (Percentages of Total Revenues)*

	INDIVIDUAL INCOME TAXES	CORPORATE INCOME TAXES	SOCIAL SECURITY RECEIPTS	EXCISE TAXES	BORROWING	OTHER SOURCES
1978	39	13	26	4	13	4
1979	43	13	28	4	8	4
1980	41	11	27	4	12	4
1981	42	9	27	6	12	4
1982	40	7	27	5	17	4
1983	36	5	26	4	26	4
1984	35	7	28	4	22	4
1985	35	6	28	4	22	4
1986	35	6	29	3	22	4

* Percentages may not total 100 because of rounding.

Data source: Executive Office of the President, Office of Management and Budget, *The United States Budget in Brief, Fiscal Year, 1988* (Washington, D.C.: Government Printing Office, 1987), pp. 100, 114.

nature. In comparison to other nations, moreover, the United States generally has spent a higher percentage of its wealth for national defense.[12]

On the income side, the largest source of federal revenue has been the income tax on individuals, which currently supplies about 35 percent of the total (Table 10–4). Other significant revenue producers have been social security insurance taxes, now at 29 percent of total revenue, and corporate income taxes. The latter declined from 13 percent of the total in 1970 to 6 percent in 1986 in part as a result of the Reagan administration's effort to stimulate the economy by providing tax incentives for business. Corporate income taxes, however, as noted earlier, were increased by tax reform legislation adopted late in 1986.

A commonly used standard of fairness of taxation is that each person should contribute according to his or her ability to pay. This standard is met by progressive taxes, which take a higher percentage of the income of the rich than of the poor. Regressive taxes, on the contrary, take a higher percentage of the income of the poor than of the rich.

The major income producer at the national level, the individual income tax, is progressive, though only moderately so. Despite considerable reform in recent years, there are still a number of loopholes and special deductions that make the tax less progressive than it might be. Deductions designed to encourage home ownership and the purchase of state and local bonds, for example, have generally been of greatest benefit to those in high-income brackets. Some economists consider special deductions to be "tax expenditures" that result in a loss of revenue that the government must make up by taking more from others.

[12] Ibid, pp. 375–378. See also Central Intelligence Agency, *Handbook of Economic Statistics* (Washington, D.C., Government Printing Office, 1985), p. 47.

Sales and property taxes, the major sources of tax revenue for state and local governments, are regressive. Social security taxes also are regressive because they do not apply to income other than wages and because there is a limit on the amount of income subject to social security taxation.

In addition to taxation, the national government finances a good part of its activity (some 20 percent of all expenditures in recent years) by borrowing. This is done primarily by selling Treasury notes and bonds to the public and to private institutions. Congress has placed a ceiling on how much debt the nation can incur, but the ceiling has been raised regularly. From 1980 to 1985, the national debt doubled from $914 billion to some $1,841 billion ($1.8 trillion), causing intense concern with balancing the budget. As suggested above, debt increases over the 1980s resulted in large part from the unwillingness of President Reagan to raise taxes or reduce defense expenditures and the unwillingness of Congress to reduce domestic expenditures to the extent proposed by the President. Many economists consider large deficits bad because government must compete with private businesses for limited funds, and this competition pushes up interest rates. High interest rates, in turn, contribute to recessions and unemployment. These problems are discussed in the following chapter.

SUMMARY

1. Government expenditures since the 1930s have grown per capita and as a percentage of the gross national product. Still, questions concerning the proper allocation of the nation's wealth between the private and public sectors have not been resolved. The allocation of funding responsibilities among levels of government and the distribution of funds among various programs are also subjects of ongoing debate.

2. Alongside the various pressures to increase spending are pressures to keep taxes at a politically safe level. This dilemma has led to some hard choices in setting spending priorities.

3. Historically, budget makers have given their primary attention to requests for unusually large increases in expenditures and have allowed ongoing programs to grow by small increments.

4. In recent years both presidents and members of Congress have attempted to limit federal spending and taxing. The most spectacular success in these areas came early in the Reagan administration, although cuts in social welfare spending were offset by increases in defense spending.

5. Along with taxation the national government finances its activities by borrowing. Great increases in the national debt during the 1980s have brought considerable pressure for a balanced budget.

GOVERNMENT, POLITICS, AND THE ECONOMY

The notion that government should have little if anything to do with the economy is widely held in the United States. Yet in fact, there is a long tradition of government involvement in the economy. Government in the United States has been deeply involved in attempting to (1) manage the economy in order to cope with macroeconomic problems such as unemployment and inflation; (2) stimulate or protect various industries or segments of the economy; (3) control adverse spillovers (by-products) of economic activity, such as air and water pollution; and (4) resolve difficulties concerning the level and distribution of income. We examine these problems and activities in this chapter.

MANAGING THE ECONOMY

At the height of the 1930s depression close to a quarter of the work force in the United States was unemployed. President Franklin Roosevelt told Congress in his second inaugural address (1937); "I see one-third of the nation ill-housed, ill-clad, ill-nourished." Several others saw that social discontent threatened the survival of the economic and political system. Nearly forty years later President Gerald Ford told the Grocery Manufacturers of America;

> There remains a deep and pervasive anxiety about rising food prices. We do not need to consult the psychologists to learn that the problem of feeding one's self and one's family through the ages has been the source of such emotionalism that governments have been toppled and political systems changed.[1]

Achieving economic stability has been a primary concern of federal officials, especially presidents, since the 1930s. This goal has been variously defined as overcoming "boom–bust" fluctuations in the business cycle, maintaining high levels of economic growth, preventing inflation (increases in the general level of prices), and striving for high levels of employment. Under the Employment Act of 1946 the national government is committed to promoting maximum employment, production, and purchasing power.[2]

Inflation and Unemployment

The most visible economic difficulties have been inflation and unemployment. Economists and public officials have found these two problems to be inversely related: to stem inflation the nation must endure relatively high levels

---

[1] Remarks printed in the *Congressional Record*, July 17, 1974, p. H6692.

[2] The act created a three-member Council of Economic Advisers to collect and examine data on economic trends and to advise the president. The act also requires the president to give annual economic report to Congress, and it established the Joint Economic Committee in Congress to consider the president's recommendations for legislative action. On the background of the act, see Stephen K. Bailey, *Congress Makes a Law: The Story Behind the Employment Act of 1946* (New York: Columbia University Press, 1950).

of unemployment; conversely, to achieve high levels of employment it must tolerate relatively high levels of inflation. The goal has been to achieve the best possible balance between inflation and unemployment.

In keeping track of inflation policy makers use key indicators such as the Consumer Price Index and the Wholesale Price Index prepared by the Bureau of Labor Statistics of the U.S. Department of Labor. These figures, which are based on the wholesale and retail prices for a number of commodities, suggest that there has been a dramatic rate of inflation since the late 1960s, though increases have been relatively slight in the 1980s.

The major effect of inflation may be to redistribute income and wealth.[3] Thus, while inflation may bring increased profits for some, it may also diminish the relative income of others. Although it is difficult to tell who is hurt the most by inflation, two groups are particularly hard hit—persons whose incomes are fixed or lag behind price increases and creditors to whom debts may be paid with money worth considerably less than when the obligation was made. The effects of inflation on income are partially offset by governmental taxes, regulations, and programs such as social security.

Each month the Bureau of Labor Statistics takes a sample of households in various areas of the country and uses these data to estimate the percentage of the labor force that is unemployed. For the purposes of data collection, people under sixteen, retirees, and others not looking for work are not included in the total labor force.

At any given time a certain percentage of those in the labor force will be seeking employment, some for the first time and some after an absence from the work force. Full employment or zero unemployment is therefore impossible. Economists have generally estimated that the "full employment" level is reached when 4 percent or less of the labor force is seeking jobs. Some economists, however, argue that the level should be put as high as 6 percent. Since the mid 1970s the unemployment rate has usually ranged between 6 and 8 percent. A major factor in this rate has been the rapid growth in the total labor force, which has resulted largely from an increase in the number of women and teenagers looking for work. Many of those seeking jobs have been able to find them. Indeed, more people were employed in the mid 1980s than ever before. At the same time, the unemployment rate has risen and blacks, Hispanics, women, and the young have had greater difficulty than others in finding work.

People worry about losing their jobs and tend to blame those in power when their sense of security is threatened by increases in the unemployment rate.[4] Thus, it is not so much the rate of unemployment that concerns politicians

---

[3] See G. L. Bach, "The Economic Effects of Inflation," in C. Lowell Harris (ed.), *Inflation: Long-Term Problems* (New York: Academy of Political Science, 1975), pp. 20–33.

[4] D. Roderick Kiewiet, *Macroeconomics and Micropolitics: The Electoral Effects of Economic Issues* (Chicago: University of Chicago Press, 1983).

as it is the direction of the rate—that is, whether it is going up or down. For those seeking reelection, "10 precent unemployment coming down is better than 6 percent unemployment going up."[5]

Worry over inflation and unemployment cuts across ideological and party lines. Even the most conservative anti–big government members of Congress are likely to vote for a public works bill if it will provide badly needed jobs for their constituents. Generally, however, Democratics have been more likely than Republicans to give priority to the unemployment problem over the inflation problem. This preference has been illustrated by the policies of Democratic presidents since World War II, though less so in the early years of the Carter administration than, for example, in the Kennedy and Johnson years. Concern with inflation was particularly evident in Republican administrations under Eisenhower, Nixon, Ford, and Reagan. Research has linked the economic policies pursued by Democratic and Republican presidents to the class composition of their parties: Democratic policies are thought to reflect the worries of low- and middle-income groups over unemployment while Republican policies mirror the anxiety of upper-income groups over inflation.[6]

Monetary and Fiscal Policies

The two major methods of managing the economy have involved the adoption of monetary or fiscal policies. *Monetary policies* affect the supply of money and the interest rate at which banks make loans. Control over national monetary policy has been vested in the Federal Reserve Board, an independent agency with close ties to the banking community. Through various devices the Federal Reserve Board can, for example, either cause an increase in interest rates in an attempt to slow borrowing or reduce interest rates in an effort to stimulate borrowing and economic activity. Board views on the needs of the economy have often conflicted with those of the president, Congress, or both. Since the 1950s this agency has often strongly championed antiinflationary moves and has openly criticized presidential and congressional policies it considers to be opposed to this objective.

Fiscal policy involves the use of governmental taxing and spending to influence economic conditions. Fiscal theory is commonly associated with British economist John Maynard Keynes and his book *The General Theory of Employment, Interest and Money* (1936). According to this theory, increased governmental spending, governmental tax cuts, or both will heighten demand for goods and services, increased employment, and pull a nation out of a general recession. To "cool down" the economy or reduce inflation government should do the

[5] James P. Gannon, "Unemployment as a Political Issue," *Wall Street Journal,* February 12, 1976, p. 12.

[6] See Douglas A. Hibbs, Jr., "Political Parties and Macroeconomic Policy," *American Political Science Review* 71 (December 1977): 1467–1487.

opposite—decrease spending, raise taxes, or both. To overcome a recession, government moves toward a budget deficit (spending more than it receives in taxes), and in fighting inflation it strives for a budget surplus (spending less than it takes in through taxation).

Some economic devices automatically operate in the direction of a budget deficit or surplus. One such *automatic stabilizer* is the U.S. income tax, which takes in more revenue as the national income increases (thus cooling the economy) and loses revenue as the national income decreases (thus helping to stimulate the economy). Another is unemployment compensation, which increases government spending in recessions and decreases spending when the economy is active. Other taxing and spending decisions intended to stabilize the economy are made at the discretion of Congress.

Political conflict over the use of monetary and fiscal policies takes place along on several lines.[7] Conflict occurs, for example, over which policy should be primarily relied upon to bring stability. This debate, as just suggested, has often focused on the policies employed by the Federal Reserve Board. On an ideological level conservatives have tended to favor monetary policy because it supposedly involves less governmental intervention in the economy than fiscal policy. They also object to the use of fiscal policy on the grounds that government should live within its means, not spending more than it takes in through taxes, and should avoid budget deficits. The belief in the virtue of a balanced budget appears to be widely shared in the United States. Though not strong enough to prevent deficit spending or unbalanced budgets, this belief has made it more difficult to implement fiscal policy fully. For instance, even if the economy may appear to need stimulation through increased spending and lower taxes, the fear that expenditures and revenues will get too far out of line may force policy makers into a compromise solution such as a tax cut with a promise to hold down expenditures. Such promises were made by Presidents Kennedy and Johnson to secure congressional approval of tax-reduction plans.

Assuming that policy makers agree that fiscal policies are to be used, they are apt to disagree over the amount of increased or decreased expenditures needed and over what specific expenditures are to be increased or decreased. Similarly, controversy is likely over the amount of a tax increase or decrease and over who should pay and who should benefit by the tax changes. As we saw in the previous chapter, a dominant norm of taxation has been that it should be progressive, taking a higher percentage of a rich person's income than of a poor individual's income. Acceptance of this norm works against tax breaks for those in the upper-income groups. Yet, while such ethical considerations play a role in tax policy, they have also been balanced against economic considerations. Thus, as was true in the Kennedy and Johnson years as well as under Reagan, tax

[7] See James E. Anderson, *Politics and the Economy* (Boston: Little, Brown, 1966), pp. 102–122.

breaks for the wealthy may be favored on the grounds that their spending (especially in terms of increased investment) is likely to be a greater stimulus to the economy than spending by lower-income groups.

Disagreement also takes place over the particular needs of the nation at any given time. Some policy makers may feel that the government should reduce interest rates, lower taxes, and increase spending to further the goal of full employment. Others may feel that the problem is inflation and that interest rates and taxes should be raised and government spending reduced. This conflict has been particularly apparent since the early 1970s, when the nation became vulnerable to both high inflation and high unemployment, a combination known as *stagflation*. During the mid 1970s disagreement over which of the two problems was more important led to considerable conflict between Republican presidents and the Democrat-controlled Congress. The former commonly vetoed proposed legislation (usually social programs) on the basis that it would contribute to inflation.

Both monetary and fiscal policies are inherently limited in their ability to control inflation and unemployment. Even if the political obstacles just noted were overcome, full use of monetary or fiscal policies to increase employment might produce more inflation and a concentrated assault on inflation might produce unbearable levels of unemployment. Other problems in the use of the two policies are (1) predicting levels of economic activity so that the proper remedy (stimulant or depressant) will be applied, and (2) evaluating the impact of the action taken—for example, whether it is a tax cut or some other factor that leads to more consumer and business spending. Policy makers have no assurance that individuals or businesses will act as they should under the proper incentives—that they will, say, spend more for goods and services if they pay less in taxes, or borrow more if interest rates are lower.

Other Policies and Approaches

The national government has a number of other ways to influence economic conditions. For instance, it may place controls on the price of specific commodities, such as oil. It may lift import quotas to permit the entry of more and lower-priced goods, encourage or discourage food production through taxing and price-support policies, and use antitrust laws to increase economic competition and thus bring reductions in the prices of certain goods and services. Antitrust laws can be used to (1) break up companies that dominate a market and thus are able to set prices for a product or a service, and (2) end agreements among independent firms that have the effect of fixing the price of products or services. Price-fixing and similar cases have been more popular than antimonopoly cases among those who enforce antitrust laws because they are easier to prove, less expensive, and more popular with the public. Some administrations, such as that of Ronald Reagan, have avoided antimonopoly cases in the belief that large corporations bring many benefits to the economy, such as greater efficiency.

According to federal statistics, there are a number of *shared monopolies* in the United States—monopolies in which no more than four firms control at least half of the production of a particular good. Shared monopolies make such commonly purchased items as automobiles, cigarettes, and breakfast cereals. They also produce steel and aluminum. The Federal Trade Commission has estimated that if such highly concentrated industries were broken up the prices of their products would fall by at least 25 percent.

From time to time Congress has empowered the president to impose general wage and price controls such as those President Nixon ordered in the early 1970s. There are, however, problems in securing compliance with these controls (especially those on prices), not to mention the possibility that price controls will cause product scarcity. The latter comes about as production is limited or products are withheld from the market by those who seek prices higher than those established by law. The lifting of controls, moreover, is likely to be followed by rapid increases in wages and prices.

Rather than implement formal controls, the president may use publicity and the resources of his office, such as the power to initiate antitrust action, to "jawbone" unions and industries to keep wage and price hikes at a minimum. Both Presidents Kennedy and Carter, for example, used these techniques to force back proposed increases in the cost of steel.

Traditional policies directed at unemployment have provided aid such as workers' compensation to people seeking work. Since the 1960s there has been an emphasis on job training programs. The national government has also adopted a number of programs aimed at creating more jobs in the public and private sectors. Some conservative economists contend that government policies have contributed to the "jobs problem." They argue, for example, that workers' compensation not only aids people while they seek work but makes it easier for them to avoid seeking work. Others claim that minimum-wage legislation is a factor in teenage unemployment. Under the existing system, they contend, employers hire older, more experienced workers because younger workers would cost them just as much. Critics respond that to abolish the minimum wage or to establish lower minimum wages for youths than for adults would encourage industries to fire adults and hire youths for lower wages.

PROMOTING AND REGULATING ECONOMIC ACTIVITIES

Promotion and Protection

As we saw in Chapter 2, the goal of developing a national economy is reflected in the Constitution. The Constitution gives Congress broad power to regulate commerce among the states, the exclusive rights to coin and print money, the authority to establish a common system of weights and measures, and the responsibilities of protecting patents and copyrights.

Since the framing of the Constitution various industries or segments of the economy have been given various special benefits. These have included tariffs to protect domestic businesses from foreign competition, favorable tax laws, government contracts, technical assistance, and direct monetary subsidies (sometimes known facetiously as "aid to dependent corporations").

These promotional policies have been defended on the grounds that the health of the affected business or industry is vital to the general economic prosperity or the national defense. Such justifications have, for example, long been cited as reasons for giving aid to nearly every segment of the transportation industry. Railroads have benefited from land grants and mail subsidies. Truckers have profited from highway expenditures, and privately owned airlines (in nearly every other country the major airlines are publicly owned) have obtained direct monetary subsidies, payments for carrying the mail, and airports. For private water carriers there have been river and harbor improvements, navigational aids (shipping terminals, lighthouses), and huge subsidies for ship construction to help U.S. vessels compete with foreign ones.

Over the years several large corporations have sought special assistance from the national government. One of the most celebrated cases involved the Penn Central Railroad, created in 1968 through a merger of the Pennsylvania and New York Central railroads. Some unusually imaginative accounting hid Penn Central's financial troubles from its board of directors and stockholders until the mid 1970s, when the corporation asked the national government to guarantee loans it was seeking. The government refused, and Penn Central went bankrupt (it later reorganized). The following year, however, Congress did pass a loan-guarantee program to assist the Lockheed Corporation, which had been facing financial losses largely because of cost overruns on defense contracts. The company eventually repaid its loan.

A dramatic corporate bailout came in December 1979, when the Chrysler Corporation received $1.5 billion in federal loan guarantees on condition that it come up with $2 billion in private concessions from bankers, suppliers, state and local governments, and workers (the last-named were to give up negotiated wage gains). Chrysler's request for aid was opposed by some unlikely allies. Both consumerist Ralph Nader and conservative economist Milton Friedman, for example, agreed that the corporation should fend for itself. So did representation of some Chrysler competitors, such as the chairman of General Motors. Allied with Chrysler was a lobby composed of the United Automobile Workers, dealers, and suppliers who did business with the corporation.

Critics of the aid proposal contended that Chrysler had caused its own problems by, for example, failing to update its facilities or to design cars that would compete effectively in the marketplace. More broadly, it was argued that government should not, as a matter of general policy, guarantee any corporation against failure or protect business people against their own incompetence. Chrysler responded that the national government was mostly to blame for the company's troubles because it had overzealously imposed automobile emission and fuel-economy standards. These regulations, Chrysler argued, hurt it more than they did Ford and General Motors—larger companies that could more easily absorb the financial costs of meeting the standards. Proponents of aid also contended that it was needed to prevent the loss of 500,000 jobs, many of which were held by blacks and other minorities who lived in distressed inner-city areas. These arguments and, in the opinion of many observers, the desire in Congress and the Carter White House to avoid economic disruptions during the upcoming election resolved the aid issue in the corporation's favor.

Although politicians have differed over many regulatory matters, there has been a consensus since the 1970s that several "regulatory" programs for specific industries serve only limited interests rather than those of the public. As former Federal Trade Commission chairman Lewis Engman stated,

> we get irate about welfare fraud. But our complex systems of regulatory subsidies make welfare fraud look like petty larceny. . . . The fact of the matter is that most regulated industries have become Federal Protectorates, living in the cozy world of cost-plus, safely protected from the ugly specters of competition, efficiency, and innovation.[8]

Such charges have brought about a reduction in agency control of various aspects of the economy since the 1970s. Some of the earliest deregulation measures came in the area of transportation: the Interstate Commerce Commission and the Civil Aeronautics Board lost their power to regulate rates, routes, and mergers. The evidence is not yet complete, but it appears that in the short run, at least, deregulation in the airline industry has brought increased competition and in turn increased efficiency and a general downward pressure on air fares. There is some indication, however, that increased competition and cost cutting have created safety problems in terms of pilot training and aircraft maintenance. From the government's viewpoint, airline deregulation may necessitate more safety inspectors and more and better-qualified air-traffic controllers.

Regulation

While there are a number of government programs designed to stimulate or protect particular industries, there are also programs intended to protect the public from the effects of certain activities. Some of the more important of the latter programs are concerned with environmental protection.

Until the 1970s environmental problems such as air and water pollution were considered the responsibility mainly of state and local governments. These

---

[8] From an address reprinted in *Congressional Record* January 28, 1975, p. E209.

governments, however, were unable or unwilling to do much about these problems. Historically, the states have been reluctant to impose rigid pollution controls, fearing that their industries would close down or move to other states. Many communities have also feared the effect pollution controls might have on their economies.

The National Environmental Policy Act of 1970 committed the national government to protect and enhance the quality of the environment. The law established the Council on Environmental Quality and charged it with preparing studies, advising the president, and working with other federal agencies on environmental matters. The act also requires federal agencies to prepare environmental-impact statements for any activity likely to have a significant impact on the environment. In practice, agencies have discretion in determining whether a statement is needed for a particular project, though their refusal to prepare one may be challenged in court. The impact-statement requirement was adopted out of the fear that agencies would not willingly implement the goals of the National Environmental Policy Act. The requirement ensure that administrative decision making was hoped, would take account of environmental factors.

Much of the responsibility for combating pollution has been taken on by the National Environmental Protection Agency, which was established in 1970. The EPA is primarily a regulatory agency authorized to develop standards for air and water quality, solid-waste disposal, radiation, noise, and pesticides. Since the 1980s the agency has also been trying to control toxic wastes. Publicity growing out of the Love Canal disaster—which involved the discovery that the health of the people in that community was jeopardized because their homes had been built on a dump site for chemical wastes—prompted Congress to establish a Superfund for cleaning up toxic-waste sites.

Air and water pollution and other environmental problems have generally eased since the early 1970s, although not always to the extent contemplated by the authors of environmental laws. Progress has been impeded somewhat by political, economic, and technological problems. Politically, the EPA's attempts to implement antipollution laws have varied with national administrators. Created in the Nixon era, the agency got off to a strong start but later encountered resistance and under Reagan lost much of its enthusiasm. At any given time, the agency is likely to encounter the resistance of state and local governments, industrial polluters, and economic conservatives who feel that controls are hurting economic productivity. The problem of getting the states to carry out national pollution-control standards has been handled by bargaining, compromise, and the extension of deadlines for state compliance.

With the election of conservative Ronald Reagan in 1980, the EPA and agencies such as the Occupational Safety and Health Administration and the Consumer Product Safety Commission appeared destined for curtailment on the grounds that they had imposed regulations overzealously, harassed industry, and increased costs for business and consumer alike. These agencies were not abolished but rather "turned around" by budget cuts and the appointment of agency personnel who shared the president's concerns. This dismantling of regulatory protections was criticized for, among other things, endangering consumers, workers, and public health.[9]

Evaluations of Regulation

The system of economic regulation in this country has long been the subject of intense criticism and debate. Regulatory agencies have been criticized by conservatives as being uncontrollable monsters that threaten the civil liberties of business people and the proper functioning of the economic system. But conservatives have also depicted regulatory agencies as inefficient, bungling bureaucracies that do little more than waste taxpayer money. Liberals have often been enthusiastic over new regulatory agencies but disappointed with their performance. To many liberals, regulatory agencies become the captives of the regulated and thus lose their willingness to pursue their public-interest obligations.

Compared with programs such as social security, regulation does not call for vast public expenditures. Yet critics have contended that many regulations, like governmental spending, contribute to inflation. This, it is charged, is largely because the regulated industries or professions use government to restrict competition and can pass the cost of complying with regulations, such as automobile safety standards, along to consumers in the form of higher prices.

Governmental regulation has also been ideologically controversial because it raises questions concerning the proper role of government in the economy. Conservative "free-enterprise" economic policy has generally called for government to keep its hands off economic activity. To economic conservatives "liberty" requires the absence of governmental restraints on an entrepreneur's use of his or her property; the same protections against regulation are to be given to corporations. The pursuit of business profits, moreover, is seen by economic conservatives as being in the best interest of the public. A common version of this theme is "What is good for business is good for the country." Liberals or progressives are more likely than conservatives to seek restrictions on the rights of business people or corporations in order to protect what they believe are the important rights of workers, consumers, and the public.

POVERTY AND THE POLITICS OF REDISTRIBUTION

The Poverty Problem

The United States, with only about 6 percent of the world's population, has about 23 percent of the world's wealth, as measured by the gross national

---

[9] Susan J. Tolchin and Martin Tolchin, *Dismantling America: The Rush to Deregulate* (Boston: Houghton Mifflin, 1983).

product of the nations of the world. Within the United States, however, there is considerable variation in income. Indeed, during the early 1980s statistics revealed both increasing affluence and rising poverty. Thus, there was a rise in the number of families making more than $50,000 per year and a rise in the number of families earning less than $10,000 a year. At the extremes, there were more millionaires than ever and, living in emergency shelters or on the streets, an estimated 3 million people without homes. As the number of rich and the number of poor have increased the middle class, customarily seen as the backbone of a stable society, has decreased.

Nearly 14 percent of the nation's population, or about 34 million people, live below the poverty level defined by the Social Security Administration. In 1985 the poverty level for a family of three in an urban area was set at $8,850. Such families earning less than this amount were classified as poor. By this measurement poverty has been greater among nonwhites than whites, greater among female-headed families than male-headed families, greater among rural inhabitants than urban residents, and greater among people in central cities than those in suburbs. The most dramatic poverty trend in recent years has been the feminization of poverty—the growth in the number of female-headed households classified as poor. For many women, poverty appears to be "only a divorce away."

Measuring poverty by an absolute standard—that is, declaring people to be poor if their income fails to reach a certain level, is merely one way of looking at the problem. A more meaningful approach is to consider poverty as a feeling of relative deprivation. In this sense some individuals who are poor by Social Security Administration standards may not consider themselves poor because they are wealthier than most other people they know. At the same time, people above the poverty line may regard themselves as poor if they do not have as much money or as many material goods as others. The distinction between absolute and relative poverty is most significant when attempts are made to remedy poverty. Absolute poverty can be overcome by raising the income of the poor above a specific level. Relative poverty, however, can be surmounted only by a redistribution of wealth. Somewhat surprisingly, survey research suggests that some 60 percent of the American people in the mid 1980s believes that this country's wealth should be more evenly distributed. Not surprisingly, those in the highest income groups showed the least enthusiasm for this idea.[10]

Though blacks have made significant income advances since the 1960s, they continue to lag behind whites in most economic areas. The average black family earns about 60 percent as much as the average white family. The jobless rate for blacks is nearly double that for whites. Blacks comprise about 11 percent of the population but account for approximately 30 percent of all persons below the poverty line and make about 40 percent of all food-stamp purchases. Many

[10] *Gallup Poll Index*, March 1985, p. 25.

of the income and quality-of-life problems faced by black Americans are also encountered by Spanish-speaking minorities (Hispanics or Latinos) and American Indians.

The plight of these minorities has generally been attributed to a long history of economic, political, and social discrimination and to problems that can be reduced by such reforms as improved education, job training, housing, and neighborhood conditions. Some observers, however, contend that such programs are unlikely to do much good because many of the poor and nonwhite supposedly do not choose to improve themselves. Political scientist Edward Banfield, for instance, claims that many of the disadvantaged whites as well as nonwhites, are trapped in a lower-class subculture that emphasis satisfying immediate needs rather than planning for the future.[11] The American public seems equally divided between lack of effort on the one hand and circumstances on the other as the explanation for poverty (see Table 11-1). Republicans and Democrats appear to be particularly divided over this issue, as the former opting for effort and the latter, circumstances.

Growth of the Federal Role in Public Assistance

Up to the 1930s local governments and private charities assumed most of the responsibility for aiding the poor. During the nineteenth century local governmental aid consisted largely of institutional care for the needy, such as orphanages for destitute children, workhouses for the able-bodied poor, and poorhouses for those unable to work. Residency requirements for aid were imposed by each local jurisdiction so that care would not be given to people who lived in other areas. Meanwhile, private charities assumed the tasks of supporting the needy with food, clothing, and shelter. During the late nineteenth and early twentieth centuries political party "machines" in large cities provided numerous charitable services to newly arrived and impoverished immigrants (who also had private social-service organizations in their own communities). Although political parties offered welfare services in exchange for votes, they provided these services on a more personal basis and with considerably less red tape than the large welfare bureaucracies that replaced them.

Until the early 1930s, the federal government played only a minimal role in helping the needy. Then, under pressure generated by the depression, it began various public employment programs, such as those administered by the Works Progress Administration (WPA) and the Civilian Conservation Corps (CCC), and adopted the Social Security Act of 1935, which has been amended several times over the years.

During the 1960s President Lyndon Johnson called for a War on Poverty, wishing to attack the causes of poverty rather than simply providing

---

[11] See Edward C. Banfield, *The Unheavenly City Revisited* (Boston: Little, Brown, 1974).

Table 11–1 Blame for Poverty

QUESTION: In your opinion, which is more often to blame if a person is poor, lack of effort on his own part or circumstances beyond his control?

	DECEMBER 7–10, 1984				
	LACK OF EFFORT	CIRCUMSTANCES	BOTH (VOL.)	NO OPINION	NUMBER OF INTERVIEWS
National	33%	34%	31%	2%	1,505
Sex					
Men	36	31	30	3	747
Women	29	37	31	3	758
Age					
Total under 30	28	37	32	3	306
18-24 years	25	34	36	5	152
25-29 years	33	41	26	*	154
30-49 years	34	34	30	2	576
Total 50 and older	34	33	31	2	618
50-64 years	34	34	30	2	342
65 and older	34	32	32	2	276
Region					
East	28	39	29	4	383
Midwest	33	35	31	1	395
South	34	31	32	3	438
West	36	33	30	1	289
Race					
Whites	35	30	33	2	1,318
Nonwhites	16	64	17	3	187
Blacks	15	67	16	2	153
Hispanics	11	44	38	7	68
Education					
College graduates	35	30	34	1	284
College incomplete	32	34	32	2	401
High school graduates	34	34	29	3	501
Less than high school graduates	29	38	30	3	315
Politics					
Republicans	45	20	32	3	483
Democrats	24	48	26	2	553
Independents	29	32	35	4	420
Occupation					
Professional and business	36	32	31	1	440
Clerical and sales	41	36	23	*	108
Manual workers	29	36	31	4	548
Nonlabor force	31	37	31	4	325
Income					
$40,000 and over	39	26	34	1	236
$30,000-$39,999	42	27	29	2	203
$20,000-$29,999	33	36	30	1	284
$10,000-$19,999	27	38	32	3	449
Under $10,000	29	41	26	4	249
Religion					
Protestants	35	33	30	2	889
Catholics	29	36	32	3	398
Labor Union					
Labor union families	30	36	33	1	298
Non labor union families	33	34	30	3	1,207

*Less than 1%.

Source: *Gallup Report* (March 1985), p. 24. Reprinted with permission.

assistance to those who happened to be in need. In actuality the War on Poverty also included medical care and educational programs for those thought to need them. The Economic Opportunity Act of 1964 established a number of other programs, such as the Jobs Corps to provide training for disadvantaged youths; Volunteers in Service to America (VISTA) to combat community poverty; a work-study program to give low-income students employment; and a legal-services program for the poor. This law also led to the establishment of local community-action agencies throughout the country. At least a third of the membership of the governing boards of these agencies have to consist of the poor in the areas served. Community-action agencies, usually located outside of city governments, have undertaken numerous projects, such as job training and health services for the disadvantaged.

Some scholars have argued that the War on Poverty was largely beneficial, helping millions of people out of poverty, its various programs improved the status of minorities in areas such as education and health.[12] Others, including many of the government sponsors of the effort, were disappointed about its lack of accomplishment.[13] On a more political level, the War on Poverty became unpopular with many public officials, who suddenly found themselves under attack by militant spokespeople for the poor. Government administrators, many of whom were accustomed to working on behalf of the disadvantaged, found it difficult to share power with representatives of the poor and to work with them toward common ends. Other factors undercutting the War on Poverty were its increasing identification as a welfare program designed to benefit a specific segment of the population (Blacks and Hispanics in large cities) and the escalation of the war in Vietnam in the late 1960s, which diverted attention and financial resources away from domestic programs. Eventually several of the poverty programs were transferred to other existing agencies and the remainder were either dropped or assumed by a new agency, the Community Services Administration.

The Public Assistance System Today

Currently the major components of the welfare or public assistance system in the United States are supplemental security income (SSI), Aid to Families with Dependent Children (AFDC), and various in-kind benefit programs. The SSI program provides cash benefits to the needy aged, blind, and disabled. The entire cost of the program is borne by the federal government, although the states may supplement national payments from their own funds.

[12] See Sar A. Levitan and Robert Taggert, *The Promise of Greatness: The Social Programs of the Last Decade and Their Major Achievements* (Cambridge, Mass.: Harvard University Press, 1976).

[13] See, for example, Daniel P. Moynihan, *Maximum Feasible Misunderstanding: Community Action in the War on Poverty* (New York: Free Press, 1969).

SSI was adopted in 1974 to relieve state governmental financial burdens and to bring uniformity to eligibility requirements and minimum payment levels. Some 4 million people are receiving benefits from this program.

The most controversial component of the public assistance package has been Aid to Families with Dependent Children. AFDC is financed by federal and state funds and is administered largely by the states. Its primary objective is to aid children who do not have adequate financial support because one parent is deceased, incapacitated, or absent from the home. About half of the states now give aid to families in which both parents are in the home but are unemployed.

Other states have emphasized the absence of one parent as a precondition of receiving aid. This has prompted them to conduct such constitutionally questionable practices as early-morning house raids to find a husband or an individual who could qualify under state law as a "substitute father." Another effect of the absent-parent provision has been to encourage fathers to desert their families. There are an estimated 1.3 million absent parents.

AFDC benefits differ greatly from state to state. Generally, however, they are higher in the North and East than in the South and West, even when differences in cost of living are taken into account. Slightly over half of the AFDC families are black. The size of the average AFDC family is smaller than commonly assumed—between three and four members. Three-fourths of the families in the AFDC program are headed by a woman, and about a third of the children in the program were conceived out of wedlock.[14] Under current regulations those able to work are required to enroll in work programs developed by the states.

In many cases the poor are entitled to multiple in-kind benefits in addition to cash benefits, though many of these programs have been cut back in recent years. In-kind benefits include food stamps, housing subsidies, free health care (medicaid), and free legal services. The provision of in-kind benefits has been based partly on the belief that the poor cannot be depended upon to spend their money (or money given to them) wisely. From this perspective, if the poor were given cash instead of food stamps the money might be wasted on gambling or alcohol and food needs would thus be neglected. Some analysts of in-kind benefits deny these assumptions about the behavior of cash recipients and contend that they, like everyone else, should be able to freely choose how they spend their money. Others have argued that some of these benefits actually hurt the poor. Some people have contended, for example, that the poor should be able to use the money spent on legal services for them to purchase food, shelter, or something more valuable to them than hiring a lawyer.

---

[14] See Howard Oberheu, "The Typical Family Compared With the AFDC Family," *Social and Rehabilitation Record,* April 1976, pp. 6–8.

Evaluation of the System

Most Americans apparently do not object to having some of their tax dollars spent on programs that benefit the aged, blind, or disabled. Benefits to other groups, however, have been more controversial. The argument has been made, for instance, that blue-collar workers, many of whom have no more than a high school education, should not have to support a food-stamp program for those who have chosen to be unemployed in order to go to college. Those who have opposed low-rent public housing have often asked hardworking homeowners, "Do you want to pay somebody else's rent?" A negative response to this question may fare badly by standards of Judeo-Christian ethics, but it is an answer many Americans have given.[15] Some researchers have found that much of the bias against welfare in general is rooted in racial bigotry. One study tentatively concluded

> that many of the objections expressed by whites to current welfare programs were in effect anti-black biases. . . . It seems possible that negative expressions about welfare and welfare recipients are a socially acceptable channel for persons with politically conservative attitudes to express basically negative attitudes toward blacks at a time when blatant expressions of prejudice are not acceptable.[16]

For whatever reason, many Americans feel that most individuals on welfare are lazy chiselers trying to live off others. Other critics have attacked the welfare system rather than those on welfare. Some have argued, for example, that welfare has purposely been made degrading to encourage people to stay at low-paying jobs.[17]

Welfare reform has ranked high on the governmental agenda since the 1960s. Some scholars and state and local officials have asked the national government to assume all or much of the responsibility for welfare expenditures. Another strongly supported proposal is to replace the present system with a negative income tax, which would guarantee a certain minimum income for all families. The latter idea was incorporated into welfare-reform proposals developed by both Presidents Nixon and Carter. President Reagan drastically cut spending on such programs as food stamps, housing subsidies, and medicaid, largely by having eligibility standards for these programs raised. Reagan also proposed that state and local governments assume major responsibility for

---

[15] Leonard Freedman, *Public Housing: The Politics of Poverty* (New York: Holt, Rinehart & Winston, 1969), p. 11.

[16] David J. Kallen and Dorothy Miller, "Public Attitudes toward Welfare," *Social Work* 16 (July 1971):83–90. See also Gerald C. Wright, Jr., "Racism and Welfare Policy in America," *Social Science Quarterly* 57 (March 1977):718–730; and Gilbert Steiner, *Social Insecurity: The Politics of Welfare* (Chicago: Rand McNally, 1966).

[17] See Frances Fox Piven and Richard A. Cloward, *Regulating the Poor* (New York: Random House, 1971).

welfare programs—a responsibility few, if any, state and local officials appear willing to assume.

SUMMARY

1. Two major economic problems of concern to national policy makers (especially the president) are inflation and unemployment. These problems are generally felt to be inversely related, though there have been periods, as in the 1970s, of both high inflation and high unemployment. Generally, Democratic administrations have been more likely to emphasize employment problems and Republican administrations have been more likely to emphasize the inflation problem.

2. Monetary and fiscal policies have been employed to manage the economy. In theory, when government wants to stimulate the economy it should lower interest rates, increase spending, and decrease taxes. When the goal is cooling down the economy, government should increase interest rates, decrease spending, and increases taxes. Monetary policies (those relating to the money supply and interest rates) are controlled by the Federal Reserve Board, which may not see eye to eye with elected officials on the needs of the economy. There also may be considerable disagreement between the president and Congress or within Congress as to what taxing and spending policies are appropriate. Both monetary and fiscal policies are limited in their capacity to control inflation and unemployment.

3. The national government may also influence economic activity through controls over specific industries or commodities, antitrust laws, general wage and price controls, and informal jawboning. Unemployment has resulted in governmental relief measures, training programs, and job-creation programs.

4. Governments in the United States have long been involved in promoting and regulating economic activity. Many regulations have the objective of protecting the interests of the consumer or the general public. Other "regulations" have been adopted to protect particular economic groups.

5. The National Environmental Policy Act of 1970 committed the national government to the protection and enhancement of the environment. Air and water quality have improved because of this commitment. Further protection, however, faces political, economic, and technological problems.

6. Welfare programs, particularly Aid to Families with Dependent Children and in-kind benefits, have been controversial. Many Americans believe that those on welfare have no one to blame but themselves for their plight and are living off the taxes paid by others. On the other hand, welfare programs are seen by some people as providing only minimal benefits in a very degrading manner.

12

GOVERNMENT,
POLITICS,
AND FOREIGN POLICY

In 1966 President Lyndon Johnson told American troops in Vietnam, "There are 3 billion people in the world and we have only 200 million of them. We are outnumbered 15 to 1. If might did make right, they would sweep over the United States and take what we have. We have what they want." The view that the United States must struggle to protect its interests in a dangerous and hostile world has commonly been reflected in decisions about military matters, international agreements, foreign aid, direct involvement in the affairs of other countries, and foreign trade. This chapter begins by reviewing basic directions and goals of American foreign policy. We then consider the roles played by various political actors in the making of foreign policy and the instruments by which that policy has been implemented.

DIRECTIONS IN FOREIGN POLICY

Isolation and Intervention

Throughout much of the early history of the United States the national government attempted to remain relatively aloof from world, especially European, politics. In his Farewell Address to the country (1796), George Washington urged that the U.S. government avoid involvement in struggles among European nations. European allies, Washington warned, should be sought only in times of crisis and never on a permanent basis. President James Monroe, in what is known as the Monroe Doctrine (1823), declared that this nation should stay out of European politics but also warned European nations against attempting to extend their influence into the Western Hemisphere.

Until the First World War the United States, aided by the broad expanse of the Atlantic Ocean, was largely able to avoid entanglement in European power struggles. At home, however, this country pursued expansionist policies through military action during the 1800s. In 1846 the United States went to war with Mexico. This resulted in the acquisition of much of what is now the American Southwest. About a half century later came the Spanish-American War (1898), which gave the United States control over Cuba, Puerto Rico, and the Philippine Islands. Nevertheless, the scope of the U.S. imperialistic activity in the late nineteenth century was small in comparison with that of European nations, who from 1875 to 1900 diligently staked out most of Africa and a large part of the Far East.

The United States was unable to avoid participation in the First and Second World Wars. After the First World War, President Woodrow Wilson attempted to arbitrate conflict between European nations and frame a lasting peace through the creation of the League of Nations. The United States Senate, however, rejected this country's participation in the League, and an isolationist policy prevailed until the Japanese attack on Pearl Harbor in Hawaii in 1941, which triggered U.S. involvement in World War II.

Until World War II the United States participated in world politics only an episodic basis. For the most part the nation confined its foreign affairs to the Western Hemisphere, being somewhat disdainful of "Old World" politics, and acted without allies in pursuing its foreign policy objectives. After the Second World War U.S. national policy makers formed numerous alliances with other countries and tended to agree with the view expressed years before by Theodore Roosevelt: "We have no choice as to whether or not we shall play a great part in the world. That has been determined for us by fate. The only question is whether we will play that part well or badly."[1]

The Cold War

Since World War II a dominant theme of U.S. foreign policy has been the need to contain communism. The spread of communism was dramatic in the years immediately following that war as the Soviet Union exerted control over Albania, Bulgaria, Czechoslovakia, Hungary, Poland, Romania, and Yugoslavia. Meanwhile communists revolutionaries took China away from Chiang Kai-Shek, who in 1949 retreated with his followers to the island of Formosa (Taiwan).

The need to contain communism, especially Soviet-led communism, was expressed by leading State Department experts such as George Kennan. This view underlays President Truman's decisions to (1) extend military and economic aid to Greece and Turkey; (2) pour billions of dollars under the Marshall Plan (named for its creator, Secretary of State George C. Marshall) into Western Europe to speed its recovery from World War II; (3) and create the North Atlantic Treaty Organization (NATO), in which the U.S. and most Western European nations agreed to come to each other's defense in case of an attack.

Concern over the spread of communism also led to the creation of a number of other military alliances, a nuclear arms race with the Soviet Union, and a steadily increasing defense budget in the 1950s and 1960s. In addition, the cold war with the Soviet Union and its communist allies prompted the United States to keep on guard against communist-inspired national wars of liberation in various parts of the world. U.S. policy makers acted on the assumption that people in other lands never voluntarily choose communism and that no matter how repressive and corrupt their noncommunist governments are they would be worse off under communism.[2] These reasons were used to justify American economic and military aid to various dictatorial governments.

Since 1945 the United States has directly confronted the Soviet Union in Berlin and Cuba and has fought two major wars in Asia against communist

---

[1] Quoted in *The Meaning of the New Panama Canal Treaties* (Washington, D.C.: Department of State, 1978), p. 14.

[2] See, for example, Richard J. Barnet, "The National-Security Managers," in Jerome H. Skolnick and Elliott Currie (eds.), *Crisis in American Institutions* (Boston: Little, Brown, 1970), pp. 198–210.

forces. After World War II the city of Berlin in East Germany was divided into two sectors: one (East Berlin) was controlled by the Soviet Union, the other (West Berlin) by the United States, England, and France. In 1948 the Soviets attempted to pressure their ex-allies out of their zone in Berlin by prohibiting the transport of food and supplies through East Germany to the western sector. This effort, however, was foiled by the ability of the Western nations to supply the zone by air.

In the Cuban missile crisis of 1962, the United States and the Soviet Union came perilously close to a nuclear confrontation. The crisis arose from the discovery that Soviet technicians had installed in Cuba, an ally of the U.S.S.R., a number of intermediate-range ballistic missiles that could carry atomic warheads into the United States. In October 1962, the Kennedy administration imposed a naval blockade on Cuba to prevent the importation of more arms and threatened to attack Cuba unless the existing missiles were removed. The Soviet Union avoided contact with the American blockade and removed its missiles.

Vietnam

Major wars against communism occurred in Korea in the early 1950s and in Vietnam in the 1960s and early 1970s.[3] The Korea conflict began after communist North Korea invaded South Korea in June 1950. The invasion was resisted by a special United Nations army in which United States troops played the major role. The conflict, though unpopular, ended in 1953 and preserved the Republic of South Korea.

The war in Vietnam was the longest war in United States history and in many respects its most disastrous. U.S. involvement in Vietnam escalated over several years. In 1950 President Truman sent a military advisory team to help France combat Vietnamese communists seeking to take control of the country. In 1954 the French withdrew from Vietnam and the country was divided into North Vietnam, controlled by the Vietnamese communists, and South Vietnam, considered pro-Western. In that same year President Eisenhower offered economic aid to South Vietnam, and a year later he agreed to help train the army of South Vietnam. Faced with growing communist activity within South Vietnam, President Kennedy began to send troops, officially known as "military advisers," to that country. By the end of 1963, there were 16,000 U.S. military advisers in South Vietnam. U.S. involvement escalated during the Johnson administration into a full-scale war against the communist National Liberation Front (Vietcong) of South Vietnam and North Vietnam. By the end of 1967

---

[3] Two other occasions in which U.S. troops were used in the 1950s and 1960s were (1) the sending of marines to Lebanon in 1958 to prevent what was seen as a plot by the Soviet Union, Egypt, and Syria to overthrow the Lebanese government; and (2) the sending of troops to the Dominican Republic in 1965 to prevent what was seen as a communist-inspired revolution.

more than 470,000 American troops were in Vietnam, and two years later the total had increased beyond 540,000.

The escalation of the war prompted several large-scale protests in the United States. Thousands protested in Washington in 1967, and hundreds of these protesters were arrested when they attacked the Pentagon. Demonstrators against the war also disrupted the 1968 Democratic convention in Chicago. In Washington the next year, more than 250,000 people participated in the largest antiwar protest in American history. President Nixon's decision in 1970 to invade Cambodia in an effort to destroy enemy supply bases prompted protests on college campuses throughout the United States. On one campus, that of Kent State University in Ohio, National Guardsmen opened fire on demonstrators, killing four and wounding nine others. The next year police broke up an antiwar protest in the nation's capital by arresting over 12,000 people.

By the time peace pacts were formally signed in Paris (1973) by the United States, North Vietnam, South Vietnam, and the Vietcong, about two million people had died because of the war, more than 46,000 of them U.S. soldiers. Public opinion surveys taken after this war demonstrated a sharp decline in support for military spending and the use of U.S. troops in other parts of the world.[4] More broadly, the Vietnam War virtually destroyed the nonpartisan consensus on foreign policy that had characterized most of the 1940s and 1950s. The focus of that policy on a cold war with communism, had become difficult to maintain.

After the war, informed opinion, as reflected in books and foreign policy journals, was divided over the proper course to follow.[5] Some concluded that the war had been lost because of poor leadership, timidity, and dissent at home. In the future, the United States had no option but to become more aggressive and strengthen its military posture toward the Soviet Union. To others, the lesson of Vietnam was the need to work with the Soviet Union toward ending the arms race and minimizing world tension. Still others, of a more isolationist bent, felt the need to withdraw as far as possible from world affairs. The immediate change in foreign policy, as we will see, was generally toward the second of these views. By the late 1970s, however, the United States had assumed a more aggressive stand.

Détente and Tension

Under the Nixon administration the United States entered a period of *détente* (literally, a relaxation of tensions) with the Soviet Union. The détente between the two superpowers is commonly regarded as having begun in a 1972

---

[4] See Bruce Russett and Miroslav Mincic, "American Opinion and the Use of Military Force Abroad," *Political Science Quarterly* 91 (Fall 1976): 411–431.

[5] See Ole R. Holsti and James N. Rosenau, *American Leadership in World Affairs: Vietnam and the Breakdown of Consensus* (Winchester, Mass.: Allen & Unwin, 1984).

summit meeting in Moscow. In this meeting President Nixon signed an agreement growing out of the Strategic Arms Limitations Talks (SALT) in which both countries placed limits on nuclear arms in an effort to obtain "essential equivalence" in weapons and reduce the costly arms race. Détente, according to a 1974 State Department report, was "based on the premise that the two nuclear superpowers must do everything in their power to spare mankind the dangers of a nuclear holocaust."[6]

Détente was continued as a goal by the Carter administration, which pressed for renewed agreement with the Soviets on limiting strategic arms. The arms treaty, however, was put on the back burner after the Soviet invasion of Afghanistan in 1979. The election of Ronald Reagan in 1980, moreover, brought into power an administration whose basic foreign policy was perhaps best summarized in the slogan "Peace and security through strength." Reagan came into office skeptical of détente (feeling it was a tactic of the Soviet Union to gain a military advantage over the United States) and weary of dealing with the Soviet Union other than through a position of absolute military superiority. In 1981 Reagan called for the largest peacetime buildup of arms since World War II, an expenditure of $1.5 trillion dollars over five years. In putting together this budget proposal the Reagan administration acted on the assumption that nuclear war was not unthinkable and that this country must be prepared to win a limited nuclear conflict. Critics of this policy contended that there can be no such thing as a "limited" nuclear war and that in preparing for one the United States and the Soviet Union were simply making a tragic confrontation more likely.

In the 1980s the United States did renew arms talks with the Soviets and President Reagan met with Russian leader Mikhail Gorbachev. Though the SALT II Treaty was rejected by the Senate, the Reagan administration agreed to its limitations on nuclear-weapons systems. This policy was changed in 1986, however, on the grounds that the Soviets had violated the agreement. Reagan's action raised the possibility of an intensified arms race.

The Reagan administration generally placed considerably more emphasis on the military than the diplomatic side of foreign policy. We have already noted Reagan's military buildup, which was designed in part to impress the Soviet Union with the sheer magnitude of the U.S. defense budget and in part to make up for a low level of prepardness following Vietnam. The buildup was accompanied by a policy of expanded support for anticommunist insurgencies in the third world (from the "freedom fighters" in Nicaragua to the guerrillas in Afghanistan; a war on terrorism (most dramatically revealed in the 1986 bombing of Libya, thought to be a leading source of state-sponsored terrorism); and investment in a space-based Strategic Defense Initiative System (SDI), known by its critics as Star Wars. Though advocated by the Reagan administra-

---

[6] *The Meaning of Détente* (Washington, D.C.: Department of State, 1974), p. 2.

tion as a means of defending against enemy missiles, SDI has been looked upon by the Soviet Union as a shield behind which the United States might feel free to launch a nuclear attack.

By 1987, covert operations under Reagan involving the selling of arms to Iran in exchange for U.S. hostages and the diversion of profits from the arms sales to Nicaraguan rebels led to a host of problems for the administration. The arms-for-hostages swap conflicted with a publicly stated policy against dealing with terrorists. The administration suffered not only a loss of credibility at home but also with its allies, many of whom had been pressured by the United States not to sell arms to Iran or make concessions to terrorists. Aside from the contradictions between stated and actual policies, trading with terrorists was criticized on the grounds that it only created an incentive for the further taking of hostages. The diversion of profits from the sale of arms to Iran to the contra forces apparently came as part of a broader effort to circumvent a congressional ban on such aid. In addition to arms sales, units in the National Security Council and the CIA that were engaged in covert operations raised funds for the contras by soliciting certain foreign governments and private parties. Such activities were criticized strongly in Congress, where doubts were raised about their legality.

THE MAKING OF FOREIGN POLICY

The Constitution divides responsibility for foreign affairs among the president, the Senate, and Congress as a whole. For a number of reasons, however, the president has come out on top in the struggle over the direction of foreign policy.

Presidential Leadership

Presidential leadership in foreign policy has resulted mainly from public expectations that the chief executive cope with international threats to this nation's security or, as in the case of oil, its economy. On a more personal level involvement in international diplomacy offers the president an opportunity to be remembered in world history an achievement such as opening relations with China or settling a Middle Eastern crisis. Dealing with world leaders is also often one of the more glamorous and pleasurable aspects of the presidency. As an aide to President Jimmy Carter remarked, "It's like being able to go outside and play. . . . It's just more fun than dealing with a Congressman whose military base is about to be closed.[7]

On a constitutional level much of the president's leadership and influence in foreign relations stems from his roles as chief administrator, commander

[7] Quoted in "What Price Candor," *Newsweek*, March 21, 1977, p. 28.

in chief of armed forces, and chief diplomat. As chief administrator the president heads a vast foreign policy apparatus composed of the departments of State and Defense and the intelligence agencies. Although presidential control over this machinery is far from complete, the president's administrative status gives him access to expertise and information that is unavailable to Congress. This status, coupled with his control over the military and diplomatic relations, also enables the president to meet a crisis swiftly and decisively.

Technically the president and Congress share control over the military. Congress has the power to control military appropriations, declare war, raise and support armies, and make rules and regulations governing the armed forces. As commander in chief of these forces, however, the president can subvert the authority vested in Congress. To cite a humorous example, Theodore Roosevelt, after being denied funds by Congress to sail the American fleet around the world, took what funds he had to start the fleet on its journey and left it up to Congress to provide the money needed to bring the fleet back home.

The most serious problem concerning the power of the president as commander in chief is that he can involve the nation in a war through his control over the movement of troops even if Congress has not declared war. In fact, the last time Congress officially declared war was in 1941, against Japan, Germany, and Italy. Since then presidents have engaged American troops in combat in Korea, Lebanon, the Dominican Republic, Vietnam, and Cambodia without a declaration of war. In the case of Vietnam the report of an attack on U.S. destroyers by North Vietnam torpedo boats in the Gulf of Tonkin (later revealed to be a purposeful distortion of a minor event) prompted Congress to adopt the Gulf of Tonkin Resolution (1964), which gave the president the power to "take all necessary measures to repel any armed attack against the forces of the U.S. and to prevent further aggression."

The conflict in Vietnam illustrated to many people the dangers of a presidential war. Following the war Congress sought to reassert its control over military matters by passing the War Powers Act of 1973. Under this law the president may commit forces to combat in emergencies without congressional authorization but must report this action to Congress within forty-eight hours; and he cannot commit troops to combat longer than sixty days (ninety days in an extreme emergency) without congressional approval. Some observers have contended that rather than increasing the control of Congress, the act in effect gives the president unlimited authority to wage war for sixty days.[8]

In his role as chief diplomat the president has the authority to recognize foreign governments, make appointments to diplomatic posts, and enter into treaties with other nations. Appointments to diplomatic posts such as ambassadorships are subject to senatorial confirmation. The Senate also has some control

---

[8] See former senator Thomas E. Eagleton's *War and Presidential Power: A Chronicle of Congressional Surrender* (New York: Liveright, 1974).

over treaties; two-thirds of that body must approve treaties before they can become effective.

The requirement of Senate approval of treaties can effectively control presidential policy making. In 1919, for example, the Senate rejected by a very narrow margin U.S. participation in the League of Nations on the basis of its infringement upon this country's sovereignty. In 1978 President Carter was barely able to secure adoption of treaties that returned the Canal Zone to Panamanian control by the year 2000 and guaranteed the neutrality of the canal (that is, that it will be open and accessible to ships of all nations). The Senate ratified both canal treaties by a vote of 68 to 32, giving the president a bare one vote more than needed.

Opponents of the treaties contended that the United States was giving away valuable property and taking another step in its decline as a world power. Proponents argued that this nation never actually owned the canal and that returning active control of it would improve the image of the United States in Latin America and the third world generally. Failure to ratify, it was also argued, would invite riotous conditions in Panama, as had occurred in 1964.

In addition to treaties, the president may enter into executive agreements with foreign heads of state. Some executive agreements, including those pertaining to trade with other nations, require authorization by Congress; the president makes others under his own constitutional authority. Presidents have entered into many more executive agreements than treaties, and some of these agreements, such as a security pact signed with Spain in 1970, have been of great potential significance. Since 1972 Congress has required notification of all executive agreements the president negotiates. Some members of Congress have pressed for legislation that would give that body the right to reject all executive agreements.

The Role of Congress

Over the last several decades Congress has vacillated between supporting presidential foreign policies and opposing them. For most of the post–World War II peroid Congress has shared the presidential view that the two branches must be united in combating international communism. A related theme in the cold war period was that the battle against communism was not a matter of partisan politics. Rather, members of both major political parties were expected to stand behind the president and present a united front to communist aggressors. Even representatives and senators who doubted the wisdom of some presidential policies or the growth of the national defense budget feared to speak out lest they be considered unpatriotic, "soft on communism," or unconcerned about national security.

More positively, the "communist threat" could be used by members of Congress to justify aid programs to developing countries and, on the domestic front, such programs as the interstate highway system (originally passed as a "defense highway act") and federal aid to education (the first such bill came shortly after the Russians launched the first artificial satellite, Sputnik I, in 1957). "National defense," in other words, became a convenient banner under which social and economic programs could be sold.[9]

The Vietnam War and détente ushered in a period in which Congress demonstrated a greater willingness to openly criticize openly defense spending and presidential performance in the foreign policy area. The legislation on war powers and executive agreements are examples of the steps taken by Congress in the early 1970s to assert its control over foreign policy. Other legislation in this direction included a requirement that the nation's chief intelligence unit, the Central Intelligence Agency (CIA), report its covert (secret) operations to Congress in "timely fashion" and a law giving Congress the authority to veto arms sales of $7 million or more to a foreign country.

While Congress is not always a rubber stamp for whatever foreign policy the president wishes to pursue, its role in this area is limited. Defense spending is related to the perception or the existence of an external threat that the nation must be prepared to meet. Members of Congress have generally had little choice but to defer to the judgment of the president and the military, or both, on the existence of a danger and the types and levels of expenditures needed. For the most part conflicts in Congress over defense matters have occurred when the experts disagree and Congress must choose among competing proposals—for example, alternate weapon systems.

Congress, like the public at large, is likely to support the president in international emergencies such as the Cuban missile crisis, the Iranian hostage crisis of 1980, or the bombing of Libya. At such times congressional leaders of both major parties are invited to emergency meetings at the White House to be informed of the situation and the administration's plan of action. Presidents seek congressional support to legitimize their action and to demonstrate to foreign adversaries that the nation is united behind this action. Usually presidents have little difficulty in getting such support.

The Role of the Bureaucracy

The bureaucracy also helps shape the direction of foreign policy. The two Cabinet-level departments most concerned with foreign-policy making and implementation are the Department of State and the Department of Defense. The former contains administrative units with such specific functions as economic and business affairs and such areas of focus as Africa and Europe.

The Department of Defense assumes broad responsibility for military policy. This agency employs about one million civilians, many of them at the

---

[9] James Clotfelter, *The Military in American Politics* (New York: Harper & Row, Pub., 1973), p. 155.

Pentagon, the "world's largest office building." Within the department are the separate departments of the Army, the Navy, and the Air Force. The Department of the Navy includes naval aviation and the U.S. Marine Corps. The senior military officers of the various services advise the civilian secretaries of the military departments. In addition, these military leaders and the chief of staff to the secretary of defense constitute the Joint Chiefs of Staff, the principal military advisory body to the president (a role to be discussed later in this chapter).

The secretaries of state and defense, as pointed out in Chapter 6 have been members of the President's inner Cabinet and are consequently in close contact with the President or his staff of advisers. These secretaries also sit on the president's National Security Council along with the vice-president, the assistance to the president for national security affairs, and, on an invitational basis, such people as the chairman of the Joint Chiefs of Staff and the director of the Central Intelligence Agency.

The policy-making role of these officials and agencies has varied over time. The post–World War II State Department under George Marshall, for example, devised innovative plans to aid Europe, Greece, and Turkey and formulated the containment policy toward Russia. Truman's second secretary of state, Dean Acheson, and Eisenhower's secretary of state, John Foster Dulles, carried out important roles as presidential advisers, but they generally did so as individuals rather than as representatives of the State Department.

In the 1950s the State Department bureaucracy became increasingly viewed as too tradition-ridden and cautious to be of much value as a source of innovation in foreign policy. President Kennedy functioned largely as his own secretary of state, relying less on the State Department bureaucracy and its secretary, Dean Rusk, than on the special groups of officials he organized for foreign policy advice. Foreign policy planning in the Nixon and Ford years centered in the White House national security staff headed by foreign policy adviser Henry Kissinger. President Carter seemed to vacillate between the advice of his secretaries of state (Cyrus Vance and Edmund Muskie) and his national security adviser Zbigniew Brzezinski. President Reagan consulted closely with his secretaries of state and defense (Alexander Haig and Caspar Weinberger, respectively), though in the early 1980s there was occasional conflict between these two; each also found himself competing with national security adviser Richard Allen for influence with the president. In recent administrations the national security adviser apparently has become as important as, if not more, than, the secretaries of state and defense in shaping national foreign policy.[10]

---

[10] Erwin C. Hargrove, *The Power of the Modern Presidency* (Philadelphia: Temple University Press, 1974), pp. 241–250. See also Barry Rubin, *Secrets of State: The State Department and the Struggle Over U.S. Foreign Policy* (New York: Oxford University Press, 1985).

The Role of the Military

Deeply imbedded in this nation's history is the desire to subject the military to civilian control. The vision of a "man on horseback" in charge of a large professional army has long been viewed as a threat to the survival of democratic government and to peace itself. The Constitution places control of the military in civilian hands—that is, with the president and Congress. The extent to which civilian authorities actually control the military has been seriously questioned. The most dramatic instance of open conflict between a president and a military leader was Truman's disagreement with the desire of General Douglas MacArthur, American commander in chief in the Far East, to escalate the Korean conflict. Truman relieved MacArthur of his command, declaring that the general had acted in defiance of U.S. policy.

On rare occasions other military leaders on active duty have publicly questioned presidential policy. In 1977, for instance, the third-ranking military officer in South Korea publicly warned the United States that a withdrawal of U.S. troops from that country could lead to war. President Jimmy Carter, who proposed to phase out U.S. ground troops there, relieved the officer of his command.

Of more concern to those who favor civilian control of the military is the possibility that continuous international tension will lead to an overreliance on the military in the shaping of foreign policy. Ultimately, some analysts have warned, an international crisis could create a "garrison state" in which the military would dominate American politics.[11]

Although the actual influence of military leaders on foreign policy has not been precisely measured, military men, especially the Joint Chiefs of Staff, are obviously heard at the highest levels of decision making. In crises their expertise, intelligence reports, position papers, and proposals give them an enormous input in decision making. One observer has concluded that since World War II the military leadership has been cautious in urging military action, often out of concern about the feasibility of fighting a particular war. Once committed to battle, however, the military has tended to pressure for escalating the conflict toward total victory.[12]

The military and those industries dependent on defense contracts for weapons development have been a force in increasing defense spending. At the same time, this so-called military-industrial complex has not had its way entirely with the president or Congress. Presidents have frequently cut Defense Department budget proposals and occasionally have rejected weapons supported by the military. A spectacular example of the latter was President Carter's decision in

---

[11] See Samuel P. Huntington, *The Soldier and the State* (New York: Vintage Books, 1964), Chapter 13.

[12] Clotfelter, op. cit., Chapter 9.

1977 to stop production of the B-1 bomber in the belief that it was unnecessary and too expensive.

INSTRUMENTS OF FOREIGN POLICY

Among the chief instruments by which U.S. policy makers have attempted to influence the behavior of foreign officials or alter conditions in other countries are military strength, foreign assistance and trade policies, diplomacy, intelligence gathering, and educational programs.

Military Strength

Historically, Americans have distrusted large standing armies. Yet two world wars and cold and hot wars against communism have led to the emergence of the United States as perhaps the greatest military power on earth. At the beginning of the 1980s about 2 million citizens of the United States were on active duty in the army, navy, Marine Corps, and air force. About one of every four served outside the United States. The number of people involved in the defense effort is considerably increased when the 2½ million members of the military reserves and the 1 million civilian employees of the Defense Department are included.

Along with its human and financial resources, the United States has the largest and most sophisticated weapons system in the world. Since the initial deployment of the atomic bomb in 1945 the government has greatly enlarged its arsenal of nuclear weapons. These now include intercontinental ballistic missiles, intercontinental bombers and, because the Soviet Union has also engaged in nuclear weaponry, antimissile missiles. While efforts have been made from time to time to limit the spread of nuclear weapons and the nuclear arms race with the Soviet Union, the United States has also striven to insure that it is prepared to conduct a nuclear exchange with other countries. Anticipating that most conflicts around the world will not involve nuclear weapons, the United States has also sought to maintain weapons with which to fight a conventional limited war such as that undertaken in Vietnam.

The basic justification for maintaining a high level of military strength in the United States has been that it is needed to deter actions that are contrary to this nation's national security interests. To deter aggression the United States has also entered into defense agreements with fifty nations under which the parties agree to defend each other in case of attack.

Military strength and alliances have commonly been viewed in this country as means of underpinning diplomatic efforts with a show of force and unity against communist aggression. But these instruments have certain limitations. In recent years, for example, the U.S. has found it difficult to maintain

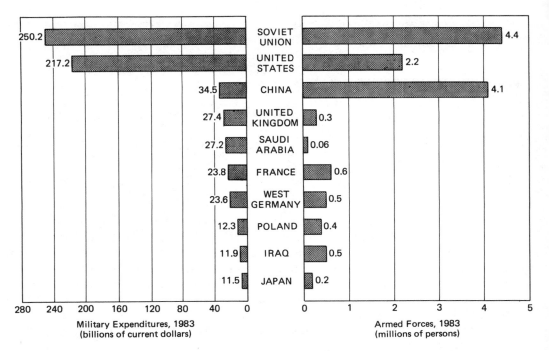

Figure 12–1 Leading Countries in Military Expenditures and Supported Armed Forces, 1983

Source: U.S. Army Control and Disarmament Agency, World Military Expenditures and Arms Transfers (Washington, D.C.: Government Printing Office, 1985), p. 5.

unity in alliances such as the North Atlantic Treaty Organization. The actual use of nuclear weapons, moreover, has been inhibited by a number of factors, not the least of which is the fear of retaliation and a nuclear holocaust.

The actual use of force, and thus its value as a credible deterrent, is also limited by domestic politics. The Vietnam experience suggests that Americans are unlikely to support a long, inconclusive war. Public opinion polls taken in the mid-1970s showed that the American people as a whole are opposed to the use of nuclear weapons and are selective about the use of U.S. troops to defend other countries. The public appears to be most willing to give military aid to those nations geographically close to the United States (for example, Canada and Mexico) and to countries subject to external attack rather than domestic insurgency.[13]

[13] See Bruce Russett and Miroslav Nimcic, "American Opinion and the Use of Military Force Abroad," *Political Science Quarterly* 1 (Fall 1976): 411–431.

Economic Instruments

The major economic instruments of foreign policy have been foreign assistance and trade policies. Foreign assistance has consisted of military and nonmilitary aid to other countries. Military equipment has been given away and sold on a credit or cash basis. This type of aid has been defended as necessary to strengthen anticommunist forces and achieve influence in the recipient countries. Also, the United States has felt compelled to provide military equipment out of fear that if it does not do so the Soviet Union will and thereby expand its influence in the world. Influence results not only from the goodwill gained from military aid but also from the dependence of the recipient country on replacement parts, which may be withheld if the supplier deems this to be necessary.

In the early 1970s the United States was clearly the world's leading supplier of military equipment. Much of the aid went to governments in the Middle East where, as in other parts of the world, the United States was arming countries that were in conflict with each other. Elsewhere military aid went to dictatorial regimes whose only virtue was that they were not communist. In the third world aid was given to military governments out of the belief that a strong military was needed to bring stability and promote modernization.[14]

In the mid 1970s the role of the United States as "arms merchant of the world" and its policy of providing military aid to governments that infringe upon the human rights of their own citizens were seriously questioned by many Americans. In 1976 Congress passed legislation giving it authority to review and veto large arms sales (though both houses of Congress must vote to do so). Both Congress and the Carter administration went on record as being opposed to sales of military equipment to nations that violate human rights. Ronald Reagan, who had criticized the Carter human-rights policy in the 1980 election as unrealistic and damaging to foreign policy, resumed arms sales to countries considered anti-Soviet, regardless of their human rights record.

Many issues involved in military aid programs are also found in other assistance programs and in trade policies. Much of the aid provided by the United States to other countries consists of money grants and long-term loans. The Agency for International Development administers most of these economic assistance programs. In addition, the United States sells or gives away agricultural surpluses to other countries.

These assistance programs reflect several motivations. In part the programs are intended to promote domestic economic interests. Economic aid programs, for example, have often included a requirement that recipient countries make most of their purchases from industries in the United States.

---

[14] The assumption that governments controlled by military leaders are better than those controlled by civilians in bringing modernization is highly questionable. See Robert W. Jackman, "Politicians in Uniform," *American Political Science Review* 70 (December 1976): 1078–1097.

Similarly, farmers directly benefit by having their surplus production purchased by the national government for disposal abroad. As in the case of military aid, economic assistance has also been used to contain communism and win over allies, or at least to keep countries from turning to the Soviet Union for aid. More humanitarian motives have been shown in donations of food to famine-stricken countries such as India.

The latest emphasis in foreign aid has been on assisting Third World countries. Aid was originally given to encourage economic growth, the assumption being that such expansion would allow wealth to "trickle down" to the poor masses. In practice, however, only a few benefited from the aid and very little wealth trickled down. As one commentator noted,

> corrupt politicians, parasitic merchants, privileged warlords, courtiers, and kings can and do divert development funds, directly or indirectly, to internal security forces, grandiose public monuments, luxury imports, excessive personal consumption, or foreign bank accounts. In such cases the effect of aid is to widen the already large gap between social classes.[15]

In 1973 Congress switched the emphasis in economic aid from economic development to direct assistance to the poor. At the same time, however, economic aid to foreign countries has not been popular in Congress, where it is commonly viewed as "pouring money down a rat hole" and, as likely as not, producing ingrates instead of friends. Skepticism about economic aid is evident in the fact that while the United States is among the world leaders in the dollar total of the aid it gives to other countries, the proportion of its national wealth devoted to this purpose has steadily declined; by this measurement it makes much less of a sacrifice than several other nations (Table 12–1).

Some objectives sought through economic aid can also be pursued through the power of the national government to control imports into this country and exports to other countries. Imports have been controlled by tariffs and quotas. *Tariffs* are taxes on imported goods. *Quotas* impose limits on the amount of a product that can be brought into a country. These limits may be imposed by legislation or as the result of negotiations with foreign leaders. Under existing law the president may, within limits, increase or decrease tariff rates and invalidate trade agreements if they are found to result in the importation of such a high level of products as to threaten American industries.

From time to time Congress has prohibited the importation of specific articles or banned trading with particular nations—for example, white-controlled Rhodesia (present-day Zimbabwe). In 1974 Congress decided that as a general principle, trade preferences should be given to less developed countries. At the same time it decided to give less-than-preferential treatment to nations

---

[15] Laurence I. Radway, *Foreign Policy and National Defense* (Glenview, Ill.: Scott, Foresman, 1969), p. 54.

Table 12–1 Ranking of 17 largest donors of Foreign aid, 1984.

VOLUME OF AID (IN MILLIONS OF US DOLLARS)	AMOUNT	SHARE (PERCENT)	PERCENTAGE OF GNP	
1. United States	8,698	30.4	1. Netherlands	1.02
2. Japan	4,319	15.1	2. Norway	0.99
3. France	3,790	13.2	3. Denmark	0.85
4. Germany	2,782	9.7	4. Sweden	0.80
5. Canada	1,625	5.7	5. France	0.77
6. United Kingdom	1,432	5.0	6. Belgium	0.56
7. Netherlands	1,268	4.4	7. Canada	0.50
8. Italy	1,105	3.9	8. Germany	0.45
9. Australia	773	2.7	8. Australia	0.45
10. Sweden	741	2.6	10. Finland	0.36
11. Norway	526	1.8	11. Japan	0.35
12. Denmark	449	1.6	12. United Kingdom	0.33
13. Belgium	434	1.5	13. Italy	0.32
14. Switzerland	286	1.0	14. Switzerland	0.30
15. Austria	181	0.6	15. Austria	0.28
16. Finland	178	0.6	16. New Zealand	0.27
17. New Zealand	59	0.2	17. United States	0.24
Total	28,647	100.0		

Source: Shahid Javed Burki and Rubert L. Ayres, "A Fresh Look at Development Aid", *Finance and Development* 23 (March 1986): 9.

that (1) withhold the supply of a needed product, such as oil, from international trade, (2) nationalize the property of U.S. corporations without adequate compensation, or (3) do not take adequate measures to prevent narcotics from entering the United States.

Tariffs were used in the early years of the nation to protect infant domestic industries. Until incorporation of the income tax into the U.S. Constitution (1913) tariffs were also a principal source of national government revenue. While at present American industry in general hardly qualifies as infant, the government remains under considerable pressure to follow protectionist policies. Attempts by foreign nations to increase exports of autos, sugar, meat, shoes, electronics, steel, and various other products to the United States have been resisted by domestic manufacturers and unions. Manufacturers have dreaded foreign competition and unions have feared the loss of jobs in industries subject to such competition.

More generally, Americans have become concerned that the United States must maintain a favorable balance of trade by importing less than it exports. Otherwise dollars and gold will flow to foreign countries. The United States has had a severe balance-of-payments problem in recent years, especially since the increases in the price of foreign oil.

On the negative side, protectionist policies mean higher prices for consumers. Such policies may also be self-defeating, because other countries may retaliate and impose tariffs or quotas on U.S. imports. From the diplomatic point of view protectionist measures may frustrate efforts to build or maintain friendly relations with other countries or to secure noneconomic concessions from them.

Within the limits imposed by domestic economic and political considerations since the 1930s, the United States has generally sought to promote foreign trade—for example, by achieving mutual reductions in tariffs.[16] In addition, it has generally sought to encourage private (corporate) investments in other countries, especially the less developed nations. Toward this end Congress created the Overseas Private Investment Corporation (OPIC) in 1969, which offers insurance to U.S. investors against certain "political risks" such as the appropriation of their foreign property.

Tax policies that, for example, allow credits against the U.S. income tax for foreign income taxes, also are intended to encourage private investment. The basic premise of these policies—that U.S. investments abroad are good for this country and for foreign nations—has been questioned in recent years. Some critics, particularly labor leaders, have complained that promotion of private investment in other countries erodes the domestic industrial base and, as companies set up shop in other nations, leads to the exportation of jobs. On the receiving end, most nations have appeared eager to attract corporate investors but have complained that U.S. corporations have too much influence on their economies. The problem from the recipients' point of view is how to minimize this influence while not discouraging foreign investors.

Diplomacy, Intelligence, and Education

Diplomacy as a tool of foreign policy involves communicating the nation's stand on policy matters to foreign officials. It also involves negotiating agreements with or, as in the case of the dispute between Israel and the Arab nations, among other governments. Meetings between presidents and heads of other nations and conferences resulting from trips by secretaries of state to foreign capitals are the most dramatic forms of diplomacy. Less visible are the activities of U.S. representatives to international organizations such as the United Nations and to disarmament conferences and the activities of those in diplomatic missions to other countries.

The time and subject matter of meetings with foreign officials vary greatly. The two sides may be eager to reach some type of agreement, or they may be unyielding in their positions and seek to embarrass each other and win a propaganda victory. In some situations U.S. officials may apply pressure to achieve concessions or policy changes from the leaders of other governments.

---

[16] This policy has been demonstrated in the Reciprocal Trade Agreement Act of 1934, the General Agreement on Tariffs and Trade of 1947, and the Trade Expansion Act of 1962.

These pressures may include threats of military action, cutoffs of foreign aid, or the erection of trade barriers. Probably more commonly the United States attempts to trade favors with foreign officials—for example, increasing aid to a country in exchange for the right to establish a military base there.

During negotiations diplomats usually try to remain flexible, and toward this end they state their objectives in ambiguous terms. Traditionally exchanges among nations have been conducted in secrecy on the grounds that the publication of details of each side's position at various stages in the bargaining process makes a final agreement more difficult. Publicity, for instance, may generate domestic political pressures that compel negotiators to adhere rigidly to a certain point of view so that they will not "lose face" that is, their nation's dignity or prestige.

While U.S. diplomacy has been characterized by secrecy, there has also been a strong theme in American society that, in the words of Woodrow Wilson, agreements among nations should be "open covenants openly arrived at." The United States, moreover, makes secrecy difficult by requiring that many (though, as noted, not all) agreements be subject to senatorial approval. Unlike officials in most other countries, U.S. officials cannot guarantee other nations that whatever agreement they reach will be honored at home. Given this legal context and the relative openness of the political system in this country, the nature and terms of U.S. agreements such as that regarding transfer of control of the Panama Canal may be subjected to public scrutiny and debate. Domestic conflict is especially likely if it should appear that the United States is getting the short end of a bargain.

The Department of State, through which much of this nation's diplomacy is conducted, also has a large measure of responsibility for foreign intelligence. This involves gathering information about such matters as a foreign country's political, economic, and military situation. Intelligence activities are also carried out by agencies such as the CIA and those connected with the Department of Defense and the several military branches.

Most information collected by intelligence agents comes from open sources such as foreign publications and contacts with foreign officials. The United States, however, has also engaged in espionage—the use of spies and various devices to obtain data other nations wish to keep secret.

The most controversial of all agencies involved in foreign intelligence is the Central Intelligence Agency. The CIA was established in 1947 to advise the National Security Council and acquire information about foreign countries. It was also expected to pursue the goal of changing the policies of foreign governments by such covert means as subsidizing friendly political parties, bribing foreign leaders, and supporting foreign secret police. The CIA's basic cadres and leadership originally came from the Office of Strategic Services (OSS), a training grounds for paramilitary operations behind enemy lines in World War II.

As with intelligence agencies in other countries, most of the activities of the CIA have been shrouded in secrecy. Until recent years very little was known about this agency. Much of what has been revealed has been negative. In the mid 1970s investigations conducted by the U.S. Senate Select Committee on Intelligence disclosed that the agency had, among other things, spied on American citizens at home and plotted assassinations of and coups (changes in government) against foreign leaders. Although presidential involvement in these activities is difficult to document, Presidents Kennedy, Johnson, and Nixon apparently did not rule out assassination as a possible tool of foreign policy.

Under Reagan the CIA's budget, the totals of which are not made public, appears to have been increased dramatically and the agency has expanded its covert paramilitary operations in other countries. Since 1976 the United States government has officially repudiated assassination as an instrument of foreign policy. President Reagan made it clear, however, that his Libya policy in the mid 1980s was designed simply to get rid of Muammar Kaddafi one way or another. It was thought that the 1986 bombing, known by the code name Operation El Dorado, might encourage dissenters within Libya to overthrow Kaddafi's regime. On the other hand, the bombing of Kaddafi's barracks was undertaken with, as Secretary of State George Shultz put it, "a reasonable expectation that he might be there."[17]

Another set of foreign policy instruments may be labeled *public diplomacy.* This term refers to educational programs through which the government attempts to create a favorable image of the United States and its policies. Various image-building programs are administered by the United States International Communication Agency (formerly the United States Information Agency). The ICA maintains agencies in several nations through which it provides information on the United States and attempts to improve relations with local economic leaders. The agency also supports the Voice of America, which produces programs heard in a variety of languages in other countries, and several cultural exchange programs. Other ICA activities have been directed toward putting other countries in a bad light. One example was the 1982 television show "Let Poland Be Poland," which was beamed to a potential audience of 400 million people worldwide in an effort to generate support for the Solidarity labor movement. The production's show-business aspects, featuring several Hollywood stars, were criticized in this and other countries for making a dangerous political situation seem trivial. The Reagan administration, assuming that the Soviets had been doing much better than the United States in the battle for the minds of people (for example, in depicting the image of the U.S. as an aggressive and imperialist threat to world peace), stepped up the government's educational and propaganda efforts.

[17] Quoted "Getting Rid of Kaddafi," *Newsweek*, April 28, 1986, p. 18.

FOREIGN POLICY: A MIXTURE OF GOALS

United States foreign policy in recent decades has been characterized by a complex mixture of security, economic, and idealistic goals. As noted earlier in this chapter, the security dimension of U.S. foreign policy for most of the period following the Second World War has focused on containing world communism.

Radical (neo-Marxist) critics have contended that this country has acted chiefly as an imperialist power bent on world domination. The basic goal of increasing United States control over the affairs of other nations has frequently been seen by these critics to be economic, particularly when such control helps United States–based corporations obtain access, on favorable terms, to raw materials and markets in other countries. Radical critics have generally been challenged for exaggerating the extent to which a business elite has influenced foreign policy decisions and the degree to which government has pursued economic goals at the expense of other objectives.[18]

Another aspect of United States foreign policy has been an emphasis on idealistic goals such as "making the world safe for democracy" and protecting human and civil rights throughout the world. Human rights was given considerable emphasis in the late 1970s by the Carter administration, even at the risk of endangering relations with neutral or friendly governments. Said one Carter spokesperson, "We finally decided we didn't have to support every son of a bitch around the world just because he was our son of a bitch."[19]

Carter's human rights policy was criticized by some on the grounds that it was inconsistently applied. Other critics contended it was wrong to apply the doctrine, no matter how justified, to governments such as Argentina and Brazil, because the United States needed their support in the fight against international communism. Disputes over the place of human rights in American foreign policy continued into the Reagan administration. While Reagan appeared less willing than Carter to emphasize human rights, several members of Congress continued to do so. Senator Charles Percy (R–Ill.), for example, put forth the following case:

> Concern for human rights is not just a policy of the United States; it is an underlying principle of our political system and a fundamental factor in the appeal of democracy to people throughout the world. Likewise, our concern for human rights in other countries is not simply a moralistic crusade to remake the world in our own image. Rather it is based on a realistic recognition that the way governments treat their citizens has a direct effect upon their own stability, their reliability as allies, and their dangers as adversaries. We cannot credibly stand up in the world as the defenders of freedom and democracy if we condone the

---

[18] A useful review of the relevant literature is found in Jerome Slater, "Is United States Foreign Policy 'Imperialist' or 'Imperial'?" *Political Science Quarterly* 91 (Spring 1976): 63–87.

[19] "A Foreign Policy in Disarray," *Newsweek*, May 12, 1980, p. 42.

violation of basic human rights and fail to speak out when serious violations occur—wherever they occur.[20]

The mixture of idealistic and national security goals has led to basic inconsistencies in United States foreign policy. The goals of national self-determination, human rights, and political freedoms have been central themes in this policy. Yet security fears have often caused the United States to resist attempts at self-determination, on the grounds that the change is communist-inspired, and to give aid to regimes that suppress human freedoms.

SUMMARY

1. Throughout much of its history the United States has sought to remain apart from world politics. After World War II, the most prominent theme of U.S. foreign policy became the need to contain communism. Concern with communism was apparent in military and economic aid programs, the creation of military alliances, an arms race with the Soviet Union, and two major wars in Asia. In the 1970s the United States entered a period of détente (a relaxation of tensions) with the Soviet Union and sought to limit the arms race. In the early 1980s, however, the cold war between the two nations reemerged.

2. Within the national government there has been a struggle between the president and Congress over the direction of foreign policy. Presidents have access to foreign policy expertise and information not available to Congress and, unlike Congress, are able to meet a crisis swiftly and decisively. Congress has generally not taken the initiative in foreign policy but has accepted or rejected proposals made by the president.

3. The bureaucracy also helps shape the direction of foreign policy. A number of agencies supply information on developments in other nations, such as what foreign leaders want from the United States and how they are likely to react to changes in U.S. foreign policy. The policy-making roles of specific advisers to the president, such as the secretary of state, have varied over time. In general, it appears that responsibility for major foreign policy decisions has evolved into the hands of the president and his national security staff. The extent to which military leaders influence foreign policy has been disputed. It is clear, however, that military advisers, especially the Joint Chiefs of Staff, are heard at the highest level of decision making and have pushed for increasing war efforts and defense spending.

4. The United States uses many methods to influence the behavior of foreign officials or alter conditions in other countries. Among them are the military strength, foreign assistance and trade policies, diplomacy, intelligence and covert operations, and "educational programs." The fundamental objective of

[20] Quoted in *Congressional Record*, June 9, 1981, p. E2844.

maintaining a high level of military strength has been to deter actions contrary to the nation's security interests. Military and economic aid has been defended as necessary means of strengthening anticommunist forces and achieving influence in the recipient countries. In addition, the United States has felt compelled to provide aid out of the apprehension that if it does not do so the Soviet Union will and thereby expand its influence in the world. Aid has also been given to foster economic development, directly assist the world's poor, and promote domestic economic interests. Similar motivations have underlain U.S. trade policies.

5. Much of the activity of U.S. officials in world affairs consists of meeting with counterparts of other nations, gathering information on foreign countries (most often from public sources), and conducting educational or public relations programs. The covert activities of the Central Intelligence Agency, which have included assassination plots against foreign leaders, have been more controversial.

6. In general, United States foreign policy over the years has been based on a complex mixture of economic, idealistic, and security motivations. The economic base of this policy, however, has been exaggerated by radical (neo-Marxist) critics. At the same time, formal commitment to idealistic values such as human rights has often been sacrificed when these values conflict with security goals.

13

GOVERNMENT,
POLITICS,
AND CIVIL RIGHTS

In this concluding chapter we focus on governmental policies, largely judicial, regarding the fundamental civil rights and liberties of citizens. The terms *civil rights* and *civil liberties* are used here interchangeably to refer to protections of individual freedom found in the Constitution. In some instances, freedom means limiting the ability of government to infringe upon basic rights, such as free speech or a fair trial. From a more positive perspective freedom means removing barriers to the exercise of individual rights, whether these barriers be imposed by government or by others in society.

Decisions made by government officials about civil rights have added importance because they not only affect the welfare of individuals but shape the general rules by which public policy is made and implemented. The freedoms of speech, press, and assembly take on particular significance in a democratic society. Without them, as George Washington once suggested, "reason is of no use to us . . . and dumb and silent we may be led, like sheep to the slaughter."[1] There is, on the other hand, no guarantee that exercising these freedoms will amount to much. There be more than a grain of truth to the observation of a world traveler: "In the Soviet Union you have to watch what you say or you will get arrested. In the United States you can say whatever you want, but nobody listens."

This chapter begins with an overview of how civil liberties are reflected in policy making. We then analyze policies affecting general freedoms (religion, speech, press, and privacy), criminal justice, and equality.

CIVIL RIGHTS AND POLICY MAKING

The Issues

Issues involving questions of civil rights stem from a variety of environmental disruptions, perceived problems, and conflicts. In time of war or increased international tension, for example, even the mildest criticism of government may be interpreted as treason and public fears of "the enemy within" may be heightened by the alarms sounded by ambitious politicans. Such abuses occurred in the Red Scare of the 1950s when Senator Joseph McCarthy (R–Wisc.), with little or no documentation, claimed that communists had infiltrated much of the federal government (including the army). On one occasion, according to an oft-told but most likely apocryphal story, a witness testifying before McCarthy shouted "But Senator, I'm an anticommunist!" McCarthy shouted back "I don't care what kind of a Communist you are!"

Other civil rights issues develop from more purely domestic disruptions. Some of the most basic of these issues, as noted earlier, arose from the discovery

---

[1] Address to Officers of the Army, March 15, 1783.

that a large segment of the population (blacks and women) were not being treated comparably to their opposites (whites and males) in the economic realm or under the laws. Feelings of relative deprivation resulted in charges of discrimination. Other groups have found themselves involved in civil liberties battles to preserve or restore cherished values and ways of life. Such motivations appear to explain the opposition of Christian conservatives and others to the Equal Rights Amendment and to Supreme Court decisions on abortion, desegregation, and school prayer.

A number of civil rights conflicts between liberals and conservatives center in the schools. The right fears that children will not learn the proper values. It therefore advocates school prayer, the purging of textbooks it considers antireligious, communistic, or pornographic, the need to prevent homosexual teachers from serving as role models, the desirability of teaching "creation science" (the biblical version of creation), the elimination of sex education on the grounds that it only encourages improper behavior, the curtailment of busing for the purpose of integration, and more public financial support for private (often segregated) schools. The left finds these proposals objectionable and worries that children, particularly minorities, will not receive a proper education because, for example, of the disparities in the amount of funds school districts can spend.

Public attitudes toward basic civil liberties are quite inconsistent.[2] Survey research shows that while a majority of citizens agree with basic constitutional guarantees such as the freedom of speech and the right of the accused to a fair trial, they do not favor thorough application of these principles. Many people for instance, have severe reservations about protecting the free-speech right of Communists, Nazis, or others with whom they violently disagree. Many others feel that procedural protections, such as the one against unlawful searches, should not hamstring the police or let the guilty go free.

Scholars have generally found that the people most active in politics are far more likely than the average citizen to favor, at least in broad principle, extending protections to minorities and politically unpopular groups. The reason for this may be the educational and socioeconomic backgrounds of the politically active and their socialization into a political process that emphasizes toleration of different points of view, bargaining, and compromise.

The extent to which those most active in politics or the elite in society differ from others in their willingness to actually apply principles, however, is not altogether clear. Studies indicate, for example, that the highly educated are more likely than the less educated to support the principle of racial equality. On the other hand, there appears to be relatively little difference between the two on support for concrete steps to bring this about. Some theorists suggest that this

---

[2] See Herbert McClosky and Alida Brill, *Dimensions of Tolerance: What Americans Believe About Civil Liberties* (New York: Russell Sage Foundation, 1983).

gap between the principles and policy preferences of the well educated has to do, at least in part, with their reluctance to take a stand on a principle they feel is not socially desirable. Education, in effect, appears to teach people to say the "right thing," even if they do not concur completely with its implications.[3]

Government Activity

Civil rights battles are fought in many forums, but nowhere more frequently than in the courts. From the court's point of view, the other branches of government frequently are a large part of the problem. It is their activity or lack thereof that prompts people to go to court in defense of their civil liberties.

Litigation involving the rights of individuals takes place in both federal and state courts and at all levels of courts within each of these two systems. In recent years state courts have become somewhat more important in handling civil liberties litigation because federal courts have been less willing to get involved in civil rights issues. State courts have been particularly active in interpreting bills or declarations of rights found in state constitutions. These provisions typically contain the same types of protections found in the Bill or Rights of the United States Constitution.

Over the years, the leading role in shaping civil rights has been played by the U.S. Supreme Court. Much of its work has consisted of interpreting the freedoms referred to in the First, Fourth, Fifth, Sixth, and Eighth amendments to the U.S. Constitution. The First Amendment freedoms are those of religion, speech, and the press; the others have to do with the rights of persons accused of crime. Other rights, such as the right of privacy, have been fashioned out of various provisions of the Constitution.

One particularly important civil rights concept in the Constitution is due process of the law. The term *due process* is found in the Fifth and Fourteenth amendments to the Constitution. The Fifth Amendment prohibits the national government from depriving any person "of life, liberty, or property, without due process of law." State governments are similarly restricted by the Fourteenth Amendment.

Although the Supreme Court has not precisely defined due process it has generally used it to protect what the justices consider to be "fundamental rights" and to prohibit what they have found to be unreasonable, arbitrary, or simply unfair government action. The protections extended by the due process provision of the Fourteenth Amendment have been interpreted by the Court to include many of the fundamental rights found in the Bill of Rights. Through this process of incorporation, for example, the states as well as the national

---

[3] See Mary R. Jackman, "Education and Policy Commitment to Racial Integration," *American Journal of Political Science* 25 (May 1981); 256–269. See also Paul M. Sniderman et al., "Policy Reasoning and Political Values: The Problem of Racial Equality," *American Journal of Political Science*, 28 (February 1984); 75–94.

government are subject to First Amendment provisions regarding the freedoms of religion and speech.[4]

Over the years courts have directly applied due process as a test of both the substance of legislation, (substantive due process) and the procedures by which governmental activities are carried out (procedural due process). Some of the most important court decisions about procedural due process have involved the rights of those accused of crime. These rights are considered later in this chapter. The courts may invalidate a law on the bases of substantive due process regardless of how the law is administered. From the late nineteenth century until the mid 1930s, the Supreme Court often employed substantive due process in striking down laws that regulated business activity. Laws regulating the hours of labor, for example, were held to be inherently unreasonable restrictions on the liberty of business people and thus a violation of due process. Over the last several decades the Court has made little use of substantive due process in cases involving government regulations of business. Substantive due process has been used, however, in striking down legislation and regulations that conflict with what the Court has considered to be basic civil liberties. It played a role, for example, in the controversial abortion decisions discussed later in the chapter.

The Supreme Court, as noted in Chapter 9, cannot enforce its decisions. Its finding that a law or practice is unconstitutional may be ignored or circumvented and thus have little actual impact. There is not even any guarantee that a Supreme Court decision will be faithfully implemented by other courts. The willingness of state courts and lower federal courts to do so may differ widely. For example, some state courts felt obligated to implement the Supreme Court's decisions in school desegregation cases (discussed later in the chapter) as quickly as possible while other state courts decided to go slow in light of local political conditions. Because of their independence from state political systems, lower federal courts may generally be better able to implement controversial Supreme Court decisions.[5] Beyond the court system the course of civil rights policy depends on how decisions are received by the public and other political actors.

FUNDAMENTAL FREEDOMS

One of the values most cherished in this country, by liberals and conservatives alike, is individual freedom. Traditionally, freedom has been viewed as limiting government interference with basic rights.

[4] Because states have similar protections in their constitutions, litigants often have a choice of bringing a case under state or federal law.

[5] See Kenneth N. Vines, "Southern Supreme Courts and Race Relations," *Western Political Quarterly* 18 (March 1985): 5–18; and Kenneth C. Haas, "The Comparative Study of State and Federal Judicial Behavior Revisited," *Journal of Politics* 44 (1982): 721–746.

Freedom of Religion

The First Amendment to the Constitution begins by forbidding the government to make any law "respecting an establishment of religion, or prohibiting the free exercise thereof." In some cases, courts have had to decide whether a certain law or practice constitutes an establishment of religion. In others, the question has been whether government has infringed upon the free exercise of religion.

The establishment clause of the First Amendment has been viewed by the courts as preventing government from establishing a state religion and or otherwise favoring one religious sect over another. According to other judicial interpretations, the clause also prohibits government from favoring religion over nonreligion. Government, in short, is to be neutral on matters of religion. Some judges have insisted upon a "wall of separation" between church and state. In practice, however, the separation between church and state has been less than complete. Two major areas of controversy under the establishment clause have been government aid to parochial schools and religious services in public schools.

The right of parents to send their children to parochial rather than public schools has long been recognized by the Supreme Court.[6] Whether, how, and to what extent government can aid parochial schools, however, have been controversial subjects. The Supreme Court has not erected a wall of complete separation in answering these questions. In 1947, for example, the Court upheld a New Jersey law that allowed the use of tax money to bus children to Catholic schools. The judges reasoned that the aid was justified because it benefited the children by providing them with safe transportation.[7]

The child-benefit theory has been used to uphold a number of other types of aid to parochial schools, such as providing nonreligious textbooks, lunches, and health services. But the Supreme Court has found some forms of aid, such as using public funds to pay the salaries of parochial school teachers, to involve an "excessive entanglement" of church and state.[8]

In total governments provide considerable assistance to parochial schools. In 1970 the Court held that state governments could give tax exemptions to church property used for religious purposes.[9] In addition, the national government provides funds for low-income students in both public and church-related schools under the Elementary and Secondary Education Act (ESEA) of 1965. The Supreme Court has not directly ruled upon the church–state questions involved in the act. It has, however, sanctioned the right of the

---

[6] *Pierce* v. *Society of Sisters of the Holy Name,* 268 U.S. 510 (1925).

[7] *Everson* v. *Board of Education,* 330 U.S. 504.

[8] See *Lemon* v. *Kurtzman,* 402 U.S. 602 (1971); and *Meek* v. *Pittenger,* 421 U.S. 349 (1975).

[9] *Walz* v. *Tax Commission of the City of New York,* 397 U.S. 664.

national government to fund church-sponsored colleges for construction of new facilities.[10]

Other than the child-benefit theory, an argument often made on behalf of government aid to parochial schools is that these schools are in financial trouble; if they are not helped, millions of students will be forced into an already inadequate public school system. Closing parochial schools, especially 12,000 Catholic elementary and secondary schools, would double the burden on public school systems in some communities.

In the first major case relating to the use of public schools for religious exercises, the Court in 1948 invalidated a practice in Illinois under which religious instruction was provided for students during school hours.[11] The Court has held, however, that religious instruction classes for public school children do not violate the Constitution if they are held on other than school property.[12]

The most controversial Supreme Court decisions involving religious exercises in public schools have been *Engel* v. *Vitale* (1962)[13] and *Abington School District v. Schempp* (1963)[14] In the *Engel* case the Court struck down a practice in New York by students recited a nondenominational prayer prepared by the State board of Regents. The Court concluded that government should not be in the business of writing prayers. The *Schempp* decision found the Court invalidating the reading or recitation of the Bible in public schools. Despite these rulings, there are a number of schools in which religious exercises are held.[15] Some states have attempted to avoid direct confrontation with Court decisions by passing laws allowing silent meditation.

The right to freely exercise one's religious convictions, like other rights contained in the Constitution, is subject to numerous limitations. Congress, for example, was allowed to prohibit the Mormon practice of polygamy as a condition for admitting Utah as a state.[16] The right of Navahjo Indians to use peyote as part of a religious ritual has been recognized by some lower courts. A federal court of appeals, however, rejected the claim of Timothy Leary that he be permitted to use marijuana because it was required in his religious practices.

Many of the most striking recognitions of free-exercise rights have related to established minority religions. The Supreme Court in 1972, for

[10] *Tilton* v. *Richardson*, 403 U.S. 672 (1971).

[11] *McCollum* v. *Board of Education*, 333 U.S. 203.

[12] *Zorach* v. *Clauson*, 343 U.S. 306 (1952).

[13] 370 U.S. 421.

[14] 374 U.S. 203.

[15] See, for example, Robert H. Birkby, "The Supreme Court and the Bible Belt: Tennessee Reaction the Schempp Decision," *Midwest Journal of Political Science* 10 (August 1966); 304–315; and, more generally, Frank J. Sorauf, *The Wall of Separation: The Constitutional Politics of Church and State* (Princeton, N.J.: Princeton University Press, 1976).

[16] See *Reynolds* v. *United States*, 98 U.S. 145 (1878).

instance, held that the efforts of the state of Wisconsin to compel Amish children to attend school beyond the eighth grade conflicted with that group's basic religious tenets and practices.[17]

In a long line of cases, the Supreme Court has also recognized the free-exercise rights of Jehovah's Witnesses. Cases decided in the 1930s and 1940s gave this sect the right to solicit door to door and to distribute religious literature on city streets even though those activities violated municipal laws and interfered with the privacy of others. During the Second World War the Court ruled that children of Jehovah's Witnesses could not refuse to salute the flag on the grounds that their religion regarded the flag to be a "graven image."[18] But after the war the Court reversed itself.

Congress and the Supreme Court have recognized the right of persons to be excluded from military service on the basis of their religious or ethical beliefs. Those who wish exemptions, however, must be opposed to war in general, not simply a particular war.[19]

A recent free-exercise issue that appeared in the lower courts involved the attempt of parents to remove their children (mostly of college age) from religious sects such as Reverend Moon's Unification Church. The abduction of "Moonies" from their sects has been made legal on the grounds that the children are not capable of making their own decisions and should be protected by a court-appointed conservator. This officer of the court is legally entitled to return the children to their families. This is often done after the children are deprogrammed from the sect's beliefs. Some lower courts, however, have reversed conservatorship orders on the grounds that parents do not have legal control over their adult children and the children have the right to choose their own religion.

Freedom of Speech

Following the clauses dealing with religion, the First Amendment forbids government from "abridging the freedom of speech, or of the press; or the right of the people peaceably to assemble, and to petition the government for a redress of grievances." The Supreme Court has also found that a general right of association may be inferred from the First Amendment.

These rights have been looked upon by many judges as occupying a preferred position among those guaranteed by the Constitution. According to this view, these rights merit special protection because they are vital to the democratic functioning of our political system. In practice, however, the Court has permitted several limitations on them. The right of free speech, for example,

---

[17] *Wisconsin* v. *Yoder,* 406 U.S. 205.

[18] See *West Virginia Board of Education* v. *Barnette,* 319 U.S. 624 (1943).

[19] See *Welsh* v. *United States,* 398 U.S. 333 (1970); and *Gillette* v. *United States* 401 U.S. 437 (1971).

has been balanced against the need for public order and national security. Under a rule promulgated by Justice Oliver Wendell Holmes, free speech may be limited when it leads to a "clear and present danger" of developments government has a right to prevent.[20] The Court has occasionally employed this "clear and present danger" test. It has also used a less liberal "bad tendency" test, under which the gravity of the action advocated—for instance, the violent overthrow of the United States government—is enough to limit speech even if the danger of this action being committed is not imminent. As a more general rule, the courts have held that speech may be limited—for example, by the police—if it contains "fighting words" that appear likely to lead to a riot.

In practice, the Supreme Court has approached freedom of expression problems case by case rather than from a consistent philosophical point of view. Generally the Court has insisted upon a compelling public interest to justify laws or practices that limit free speech. A "compelling public interest," like many other judicial tests, is, of course, what the judges decide it to be. As a result, many free-speech and assembly cases have been controversial. An example is a 1978 decision by a U.S. district court judge that a group of American Nazis had the right to march through Skokie, Illinois, a suburb of Chicago containing many Jews, some of them survivors of concentration camps run by German Nazis during World War II. Skokie officials had attempted to prevent the march on the grounds that it would likely lead to violence. The court found that the measures taken by city officials to prevent the march (which included the posting of high personal-liability bonds) interfered with the Nazis' rights to free speech and assembly. The anticipated conflict was avoided, however, when the Nazi group decided to rally elsewhere in Chicago.

Among the laws that limit free expression are those relating to sedition, libel, slander, and obscenity. Sedition is an attempt to overthrow government. In the 1940s and 1950s, Congress adopted a number of laws aimed at political conspiracies. The Supreme Court in 1951 upheld one of these, the Smith Act of 1940, which makes it illegal for any group or individual to advocate the use of force or violence to overturn the government.[21] But in a later case the Court concluded that simply preaching communist doctrine in the abstract, without urging people to rebel, did not constitute sedition.[22]

Libel and slander defame the character of an individual or a group. Libel is carried out in written statements, slander to in oral ones. Public officials enjoy immunity from libel and slander suits for remarks made while performing their official duties. On the other hand, judicial rulings have made it difficult for governmental officials and other prominent public figures to sue those who defame them. Newspapers and individuals may even make false statements

---

[20] *Schenck* v. *United States*, 249 U.S. 47 (1919).

[21] *Dennis* v. *United States*, 341 U.S. 494.

[22] *Yates* v. *United States*, 354 U.S. 298 (1957).

about such individuals. To win a libel or slander suit, a plaintiff must prove that the false statements were made with deliberate malice or with reckless disregard for the truth.[23]

Material judged obscene does not quality for constitutional protection. Thus the production, sale, or transportation of obscene material may be prohibited and punished by law. Mere possession of obscene material for private use, however, is not a crime.[24] The Supreme Court has employed several standards in judging what is obscene and what is not. Material (movies, books, magazines) considered to have some redeeming social value or whose basic theme does not appeal to prurient interests is not judged obscene.[25] In the 1973 case of *Miller* v. *California*,[26] the Court decided that the task of judging obscenity should be assumed by local courts in light of community standards. Under this ruling, what is obscene varies from area to area. The Court, however, has not always honored local discretion and on occasion has exerted its right to review lower court decisions on this subject. In the case of *Jenkins* v. *Georgia* (1974), for example, the Court reversed the decision of a jury in Albany, Georgia, and held that the movie *Carnal Knowledge* was not obscene under the Constitution.[27] In the end, what is obscene is a matter of highly subjective judgment. Former Supreme Court justice Potter Stewart once declared that he could not define obscenity but that he knew it when he saw it.

Freedom of the Press

Under the First Amendment Congress, and by interpretation state governments, is prohibited from abridging the freedom of the press. This freedom, like that of speech, is not absolute. The press in this country has, however, generally enjoyed constitutional protection against censorship or prior restraints on what it may publish. This point was reemphasized in *New York Times Company* v. *United States* (1971), in which the Supreme Court rejected the efforts of the Nixon administration to prevent the *New York Times* and other newspapers from publishing *The Pentagon Papers*.[28] This "classified" study of policies on the war in Vietnam had been leaked to the press by Daniel Ellsberg a former Pentagon employee. The government in this case failed to convince a majority of the justices that censorship was necessary in the interest of national security.

For much of the nation's history the press has been relatively free to criticize government officials and prominent citizens without risking a libel suit. This broad right of the press—a right thought by some to be essential in an open

[23] See *New York Times* v. *Sullivan,* 376 U.S. 254 (1964).

[24] *Stanley* v. *Georgia,* 394 U.S. 557 (1969).

[25] See *Roth* v. *United States,* 354 U.S. 476 (1957).

[26] 413 U.S. 15.

[27] 418 U.S. 153.

[28] 403 U.S. 713.

society—was recognized by the Supreme Court in *New York Times* v. *Sullivan* (1964). In this case the Court declared that the press could be subject to libel damages only if what it wrote about a public official was false *and* the official involved proved that the publisher or editor knew that the story was false or did not care if it was false. For several years the *Sullivan* rule kept the press all but immune from libel suits, not only by public officials but by celebrities outside of government. Since the mid 1970s, however, libel suits have become more common and the courts have restricted the category of "public figures" whose right to sue is limited by the *Sullivan* ruling. Broadcasters, who have enjoyed protections against suits comparable to that given the print media, have also become more vulnerable to litigation.

A broad area in which attempts have been made to limit what may be printed (or broadcast or telecast) is that of criminal trials. In any given trial, the freedom of the press or the people's right to know may conflict with the right, under the Sixth Amendment, of an accused person to a fair trial by an impartial jury. Prejudicial publicity before or during a trial may serve as grounds on which a conviction can be set aside. In 1966, for example, prejudicial publicity prompted the Supreme Court to reverse the conviction of Dr. Samuel Sheppard on the charge of murdering his wife.[29] Retried in an Ohio court, Sheppard was acquitted.

Concern with prejudicial publicity has prompted some lower court judges to exclude the press from preliminary hearings and to forbid it from reporting the evidence presented at trial. In a 1976 case, *Nebraska Press Association* v. *Stuart*,[30] the Supreme Court ruled that such restrictions on the press violated the First Amendment. The Court suggested that trial courts should attempt to avoid publicity by such means as delaying the trial, holding it in a different location, or sequestering (isolating) the jury.

Other constitutional issues involving freedom of the press concern the right of reporters to refuse to disclose the sources of their stories or unpublished interviews and the access of individuals to the media themselves. Reporters have commonly based their refusal to disclose their sources to a judicial body or a governmental agency on the grounds that the sources would dry up if unprotected and they would then be unable to secure information. Several states have adopted laws giving reporters some protection from disclosing their sources. The Supreme Court, however, has held that reporters must reveal their sources if asked to do so by a grand jury.[31] In several instances, reporters who have refused to disclose their sources have been sent to jail.

More to the liking of the press was a decision in 1974 in which the Court

---

[29] *Sheppard* v. *Maxwell*, 384 U.S. 333.

[30] 427 U.S. 539.

[31] *United States* v. *Caldwell*, 408 U.S. 665 (1972). See also *Branzburg* v. *Hayes*, 408 U.S. 665 (1972); and *In the Matter of Paul Pappas*, 408 U.S. 665 (1972).

invalidated a Florida "right-to-reply" law.[32] The law, passed in 1913, required newspapers to print the replies of candidates for public office whom they had assailed in their columns. Pat Tornillo, a candidate for the state legislature, had been severely criticized by editorials in the *Miami Herald* and, citing the 1913 law, had requested that the paper print his response. In invalidating that law under the First Amendment, the Court concluded that states could not tell editors what to print. This, like telling them what they could not print, amounted to censorship.

The broader argument, rejected by the Court in this case, was that the First Amendment was meant to allow people a diversity of views. Advocates of this positive interpretation of the First Amendment have argued that there is a concentration of power in the newspapers that makes it difficult, if not impossible, for those who disagree with an editor's viewpoint to present their own views.[33]

The Right to Privacy

Though the Constitution does not specifically mention a general right to privacy, the Supreme Court has derived such a right from its reading of a number of constitutional provisions. One of the most controversial Supreme Court cases in recent years involved the application of this principle to limit the power of state governments to control abortions. In the 1973 cases of *Roe* v. *Wade*[34] and *Doe* v. *Bolton*[35] the Court overturned abortion laws in Texas and Georgia and concluded that the right of privacy under the fourteenth Amendment is "broad enough to encompass a woman's decision whether or not to terminate her pregnancy." In so ruling the Court rejected the argument that unborn children are persons with constitutional rights.

The right to terminate a pregnancy, however, was not viewed as absolute: the Court held that states could regulate abortions after the third month of pregnancy. Decisions made in the first three months about abortion are of concern only to the woman and her physician. States may regulate abortion in the second three months of pregnancy only to protect the health of the woman. During this period they may regulate the persons and facilities involved in an abortion. States may prohibit abortions in the last three months of pregnancy except when such prohibition would interfere with the health of the mother.

Survey data reveal that the public has been about evenly divided on the abortion issue. Policies liberlizing abortion laws have had greater support among

---

[32] *Miami Herald Publishing Company* v. *Tornillo*, 418 U.S. 241.

[33] See Jerome A. Barron, *Freedom of the Press for Whom?* (Bloomington: Indiana University Press, 1973).

[34] 410 U.S. 113.

[35] 410 U.S. 179.

men than women, Protestants than Catholics, persons with college backgrounds than those without, persons under thirty than those thirty or over, and single persons than married persons. The views of women vary with age and education, young women possessing college educations being particularly inclined toward liberalization. Catholics in all segments of the population overwhelming oppose judicial decisions that make it easier to obtain an abortion.

Opposition to the 1973 rulings has been based mainly on moral and religious grounds. From the viewpoint of the opposition, the Supreme Court has sanctioned the killing of children. Some opponents of the Court's decision have looked upon the abortion issue s a crusade, somewhat comparable to the antiwar movement of the 1960s and early 1970s. As such, it justifies illegal activity such as setting abortion clinics on fire as well as the more conventional approaches of lobbying and litigation. Proponents of liberalized abortion laws, among when population control and women's liberation groups have been prominent, have defended the right of women to choose whether they want an abortion, contending that their opponents are simply trying to impose their religious views on others. Many politicians, caught between two intense and vocal camps, have found it difficult to take a clear stand on the issue.

Since 1973 the Supreme Court has reaffirmed its basic ruling in the *Roe* case on several occasions, though some of these decisions have been by a five-to-four margin. However, the Court has also upheld a congressional decision not to provide funds for abortions under the medicaid program as "medically necessary services" for the poor.

Over the years the Court has found other state law—for example, those banning interracial marriages or the distribution of contraceptives—to violate the constitutional right to privacy. A departure from this line of rulings came in 1986 when the Court, in *Bowers* v. *Hardwick*, upheld a Georgia law making sodomy (oral or anal sex) a felony. This five to four ruling is expected to have little more than a symbolic effect. Over half of the states have decriminalized consensual sodomy, and even where such laws remain on the books they are not well enforced—in large part because they are extremely difficult to enforce. Opinion polls suggest that a large majority of people feel that the government has no business prohibiting sexual practices between consenting adults, be they homosexual or heterosexual. On the other hand, fear of the spread of AIDS, a deadly disease apparently spread in large part by sodomy, may prompt more restrictions on sexual activity.

CRIMINAL JUSTICE

G. Gordon Liddy, one of those sentenced to jail for involvement in the Watergate scandal, once concluded, "Obviously crime pays, or there'd be no crime."[36] Whether or not it actually pays, crime does appear to be as American as cherry pie. Recent statistics from the Federal Bureau of Investigation indicate that one property crime occurs in the United States every three seconds and one violent crime every twenty-four seconds. From most accounts there is much organized criminal activity in the United States, such as illegal gambling, loan sharking (lending money above the maximum interest rate established by state law), prostitution, narcotics, land frauds, and corruption of public officials. The crime problem is considerably widened by the inclusion of white-collar crimes such as price fixing, securities frauds, and tax evasion. Most Americans appear particularly bothered by crime in the streets (compared with crime in the suites) because it involves direct threats to their security and physical well-being.

Americans, as suggested earlier in the chapter, also appear skeptical of procedural protections given to people accused of crime. These are regarded by many people as mere technicalities that allow the guilty to go free. On the other hand, they are essential safeguards against arbitrary governmental action. As former Supreme Court justice Felix Frankfurter said, "the history of American freedom is, in no small measure, the history of procedure."[37]

Provisions relating to the right of people accused of crime are found in the basic text of the Constitution and several of its amendments. The former protects individuals against bills of attainder, ex post facto laws, and suspension of the writ of habeas corpus except in times of emergency. The Constitution also guarantees a jury trial to persons accused of committing a federal crime.

A bill of attainder is a legislative act that directly punishes an individual or a group without giving it the benefit of a judicial trial. An ex post facto law punishes someone for something that was not a crime when he or she did it or increases the penalty for a crime after it was committed. A writ of habeas corpus is a court order directing an arresting officer or another official to bring a prisoner to court and to explain why this person is being held.

Additional provisions concerning criminal matters are found in the Fourth, Fifth, Sixth, and Eighth amdnements to the Constitution. With a few exceptions, the protections contained in these amendments apply to the activities of both the states and the national government. The remainder of this section considers the basic safeguards provided by these amendments.

Protections Against Search and Seizure

The Fourth Amendment of the Constitution is intended to make people secure "in their persons, houses, papers, and effects, against unreasonable searches and seizures." Until the early 1970s the Supreme Court generally required police to secure a search warrant from a judicial officer that described

---

[36] Quoted in "Overheard," *Newsweek*, November 10, 1986, p. 19.

[37] *Malinski* v. *New York,* 324 U.S. 401 (1945), p. 414.

the place to be searched and the person or evidence to be seized. The Warren Court (1953–69) tended to look upon searches made without a warrant as unreasonable and thus in violation of the Fourth Amendment. The Court under Chief Justice Warren Burger (1969–86) greatly expanded the exceptions to the rule requiring a warrant; it was more concerned with whether in a given set of circumstances the search itself is reasonable.[38]

In many situations police do not have to secure a search warrant. The Supreme Court, for example, has not required police to secure a warrant to stop and frisk a suspect, search a vehicles (if they have reason to believe it was involved in a crime or contains evidence of a crime), or search people who have been lawfully arrested. A search may even be made of an individual arrested on a minor traffic violation. The danger is that a traffic arrest may serve simply as a pretext for a search. In 1986 the Court also ruled that a warrant is not needed by police using airplanes to search for marijuana growing in fenced-in residential yards. While the search of a home may generally require a warrant, the search of a private back yard, like that of an open field, does not.

It is difficult to tell whether a specific search and seizure will, if challenged, be upheld by the Supreme Court. If it is determined that evidence was illegally obtained, the evidence may not be used in court. This *exclusionary rule* has been the major deterrent to unreasonable searches and seizures. On the other hand, it has not prevented as many confictions as is commonly assumed. Courts, particularly in recent years, have been reluctant to disallow evidence, even in the presence of doubt about how it was obtained. Under an *inevitable discovery* rule, for example, evidence that courts feel the police were bound to find anyway is acceptable even if secured through procedural shortcuts.

Governmental use of wiretapping and eavesdropping devices generally require a court warrant. The chief exception recognized in law is the president's authority to order bugging and tapping in cases involving national security. The phrase *national security,* of course, is vague enough to justify a wide range of actions. In 1972, however, the Supreme Court rejected an argument by the Nixon administration tht it did not have to obtain a warrant to tap and bug private citizens suspected of being a threat to internal security.[39] Left open in this decision was the question of whether a warrant was needed to maintain electronic surveillance of foreign agents.

The extent to which Supreme Court decisions and acts of Congress have actually protected private citizens against violations of the Fourth Amendment has been far less than one might expect. Disclosures have made it dramatically clear, for example, that the Federal Bureau of Investigation has long engaged in illegal burglaries, wiretaps, and buggings. The Watergate scandals are testimony

[38] See J. W. Peltason, *Understanding the Constitution,* 7th ed. (Hinsdale, Ill.: Dryden Press, 1976), pp. 145-147.

[39] *United States* v. *United States District Court,* 407 U.S. 297.

that a president of the United States may not be above using these methods to punish his political enemies.

Fifth Amendment Protections

In addition to a general guarantee of due process, the Fifth Amendment of the Constitution contains three provisions that affect the rights of those accused of crime: (1) no person is to be tried on a federal offense unless first indicted by a grand jury; (2) no person may be placed in double jeopardy; and (3) no person "shall be compelled in any criminal case to be a witness against himself" or herself.

A grand jury is a group of not more than twenty-three citizens that, after hearing evidence presented by a prosecuting attorney, determines whether persons will be tried for alleged crimes. The states are not required to indict (formally accuse) persons through grand-jury proceedings. Usually state and local prosecutors file an *information* (sworn affidavit) that the evidence is sufficient to justify a trial.

The double jeopardy provision means that once a person has been found innocent of a specific charge, he or she cannot be tried again for the same offense. The ban, however, applies only to trials by the same government. Thus an individual may be tried for the same offense by the national government and the various state governments.

The protection against self-incrimination is intended to prevent coerced (forced) confessions. The right is frequently exercised in courtrooms or before congressional committees: defendants or witnesses "take the fifth" and refuse to answer questions. However, they may face punishment if they refuse to testify after having been given immunity from prosecution for what they say.

The danger of coerced confessions has been greater during interrogation in the police station than at trial. Confessions during interrogation may be coerced by physical means or by psychological pressure—for example, long periods of questioning that wear down the accused. Evidence secured through coercion may not be used in a trial. This assumes, of course, that the coercion is discovered and brought to the attention of a court, and that the court (ultimately the Supreme Court) agrees that the coercion violated the Fifth Amendment.

In the case of *Miranda* v. *Arizona* (1966),[40] the Warren Court set off a wave of controversy by reversing the conviction of a man (Miranda) for kidnapping and rape on the grounds that his confession to police was made in violation of the privilege against self-incrimination. Miranda, it should be noted, was reconvicted by the state of Arizona on the basis of evidence other than his confession. In deciding the *Miranda* case, the Court ruled that statements made by an accused to the police can be used as evidence only if the police, prior to any

[40] 384 U.S. 436.

questioning, do two things. One is to warn the accused that he or she has the right to remain silent and that anything the individual chooses to say may be used against him or her in court. The second is to inform the accused that he or she has the right to have an attorney present during interrogation and that an attorney will be provided if he or she cannot afford one.

Critics of the decision feared it would greatly reduce the ability of the police to secure confessions. Research on the subject suggests that the ruling has had little effect on the percentage of cases decided on the basis of a confession and, indeed, little effect on police interrogation in general.[41] Since the early 1970s the Supreme Court has nibbled away at the *Miranda* ruling by holding that statements made in violation of the warning and informational requirements may be used at the trial in certain circumstances, such as to discredit the testimony of the accused.[42]

Right to a Fair Trial

Protection against self-incrimination and the exclusion of evidence illegally obtained have been central elements in the legal concept of a fair trial. The Sixth Amendment contains additional elements of a fair trial, requiring trials to be speedy, public, and heard by an impartial jury. The amendment also requires the accused to be allowed to confront witnesses against them and have the right to legal assistance.

The provisions of the Sixth Amendment, like others in the Constitution, have been modified by judicial interpretation. The Supreme Court has recognized, for example, that the goal of speed does not have priority over the right of accused persons to procedural fairness. The guarantee of a public trial is intended to eliminate secret proceedings against an individual. The provision protects the rights of the accused, not the right of media to cover trials. Publicity, on the other hand, may be deemed by the courts to be detrimental to the accused, particularly to their right to trial by an impartial jury. The goal of an impartial jury has also led the Court to hold that specific groups of people, such as women, cannot be excluded from jury service.[43] In a recent case, however, the Court ruled that the right to a trial by an impartial jury is not denied if people strongly opposed to capital punishment are excluded from jury duty. The decision (*Lockhart* v. *McCree*, 1986), upholding the use of "death-qualified" juries, removed a barrier to the use of the death penalty.

As for the provision of legal services, the Court has decided that governments have an obligation to see that accused persons have counsel if they

---

[41] See David Fellman, "The Supreme Court's Changing Views of Criminal Defendants' Rights," in Barbara N. McLennan (ed.), *Crime in Urban Society* (New York: Dunnellen, 1970), pp. 110–113.

[42] See *Harris* v. *New York,* 401 U.S. 222 (1971).

[43] *Taylor* v. *Louisiana,* 419 U.S. 522 (1975).

so wish and that counsel be provided at public expense to those unable to hire their own. Legal assistance is to be given in any case where there is a possibility of a jail sentence[44] and extends not only to the trial but also to the pretrial and appeal stages.

Protections Concerning Bail and Punishment

The Eighth Amendment to the Constitution provides that "excessive bail shall not be required, nor excessive fines imposed, nor cruel and unusual punishments inflicted." In many cases judges or magistrates will order an accused person to post bail (a sum of money) as a condition of pretrial release. The basic purpose of bail is to help ensure that the accused will appear in court when his or her trial comes up. The inability of individuals to raise bail has often meant that they are forced to stay in jail for weeks or months pending their trial. In effect, they are punished without having been proved guilty of any crime. The constitutional prohibition of excessive bail is designed to elleviate this problem and minimize the advantages the bail system gives to the rich over the poor.

Magistrates and trial court judges have considerable discretion in determining whether an individual will be allowed to raise bail and, if so, what amount of bail will be required. Further opportunities to avoid pretrial detention, however, have been provided by federal and state legislation that permits magistrates and trial court judges to release accused persons simply on their own recognizance (their promise to appear at trial). Such releases are made in light of such factors as the seriousness of the crime and the record and community ties of the accused.

The Eighth Amendment ban on cruel and unusual punishments has been used to review the sentences given for particular crimes by legislatures and judges. Since the mid 1960s, it has also been used by the courts in reviewing prison practices and regulations.[45] Historically the amendment has been used to prohibit punishments that are disproportionate to the crime (for instance, a twenty-year prison sentence for selling marijuana) and punishments that are in themselves cruel and unusual, such as mutilation and burning.

The major methods of imposing the death penalty (hanging, shooting, electrocution, and gaseous asphyxiation) have been upheld under the Eighth Amendment. In 1972, the Supreme Court decided that existing death-penalty or capital-punishment laws were themselves applied in an arbitrary and capri-

---

[44] *Argersinger* v. *Hamlin,* 407 U.S. 25 (1972).

[45] See Larry C. Berkson, "The Eighth Amendment: A New Frontier of Creative Constitutional Law," in Stephen L. Wasby (ed.), *Civil Liberties: Policy and Policy Making* (Lexington, Mass.: Heath, Lexington Books, 1976), pp. 107–118.

cious manner and thus constituted cruel and unusual punishment.[46] Among those who have received the death penalty the most have been blacks and poor whites.

State governments responded to the 1972 decision by making laws that reserved capital punishment for specially defined offenses. In 1976 the Supreme Court upheld new laws in three states that imposed capital punishment for those found guilty of murder.[47] The Court has decided, however, that states cannot automatically impose the death penalty for murder or any other crime. Though Supreme Court justices have disagreed on what procedures are necessary for imposing the penalty, the trial courts are to consider the nature of the crime, the record of the defendant, and other mitigating circumstances in each case.

The cruel and unusual punishment clause also received increased interest in the 1970s because of its application to prison practices and conditions. Courts have insisted, for example, that prison administrators may impose solitary confinement but that those so confined are entitled to adequate clothing, a ventilated room, and a mattress during sleeping hours.[48] In some cases judges have found that entire penal systems or specific facilities within systems are so overcrowded that they violate the Eighth Amendment's prohibition of cruel and unusual punishment.

EQUAL JUSTICE

The word *equality,* like other value-laden words, has been variously interpreted. In one sense the term has reflected the notion that no person, despite his or her inherited characteristics or social status, is inherently better than or inferior to another person. This in essence is the view expressed in the Declaration of Independence that all people "are created equal." Closely tied to this view is one that governments in the United States should treat everyone equally (or, in a negative sense, should not give some better treatment than others). This viewpoint was admirably articulated in a Supreme Court case late in the previous century:

> In view of the Constitution, in the eye of the law, there is in this country no superior, dominant ruling class of citizens. There is no caste here. Our Constitution is color-blind, and neither knows nor tolerates classes among citizens. In respect of civil rights, all citizens are equal before the law. The humblest is the peer of the most powerful.[49]

[46] *Furman* v. *Georgia,* 408 U.S. 238.
[47] *Gregg* v. *Georgia,* 428 U.S. 513.
[48] Berkson, op. cit., p. 111.
[49] John Marshall Harlan, dissenting opinion, *Plessy* v. *Ferguson,* 163 U.S. 537, 559, (1896).

A third view of equality emphasizes the goal of insuring that all people have an equal opportunity to go as far as their talents and abilities may take them. Advancement in life should not be denied because of barriers that have nothing to do with merit. A fourth view of equality is that people should be given equal benefits. Achieving this goal requires some discrimination against the haves in favor of the have-nots.

Obviously the concept of inherent equality has been rejected by those who have regarded large groups of people, such as racial minorities, as somehow inferior and thus less less deserving of the benefits of society and of equality under the law. Many Americans now agree, in broad principle at least, that people should not be discriminated against on the basis of such characteristics as race, sex, national origin, or religion. There is considerable controversy, however, over whether various groups should have equal benefits—for example, the right to employment or education in proportion to their numbers in the general population.

The principal constitutional protections against governmental discrimination are the equal protection clause of the Fourteenth Amendment, which applies to the states, and the due process clause of the Fifth Amendment, which applies to the national government. These provisions, as interpreted by the courts, allow governments to classify people for various purposes as long as the classifications are not unreasonable. Courts, for example, will not find fault with state laws that deny a driver's license to blind people. Laws that deny a driver's license to people with red hair, on the other hand, would be found unreasonable or arbitrary. What is "unreasonable" or "abritrary" may vary from court to court. Much depends on who is discriminated against and in what areas the discrimination takes place. Discrimination based on race and, in recent years, sex are particularly likely to be reviewed by the courts. Also likely to be reviewed are discriminatory practices involving such fundamental rights as voting.

In addition to court decisions, numerous federal and state laws forbid discrimination on the basis of race, color, religion, national origin, or sex in such spheres as voting, housing, use of public accommodations, and employment. Federal regulations have also required public and many private employers to avoid discrimination against women and disadvantaged groups (for example, blacks, American Indians, and Hispanics) and to take positive steps to recruit, employ, and promote members of these groups.

School Desegregation

Two of the most controversial types of cases involving equality have been school desegregation and affirmative action. Controversy over school desegregation stems from the Supreme Court's decision in *Brown* v. *Board of Education* (1954), in which the Court unanimously held that segregation violated the equal protection clause of the Fourteenth Amendment[50] The Court initially took a cautious approach to the problem of implementing its decision. Rejecting the advice of the National Association for the Advancement of Colored People and others, the Court decided to give the states, especially those in the South, time to adjust to the new standard. The states were asked to comply "with all deliberate speed." From 1954 to 1964 there was considerably more deliberation than speed. By 1964 only about one of every hundred black students attended an integrated school. The rate of integration began to increase in the mid 1960s after Congress threatened to cut off aid to segregated facilities. By the early 1970s about 40 percent of all black students were enrolled in schools in which at least half of the students were white.

While the vast majority of white parents have kept their children in desegregated schools, many have sent their children to private schools to avoid desegregation. Research suggests, moreover, that many white parents who continue to send their children to integrated schools would transfer them to private schools if they could afford to do so. In this situation, government aid to private education such as grants or tax credits for tuition, could be expected to work against the integration cause.[51]

Since the 1970s the Supreme Court has been faced with problems of de facto segregation caused by segregated housing patterns, particularly in northern cities. Much controversy has grown from lower court orders to bus children from one neighborhood to another as a means of achieving racial balance in schools. The Supreme Court has upheld the right of lower court judges to order busing but has not approved of court-ordered busing across school-district lines—for example, from central cities, where much of the black population is concentrated, to white suburban areas.[52]

Many people dislike the idea of busing to achieve racial integration, even though they may consider themselves opposed to school segregation. Research suggests that attitudes toward busing have little effect on those having a personal stake in the issue. Adults who have children in public schools, for example, are neither more nor less opposed to busing than those who do not have children in public schools. Perhaps more important than considerations of self-interest (that is, how busing affects an individual's life) in explaining adult opposition to busing are attitudes formed in childhood reflecting political conservatism (opposition to change) and racial prejudice. As black leader Jesse Jackson once put it, "It ain't the bus, it's us."[53] Only about 3 percent of all busing done in this

[50] 347 U.S. 483.

[51] Michael W. Giles and Douglas S. Gatlin, "Mass-Level Compliance with Public Policy: The Case of School Desegregation," *Journal of Politics* 42 (1980): 722–746.

[52] *Swann* v. *Charlotte-Mecklenberg Board of Education*, 402 U.S. 1 (1971).

[53] Quoted in H. Frank Way, Jr., *Liberty in the Balance: Current Issues in Civil Liberties* (New York: McGraw-Hill, 1976), p. 1. See also David O. Sears, Carl P. Hensler, and Leslie K. Speer, "Whites' Opposition to 'Busing': Self-Interest or Symbolic Politics?" *American*

nation results from desegregation efforts. Considerable busing is undertaken to get away from integrated schools.

The actual effects of school integration on the education of minorities, however, have been disputed. Some researchers have found that school integration encourages a white flight to the suburbs, which means that schools will ultimately be resegregated. Others have discovered that school integration in itself is not a major cause of white movement to the suburbs.[54] A general consensus does exist, however, on the danger of resegregation, and those who oppose this trend have called for integration plans that cut across school-district lines and extend into the suburbs.

Another dispute is whether blacks benefit from attending racially integrated schools. the 1965 ruling in *Brown* v. *Board of Education* rested in part on social science research indicating that segregation reinforced black children's feelings of inferiority and thus inhibited their academic achievement. Some studies suggest that blacks actually do better in integrated schools. Another line of research, however, argues that integration has not significantly raised black achievement or self-esteem.[55]

Affirmative Action

Affirmative action in employment and preferential treatment of women and minorities in such areas as education have been among the most explosive civil rights issues. Opponents of affirmative action have generally claimed that opportunity should be based on a person's ability rather than a person's race or sex and that the practice amounts to reverse discrimination against white males. Defenders of affirmative action contend that it is needed to make up for years of discrimination against women and minorities and to help insure that unfair barriers to their economic and social mobility will be removed. Proponents of affirmative action have also argued that methods of determining whether an applicant for a job or for advancement is qualified, such as written tests and personal evaluations, are often biased and unrelated to job performance.[56]

Political Science Review 79 (June 1979): 368–384; and John B. McConahy, "Self-Interest Versus Racial Attitudes As Correlates of Anti-Busing Attitudes in Louisville: Is It The Buses Or The Blacks?" *Journal of Politics* 44 (1982): 692–720.

[54] See James S. Coleman and others, *Equality of Educational Opportunity* (Washington, D.C.: Government Printing Office, 1966); Christine H. Rossell, "School Desegregation and White Flight," *Political Science Quarterly* 90 (Winter 1975–1976); 675–695; and U.S. Commission on Civil Rights, op. cit.

[55] For a negative view of the effects of integration, see David J. Armor, "The Evidence on Busing," *Public Interest,* Summer 1972, pp. 90–126. U.S. Commission on Civil Rights, op. cit.

[56] The Supreme Court has held that employment tests may be invalid under Title 7 of the Civil Rights Act of 1964 if they are not relevant to the qualifications needed to perform the job in question. *Griggs* v. *Duke Power Co.,* 401 U.S. 424 (1971).

The Supreme Court in *The Regents of the University of California* v. *Allan Bakke* (1978) showed itself to be badly divided over affirmative action.[57] The case involved the rights of a white male, Bakke, who had been rejected for admission to the University of California's medical school at Davis even though his grades and test scores were above those of several minority students who were admitted. This happened because the medical school employed an affirmative action plan that reserved 16 of every 100 admissions each year for members of minority groups. Bakke claimed he had been discriminated against because he was white. The university and the Justice Department (the latter filing a separate brief as amicus curiae, or friend of the court) argued that affirmative action was necessary to overcome past discrimination.

Five Supreme Court justices, a majority, declared that the university had erred in its particular affirmative action plan and had to admit Bakke to the medical school. A reading of the opinions in the case (six were written), however, leads to the conclusion that a majority of the justices found nothing wrong with the principle of affirmative action and that a more flexible plan (that is, one that did not have a specific numerical cutoff) could pass the test of constitutionality. The Court in *Bakke* left unsettled the question of how far employers could go with affirmative action programs designed to help minorities find better jobs. That issue reached the Supreme Court in a case involving Brian Weber, a white employee who filed suit after two blacks with less seniority were promoted ahead of him. Weber failed to get the promotion because his company had implemented a system that favored minorities. The Court concluded that the practice used by the company was in keeping with the 1964 Civil Rights Act, which was designed to aid minorities, and with the Constitution.[58]

Though sometimes limiting the scope of affirmative action programs in the work place, the Supreme Court has generally upheld in the principle of affirmative action and rejected the position, advanced by conservatives, including the Reagan administration, that only actual victims of discrimination should be given preferential treatment in employment. Decisions upholding affirmative action have been made by a divided court, however, and are probably not the last word on this topic.

CONCLUDING OBSERVATIONS

Civil rights struggles often involved deeply rooted conflicts between groups with different aspirations, life styles, and values. Often, as in the example of affirmative action, lawmakers are faced with a no-win situation because they cannot confer benefits to one party without denying benefits to another. In the United States, such conflicts ultimately wind up in the courts. More broadly,

[57] 438 U.S. 265.
[58] *Steelworkers* v. *Weber*, 443 U.S. 193 (1979).

courts have been faced with the tasks of protecting minorities (whether economic, political, or social) and drawing a balance between the need for individual freedom and the need for order.

One prominent judicial scholar has concluded that "the Supreme Court of the United States is beyond question the great and ultimate defender of the basic freedoms of the American People."[59] While many would agree with this sentiment, it should also be noted that the Court, as well as other participants in the political system, has sometimes been lax in performing its function as defender of freedom. One flagrant example, mentioned in Chapter 9, was the refusal of the court to intervene on behalf of some 120,000 Japanese–Americans who were forced into concentration camps in the western United States during World War II. These people were judged national security risks not because of anything they had done but simply because of their heritage. Basic rights and liberties found in the Constitution cannot be taken for granted but require, in the words of nineteenth century abolitionist Wendell Phillips, "eternal vigilance."

SUMMARY

1. Civil rights cases reflect a variety of dislocations. These include international tensions, conflicts stemming from feelings of relative deprivation, and perceived threats to cherished values or ways of life.

2. Americans have been divided over the extension of basic civil liberties to minorities and unpopular groups. Generally the better educated and those most active in politics have been most likely, in principle at least, to favor constitutional guarantees.

3. One of the most basic civil liberties is due process. This concept has been used by the courts to protect fundamental rights from unreasonable or arbitrary governmental action. Often, the courts have insisted upon procedural due process—for example, that those accused of a crime be given the opportunity to defend themselves. Courts also have applied due process substantively, striking down laws found to be unreasonable or arbitrary regardless of how they are administered.

4. The First Amendment guarantees the freedoms of speech, assembly, and the press. These rights have generally been considered so fundamental to the functioning of a democratic political system that they have a preferred position among the rights guaranteed by the Constitution. Yet, even these rights are not absolute. Speech, for example, may be limited by laws regarding sedition, libel, slander, and obscenity.

[59] Henry J. Abraham, *The Judiciary* (Boston: Allyn and Bacon, 1985), p. 95.

5. The press (including the electronic as well as the print media) is relatively free to criticize public officials without risking libel or slander suits, and it enjoys a general protection against censorship. Courts have, however, attempted to restrict media coverage that interferes with the rights of individuals to a fair trial and have often required reporters to disclose the sources of their news stories.

6. The "right to privacy" limits the power of government to interfere with several matters, including abortion. The Supreme Court's 1973 abortion rulings reflect the difficult political position in which the courts sometimes find themselves.

7. Both the basic text of the Constitution and several of its amendments extend protections to people accused of crime. Central among these are the following: unreasonable searches and seizures are prohibited; no one in a criminal case is compelled to testify against himself or herself; trials are to be speedy, public, and heard by an impartial jury; the accused is allowed to confront witnesses against him or her and to have legal assistance; and those who are found guilty are not to be subject to cruel and unusual punishment. The implementation of these as well as other rights has depended mainly on judicial interpretations, and has involved much public controversy over the rights of society versus those of the accused.

8. The principle of equality is contained in a number of congressional acts and Supreme Court decisions that prohibit government or citizens from discriminating against others on the basis of their race, sex, religion, or national origin. Since the mid 1970s one of the most controversial civil rights areas has been affirmative action laws and regulations, which require that advantages be given to women and disadvantaged groups in such matters as jobs and admission to universities. Some have argued that affirmative action is wrong because it rewards people on the basis of sex or race rather than ability. Others have contended that such action is necessary to make up for decades of discrimination against these groups.

SELECTED READINGS

CHAPTER 2:
CONSTITUTIONAL CONDITIONS

BEARD, CHARLES A. *An Economic Interpretation of the Constitution.* New York: Macmillan, 1969.

BECKER, CARL L. *The Declaration of Independence.* New York: Vintage Books, 1942.

BOWEN, CATHERINE DRINKER. *Miracle at Philadelphia.* Boston: Little, Brown, 1966.

CHOPER, JESSE H. *Judicial Review and the National Political Process: A Functional Reconsideration of the Role of the Supreme Court.* Chicago: University of Chicago Press, 1980.

ELAZAR, DANIEL J. *American Federalism: A View From the States.* New York: Thomas Y. Crowell, 1972.

FARRAND, MAX. *The Framing of the Constitution of the United States.* New Haven: Yale University Press, 1962.

The Federalist. (available in several editions).

"GENERAL REVENUE SHARING AND FEDERALISM," *Annals* 419 (May 1975).

GLENDENING, PARRIS, AND MAVIS REEVES. *Pragmatic Federalism.* Pacific Palisades, Calif.: Palisades Publishers, 1977.

GOODWIN, ROBERT A., ED. *A Nation of States.* Chicago: Rand McNally, 1963.

GRODZIN, MORTON. *The American System.* Chicago: Rand McNally, 1966.

HOFSTADTER, RICHARD. *The American Political Tradition and the Men Who Made It.* New York: Knopf, 1973.

"INTERGOVERNMENTAL RELATIONS IN AMERICA TODAY," *Annals* 416 (November 1974).

JENSEN, MERRILL. *The Articles of Confederation.* Madison: University of Wisconsin Press, 1940.

——. *The Making of the American Constitution.* New York: D. Van Nostrand, 1964.

KELLY, ALFRED H., AND WINFRED A. HARBINSON. *The American Constitution: Its Origins and Development.* New York: W. W. Norton & Co., Inc., 1976.

MCDONALD, FORREST. *We the People: The Economic Origins of the Constitution.* Chicago: University of Chicago Press, 1958.

MARTIN, ROSCOE. *The Cities in the Federal System.* New York: Atherton, 1965.

MASON, ALPHEUS THOMAS, ED. *Free Government in the Making.* New York: Oxford University Press, 1972.

REAGAN, MICHAEL D., AND JOHN G. SANZONE. *The New Federalism.* New York: Oxford University Press, 1980.

RIKER, WILLIAM H. *Federalism: Origin, Operation, Significance.* Boston: Little, Brown, 1964.

ROSSITER, CLINTON L. *Seedtime of the Republic.* New York: Harcourt, Brace, 1953.

SHARKANSKY, IRA. *The Maligned States.* New York: McGraw-Hill, 1978.

SUNDQUIST, JAMES L, AND DAVID W. DAVIS. *Making Federalism Work.* Washington D.C.: Brookings Institution, 1969.

CHAPTER 3: CITIZEN INPUTS:
OPINION, PARTICIPATION, AND CONTROL

ABRAMSON, PAUL R. *Political Attitudes in America.* San Francisco: W. H. Freeman & Company Publishers, 1983.

CARROLL, SUSAN. *Women as Candidates in American Politics.* Bloomington: Indiana University Press, 1985.

DAWSON, RICHARD E., AND OTHERS. *Political Socialization.* Boston: Little, Brown, 1977.

EDELMAN, MURRAY. *Politics and Symbolic Action.* Chicago: Markham, 1971.

KEY, V. O., JR. *Public Opinion and American Democracy.* New York: Knopf, 1961.

LIPPMAN, WALTER. *The Public Philosophy.* Boston: Little, Brown, 1950.

MCCLOSKEY, HERBERT, AND JOHN ZALLER. *The American Ethos: Public Attitudes Toward Capitalism and Democracy.* Cambridge, Mass.: Harvard University Press, 1984.

SCHATTSCHNEIDER, E. E. *The Semi-Sovereign People.* New York: Holt, Rinehart & Winston, 1960.

VERBA, SIDNEY, AND NORMAN N. NIE. *Participation in America.* New York: Harper & Row, Pub., 1972.

WEISSBERG, ROBERT. *Public Opinion and Popular Government.* Englewood Cliffs, N.J.: Prentice-Hall, 1976.

CHAPTER 4:
GROUP POLITICS AND THE MEDIA

BAUER, RAYMOND, AND OTHERS. *American Business and Public Policy.* New York: Atherton, 1964.

BERRY, JEFFREY. *Lobbying for the People.* Princeton, N.J.: Princeton University Press, 1977.

———. *The Interest Group Society.* Boston: Little, Brown, 1984.

CARROLL, SUSAN. *Women as Candidates in American Politics.* Bloomington: Indiana University Press, 1985.

DAHL, ROBERT A. *Pluralist Democracy in the United States.* Chicago: Rand McNally, 1967.

EPSTEIN, EDWARD. *News From Nowhere.* New York: Random House, 1973.

FREEMAN, JO. *The Politics of Women's Liberation.* New York: D. McKay, 1975.

GAMSON, WILLIAM A. *The Strategy of Social Protest.* Homewood, Ill.: Dorsey, 1975.

GARDNER, JOHN. *In Common Cause.* New York: W. W. Norton & Co., Inc., 1972.

GREENWALD, CAROL S. *Group Power: Lobbying and Public Policy.* New York: Praeger, 1977.

JAQUETTE, JANE S., ED. *Women in Politics.* New York: John Wiley, 1974.

KELLER, SUZANNE. *Beyond the Ruling Class.* New York: Random House, 1968.

KEY, V. O., JR. *Politics, Parties, and Pressure Groups,* 5th ed. New York: Thomas Y. Crowell, 1964.

LIPSKY, MICHAEL. *Protest in City Politics: Rent Strikes, Housing and the Power of the Poor.* Chicago: Rand McNally, 1970.

LOWI, THEODORE J. *The End of Liberalism.* New York: W. W. Norton & Co., Inc., 1969.

MCCONNELL, GRANT. *Private Power and American Democracy.* New York: Knopf, 1967.

MILBRATH, LESTER W. *The Washington Lobbyist.* Chicago: Rand McNally, 1967.

MILLS, C. WRIGHT. *The Power Elite.* New York: Oxford University Press, 1956.

MINOW, NEWTON N., AND OTHERS. *Presidential Television.* New York: Basic Books, 1973.

MOSCA, GAETANO. *The Ruling Class.* New York: McGraw-Hill, 1939.

OLSON, MANCUR, JR. *The Logic of Collective Action.* New York: Schocken, 1968.

ORNSTEIN, NORMAN J., AND SHIRLEY EDLER. *Interest Groups, Lobbying and Policymaking.* Washington, D.C.: Congressional Quarterly Press, 1978.

PREWITT, KENNETH, AND ALAN STONE. *The Ruling Elites.* New York: Harper & Row, Pub., 1973.

TRUMAN, DAVID. *The Governmental Process.* New York: Knopf, 1951.

VERBA, SIDNEY, AND NORMAN N. NIE. *Participation in America.* New York: Harper & Row, Pub., 1972.

WILSON, JAMES Q. *Political Organizations.* New York: Basic Books, 1973.

CHAPTER 5:
PARTIES, CAMPAIGNS, AND ELECTIONS

ADAMANY, DAVID W. *Campaign Finance in America.* North Scituate, Mass.: Duxbury Press, 1972.

ADAMANY, DAVID W. AND GEORGE E. AGREE. *Political Money.* Baltimore: John Hopkins, 1975.

ALEXANDER, HERBERT E. *Financing the 1972 Election.* Lexington, Mass.: Health, 1976.

———. *Financing Politics.* Washington, D.C.: Congressional Quarterly Press, 1980.

ASHER, HERBERT. *Presidential Elections and American Politics.* Homewood, Ill.: Dorsey, 1980.

BARBER, JAMES DAVID. *The Pulse of Politics: Electing Presidents in the Media Age.* New York: W. W. Norton & Co., Inc., 1980.

BARBER, JAMES DAVID, ED. *Race for the Presidency: The Media and the Nominating Process.* Englewood Cliffs, N.J.: Prentice-Hall, 1978.

BINKLEY, WILFRED E. *American Political Parties.* New York: Knopf, 1963.

BOLLENS, JOHN C., AND G. ROBERT WILLIAMS. *Jerry Brown: In a Plain Brown Wrapper.* Pacific Palisades, Calif.: Palisades Publishers, 1978.

BONE, HUGH A. *American Politics and the Party System.* New York: McGraw-Hill, 1971.

BRODER, DAVID. *The Party's Over.* New York: Harper & Row, Pub., 1972.

BURNHAM, W. DEAN. *Critical Elections: The Mainsprings of American Politics.* New York: W. W. Norton & Co., Inc., 1970.

CAMPBELL, ANGUS, AND OTHERS. *The American Voter.* New York: John Wiley, 1960.

COTTER, CORNELIUS P., AND OTHERS. *Party Organizations in American Politics.* New York: Praeger, 1984.

CROTTY, WILLIAM J., AND GARY C. JACOBSON. *American Parties in Decline.* Boston: Little, Brown, 1980.

DUVERGER, MAURICE. *Political Parties.* New York: John Wiley, 1963.

FISHEL, JEFF. *Party and Opposition.* New York: D. McKay, 1973.

GIBB, JOYCE, AND MARIAN L. PALLEY. *Tradition and Change in American Politics.* New York: Thomas Y. Crowell, 1975.

HOFSTADTER, RICHARD. *The Idea of a Party System.* Berkeley: University of California Press, 1969.

JACOBSON, GARY C. *The Politics of Congressional Elections.* Boston: Little, Brown, 1983.

KEECH, WILLIAM R., AND DONALD R. MATTHEWS. *The Party's Choice.* Washington, D.C.: Brookings Institution, 1976.

KEY, V. O., JR. *Politics, Parties, and Pressure Groups,* 5th ed. New York: Thomas Y. Crowell, 1964.

————. *The Responsible Electorate.* Cambridge, Mass.: Harvard Unniversity Press, 1966.

————. *Southern Politics in State and Nation.* New York: Knopf, 1949.

LADD, EVERETT, AND CHARLES D. HADLEY. *Transformation of the American Party System.* New York: W. W. Norton & Co., Inc., 1978.

LAMIS, ALEXANDER P. *The Two-Party South.* New York: Oxford University Press, 1984.

LEBLANC, HUGH L. *American Political Parties.* New York: St. Martin's Press, 1982.

LONGLEY, LAURENCE D., AND ALAN C. BRAUN. *The Politics of Electoral College Reform.* New Haven: Yale Univerity Press, 1972.

MARTIN, JOHN FREDERICK. *Civil Rights and the Crisis of Liberalism: The Democratic Party 1945–1976.* Boulder, Colo.: Westview Press, 1979.

MAZMANIAN, DANIEL A. *Third Parties in Presidential Elections.* Washington, D.C.: Brookings Institution, 1974.

NIE, NORMAN H., SIDNEY VERBA, AND JOHN PETROCIK. *The Changing American Voter.* Cambridge, Mass.: Harvard University Press, 1979.

NIMMO, DAN. *The Political Persuaders: The Techniques of Modern Election Campaigns.* Englewood Cliffs, N.J.: Prentice-Hall, 1970.

PATTERSON, THOMAS W. *The Mass Media Election.* New York: Praeger, 1980.

POLSBY, NELSON W., AND AARON B. WILDAVSKY. *Presidential Elections.* New York: Scribner's, 1976.

POMPER, GERALD M. *Elections in America.* New York: Dodd, Mead, 1971.

————. *Voter's Choice.* New York: Dodd, Mead, 1975.

ROSENBLOOM, DAVID. *The Election Men: Professional Campaign Managers and American Democracy.* New York: Quadrangle, 1972.

ROSSITER, CLINTON. *Parties and Politics in America.* Ithaca, N.Y.: Cornell University Press, 1960.

ROYKO, MIKE. *Boss: Richard J. Daley of Chicago.* New York: New American Library, 1971.

RUBIN, RICHARD L. *Party Dynamics: The Democratic Coalition and the Politics of Change.* New York: Oxford University Press, 1976.

SORAUF, FRANK J. *Party Politics in America.* Boston: Little, Brown, 1981.

WEISS, NANCY J. *Farewell to the Party of Lincoln.* Princeton, N.J.: Princeton University Press, 1983.

WOLFINGER, RAYMOND E., AND STEVEN J. ROSENSTONE. *Who Votes?* New Haven: Yale University Press, 1980.

CHAPTER 6: PRESIDENTIAL POLITICS AND POLICY MAKING

BARBER, JAMES DAVID. *The Presidential Character. Predicting Performance in the White House,* 3rd ed. Englewood Cliffs, N.J.: Prentice-Hall, 1985.

BERGER, RAOUL. *Executive Privilege.* Cambridge, Mass.: Harvard University Press, 1974.

————. *Impeachment: The Constitutional Problems.* Cambridge, Mass.: Harvard University Press, 1974.

BUCHANAN, BRUCE. *The Presidential Experience.* Englewood Cliffs, N.J.: Prentice-Hall, 1978.

CALIFANO, JOSEPH A., JR. *A Presidential Nation.* New York: W. W. Norton & Co., Inc., 1975.

CORNWELL, ELMER E., JR. *Presidential Leadership of Public Opinion.* Bloomington: Indiana University Press, 1965.

CORNWIN, EDWARD S. *The President: Office and Powers.* New York: New York University Press, 1957.

CRONIN, THOMAS. *The State of the Presidency,* 2nd ed. Boston: Little, Brown, 1980.

DALLEK, ROBERT. *Ronald Reagan: The Politics of Symbolism.* Cambridge, Mass.: Harvard University Press, 1984.

EDWARDS, GEORGE C. *Presidential Influence in Congress.* San Francisco: W. H. Freeman & Company Publishers, 1980.

FENNO, RICHARD F., JR. *The President's Cabinet.* Cambridge, Mass.: Harvard University Press, 1959.

FISHER, LOUIS. *President and Congress.* New York: Free Press, 1972.

HALPERN, PAUL J., ED. *Why Watergate?* Pacific Palisades, Calif.: Palisades Publishers, 1973.

HARDIN, CHARLES M. *Presidential Power and Accountability.* Chicago: University of Chicago Press, 1974.

HARGROVE, ERWIN D. *The Power of the Modern Presidency.* New York: Knopf, 1974.

——. *Presidential Leadership: Personality and Political Style.* New York: Macmillan, 1966.

HARGROVE, ERWIN C., AND MICHAEL NELSON. *Presidents, Politics, and Policy.* Baltimore: Johns Hopkins, 1984.

HESS, STEPHEN. *Organizing the Presidency.* Washington, D.C.: Brookings Institution, 1976.

HOY, JOHN, AND MELVIN BERNSTEIN, EDS. *The Effective President.* Palisades, Calif.: Palisades Publishers, 1976.

HUGHES, EMMETT JOHN. *The Living Presidency.* Baltimore: Penguin, 1974.

JANIS, IRVING L. *Victims of Groupthink.* Boston: Houghton Mifflin, 1972.

KEARNS, DORIS. *Lyndon Johnson and the American Dream.* New York: Harper & Row, Pub., 1976.

KOENIG, LOUIS W. *The Chief Executive.* New York: Harcourt Brace Jovanovich, Inc., 1981.

LAMMERS, WILLIAM W. *Presidential Politics.* New York: Harper & Row, Pub., 1976.

LIGHT, PAUL C. *Vice-Presidential Power: Advice and Influence in the White House.* Baltimore: Johns Hopkins, 1984.

MUELLER, JOHN E. *War, Presidents and Public Opinion.* New York: John Wiley, 1973.

NATHAN, RICHARD P. *The Plot That Failed: Nixon and the Administrative Presidency.* New York: John Wiley, 1975.

NEUSTADT, RICHARD E. *Presidential Power.* New York: John Wiley, 1980.

POLSBY, NELSON W., ED. *The Modern Presidency.* New York: Random House, 1973.

REEDY, GEORGE E. *The Presidency in Flux.* New York: Columbia University Press, 1973.

——. *The Twilight of the Presidency.* New York: World Publishing, 1970.

ROSE, RICHARD. *Managing Presidential Objectives.* New York: Free Press, 1976.

ROSSITER, CLINTON. *The American Presidency,* 2nd ed. New York: Harcourt, Brace & World, 1960.

SCHLESINGER, ARTHUR M. *The Imperial Presidency.* Boston: Houghton Mifflin, 1973.

SORENSON, THEODORE C. *Decision-Making in the White House.* New York: Columbia University Press, 1963.

SUNDQUIST, JAMES. *Politics and Policy: The Eisenhower, Kennedy, and Johnson Years.* Washington, D.C.: Brookings Institution, 1968.

WOLAMIN, THOMAS R. *Presidential Advisory Commissions: Truman to Nixon.* Madison: University of Wisconsin Press, 1975.

CHAPTER 7: CONGRESSIONAL POLITICS AND POLICY MAKING

BAUER, RAYMOND, AND OTHERS. *American Business and Public Policy.* New York: Atherton, 1963.

CLAPP, CHARLES L. *The Congressman: His Work as He Sees It.* Washington, D.C.: Brookings Institution, 1964.

CLAUSEN, AAGE R. *How Congressmen Decide: A Policy Focus.* New York: St. Martin's Press, 1973.

DAVIDSON, ROGER H. *The Role of the Congressman.* New York: Pegasus, 1969.

FENNO, RICHARD F., JR. *Home Style: House Members in Their Districts.* Boston: Little, Brown, 1978.

FROMAN, LEWIS A., JR. *Congressmen and Their Constituencies.* Chicago: Rand McNally, 1963.

——. *The Congressional Process.* Boston: Little, Brown, 1967.

HINCKLEY, BARBARA. *Stability and Change in Congress.* New York: Harper & Row, Pub., 1978.

KEEFE, WILLIAM J., AND MORRIS S. OGUL. *The American Legislative Process.* Englewood Cliffs, N.J.: Prentice-Hall, 1981.

KINGDON, JOHN W. *Congressional Voting Decisions.* New York: Harper & Row, Pub., 1980.

MANSFIELD, HARVEY C., SR., ED. *Congress Against the President.* New York: Academy of Political Science, 1975.

MATTHEWS, DONALD R. *U.S. Senators and Their World.* New York: Vintage Books, 1960.

MATTHEWS, DONALD P., AND JAMES A. STIMSON. *Yeas and Nays: Normal Decision-Making in the U.S. House of Representatives.* New York: John Wiley, 1975.

MAYHEW, DAVID R. *Congress: The Electoral Connection.* New Haven: Yale University Press, 1974.

MILBRATH, LESTER. *The Washington Lobbyists.* Chicago: Rand McNally, 1963.

OLESZEK, WALTER J. *Congressional Procedures and the Policy Process.* Washington, D.C.: CQ, Inc.., 1978.

ORFIELD, GARY. *Congressional Power: Congress and Social Change.* New York: Harcourt Brace Jovanovich, Inc., 1975.

POLSBY, NELSON W. *Congress and the Presidency.* Englewood Cliffs, N.J.: Prentice-Hall, 1976.

PRICE, DAVID. *Who Makes the Laws?* Cambridge, Mass.: Schenkman, 1972.

RINGLE, DONALD. *O Congress.* Garden City, N.Y.: Doubleday, 1972.

SINCLAIR, BARBARA. *Congressional Realignment: 1925–1978.* Austin: University of Texas Press, 1982.

TACHERON, DONALD G., AND MORRIS K. UDALL. *The Job of the Congressman.* Indianapolis: Bobbs-Merrill, 1966.

VOLGER, DAVID. *The Third House: Conference Committees in the United States.* Evanston, Ill.: Northwestern University Press, 1971.

YOUNG, STEPHEN M. *Tales Out of Congress.* Philadelphia: Lippincott, 1964.

CHAPTER 8: BUREAUCRATIC POLITICS AND POLICY MAKING

ALTSHULER, ALAN A., ED. *The Politics of the Federal Bureaucracy.* New York: Dodd, Mead, 1968.

BERKLEY, GEORGE E. *The Craft of Public Administration.* Boston: Allyn & Bacon, 1975.

BERNSTEIN, MARVER H. *Regulating Business by Independent Commission.* Princeton, N.J.: Princeton University Press, 1955.

CAIDEN, GERALD. *Public Administration,* 2d. ed. Pacific Palisades, Calif.: Palisades Publishers, 1982.

DOWNS, ANTHONY. *Inside Bureaucracy.* Boston: Little, Brown, 1967.

FRITSCHLER, A. LEE. *Smoking and Politics: Policy-Making and the Federal Bureaucracy.* Englewood Cliffs, N.J.: Prentice-Hall, 1975.

HALPERIN, MORTON H. *Bureaucratic Politics and Foreign Policy.* Washington D.C.: Brookings Institution, 1974.

HARRIS, JOSEPH P. *Congressional Control of Administration.* Garden City, N.Y.: Doubleday, 1964.

HELCO, HUGH. *A Government of Strangers: Executive Politics in Washington.* Washington, D.C.: Brookings Institution, 1977.

HERSHEY, CARY. *Protest in the Public Service.* Lexington, Mass.: Health, Lexington Books, 1973.

HUMMEL, RALPH P. *The Bureaucratic Experience.* New York: St. Martin's Press, 1977.

KAUFMAN, HERBERT. *Are Government Organizations Immortal?* Washington, D.C.: Brookings Institution, 1976.

KOHLMEIER, LOUIS M., JR. *The Regulators.* New York: Harper & Row, Pub., 1969.

LANDIS, JAMES M. *The Administrative Process.* New Haven: Yale University Press, 1938.

MEIER, KENNETH J. *Politics and Bureaucracy: Policymaking in the Fourth Branch of Government.* North Scituate, Mass.: Duxbury Press, 1979.

MOSHER, FREDERICK C. *Democracy and the Public Service,* 2nd ed. New York: Oxford University Press, 1982.

NESBITT, MURRAY B. *Labor Relations in the Federal Government Service.* Washington, D.C.: Bureau of National Affairs, 1976.

OGUL, MORRIS S. *Congress Oversees the Bureaucracy.* Pittsburgh: University of Pittsburgh Press, 1976.

PETER, LAURENCE J., AND RAYMOND HULL. *The Peter Principle.* New York: Morrow, 1968.

REAGAN, MICHAEL D. *The Administration of Public Policy.* Glenview, Ill.: Scott, Foresman, 1969.

REDFORD, EMMETTE S. *Democracy in the Administrative State.* New York: Oxford University Press, 1969.

ROURKE, FRANCIS E. *Bureaucracy, Politics and Public Policy.* Boston: Little, Brown, 1976.

SEIDMAN, HAROLD. *Politics, Position, and Power.* New York: Oxford University Press, 1980.

SIMON, HERBERT A. *Administrative Behavior.* New York: Free Press, 1957.

VAN RIPER, PAUL. *History of the United States Civil Service.* New York: Row, Peterson, 1958.

WARNER, W. L., AND OTHERS. *The American Federal Executive.* New Haven: Yale University Press, 1963.

WOLL, PETER. *American Bureaucracy.* New York: W. W. Norton & Co., Inc., 1977.

CHAPTER 9: JUDICIAL POLITICS AND POLICY MAKING

ABRAHAM, HENRY J. *The Judicial Process.* New York: Oxford University Press, 1975.

———. *Justices and Presidents.* New York: Oxford University Press, 1974.

BAUM, LAWRENCE C. *The Supreme Court.* Washington, D.C.: Congressional Quarterly Press, 1981.

BECKER, THEODORE L., AND MALCOLM M. FEELEY, EDS. *The Impact of Supreme Court Decisions.* New York: Oxford University Press, 1973.

BICKEL, ALEXANDER M. *The Last Dangerous Branch.* Indianapolis: Bobbs-Merrill, 1962.

———. *Politics and the Warren Court.* New York: Harper & Row, Pub., 1965.

CARDOZO, BENJAMIN N. *The Nature of the Judicial Process.* New Haven: Yale University Press, 1921.

CHASE, HAROLD W. *Federal Judges: The Appointing Process.* Minneapolis: University of Minnesota Press, 1972.

CORP, ROBERT A., AND C. K. ROWLAND. *Policymaking and Politics in the Federal Courts.* Knoxville: University of Tennessee Press, 1983.

COX, ARCHIBALD. *The Role of the Supreme Court in American Government.* New York: Oxford University Press, 1976.

GLICK, HENRY ROBERT, AND KENNETH N. VINES. *State Court Systems.* Englewood Cliffs, N.J.: Prentice-Hall, 1973.

GOLDMAN, SHELDON, AND THOMAS R. JAHNIGE, *The Federal Courts as a Political System.* New York: Harper & Row, Pub., 1976.

GROSSMAN, JOE B. *Lawyers and Judges: The ABA and the Politics of Judicial Selection.* New York: John Wiley, 1965.

HOROWITZ, DONALD L. *The Courts and Social Policy.* Washington: Brookings Institution, 1977.

JACOB, HERBERT, ED. *Law, Politics and the Federal Courts.* Boston: Little, Brown, 1967.

KRISLOV, SAMUEL. *The Supreme Court in the Political Process.* New York: Macmillan, 1965.

KURLAND, PHILIP. *Politics, the Constitution, and the Warren Court.* Chicago: University of Chicago Press, 1970.

MILLER, ARTHUR SELWYN. *The Supreme Court and American Capitalism.* New York: Free Press, 1968.

MURPHY, WALTER F. *Congress and the Court.* Chicago: University of Chicago Press, 1962.

——. *Elements of Judicial Strategy.* Chicago: University of Chicago Press, 1964.

MURPHY, WALTER F., AND C. HERMAN PRITCHETT. *Courts, Judges and Politics.* New York: Random House, 1974.

NAGEL, STUART. *The Legal Process From a Behavioral Perspective.* Homewood, Ill.: Dorsey, 1969.

PRITCHETT, C. HERMAN. *Congress Versus the Supreme Court.* Minneapolis: University of Minnesota Press, 1961.

RHODE, DAVID, AND HAROLD J. SPAETH. *Supreme Court Decision Making.* San Francisco: W. H. Freeman & Company Publishers, 1976.

SCHMANDT, HENRY J. *Courts in the American Political System.* Belmont, Calif.: Dickenson, 1968.

SCHMIDHAUSER, JOHN R. *The Supreme Court and Congress.* New York: Free Press, 1972.

SCIGLIANO, ROBERT. *The Supreme Court and the Presidency.* New York: Free Press, 1971.

SHAPIRO, MARTIN. *The Supreme Court and Administrative Agencies.* New York: Macmillan, 1968.

ULMER, SIDNEY S. *Courts as Small and Not So Small Groups.* New York: General Learning Press, 1971.

VOSS, CLEMENT E. *Caucasians Only.* Berkeley: University of California Press, 1959.

WARREN, CHARLES. *Congress, the Constitution and the Supreme Court.* Boston: Little, Brown, 1925.

WASBY, STEPHEN L. *Continuity and Change: From the Warren Court to the Burger Court.* Santa Monica, Calif.: Goodyear, 1976.

——. *The Impact of the United States Supreme Court.* Homewood, Ill.: Dorsey, 1970.

WESTIN, ALAN F., ED. *The Supreme Court: Views From Inside.* New York: W. W. Norton & Co., Inc., 1961.

WOODWARD, BOB, AND SCOTT ARMSTRONG. *The Brethren.* New York: Simon & Schuster, 1979.

CHAPTER 10: GOVERNMENT, POLITICS, SPENDING, AND TAXING

BERMAN, LARRY. *The Office of Management and Budget and the Presidency, 1921–1979.* Princeton, N.J.: Princeton University Press, 1979.

BREAK, GEORGE R. *Financing Government in a Federal System.* Washington, D.C.: Brookings Institution, 1980.

FENNO, RICHARD. *The Power of the Purse: Appropriations Politics in Congress.* Boston: Little, Brown, 1966.

FISHER, LOUIS. *Presidential Spending Power.* Princeton, N.J.: Princeton University Press, 1975.

HAVEMANN, JOEL. *Congress and the Budget.* Bloomington: Indiana University Press, 1978.

WILDAVSKY, AARON. *The Politics of the Budgetary Process,* 4th ed. Boston: Little, Brown, 1983.

CHAPTER 11: GOVERNMENT, POLITICS, AND THE ECONOMY

ANDERSON, JAMES E., ED. *Economic Regulatory Policies.* Lexington, Mass.: Health, Lexington Books, 1976.

——. *Politics and the Economy.* Boston: Little, Brown, 1966.

ARNOLD, THURMAN. *The Folklore of Capitalism.* New Haven: Yale University Press, 1937.

BAILEY, STEPHEN K. *Congress Makes a Law: The Story Behind the Employment Act of 1946.* New York: Columbia University Press, 1950.

BERNSTEIN, MARVER H. *Regulating Business by Independent Commission.* Princeton, N.J.: Princeton University Press, 1955.

DAVIS, DAVID HOWARD. *Energy Politics.* New York: St. Martin's Press, 1978.

DONOVAN, JOHN C. *The Politics of Poverty.* New York: Pegasus, 1967.

ENGLER, ROBERT. *The Brotherhood of Oil.* Chicago: University of Chicago Press, 1977.

——. *The Politics of Oil.* New York: Macmillan, 1961.

EYESTONE, ROBERT. *Political Economy: Politics and Policy Analysis.* Chicago: Markham, 1972.

FLASH, EDWARD S., JR. *Economic Advice and Presidential Leadership.* New York: Columbia University Press, 1965.

FREEDMAN, LEONARD. *Public Housing: The Politics of Poverty.* New York: Holt, Rinehart & Winston, 1969.

GALBRAITH, JOHN K. *The New Industrial State.* Boston: Houghton Mifflin, 1967.

HARRINGTON, MICHAEL. *The Other America: Poverty in the United States.* New York: Macmillan, 1964.

KIEWIET, D. RODERICK. *Macroeconomics and Micropolitics: The Electoral Effects of Economic Issues.* Chicago: University of Chicago Press, 1983.

LEVITAN, SAR A., AND ROBERT TAGGERT, *The Promise of Greatness: The Social Programs of the Last Decade and Their Major Achievements.* Cambridge, Mass.: Harvard University Press, 1976.

LOWI, THEODORE J. *The End of Liberalism.* New York: W. W. Norton & Co., Inc., 1970.

MCCONNELL, GRANT. *Steel and the Presidency.* New York: W. W. Norton & Co., Inc., 1963.

MOYNIHAN, DANIEL P. *Maximum Feasible Misunderstanding: Community Action in the War on Poverty.* New York: Free Press, 1969.

———. *The Politics of a Guaranteed Income.* New York: Random House, 1973.

NOLL, ROGER G. *Reforming Regulation.* Washington, D.C.: Brookings Institution, 1971.

PIERCE, LAURENCE C. *The Politics of Policy Formulation.* Santa Monica, Calif.: Goodyear, 1971.

PIVEN, FRANCES FOX, AND RICHARD A. CLOWARD. *Regulating the Poor.* New York: Random House, 1971.

ROSENBAUM, WALTER. *The Politics of Environmental Concern.* New York: Praeger, 1977.

STEINER, GILBERT Y. *Social Insecurity: The Politics of Welfare.* Chicago: Rand McNally, 1966.

———. *The State of Welfare.* Washington, D.C.: Brookings Institution, 1971.

TOLCHIN, SUSAN J., AND MARTIN TOLCHIN. *Dismantling America: The Rush to Deregulate.* Boston: Houghton Mifflin, 1983.

VERNON, RAYMOND, ED. *The Oil Crisis.* New York: W. W. Norton & Co., Inc., 1976.

WILSON, JAMES Q., ED. *The Politics of Regulation.* New York: Basic Books, 1980.

CHAPTER 12: GOVERNMENT, POLITICS, AND FOREIGN POLICY

ALIANO, RICHARD A. *American Defense Policy From Eisenhower to Kennedy.* Athens: Ohio University Press, 1975.

ALLISON, GRAHAM T. *Essence of Decision: Explaining the Cuban Missile Crisis.* Boston: Little, Brown, 1971.

ALMOND, GABRIEL. *The American People and Foreign Policy.* New York: Praeger, 1960.

BALL, GEORGE. *Diplomacy for a Crowded World.* Boston: Little, Brown, 1977.

BAUER, RAYMOND, AND OTHERS. *American Business and Public Policy: The Politics of Foreign Trade.* Chicago: Aldine, 1972.

BLOOMFIELD, LINCOLN P. *In Search of American Foreign Policy.* New York: Oxford University Press, 1972.

BLUM, RICHARD H., ED. *Surveillance and Espionage in a Free Society.* New York: Praeger, 1972.

CAMPBELL, CHARLES S. *The Transformation of American Foreign Relations, 1865–1900.* New York: Harper & Row, Pub., 1976.

CARIDI, RONALD J. *Twentieth Century American Foreign Policy: Security and Self Interest.* Englewood Cliffs, N.J.: Prentice-Hall, 1974.

CLOTFELTER, JAMES. *The Military in American Politics.* New York: Harper & Row, Pub., 1973.

COHEN, BERNARD C. *The Public's Impact on Foreign Policy.* Boston: Little, Brown, 1973.

COPLIN, WILLIAM D., AND OTHERS. *American Foreign Policy.* North Scituate, Mass.: Duxbury Press, 1974.

CRABB, CECIL V., JR. *American Foreign Policy in the Nuclear Age.* New York: Harper & Row, Pub., 1972.

———. *Policy-Makers and Critics: Conflicting Theories of American Foreign Policy.* New York: Praeger, 1976.

EAGLETON, THOMAS E. *War and Presidential Power.* New York: Liveright, 1974.

ESTERLINE, JOHN H., AND ROBERT B. BLACK. *Inside Foreign Policy: The Department of State Political System and Its Subsystems.* Palo Alto, Calif.: Mayfield, 1975.

GEORGE, ALEXANDER L. *Presidential Decisionmaking in Foreign Policy.* Boulder, Colo.: Westview Press, 1980.

HALPERIN, MORTON. *Bureaucratic Politics and Foreign Policy.* Washington, D.C.: Brookings Institution, 1974.

HOLSTI, OLE R., AND JAMES N. ROSENAU. *American Leadership in World Affairs: Vietnam and the Breakdown of Consensus.* Winchester, Mass.: Allen & Unwin, 1984.

HOOPES, TOWNSEND. *The Devil and John Foster Dulles.* Boston: Atlantic–Little, Brown, 1973.

HOWE, IRVIN, ED. *A Dissenter's Guide to Foreign Policy.* New York: Praeger, 1968.

HUNTINGTON, SAMUEL P. *The Soldier and the State.* New York: Vintage Books, 1964.

IRISH, MARIAN, AND ELKE FRANK. *U.S. Foreign Policy.* New York: Harcourt Brace Jovanovich, Inc., 1975.

KAHAN, JEROME H. *Security in the Nuclear Age.* Washington, D.C.: Brookings Institution, 1975.

KENNAN, GEORGE F. *American Diplomacy 1900–1950.* Chicago: University of Chicago Press, 1951.

———. *Memories.* Boston: Atlantic–Little, Brown, 1967.

MADDOX, ROBERT JAMES. *The New Left and Origins of the Cold War.* Princeton, N.J.: Princeton University Press, 1973.

MORGENTHAU, HANS J. *A New Foreign Policy for the United States.* New York: Praeger, 1969.

MUELLER, JOHN E. *War, Presidents, and Public Opinion.* New York: John Wiley, 1973.

NEWHOUSE, JOHN. *Cold Dawn: The Story of SALT.* New York: Holt, Rinehart & Winston, 1973.

RADWAY, LAURENCE I. *Foreign Policy and National Defense.* Glenview, Ill.: Scott, Foresman, 1969.

RAINEY, GENE E. *Patterns of American Foreign Policy.* Boston: Allyn & Bacon, 1975.

ROSECRANCE, RICHARD, ED. *America as an Ordinary Country: U.S. Foreign Policy and the Future.* Ithaca, N.Y.: Cornell University Press, 1976.

RUBIN, BARRY. *Secrets of State: The State Department and the Struggle Over U.S. Foreign Policy.* New York: Oxford University Press, 1985.

RUSSETT, BRUCE M. *What Price Vigilance?* New Haven: Yale University Press, 1970.

SPANIER, JOHN. *American Foreign Policy Since World War II.* New York: Praeger, 1973.

SPANIER, JOHN, AND ERIC M. USLANER. *How American Foreign Policy Is Made.* New York: Praeger, 1974.

STOCKFISH, J. A. *Plowshares Into Swords: Managing the American Defense Establishment.* New York: Mason & Lipscomb, 1973.

WHITE, JOHN. *The Politics of Foreign Aid.* New York: St. Martin's Press, 1974.

WILCOX, FRANCIS, O. *Congress, the Executive, and Foreign Policy.* New York: Harper & Row, Pub., 1972.

CHAPTER 13: GOVERNMENT, POLITICS, AND CIVIL RIGHTS

ABRAHAM, HENRY J. *Freedom and the Court.* New York: Oxford University Press, 1977.

BARKER, LUCIUS J., AND TWILEY W. BARKER, JR., EDS. *Civil Liberties and the Constitution: Cases and Commentaries.* Englewood Cliffs, N.J.: Prentice-Hall, 1978.

BARRON, JEROME A. *Freedom of the Press for Whom?* Bloomington: Indiana University Press, 1973.

BEDAU, HUGO ADAM. *The Death Penalty in America.* Garden City, N.Y.: Doubleday, 1967.

BLUMBERG, ABRAHAM S. *Criminal Justice.* Chicago: Quadrangle, 1967.

CASPER, JONATHAN D. *American Criminal Justice: The Defendant's Perspective.* Englewood Cliffs, N.J.: Prentice-Hall, 1972.

———. *The Politics of Civil Liberties.* New York: Harper & Row, Pub., 1972.

CHAFFE, ZECHARIAH. *Free Speech in the United States.* Cambridge, Mass.: Harvard University Press, 1941.

CLOR, HARRY M. *Obscenity and Public Morality.* Chicago: University of Chicago Press, 1969.

DYE, THOMAS R. *The Politics of Equality.* Indianapolis: Bobbs-Merrill, 1971.

FELLMAN, DAVID. *The Defendant's Rights Today.* Madison: University of Wisconsin Press, 1977.

KLUGER, RICHARD. *Simple Justice: The History of Brown v. Board of Education and Black America's Struggle for Equality.* New York: Knopf, 1976.

KRASNOW, ERWIN G., AND LAWRENCE D. LONGELY. *The Politics of Broadcast Regulation.* New York: St. Martin's Press, 1973.

LEWIS, ANTHONY. *Gideon's Trumpet.* New York: Random House, 1964.

McCLOSKY, HERBERT, AND ALIDA BRILL. *Dimensions of Tolerance: What Americans Believe About Civil Liberties.* New York: Russell Sage Foundation, 1983.

MELTSNER, MICHAEL. *Cruel and Unusual: The Supreme Court and Capital Punishment.* New York: Random House, 1973.

MILLER, JOHN STUART. *On Liberty.* New York: Appleton-Century-Crofts, 1947.

MILLER, ARTHUR R. *The Assault on Privacy.* Ann Arbor: University of Michigan Press, 1971.

MITFORD, JESSICA. *Kind and Usual Punishment: The Prison Business.* New York: Vintage Books, 1974.

MORGAN, RICHARD E. *The Supreme Court and Religion.* New York: Free Press, 1975.

PRITCHETT, C. HERMAN. *The American Constitution.* New York: McGraw-Hill, 1976.

REITMAN, ALAN, ED. *The Pulse of Freedom: American Civil Liberties, 1920–1970.* New York: W. W. Norton & Co., Inc.

Report of the Commission on Obscenity and Pornography. Washington, D.C.: Government Printing Office, 1970.

SHAPIRO, MARTIN. *Freedom of Speech: The Supreme Court and Judicial Review.* Englewood Cliffs, N.J.: Prentice-Hall, 1966.

SINDLER, ALLAN. *Bakke, De Funis, and Minority Admission.* New York: Longman, 1978.

SNORTUM, JOHN R., AND ILANA HADAR, EDS. *Criminal Justice: Allies and Adversaries.* Pacific Palisades, Calif.: Palisades Publishers, 1978.

SORAUF, FRANK J. *The Wall of Separation: The Constitutional Politics of Church and State.* Princeton, N.J.: Princeton University Press, 1976.

U.S. COMMISSION ON CIVIL RIGHTS. *Fulfilling the Letter and Spirit of the Law.* Washington, D.C.: Government Printing Office, 1976.

WASBY, STEPHEN L., ED. *Civil Liberties: Policy and Policy Making.* Lexington, Mass.: Heath, Lexington Books, 1976.

WAY, FRANK H. *Liberty in the Balance: Current Issues in Civil Liberties.* New York: McGraw-Hill, 1976.

WESTIN, ALAN F. *Privacy and Freedom.* New York: Atheneum, 1967.

WOODWARD, C. VANN. *The Strange Career of Jim Crow.* New York: Oxford University Press, 1974.

CONSTITUTION OF THE UNITED STATES

We the People of the United States, in Order to form a more perfect Union, establish Justice, insure domestic Tranquility, provide for the common defence, promote the general Welfare, and secure the Blessings of Liberty to ourselves and our Posterity, do ordain and establish this Constitution for the United States of America.

ARTICLE I.

Section 1.

All legislative Powers herein granted shall be vested in a Congress of the United States, which shall consist of a Senate and House of Representatives.[1]

---

[1] This text of the Constitution follows the engrossed copy signed by George Washington and the deputies from twelve states. The superior numbers preceding the paragraphs designate clause numbers, they were not in the original.

Section 2.

[1] The House of Representatives shall be composed of Members chosen every second Year by the People of the several States, and the Electors in each State shall have the Qualifications requisite for Electors of the most numerous Branch of the State Legislature.

[2] No person shall be a Representative who shall not have attained to the Age of twenty five Years, and been seven Years a Citizen of the United States, and who shall not, when elected, be an Inhabitant of that State in which he shall be chosen.

[3] [Representatives and direct Taxes shall be

apportioned among the several States which may be included within this Union, according to their respective Numbers, which shall be determined by adding to the whole Number of free Persons, including those bound to Service for a Term of Years, and excluding Indians not taxed, three fifths of all other Persons.][2] The actual enumeration shall be made within three Years after the first Meeting of the Congress of the United States, and within every subsequent Term of ten Years, in such Manner as they shall by Law direct. The Number of Representatives shall not exceed one for every thirty Thousand, but each State shall have at Least one Representative; and until such enumeration shall be made, the State of New Hampshire shall be entitled to chuse three, Massachusetts eight, Rhode-Island and Providence Plantations one, Connecticut five, New-York six, New Jersey four, Pennsylvania eight, Delaware one, Maryland six, Virginia ten, North Carolina five, South Carolina five, and Georgia three.

[4] When vacancies happen in the Representation from any State, the Executive Authority thereof shall issue Writs of Election to fill such Vacancies.

[5] The House of Representatives shall chuse their Speaker and other Officers; and shall have the sole Power of Impeachment.

Section 3.

[1] The Senate of the United States shall be composed of two Senators from each State, [chosen by the Legislature thereof,][3] for six Years; and each Senator shall have one Vote.

[2] Immediately after they shall be assembled in Consequence of the first Election, they shall be divided as equally as may be into three Classes. The Seats of the Senators of the first Class shall be vacated at the Expiration of the second Year, of the second Class at the Expiration of the fourth Year, and of the third Class at the Expiration of the sixth Year, so that one third may be chosen every second Year [; and if Vacancies happen by Resignation, or otherwise, during the Recess of the Legislature of any State, the Executive thereof may make temporary Appointments until the next Meeting of the Legislature, which shall then fill such Vacancies][4]

[3] No Person shall be a Senator who shall not have attained to the Age of thirty Years, and been nine Years a Citizen of the United States, and who shall not, when elected, be an Inhabitant of that State for which he shall be chosen.

[4] The Vice President of the United States shall be President of the Senate, but shall have no Vote, unless they be equally divided.

[5] The Senate shall chuse their other Officers, and also a President pro tempore, in the Absence of the Vice President, or when he shall exercise the Office of President of the United States.

[6] The Senate shall have the sole Power to try all Impeachments. When sitting for that Purpose, they shall be on Oath or Affirmation. When the President of the United States is tried, the Chief Justice shall preside: And no Person shall be convicted without the Concurrence of two thirds of the Members present.

[7] Judgment in Cases of Impeachment shall not extend further than to removal from Office, and disqualification to hold and enjoy any Office of honor, Trust or Profit under the United States: but the Party convicted shall nevertheless be liable and subject to Indictment, Trial, Judgment and Punishment, according to Law.

Section 4.

[1] The Times, Places, and Manner of holding Elections for Senators and Representatives, shall be precribed in each State by the Legislature thereof; but the Congress may at any time

---

[2] The part in brackets was changed by Section 2 of the Fourteenth Amendment.

[3] The part in brackets was changed by Section 1 of the Seventeenth Amendment.

[4] The part in brackets was changed by clause 2 of the Seventeenth Amendment.

by Law make or alter such Regulations, except as to the Places of chusing Senators.

² The Congress shall assemble at least once in every Year, and such Meetings shall [be on the first Monday in December,]⁵ unless they shall by Law appoint a different Day.

Section 5.

¹ Each House shall be the Judge of the Elections, Returns and Qualifications of its own Members, and a Majority of each shall constitute a Quorum to do Business; but a smaller Number may adjourn from day to day, and may be authorized to compel the Attendance of absent members, in such Manner, and under such Penalties as each House may provide.

² Each House may determine the Rules of its Proceedings, punish its members for disorderly Behaviour, and, with the Concurrence of two thirds, expel a member.

³ Each House shall keep a Journal of its Proceedings, and from time to time publish the same, excepting such Parts as may in their Judgment require Secrecy; and the Yeas and Nays of the Members of either House on any question shall, at the Desire of one fifth of those Present, be entered on the Journal.

⁴ Neither House, during the Session of Congress, shall, without the Consent of the other, adjourn for more than three days, nor to any other Place than that in which the two Houses shall be sitting.

Section 6.

¹ The Senators and Representatives shall receive a Compensation for their Services, to be ascertained by Law, and paid out of the Treasury of the United States. They shall in all Cases, except Treason, Felony and Breach of the Peace, be privileged from Arrest during their Attendance at the Session of their respective Houses, and in going to and returning

⁵ The part in brackets was changed by Section 2 of the Twentieth Amendment.

from the same; and for any Speech or Debate in either House, they shall not be questioned in any other Place.

² No Senator or Representative shall, during the Time for which he was elected, be appointed to any civil Office under the Authority of the United States, which shall have been created, or the Emoluments whereof shall have been encreased during such time; and no Person holding any Office under the United States, shall be a Member of either House during his Continuance in Office.

Section 7.

¹ All Bills for raising Revenue shall originate in the House of Representatives; but the Senate may propose or concur with Amendments as on other Bills.

² Every Bill which shall have passed the House of Representatives and the Senate, shall, before it become a Law, be presented to the President of the United States; If he approve he shall sign it, but if not he shall return it, with his Objections to that House in which it shall have originated, who shall enter the Objections at large on their Journal, and proceed to reconsider it. If after such Reconsideration two thirds of that House shall agree to pass the Bill, it shall be sent, together with the Objections, to the other House, by which it shall likewise be reconsidered, and if approved by two thirds of that House, it shall become a Law. But in all such Cases the Votes of both Houses shall be determined by Yeas and Nays, and the Names of the Persons voting for and against the Bill shall be entered on the Journal of each House respectively. If any Bill shall not be returned by the President within ten Days (Sundays excepted) after it shall have been presented to him, the Same shall be a Law, in like Manner as if he had signed it, unless the Congress by their Adjournment prevent its Return, in which Case it shall not be a Law.

³ Every Order, Resolution, or Vote to which the Concurrence of the Senate and House of

Representatives may be necessary (except on a question of Adjournment) shall be presented to the President of the United States; and before the Same shall take Effect, shall be approved by him, or being disapproved by him, shall be repassed by two thirds of the Senate and House of Representatives, according to the Rules and Limitations prescribed in the Case of a Bill.

Section 8.

1 The Congress shall have power To lay and collect Taxes, Duties, Imposts and Excises, to pay the Debts and provide for the common Defence and general Welfare of the United States; but all Duties, Imposts and Excises shall be uniform throughout the United States;

2 To borrow Money on the credit of the United States;

3 To regulate Commerce with foreign Nations, and among the several States and with the Indian Tribes;

4 To establish an uniform Rule of Naturalization, and uniform Laws on the subject of Bankruptcies throughout the United States;

5 To coin Money, regulate the Value thereof, and of foreign Coin, and fix the Standard of Weights and Measures;

6 To provide for the Punishment of counterfeiting the Securities and current Coin of the United States;

7 To establish Post Offices and post Roads;

8 To promote the Progress of Science and useful Arts, by securing for limited Times to Authors and Inventors the exclusive right to their respective Writings and Discoveries;

9 To constitute Tribunals inferior to the supreme Court;

10 To define and punish Piracies and Felonies committed on the high Seas, and Offences against the Law of Nations;

11 To declare War, grant Letters of Marque and Reprisal, and make Rules concerning Captures on land and water.

12 To raise and support Armies, but no Appropriation of Money to that Use shall be for a longer Term than two years;

13 To provide and maintain a Navy;

14 To make Rules for the Government and Regulation of the land and naval Forces;

15 To provide for calling forth the Militia to execute the Laws of the Union, suppress insurrections and repel Invasions;

16 To provide for organizing, arming, and disciplining the Militia, and for governing such Part of them as may be employed in the Service of the United States, reserving to the States respectively, the Appointment of the Officers, and the Authority of training the Militia according to the discipline prescribed by Congress;

17 To exercise exclusive Legislation in all Cases whatsoever, over such District (not exceeding ten Miles square) as may, by Cession of particular States, and the Acceptance of Congress, become the Seat of the Government of the United States, and to exercise like Authority over all Places purchased by the Consent of the Legislature of the State in which the Same shall be, for the Erection of Forts, Magazines, Arsenals, dock-Yards, and other needful Buildings;—And

18 To make all Laws which shall be necessary and proper for carrying into Execution the foregoing Powers, and all other Powers vested by this Constitution in the Government of the United States, or in any Department or Officer thereof.

Section 9.

1 The Migration or Importation of such Persons as any of the States now existing shall think proper to admit, shall not be prohibited by the Congress prior to the Year one thousand eight hundred and eight, but a Tax or duty may be imposed on such Importation, not exceeding ten dollars for each Person.

2 The Privilege of the Writ of Habeas Corpus shall not be suspended, unless when in Cases of Rebellion or Invasion the public Safety may require it.

3 No Bill of Attainder or ex post facto Law shall be passed.

4 No Capitation, or other direct, Tax shall be laid, unless in Proportion to the Census or Enumeration herein before directed to be taken.[6]

5 No Tax or Duty shall be laid on Articles exported from any State.

6 No Preference shall be given by any Regulation of Commerce or Revenue to the Ports of one State over those of another: nor shall Vessels bound to, or from one State, be obliged to enter, clear, or pay Duties in another.

7 No Money shall be drawn from the Treasury, but in Consequence of Appropriations made by Law; and a regular Statement and Account of the Receipts and Expenditures of all public Money shall be published from time to time.

8 No Title of Nobility shall be granted by the United States: And no Person holding an Office of Profit or Trust under them, shall, without the Consent of the Congress, accept of any present, Emolument, Office, or Title, of any kind whatever, from any King, Prince, or foreign State.

Section 10.

1 No State shall enter into any Treaty, Alliance, or Confederation; grant Letters of Marque and Reprisal; coin Money; emit Bills of Credit; make any Thing but gold and silver Coin a Tender in Payment of Debts; pass any Bill of Attainder, ex post facto Law, or Law impairing the Obligation of Contracts, or grant any Title of Nobility.

2 No State shall, without the Consent of the Congress, lay any Imposts or Duties on Imports or Exports, except what may be absolutely necessary for executing it's inspection Laws: and the net Produce of all Duties and Imposts, laid by any State on Imports or Exports, shall be for the Use of the Treasury of the United

---

[6] See also the Sixteenth Amendment.

States; and all such Laws shall be subject to the Revision and Controul of the Congress.

3 No state shall, without the Consent of Congress, lay any Duty of Tonnage, keep Troops, or Ships of War in time of Peace, enter into any Agreement or Compact with another State, or with a foreign Power, or engage in War, unless actually invaded, or in such imminent Danger as will not admit of delay.

ARTICLE II.

Section 1.

1 The executive Power shall be vested in a President of the United States of America. He shall hold his Office during the Term of four Years, and, together with the Vice President, chosen for the same Term, be elected, as follows

2 Each State shall appoint, in such Manner as the Legislature thereof may direct, a Number of Electors, equal to the whole Number of Senators and Representatives to which the State may be entitled in the Congress; but no Senator or Representative, or Person holding an Office of Trust or Profit under the United States, shall be appointed an Elector.

[The Electors shall meet in their respective States, and vote by Ballot for two Persons, of whom one at least shall not be an Inhabitant of the same State with themselves. And they shall make a List of all the Persons voted for, and of the Number of Votes for each; which List they shall sign and certify, and transmit sealed to the Seat of the Government of the United States, directed to the President of the Senate. The President of the Senate shall, in the Presence of the Senate and House of Representatives, open all the Certificates, and the Votes shall then be counted. The Person having the greatest Number of Votes shall be the President, if such Number be a Majority of the whole Number of Electors appointed; and if there be more than one who have such Majority, and have an equal Number of Votes, then the House of Representatives shall immediately chuse by Ballot one of them for President; and if no Person have a Majority, then from the five highest on the List the said House shall in like Manner chuse the President. But in chusing the President, the Votes shall be taken by States, the Representation from each State having one Vote; A quorum for this Purpose shall consist of a Member or Members from two thirds of the States, and a Majority of all the States shall be necessary to a Choice. In every Case, after the Choice of the President, the Person having the greatest Number of Votes of the Electors shall be the Vice President. But if there should remain two or more who have equal votes, the Senate shall chuse from them by Ballot the Vice President.][7]

[3] The Congress may determine the Time of chusing the Electors, and the Day on which they shall give their Votes; which Day shall be the same throughout the United States.

[4] No Person except a natural born Citizen, or a Citizen of the United States, at the time of the Adoption of this Constitution, shall be eligible to the Office of President; neither shall any Person be eligible to that Office who shall not have attained to the Age of thirty-five Years, and been fourteen Years a Resident within the United States.

[5] In Case of the Removal of the President from Office, or of his Death, Resignation, or Inability to discharge the Powers and Duties of the said Office,[8] the Same shall devolve on the Vice President, and the Congress may by Law provide for the Case of Removal, Death, Resignation or Inability, both of the President and Vice President, declaring what Officer shall then act as President, and such Officer shall act accordingly, until the Disability be removed, or a President shall be elected.

[6] The President shall, at stated Times, receive for his Services, a Compensation, which shall neither be encreased nor diminished dur-

ing the Period for which he shall have been elected, and he shall not receive within that Period any other Emolument from the United States, or any of them.

[7] Before he enter on the Execution of his Office, he shall take the following Oath or Affirmation:—"I do solemnly swear (or affirm) that I will faithfully execute the Office of President of the United States, and will to the best of my Ability, preserve, protect and defend the Constitution of the United States."

Section 2.

[1] The President shall be Commander in Chief of the Army and Navy of the United States, and of the Militia of the several States, when called into the actual Service of the United States; he may require the Opinion, in writing, of the principal Officer in each of the executive Departments, upon any Subject relating to the Duties of their respective Offices, and he shall have Power to grant Reprieves and Pardons for Offences against the United States, except in Cases of Impeachment.

[2] He shall have Power, by and with the Advice and Consent of the Senate, to make Treaties, provided two thirds of the Senators present concur; and he shall nominate, and by and with the Advice and Consent of the Senate, shall appoint Ambassadors, other public Ministers and Consuls, Judges of the supreme Court, and all other Officers of the United States, whose Appointments are not herein otherwise provided for, and which shall be established by Law; but the Congress may by Law vest the Appointment of such inferior Officers, as they think proper, in the President alone, in the Courts of Law, or in the Heads of Departments.

[3] The President shall have Power to fill up all Vacancies that may happen during the Recess of the Senate, by granting Commissions which shall expire at the End of their next Session.

Section 3.

He shall from time to time give to the Congress Information of the State of the

---

[7] This paragraph has been superseded by the Twelfth Amendment.

[8] This provision has been affected by the Twenty-fifth Amendment.

Union, and recommend to their Consideration such measures as he shall judge necessary and expedient; he may, on extraordinary Occasions, convene both Houses, or either of them, and in Case of Disagreement between them, with Respect to the Time of Adjournment, he may adjourn them to such Time as he shall think proper; he shall receive Ambassadors and other public Ministers: he shall take Care that the Laws be faithfully executed, and shall Commission all of the Officers of the United States.

Section 4.

The President, Vice President and all civil Officers of the United States, shall be removed from Office on Impeachment for, and Conviction of, Treason, Bribery, or other high Crimes and Misdemeanors.

ARTICLE III.

Section 1.

The judicial Power of the United States, shall be vested in one supreme Court, and in such inferior Courts as the Congress may from time to time ordain and establish. The Judges, both of the supreme and inferior Courts, shall hold their Offices during good Behaviour, and shall, at stated Times, receive for their Services, a Compensation, which shall not be diminished during their Continuance in Office.

Section 2.

[1] The judicial Power shall extend to all Cases, in Law and Equity, arising under this Constitution, the Laws of the United States, and Treaties made, or which shall be made, under their Authority;—to all Cases affecting Ambassadors, other public Ministers and Consuls;—to all Cases of admiralty and maritime Jurisdiction;—to Controversies to which the United States shall be a Party;—to Controversies between two or more States;—between a State and citizens of another State;[9]—between Citizens of different States,—between Citizens of the same State claiming Lands under Grants of different States, and between a State, or the Citizens thereof, and foreign States, Citizens or Subjects.

[2] In all Cases affecting Ambassadors, other public Ministers and consuls, and those in which a State shall be Party, the supreme Court shall have original Jurisdiction. In all the other Cases before mentioned, the supreme Court shall have appellate Jurisdiction, both as to Law and Fact, with such Exceptions, and under such Regulations as the Congress shall make.

[3] The Trial of all Crimes, except in Cases of Impeachment, shall be by Jury; and such Trial shall be held in the State where the said Crimes shall have been committed; but when not committed within any State, the Trial shall be at such Place or Places as the Congress may by Law have directed.

Section 3.

[1] Treason against the United States, shall consist only in levying War against them, or in adhering to their Enemies, giving them Aid and Comfort. No Person shall be convicted of Treason unless on the Testimony of two Witnesses to the same overt Act, or on Confession in open Court.

[2] The Congress shall have Power to declare the Punishment of Treason, but no Attainder of Treason shall work Corruption of Blood, or Forfeiture except during the Life of the Person attainted.

ARTICLE IV.

Section 1.

Full Faith and Credit shall be given in each State to the public Acts, Records, and judicial

---

[9] This clause has been affected by the Eleventh Amendment.

Proceedings of every other State. And the Congress may by general Laws prescribe the Manner in which such Acts, Records and Proceedings shall be proved, and the Effect thereof.

Section 2.

[1] The Citizens of each State shall be entitled to all Privileges and Immunities of Citizens in the several States.

[2] A Person charged inany State with Treason, Felony, or other Crime, who shall flee from Justice, and be found in another State, shall on fled, be delivered up, to be removed to the State having Jurisdiction of the Crime.

[3] [No Person held to Service or Labour in one State, under the Laws thereof, escaping into another, shall, in Consequence of any Law or Regulation therein, be discharged from such Service or Labour, but shall be delivered up on Claim of the Party to whom such Service or Labour may be due.][10]

Section 3.

[1] New States may be admitted by the Congress into this Union; but no new State shall be formed or erected within the Jurisdiction of any other State; nor any State be formed by the Junction of two or more States, or Parts of States, without the Consent of the Legislatures of the States concerned as well as of the Congress.

[2] The Congress shall have Power to dispose of and make all needful Rules and Regulations respecting the Territory of other Property belonging to the United States; and nothing in this Constitution shall be so construed as to Prejudice any Claims of the United States, or of any particular State.

Section 4.

The United States shall guarantee to every State in this Union a Republican Form of Government, and shall protect each of them against Invasion; and on Application of the Legislature, or of the Executive (when the Legislature cannot be convened) against domestic Violence.

ARTICLE V.

The Congress, whenever two thirds of both Houses shall deem it necessary, shall propose Amendments to this Constitution, or, on the Application of the Legislatures of two thirds of the several States, shall call a Convention for proposing Amendments, which, in either Case, shall be valid to all Intents and Purposes, as Part of this Constitution, when ratified by the Legislatures of three fourths of the several States, or by conventions in three fourths thereof, as the one or the other Mode of Ratification may be proposed by the Congress; Provided [that no Amendment which may be made prior to the Year One thousand eight hundred and eight shall in any Manner affect the first and fourth Clauses in the Ninth Section of the first Article; and][11] that no State, without its consent, shall be deprived of its equal suffrage in the Senate.

ARTICLE VI.

[1] All Debts contracted and Engagements entered into, before the Adoption of this Constitution, shall be as valid against the United States under this Constitution, as under the Confederation.

[2] This Constitution, and the Laws of the United States which shall be made in Pursuance thereof; and all Treaties made, or which shall be made, under the Authority of the United States, shall be the supreme Law of the Land; and the Judges in every State shall be bound thereby, any Thing in the Constitution or Laws of any State to the Contrary notwithstanding.

[10] This paragraph has been superseded by the Thirteenth Amendment.

[11] Obsolete.

[3] The Senators and Representatives before mentioned, and the Members of the several State Legislatures, and all executive and judicial Officers, both of the United States and of the several States, shall be bound by Oath or Affirmation, to support this Constitution; but no religious Test shall ever be required as a qualification to any Office or public Trust under the United States.

ARTICLE VII.

The Ratification of the Conventions of nine States, shall be sufficient for the Establishment of this Constitution between the States so ratifying the Same.

DONE in Convention by the Unanimous Consent of the States present the Seventeenth Day of September in the Year of our Lord one thousand seven hundred and Eighty seven and of the Independence of the United States of America the Twelfth IN WITNESS whereof We have hereunto subscribed our Names,

Go WASHINGTON—
Presidt. and deputy from Virginia.

[Signed also by the deputies of twelve states.]
New Hampshire
John Langdon, Nicholas Gilman
Massachusetts

Nathaniel Gorham, Rufus King
Connecticut
Wm. Saml. Johnson, Roger Sherman
New York
Alexander Hamilton
Pennsylvania
B. Franklin, Thomas Mifflin
Robt. Morris, Geo. Claymer
Thos. FitzSimons, Jared Ingersoll
James Wilson, Gouv. Morris
New Jersey
Wil Livingston, David Brearley
Wm. Paterson, Jona Dayton
Delaware
Geo. Read, Gunning Bedford, Jun.
John Dickinson, Richard Bassett
Jaco. Broom
Maryland
James McHenry, Dan of St. Thos. Jenifer
Virginia
John Blair, James Madison Jr.
North Carolina
Wm. Blount, Rich'd Dobbs Spaight
South Carolina
J. Rutledge, Charles Cotesworth Pinckney
Charles Pinckney, Pierce Butler
Georgia
William Few, Abr. Baldwin

Attest: William Jackson, Secretary

RATIFICATION
OF THE CONSTITUTION

The Constitution was adopted by a convention of the states on September 17, 1787, and was subsequently ratified by the several states, on the following dates: Delaware, December 7, 1787; Pennsylvania, December 12, 1787; New Jersey, December 18, 1787; Georgia, January 2, 1788; Connecticut, January 9, 1788; Massachusetts, February 6, 1788; Maryland, April 28, 1788; South Carolina, May 23, 1788; New Hampshire, June 21, 1788.

Ratification was completed on June 21, 1788.

The Constitution was subsequently ratified by Virginia, June 25, 1788; New York, July 26, 1788; North Carolina, November 21, 1789; Rhode Island, May 29, 1790; and Vermont, January 10, 1791.

Articles in addition to, and amendment of, the constitution of the United States of America proposed by Congress and ratified by the legislatures of the several states pursuant to the fifth article of the original constitution.

ARTICLE [I][12]

Congress shall make no law respecting an establishment of religion, or prohibiting the free exercise thereof; or abridging the freedom of speech, or of the press; or the right of the people peaceably to asemble and to petition the Government for a redress of grievances.

ARTICLE [II]

A well regulated Militia, being necessary to the security of a free State, the right of the people to keep and bear Arms, shall not be infringed.

[12] Only the thirteenth, fourteenth, fifteenth, and sixteenth articles of amendment had numbers assigned to them at the time of ratification.

ARTICLE [III]

No Soldier shall, in time of peace be quartered in any house, without the consent of the Owner, nor in time of war, but in a manner to be prescribed by law.

ARTICLE [IV]

The right of the people to be secure in their persons, houses, papers, and effects, against unreasonable searches and seizures, shall not be violated, and no Warrants shall issue, but upon probable cause, supported by Oath or affirmation, and particularly describing the place to be searched, and th peerson or things to be seized.

ARTICLE [V]

No person shall be held to answer for a capital, or otherwise infamous crime, unless on a presentment or indictment of a Grand Jury, except in cases arising in the land or naval forces, or in the Militia, when in actual service in time of War or public danger; nor shall any person be subject for the same offence to be twice put in jeopardy of life or limb; nor shall be compelled in any criminal case to be a witness against himself, nor be deprived of life, liberty, or property, without due process of law; nor shall private property be taken for public use without just compensation.

ARTICLE [VI]

In all criminal prosecutions, the accused shall enjoy the right to a speedy and public trial, by an impartial jury of the State and district wherein the crime shall have been committed, which district shall have been previously ascertained by laws, and to be informed of the nature and cause of the accusation; to be confronted with the witnesses against him; to have compulsory process for obtaining Witnesses in his favor, and to have the assistance of counsel for his defence.

ARTICLE [VII]

In Suits at common law, where the value in controversy shall exceed twenty dollars, the right of trial by jury shall be preserved, and fact tried by a jury, shall be otherwise reexamined in any Court of the United States, than according to the rules of the common law.

ARTICLE [VIII]

Excessive bail shall not be required, nor excessive fines imposed, nor cruel and unusual punishments inflicted.

ARTICLE [IX]

The enumeration in the Constitution, of certain rights, shall not be construed to deny or disparage others retained by the people.

ARTICLE [X]

The powers not delegated to the United States by the Constitution, nor prohibited by it to the States, are reserved to the States respectively, or to the people.

The first ten amendments to the Constitution, and by the Congress on September 25, 1789. They were ratified by the following states, and the notifications of the ratification by the governors thereof were successively communicated by the president to the Congress: New Jersey, November 20, 1789; Maryland, December 19, 1789; North Carolina, December 22, 1789; Delaware, January 28, 1790; New York, February 24, 1790; Pennsylvania, March 10, 1790; Rhode Island, June 7, 1790; Vermont, November 3, 1791; and Virginia, December 15, 1791.

Ratification was completed on December 15, 1791.

The amendments were subsequently ratified by Massachusetts, March 2, 1939. Georgia, March 18, 1939; and Connecticut, April 19, 1939.

ARTICLE [XI]

The Judicial power of the United States shall not be construed to extend to any suit in law or equity, commenced or prosecuted against one of the United States by Citizens of another State, or by Citizens or Subjects of any Foreign State.

The Eleventh Amendment to the Constitution was proposed by the Congress on March 4, 1794. It was declared, in a message from the president to Congress, dated January 8, 1798 to have been ratified by the legislatures of twelve of the fifteen states. The dates of ratification were: New York, March 27, 1794; Rhode Island, March 31, 1794; Connecticut, May 8, 1794; New Hampshire, June 16, 1794; Massachusetts, June 26, 1794; Vermont, between October 9, 1794 and November 9, 1894; Virginia, November 18, 1794; Georgia, November 29, 1794; Kentucky, December 7, 1794; Maryland, December 26, 1794; Delaware, Janaury 23, 1794; North Carolina, February 7, 1795.

Ratification was completed on February 7, 1795.

The amendment was subsequently ratified by South Carolina on December 4, 1797. New Jersey and Pennsylvania did not take action on the amendment.

ARTICLE [XII]

The electors shall meet in their respective states and vote by ballot for President and Vice-President, one of whom, at least, shall not be an inhabitant of the same state with themselves; they shall name in their ballots the person voted for as President, and in distinct ballots the person voted for as Vice-President, and they shall make distinct lists of all persons voted for as President, and of all persons voted for as Vice-President, and of the number of votes for each, which lists they shall sign and certify, and transmit sealed to the seat of the government of the United States, directed to the President of the Senate;—The President of the Senate shall, in the presence of the Senate and House of Representatives, open all the certificates and the votes shall then be counted;—The person having the greatest number of votes for President, shall be the President, if such number be a majority of the whole number of Electors appointed; and if no person have such majority, then from the persons having the highest numbers not exceeding three on the list of those voted for as President, the House of Representatives shall choose immediately, by ballot, the President. But in choosing the President, the votes shall be taken by states, the representation from each state having one vote; a quorum for this purpose shall consist of a member or members from two-thirds of the states, and a majority of all the states shall be necessary to a choice. [And if the House of Representatives shall not choose a President whenever the right of choice shall devolve upon them, before the fourth day of March next following, then the Vice-President shall act as President, as in the case of the death or other constitutional disability of the President.][13] The person having the greatest number of votes as Vice-President, shall be the Vice-President, if such number be a majority of the whole number of Electors appointed, and if no person have a majority, then from the two highest numbers on the list, the Senate shall choose the Vice-President; a quorum for the purpose shall consist of two-thirds of the whole number of Senators, and a majority of the whole number shall be necessary to a choice. But no person constitutionally ineligible to the office of President shall be eligible to that of Vice-President of the United States.

The twelfth Amendment to the Constitution was proposed by the Congress on December 9, 1803. It

---

[13] The part in brackets has been superseded by Section 3 of the Twentieth Amendment.

was declared, in a proclamation of the secretary of State dated September 25, 1804, to have been ratified by the legislatures of thirteen of the seventeen states. The dates of ratification were: North Carolina, December 21, 1803; Maryland, December 24, 1803; Kentucky, December 27, 1803; Ohio, December 30, 1803; Pennsylvania, January 5, 1804; Vermont, January 30, 1804; Virginia, February 3, 1804; New York, February 10, 1804; New Jersey, February 22, 1804; Rhode Island, March 12, 1804; South Carolina, May 15, 1804; Georgia, May 19, 1804; New Hampshire, June 15, 1804.

Ratification was completed on June 15, 1804.

The amendment was subsequently ratified by Tennessee, July 27, 1804.

The amendment was rejected by Delaware, January 18, 1804; Massachusetts, February 3, 1804; Connecticut, at its session begun May 10, 1804.

ARTICLE XIII

Section 1.

Neither slavery nor involuntary servitude, except as a punishment for crime whereof the party shall have been duly convicted, shall exist within the United States, or any place subject to their jurisdiction.

Section 2.

Congress shall have power to enforce this article by appropriate legislation.

The thirteenth Amendment to the Constitution was proposed by the Congress on January 31, 1865. It was declared, in a proclamation of the secretary of state, dated December 18, 1865, to have been ratified by the legislatures of twenty-seven of the thirty-six states. The dates of ratification were: Illinois, February 1, 1865; Rhode Island, February 2, 1865; Michigan, February 2, 1865; Maryland, February 3, 1865; New York, February 3, 1865; Pennsylvania, February 3, 1865; West Virginia, February 3, 1865; Missouri, February 6, 1865; Maine, February 7, 1865; Kansas, February 7, 1865; Massachu-

setts, February 7, 1865; Virginia, February 9, 1865; Ohio, February 10, 1865; Indiana, February 13, 1865; Nevada, February 16, 1865; Louisiana, February 17, 1865; Minnesota, February 23, 1865; Wisconsin, February 24, 1865; Vermont, March 9, 1865; Tennessee, April 7, 1865; Arkansas, April 14, 1865; Connecticut, May 4, 1865; New Hampshire, July 1, 1865; South Carolina, November 13, 1865; Alabama, December 2, 1865; North Carolina, December 4, 1865; Georgia, December 6, 1865.

Ratification was completed on December 6, 1865.

The amendment was subsequently ratified by Oregon, December 8, 1865; California, December 19, 1865; Florida, December 28, 1865 (Florida again ratified on June 9, 1868, upon its adoption of a new constitution); Iowa, January 15, 1866; New Jersey, January 23, 1866 (after having rejected it on March 16, 1865); Texas, February 18, 1870; Delaware, February 12, 1901 (after having rejected it on February 8, 1865; Kentucky, March 18, 1976 (after having rejected it on February 24, 1865).

The amendment was rejected (and not subsequently ratified) by Mississippi, December 4, 1865.

ARTICLE XIV

Section 1.

All persons born or naturalized in the United States, and subject to the jurisdiction thereof, are citizens of the United States and of the State wherein they reside. No State shall make or enforce any law which shall abridge the privileges or immunities of citizens of the United States; nor shall any State deprive any person of life, liberty, or property, without due process of law; nor deny to any person within its jurisdiction the equal protection of the laws.

Section 2.

Representatives shall be apportioned among the several States according to their respective numbers, counting the whole number of persons in each State, excluding Indians not taxed. But when the right to vote at any election for the choice of electors for President and Vice President of the United States, Representatives in Congress, the Executive and Judicial officers of a State, or the members of the Legislature thereof, is denied to any of the male inhabitants of such State, being twenty-one years of age[14] and citizens of the United States, or in any way abridged, except for participation in rebellion, or other crime, the basis of representation therein shall be reduced in the proportion which the number of such male citizens shall bear to the whole number of male citizens twenty-one years of age in such State.

Section 3.

No person shall be a Senator or Representative in Congress, or elector of President and Vice President, or hold any office, civil or military, under the United States, or under any State, who having previously taken an oath, as a member of Congress, or as an officer of the United States, or as a member of any State legislature, or as an executive or judicial officer of any State, to support the Constitution of the United States, shall have engaged in insurrection or rebellion against the same, or given aid or comfort to the enemies thereof. But Congress may by a vote of two-thirds of each House, remove such disability.

Section 4.

The validity of the public debt of the United States, authorized by law, including debts incurred for payment of pensions and bounties for services in suppressing insurrection or rebellion, shall not be questioned. But neither the United States nor any State shall assume or pay any debt or obligation incurred in aid of insurrection or rebellion against the United States, or any claim for the loss or emancipation of any slave; but all debts, obligations and claims shall be held illegal and void.

[14] See the Twenty-sixth Amendment.

Section 5.

The Congress shall have power to enforce, by appropriate legislation, the provisions of this article.

The fourteenth Amendment to the Constitution was proposed by the Congress on June 13, 1866. It was declared, in a certificate by the secretary of state dated July 28, 1868, to have been ratified by the legislatures of twenty-eight of the thirty-seven states. The dates of ratification were: Connecticut, June 25, 1866; New Hampshire, July 6, 1866; Tennessee, July 19, 1866; New Jersey, September 11, 1866 (subsequently the legislature rescinded its ratification, and on March 5, 1868, readopted its resolution of rescission over the Governor's veto); Oregon, September 19, 1866 (and rescinded its ratification on October 15, 1868); Vermont, October 30, 1866; Ohio, January 4, 1867 (and rescinded its ratification on January 15, 1868); New York, January 10, 1867; Kansas, January 11, 1867; Illinois, January 15, 1867; West Virginia, January 16, 1867; Michigan, January 16, 1867; Minnesota, January 16, 1867; Maine, January 19, 1867; Nevada, January 22, 1867; Indiana, January 23, 1867; Missouri, January 25, 1867; Rhode Island, February 7, 1867; Wisconsin, February 7, 1867; Pennsylvania, February 12, 1867; Massachusetts, March 20, 1867; Nebraska, June 15, 1867; Iowa, March 16, 1868; Arkansas, April 6, 1868; Florida, June 9, 1868; North Carolina, July 4, 1868 (after having rejected it on December 14, 1866); Louisiana, July 9, 1868 (after having rejected it on February 6, 1867); South Carolina, July 9, 1868 (after having rejected it on December 20, 1866).
Ratification was completed on July 9, 1868.[15]
The amendment was subsequently ratified by Ala-

[15]The certificate of the secretary of state, dated July 20, 1868 [15 Stat. 706,707], was based on the assumption of invalidity of the rescission of ratification by Ohio and New Jersey. The following day, the Congress adopted a joint resolution declaring the amendment a part of the Constitution. On July 28, 1868, the secretary of state issued a proclamation of ratification without reservation [15 Stat. 807-711]. In the interim, two other states, Alabama on July 13 and Georgia on July 21, 1868, had added their ratifications.

bama, July 13, 1868; Georgia, July 21, 1868 (after having rejected it on November 9, 1866); Virginia, October 8, 1869 (after having rejected it on January 9, 1867); Mississippi, January 17, 1870; Texas, February 18, 1870 (after having rejected it on October 27, 1866); Delaware, February 12, 1901 (after having rejected it on February 8, 1867); Maryland, April 4, 1959 (after having rejected it on March 23, 1867); California, May 6, 1959; Kentucky, March 18, 1976 (after having rejected it on January 8, 1867).

ARTICLE XV

Section 1.

The right of citizens of the United States to vote shall not be denied or abridged by the United States or by any State on account of race, color, or previous condition of servitude.

Section 2.

The Congress shall have power to enforce this article by appropriate legislation.

The fifteenth Amendment to the Constitution was proposed by the Congress on February 26, 1869. It was declared, in a proclamation of the secretary of state, dated March 30, 1870, to have been ratified by the legislatures of twenty-nine of the thirty-seven states. The dates of ratification were: Nevada, March 1, 1869; West Virginia, March 3, 1869; Illinois, March 5, 1869; Louisiana, March 5, 1869; North Carolina, March 5, 1869; Michigan, March 8, 1869; Wisconsin, March 9, 1869; Maine, March 11, 1869; Massachusetts, March 12, 1869; Arkansas, March 15, 1869; South Carolina, March 15, 1869, Pennsylvania, March 25, 1869; New York, April 14, 1869 (and the legislature of the same State passed a resolution January 5, 1870, to withdraw its consent to it, which action it rescinded on March 30, 1970); Indiana, May 14, 1869; Connecticut, May 19, 1869; Florida, June 14, 1869; New Hampshire, July 1, 1869; Virginia, October 8, 1869; Vermont, October 20, 1869; Missouri, January 7, 1870;

Minnesota, January 13, 1870; Mississippi, January 17, 1870; Rhode Island, January 18, 1870; Kansas, January 19, 1870; Ohio, January 27, 1870 (after having rejected it on April 30, 1869); Georgia, February 2, 1870; Iowa, February 3, 1870.

Ratification was completed on February 3, 1870, unless the withdrawal of ratification by New York was effective; in which event ratification was completed on February 17, 1870, when Nebraska ratified.

The amendment was subsequently ratified by Texas, February 18, 1870; New Jersey, February 15, 1871 (after having rejected it on February 7, 1870); Delaware, February 12, 1901 (after having rejected it on March 18, 1869); Oregon, February 24, 1959; California, April 3, 1962 (after having rejected it on January 28, 1870); Kentucky, March 18, 1976 (after having rejected it on March 12, 1869).

The amendment was approved by the governor of Maryland, May 7, 1973; Maryland having previously rejected it on February 26, 1870.

The amendment was rejected (and not subsequently ratified) by Tennessee, November 16, 1869.

ARTICLE XVI

The Congress shall have power to lay and collect taxes on incomes, from whatever source derived, without apportionment among the several States, and without regard to any census or enumeration.

The sixteenth Amendment to the Constitution was proposed by the Congress on July 12, 1909. It was declared, in a proclamation of the secretary of state, dated February 25, 1913, to have been ratified by thirty-six of the forty-eight states. The dates of ratification were: Alabama, August 10, 1909; Kentucky, February 8, 1910; South Carolina, February 19, 1910; Illinois, March 1, 1910; Mississippi, March 7, 1910; Oklahoma, March 10, 1910; Maryland, April 8, 1910; Georgia, August 3, 1910; Texas, August 16, 1910; Ohio, January 19, 1911; Idaho, January 20, 1911; Oregon, January 23, 1911; Washington, January 26, 1911; Montana, January 30, 1911; Indiana, January 30, 1911; California, January 31, 1911; Nevada, January 31, 1911;

South Dakota, February 3, 1911; Nebraska, February 9, 1911; North Carolina, February 11, 1911; Colorado, February 15, 1911; Michigan, February 23, 1911; Iowa, February 24, 1911; Missouri, March 16, 1911; Maine, March 31, 1911; Tennessee, April 7, 1911; Arkansas, April 22, 1911 (after having rejected it earlier); Wisconsin, May 26, 1911; New York, July 12, 1911; Arizona, April 6, 1912; Minnesota, June 11, 1912; Louisiana, June 28, 1912; West Virginia, January 31, 1913; New Mexico, February 3, 1913.

Ratification was completed on February 3, 1913.

The amendment was subsequently ratified by Massachusetts, March 4, 1913; New Hampshire, March 7, 1913 (after having rejected it on March 2, 1911).

The amendment was rejected (and not subsequently ratified) by Connecticut, Rhode Island, and Utah.

ARTICLE [XVII]

The Senate of the United States shall be composed of two Senators from each State, elected by the people thereof, for six years; and each Senator shall have one vote. The electors in each State shall have the qualifications requisite for electors of the most numerous branch of the State legislatures.

When vacancies happen in the representation of any State in the Senate, the executive authority of such State shall issue writs of election to fill such vacancies: Provided, That the legislature of any State may empower the executive thereof to make temporary appointments until the people fill the vacancies by election as the legislature may direct.

This amendment shall not be so construed as to affect the election or term of any Senator chosen before it becomes valid as part of the Constitution.

The seventeenth Amendment to the Constitution was proposed by the Congress on May 13, 1912. It was declared, in a proclamation by the secretary of state, dated May 31, 1913, to have been ratified by the legislatures of thirty-six of the forty-eight states.

The dates of ratification were: Massachusetts, May 22, 1912; Arizona, June 3, 1912; Minnesota, June 10, 1912; New York, January 15, 1913; Kansas, January 17, 1913; Oregon, January 23, 1913; North Carolina, January 25, 1913; California, January 28, 1913; Michigan, January 28, 1913; Iowa, January 30, 1913; Montana, January 30, 1913; Idaho, January 31, 1913; West Virginia, February 4, 1913; Colorado, February 5, 1913; Nevada, February 6, 1913; Texas, February 7, 1913; Washington, February 7, 1913; Wyoming, February 8, 1913; Arkansas, February 11, 1913; Maine, February 11, 1913; Illinois, February 13, 1913; North Dakota, February 14, 1913; Wisconsin, February 18, 1913; Indiana, February 19, 1913; New Hampshire, February 19, 1913; Vermont, February 19, 1913; South Dakota, February 19, 1913; Oklahoma, February 24, 1913; Ohio, February 25, 1913; Missouri, March 7, 1913; New Mexico, March 13, 1913; Nebraska, March 14, 1913; New Jersey, March 17, 1913; Tennessee, April 1, 1913; Pennsylvania, April 2, 1913; Connecticut, April 8, 1913. Ratification was completed on April 8, 1913. The amendment was subsequently ratified by Louisiana, June 11, 1914. The amendment was rejected (and not subsequently ratified) by Utah, February 26, 1913.

ARTICLE [XVIII]

[Section 1. After one year from the ratification of this article, the manufacture, sale, or transportation of intoxicating liquors within, the importation thereof into or the exportation thereof from the United States and all territory subject to the jurisdictions thereof for beverage purposes is hereby prohibited.

[Section 2. The Congress and the several States shall have concurrent power to enforce this article by appropriate legislation.

[Section 3. This article shall be inoperative unless it shall have been ratified as an amendment to the Constitution by the legislatures of the several States, as provided in the Constitution, within seven years from the date of the submission hereof to the States by the Congress.[16]

The eighteenth Amendment to the Constitution was proposed by the Congress on December 18, 1917. It was declared, in a proclamation by the acting secretary of state, dated January 29, 1919, to have been ratified by the legislatures of thirty-six of the forty-eight states. The dates of ratification were: Mississippi, January 8, 1918; Virginia, January 11, 1918; Kentucky, January 14, 1918; North Dakota, January 25, 1918; South Carolina, January 29, 1918; Maryland, February 13, 1918; Montana, February 19, 1918; Texas, March 4, 1918; Delaware, March 18, 1918; South Dakota, March 20, 1918; Massachusetts, April 2, 1918; Arizona, May 24, 1918; Georgia, June 26, 1918; Louisiana, August 3, 1918; Florida, December 3, 1918; Michigan, January 2, 1919; Ohio, January 7, 1919; Oklahoma, January 7, 1919; Idaho, January 8, 1919; Maine, January 8, 1919; West Virginia, January 9, 1919; California, January 13, 1919; Tennessee, January 13, 1919; Washington, January 13, 1919; Arkansas, January 14, 1919; Kansas, January 14, 1919; Alabama, January 15, 1919; Colorado, January 15, 1919; Iowa, January 15, 1919; New Hampshire, January 15, 1919; Oregon, January 15, 1919; Nebraska, January 16, 1919; North Carolina, January 16, 1919; Utah, January 16, 1919; Missouri, January 16, 1919; Wyoming, January 16, 1919.

Ratification was completed on January 16, 1919.[17]

The amendment was subsequently ratified by Minnesota on January 17, 1917; Wisconsin, January 17, 1919; New Mexico, January 20, 1919; Nevada, January 21, 1919; New York, January 29, 1919; Vermont, January 29, 1919; Pennsylvania, February 25, 1919; Connecticut, May 6, 1919; and New Jersey, March 9, 1922.

The amendment was rejected (and not subsequently ratified) by Rhode Island.

---

[16] Repealed by Section 1 of the Twenty-first Amendment.
[17] See *Dillon* v. *Gloss*, 256 U.S. 368, 376 (1921).

ARTICLE [XIX]

The right of citizens of the United States to vote shall not be denied or abridged by the United States or by any State on account of sex.

Congress shall have power to enforce this article by appropriate legislation.

The nineteenth Amendment to the Constitution was proposed by the Congress on June 4, 1919. It was declared, in a certificate by the secretary of state, dated August 26, 1920, to have been ratified by the legislatures of thirty-six of the forty-eight states. The dates of ratification were: Illinois, June 10, 1919 (and that state readopted its resolution of ratification June 17, 1919); Michigan, June 10, 1919; Wisconsin, June 10, 1919; Kansas, June 16, 1919; New York, June 16, 1919; Ohio, June 16, 1919; Pennsylvania, June 24, 1919; Massachusetts, June 25, 1919; Texas, June 28, 1919; Iowa, July 2, 1919; Missouri, July 3, 1919; Nebraska, August 2, 1919; Minnesota, September 8, 1919; New Hampshire, September 10, 1919; Utah, October 2, 1919; California, November 1, 1919; Maine, November 5, 1919; North Dakota, December 1, 1919; South Dakota, December 4, 1919; Colorado, December 15, 1919; Kentucky, January 6, 1920; Rhode Island, January 6, 1920; Oregon, January 13, 1920; Indiana, January 16, 1920; Wyoming, January 27, 1920; Nevada, February 7, 1920; New Jersey, February 9, 1920; Idaho, February 11, 1920; Arizona, February 12, 1920; New Mexico, February 21, 1920; Oklahoma, February 28, 1920; West Virginia, March 10, 1920; Washington, March 22, 1920; Tennessee, August 18, 1920.

Ratification was completed on August 18, 1920.

The amendment was subsequently ratified by Connecticut on September 13, 1920 (and that state reaffirmed on September 21, 1920); Vermont, February 8, 1921; Maryland, March 29, 1941 (after having rejected it on February 24, 1920; ratification certified on February 25, 1958); Virginia, February 21, 1952 (after rejecting it on February 12, 1920); Alabama, September 8, 1953 (after rejecting it on September 22, 1919); Florida, May 13, 1969; South Carolina, July 1, 1969 (after rejecting it on January 28, 1920; ratification certified on August 22, 1973);

Georgia, February 20, 1970 (after rejecting it on July 24, 1919); Louisiana, June 11, 1970 (after rejecting it on July 1, 1920); North Carolina, May 6, 1971.

The amendment was rejected (and not subsequently ratified) by Mississippi, March 20, 1920; Delaware, June 2, 1920.

ARTICLE [XX]

Section 1.

The terms of the President and Vice President shall end at noon on the 20th day of January, and the terms of Senators and Representatives at noon on the 3d day of January, of the years in which such terms would have ended if this article had not been ratified; and the terms of their successors shall then begin.

Section 2.

The Congress shall assemble at least once in every year, and such meeting shall begin at noon on the 3d day of January, unless they shall by law appoint a different day.

Section 3.[18]

If, at the time fixed for the beginning of the term of the President, the President elect shall have died, the Vice President elect shall become President. If a President shall not have been chosen before the time fixed for the beginning of his term, or if the President elect shall have failed to qualify, then the Vice President elect shall act as President until a president shall have qualified; and the Congress may by law provide for the case wherein neither a President elect nor a Vice President elect shall have qualified, declaring who shall then act as President, or the manner in which one who is to act shall be selected, and such person shall act accordingly until a President or Vice President shall have qualified.

[18] See the Twenty-fifth Amendment.

Section 4.

The Congress may by law provide for the case of the death of any of the persons from whom the House of Representative may choose a President whenever the right of choice shall have devolved upon them, and for the case of the death of any of the persons from whom the Senate may choose a Vice President whenever the right of choice shall have devolved upon them.

Section 5.

Sections 1 and 2 shall take effect on the 15th day of October following the ratification of this article.

Section 6.

This article shall be inoperative unless it shall have been ratified as an amendment to the Constitution by the legislatures of three-fourths of the several States within seven years from the date of its submission.

The twentieth Amendment to the Constitution was proposed by the Congress on March 2, 1932. It was declared, in a certificate by the secretary of state, dated February 6, 1933, to have been ratified by the legislatures of thirty-six of the forty-eight states. The dates of ratification were: Virginia, March 4, 1932; New York, March 11, 1932; Mississippi, March 16, 1932; Arkansas, March 17, 1932; Kentucky, March 17, 1932; New Jersey, March 21, 1932; South Carolina, March 25, 1932; Michigan, March 31, 1932; Maine, April 1, 1932; Rhode Island, April 14, 1932; Illinois, April 21, 1932; Louisiana, June 22, 1932; West Virginia, July 30, 1932; Pennsylvania, August 11, 1932; Indiana, August 15, 1932; Texas, September 7, 1932; Alabama, September 13, 1932; California, January 4, 1933; North Carolina, January 5, 1933; North Dakota, January 9, 1933; Minnesota, January 12, 1933; Arizona, January 13, 1933; Montana, January 13, 1933; Nebraska, January 13, 1933; Oklahoma, January 13, 1933; Kansas, January 16, 1933; Oregon,

January 19, 1933; Delaware, January 19, 1933; Washington, January 19, 1933; Wyoming, January 19, 1933; Iowa, January 20, 1933; South Dakota, January 20, 1933; Tennessee, January 20, 1933; Idaho, January 21, 1933; New Mexico, January 21, 1933; Georgia, January 23, 1933; Missouri, January 23, 1933; Ohio, January 23, 1933; Utah, January 23, 1933.

Ratification was completed on January 23, 1933.

The amendment was subsequently ratified by Massachusetts on January 24, 1933; Wisconsin, January 24, 1933; Colorado, January 24, 1933; Nevada, January 26, 1933; Connecticut, January 27, 1933; New Hampshire, January 31, 1933; Vermont, February 2, 1933; Maryland, March 24, 1933; Florida, April 26, 1933.

ARTICLE [XXI]

Section 1.

The eighteenth article of amendment to the Constitution of the United States is hereby repealed.

Section 2.

The transportation or importation into any State, Territory, or possession of the United States for delivery or use therein of intoxicating liquors, in violation of the laws thereof, is hereby prohibited.

Section 3.

This article shall be inoperative unless it shall have been ratified as an amendment to the Constitution by conventions in the several States, as provided in the Constitution, within seven years from the date of the submission hereof to the States by the Congress.

The Twenty-first Amendment to the Constitution was proposed by the Congress on February 20, 1933. It was declared, in a certificate of the acting secretary of state, dated December 5, 1933, to have been

ratified by conventions in thirty-six of the forty-eight states. The dates of ratification were: Michigan, April 10, 1933; Wisconsin, April 25, 1933; Rhode Island, May 8, 1933; Wyoming, May 25, 1933; New Jersey, June 1, 1933; Delaware, June 24, 1933; Indiana, June 26, 1933; Massachusetts, June 26, 1933; New York, June 27, 1933; Illinois, July 10, 1933; Iowa, July 10, 1933; Connecticut, July 11, 1933; New Hampshire, July 11, 1933; California, July 24, 1933; West Virginia, July 25, 1933; Arkansas, August 1, 1933; Oregon, August 7, 1933; Alabama, August 8, 1933; Tennessee, August 11, 1933; Missouri, August 29, 1933; Arizona, September 5, 1933; Nevada, September 5, 1933; Vermont, September 23, 1933; Colorado, September 26, 1933; Washington, October 3, 1933; Minnesota, October 10, 1933; Idaho, October 17, 1933; Maryland, October 18, 1933; Virginia, October 25, 1933; New Mexico, November 2, 1933; Florida, November 14, 1933; Texas, November 24, 1933; Kentucky, November 27, 1933; Ohio, December 5, 1933; Pennsylvania, December 5, 1933; Utah, December 5, 1933.

Ratification was completed on December 5, 1933.

The amendment was subsequently ratified by Maine, December 6, 1933; Montana, August 6, 1934.

The amendment was rejected (and not subsequently ratified) by South Carolina, December 4, 1933.

ARTICLE [XXII]

Section 1.

No person shall be elected to the office of the President more than twice, and no person who has held the office of President, or acted as President, for more than two years of a term to which some other person was elected President shall be elected to the office of the President more than once. But this Article shall not apply to any person holding the office of President when this Article was proposed by the Congress, and shall not prevent any person who may be holding the office of President, or acting as President, during the term within which this Article becomes operative from holding the office of President or acting as President during the remainder of such term.

Section 2.

This article shall be inoperative unless it shall have been ratified as an amendment to the Constitution by the legislatures of three-fourths of the several States within seven years from the date of its submission to the States by the Congress.

The twenty-second Amendment to the Constitution was proposed by the Congress on March 21, 1947. It was declared, in a certificate by the administrator of general services, dated March 1, 1951, to have been ratified by the legislatures of twenty-six of the forty-eight states. The dates of ratification were: Maine, March 31, 1947; Michigan, March 31, 1947; Iowa, April 1, 1947; Kansas, April 1, 1947; New Hampshire, April 1, 1947; Delaware, April 2, 1947; Illinois, April 3, 1947; Oregon, April 3, 1947; Colorado, April 12, 1947; California, April 15, 1947; New Jersey, April 15, 1947; Vermont, April 15, 1947; Ohio, April 16, 1947; Wisconsin, April 16, 1947; Pennsylvania, April 29, 1947; Connecticut, May 21, 1947; Missouri, May 22, 1947; Nebraska, May 23, 1947; Virginia, January 28, 1948; Mississippi, February 12, 1948; New York, March 9, 1948; South Dakota, January 21, 1949; North Dakota, February 25, 1949; Louisiana, May 17, 1950; Montana, January 25, 1951; Indiana, January 29, 1951; Idaho, January 30, 1951; New Mexico, February 12, 1951; Wyoming, February 12, 1951; Arkansas, February 15, 1951; Georgia, February 17, 1951; Tennessee, February 20, 1951; Texas, February 22, 1951; Nevada, February 26, 1951; Utah, February 26, 1951; Minnesota, February 27, 1951.

Ratification was completed on February 27, 1951.

The amendment was subsequently ratified by North Carolina on February 28, 1951; South Carolina, March 13, 1951; Maryland, March 14, 1951; Florida, April 16, 1951; Alabama, May 4, 1951.

The amendment was rejected (and not subsequently ratified) by Oklahoma in June 1947; Massachusetts, June 9, 1949.

ARTICLE [XXIII]

Section 1.

The District constituting the seat of Government of the United States shall appoint in such manner as the Congress may direct:

A number of electors of President and Vice President equal to the whole number of Senators and Representatives in Congress to which the District would be entitled if it were a State, but in no event more than the least populous State, they shall be in addition to those appointed by the States, but they shall be considered, for the purposes of the election of President and Vice President, to be electors appointed by a State; and they shall meet in the District and perform such duties as provided by the twelfth article of amendment.

Section 2.

The Congress shall have power to enforce this article by appropriate legislation.

The twenty-third Amendment to the Constitution was proposed by the Congress on June 17, 1960. It was declared, in a certificate by the administrator of general services, to have been ratified by thirty-eight of the fifty states. The dates of ratification were: Hawaii, June 23, 1960 (and that state made a technical correction to its resolution on June 30, 1960); Massachusetts, August 22, 1960; New Jersey, December 19, 1960; New York, January 17, 1961; California, January 19, 1961; Oregon, January 27, 1961; Maryland, January 30, 1961; Idaho, January 31, 1961; Maine, January 31, 1961; Minnesota, January 31, 1961; New Mexico, February 1, 1961; Nevada, February 2, 1961; Montana, February 6, 1961; South Dakota, February 6, 1961; Colorado, February 8, 1961; Washington, February 9, 1961; West Virginia, February 9, 1961; Alaska, February

10, 1961; Wyoming, February 13, 1961; Delaware, February 20, 1961; Utah, February 21, 1961; Wisconsin, February 21, 1961; Pennsylvania, February 28, 1961; Indiana, March 3, 1961; North Dakota, March 3, 1961; Tennessee, March 6, 1961; Michigan, March 8, 1961; Connecticut, March 9, 1961; Arizona, March 10, 1961; Illinois, March 14, 1961; Nebraska, March 15, 1961; Vermont, March 15, 1961; Iowa, March 16, 1961; Missouri, March 20, 1961; Oklahoma, March 21, 1961; Rhode Island, March 22, 1961; Kansas, March 29, 1961; Ohio, March 29, 1961.

Ratification was completed on March 29, 1961.

The amendment was subsequently ratified by New Hampshire on March 30, 1961 (when that State annulled and then repeated its ratification of March 29, 1961).

The amendment was rejected (and not subsequently ratified) by Arkansas on January 24, 1961.

ARTICLE [XXIV]

Section 1.

The right of citizens of the United States to vote in any primary or other election for President or Vice President, for electors for President or Vice President, or for Senator or Representative in Congress, shall not be denied or abridged by the United States or any State by reason of failure to pay any poll tax or other tax.

Section 2.

The Congress shall have power to enforce this article by appropriate legislation.

The twenty-fourth Amendment to the Constitution was proposed by the Congress on August 27, 1962. It was declared, in a certificate of the administrator of general services, dated February 4, 1964, to have been ratified by the legislatures of thirty-eight of the fifty states. The dates of ratification were: Illinois, November 14, 1962, New Jersey, December 3, 1962; Oregon, January 25, 1963, Montana, January 28,

1963; West Virginia, February 1, 1963; New York, February 4, 1963; Maryland, February 6, 1963; California, February 7, 1963; Alaska, February 11, 1963; Rhode Island, February 14, 1963; Indiana, February 19, 1963, Utah, February 20, 1963; Michigan, February 20, 1963; Colorado, February 21, 1963; Ohio, February 27, 1963; Minnesota, February 27, 1963; New Mexico, March 5, 1963; Hawaii, March 6, 1963; North Dakota, March 7, 1963; Idaho, March 8, 1963; Washington, March 14, 1963; Vermont, March 15, 1963; Nevada, March 19, 1963; Connecticut, March 20, 1963; Tennessee, March 21, 1963; Pennsylvania, March 25, 1963; Wisconsin, March 26, 1963; Kansas, March 28, 1963; Massachusetts, March 28, 1963; Nebraska, April 4, 1963; Florida, April 18, 1963; Iowa, April 24, 1963; Delaware, May 1, 1963; Missouri, May 13, 1963; New Hampshire, June 12, 1963; Kentucky, June 27, 1963; Maine, January 16, 1964; South Dakota, January 23, 1964.

Ratification was completed on January 23, 1964.

The amendment was rejected (and not subsequently ratified) by Mississippi on December 20, 1962.

ARTICLE [XXV]

Section 1.

In case of the removal of the President from office or of his death or resignation, the Vice President shall become President.

Section 2.

Whenever there is a vacancy in the office of the Vice President, the President shall nominate a Vice President who shall take office upon confirmation by a majority vote of both Houses of Congress.

Section 3.

Whenever the President transmits to the President pro tempore of the Senate and the Speaker of the House of Representatives his written declaration that he is unable to discharge the powers and duties of his office, and until he transmits to them a written declaration to the contrary, such powers and duties shall be discharged by the Vice President as Acting President.

Section 4.

Whenever the Vice President and a majority of either the principal officers of the executive departments or of such other body as Congress may by law provide, transmit to the president pro tempore of the Senate and the Speaker of the House of Representatives their written declaration that the President is unable to discharge the powers and duties of his office, the Vice President shall immediately assume the powers and duties of the office as Acting President.

Thereafter, when the President transmits to the President pro tempore of the Senate and the Speaker of the House of Representative his written declaration that no inability exists, he shall resume the powers and duties of his office unless the Vice President and a majority of either the principal officers of the executive department or of such other body as Congress may by law provide, transmit within four days to the President pro tempore of the Senate and the Speaker of the House of Representatives their written declaration that the President is unable to discharge the powers and duties of his office. Thereupon Congress shall decide the issue, assembling within forty-eight hours for that purpose if not in session. If the Congress, within twenty-one days after receipt of the latter written declaration, or, if Congress is not in session, within twenty-one days after Congress is required to assemble, determines by two-thirds vote of both Houses that the President is unable to discharge the powers and duties of his office, the Vice President shall continue to discharge the same as Acting President; otherwise, the President shall resume the powers and duties of his office.

The twenty-fifth Amendment to the Constitution was proposed by the Congress on July 6, 1965. It was declared, in a certificate of the administrator of general services, dated February 23, 1967, to have been ratified by the legislatures of thirty-nine of the fifty states. The dates of ratification were: Nebraska, July 12, 1965; Wisconsin, July 13, 1965; Oklahoma, July 16, 1965; Massachusetts, August 9, 1965; Pennsylvania, August 18, 1965; Kentucky, September 15, 1965; Arizona, September 22, 1965; Michigan, October 5, 1965; Indiana, October 20, 1965; California, October 21, 1965; Arkansas, November 4, 1965; New Jersey, November 29, 1965; Delaware, December 7, 1965; Utah, January 17, 1966; West Virginia, January 20, 1966; Maine, January 24, 1966; Rhode Island, January 28, 1966; Colorado, February 3, 1966; New Mexico, February 3, 1966; Kansas, February 8, 1966; Vermont, February 10, 1966; Alaska, February 18, 1966; Idaho, March 2, 1966; Hawaii, March 3, 1966; Virginia, March 8, 1966; Mississippi, March 10, 1966; New York, March 14, 1966; Maryland, March 23, 1966; Missouri, March 30, 1966; New Hampshire, June 13, 1966; Louisiana, July 5, 1966; Tennessee, January 12, 1967; Wyoming, January 25, 1967; Washington, January 26, 1967; Iowa, January 26, 1967; Oregon, February 2, 1967; Minnesota, February 10, 1967; Nevada, February 10, 1967.

Ratification was completed on February 10, 1967.

The amendment was subsequently ratified by Connecticut, February 14, 1967; Montana, February 15, 1967; South Dakota, March 6, 1967; Ohio, March 7, 1967; Alabama, March 14, 1967; North Carolina, March 22, 1967; Illinois, March 22, 1967; Texas, April 25, 1967; Florida, May 25, 1967.

ARTICLE [XXVI]

Section 1.

The right of citizens of the United States, who are eighteen years of age or older, to vote shall not be denied or abridged by the United States or by any State on account of age.

Section 2.

The Congress shall have power to enforce this article by appropriate legislation.

The twenty-sixth Amendment to the Constitution was proposed by the Congress on March 23, 1971. It was declared in a certificate of the administrator of general services, dated July 5, 1971, to have been ratified by the legislatures of thirty-nine of the fifty states. The dates of ratification were: Connecticut, March 23, 1971; Delaware, March 23, 1971; Minnesota, March 23, 1971; Tennessee, March 23, 1971; Washington, March 23, 1971; Hawaii, March 24, 1971; Massachusetts, March 24, 1971; Montana, March 29, 1971; Arkansas, March 30, 1971; Idaho, March 30, 1971; Iowa, March 30, 1971; Nebraska, April 2, 1971; New Jersey, April 3, *1971; Kansas, April 7, 1971; Michigan, April 7, 1971; Alaska, April 8, 1971; Maryland, April 8, 1971; Indiana, April 8, 1971; Maine, April 9, 1971; Vermont, April 16, 1971; Louisiana, April 17, 1971; California, April 27, 1971; South Carolina, April 28, 1971; West Virginia, April 28, 1971; New Hampshire, May 13, 1971; Arizona, May 14, 1971; Rhode Island, May 27, 1971; New York, June 2, 1971; Oregon, June 4, 1971; Missouri, June 14, 1971; Wisconsin, June 22, 1971; Illinois, June 29, 1971; Alabama, June 30, 1971; Ohio, June 30, 1971; North Carolina, July 1, 1971; Oklahoma, July 1, 1971.*

Ratification was completed on July 1, 1971.

The amendment was subsequently ratified by Virginia, July 8, 1971; Wyoming, July 8, 1971; Georgia, October 4, 1971.

[Editorial note: There is some conflict as to the exact dates of ratification of the amendments by the several states. In some cases, the resolutions of ratification were signed by the officers of the legislature on dates subsequent to that on which the second house acted. In other cases, the governors of several of the states "approved" the resolutions (on a subsequent date), although action by the governor is not contemplated by Article V, which requires ratification by the legislatures (or conventions) only. In a number of cases, the journals of the state legislatures are not available. The dates set out in this document are based upon the best information available.]

NAME INDEX

SUBJECT INDEX